THE AMERICAN LAW INSTITUTE

THE WTO CASE LAW OF 2011

LEGAL AND ECONOMIC ANALYSIS

This book is the ninth report of the American Law Institute (ALI) project on World Trade Organization Law. The project undertakes yearly analysis of the case law from the adjudicating bodies of the WTO. These studies cover a wide range of WTO law: this volume focuses on the year 2011. Each case is jointly evaluated by well-known experts in trade law and international economics. The contributors critically review the jurisprudence of WTO adjudicating bodies and evaluate whether the ruling 'makes sense' from an economic as well as a legal point of view, and, if not, whether the problem lies in the interpretation of the law or in the law itself. The studies do not cover all issues discussed in a case, but they seek to discuss both the procedural and the substantive issues that form the 'core' of the dispute.

CHAD P. BOWN, Senior Economist, joined the World Bank in September 2009 in the Development Research Group, Trade and International Integration (DECTI). He served as Senior Economist in the White House on the President's Council of Economic Advisers (CEA) during 2010–2011. Formerly a tenured Professor of Economics at Brandeis University in Waltham, Massachusetts, he is currently a member of the Council on Foreign Relations, an Associate Editor for the *Journal of World Trade*, and he serves as the Book Review Editor and on the editorial board for the *World Trade Review*.

PETROS C. MAVROIDIS is Edwin B. Parker Professor at Columbia Law School and Professor at the University of Neuchatel. He is currently on leave at the European University Institute (EUI), in Florence.

THE AMERICAN LAW INSTITUTE

THE WTO CASE LAW OF 2011

LEGAL AND ECONOMIC ANALYSIS

Edited By

CHAD P. BOWN

AND

PETROS C. MAVROIDIS

CAMBRIDGE
UNIVERSITY PRESS

CAMBRIDGE
UNIVERSITY PRESS

University Printing House, Cambridge CB2 8BS, United Kingdom

One Liberty Plaza, 20th Floor, New York, NY 10006, USA

477 Williamstown Road, Port Melbourne, VIC 3207, Australia

314-321, 3rd Floor, Plot 3, Splendor Forum, Jasola District Centre, New Delhi-110025, India

79 Anson Road, #06-04/06, Singapore 079906

Cambridge University Press is part of the University of Cambridge.

It furthers the University's mission by disseminating knowledge in the pursuit of education, learning and research at the highest international levels of excellence.

www.cambridge.org
Information on this title: www.cambridge.org/9781107617223

A catalogue record for this publication is available from the British Library

ISBN 978-1-107-61722-3 Paperback

CONTENTS

Foreword

In a series of books published by Cambridge University Press, scholars sponsored by The American Law Institute have discussed and criticized all important legal decisions rendered by the World Trade Organization since 2000. This volume is the ninth in the series. This was an especially busy year for WTO dispute settlement, as the adjudicating bodies confronted new issues and thus challenged the economists and lawyers who wrote our reports.

The ALI appreciates the leadership of Chad Bown and Petros Mavroidis, the hard work by our authors, and the helpful criticism they received as their drafts were discussed. We also appreciate the financial support we received for this work from The Jan Wallander and Tom Hedelius Foundation and from the Milton and Miriam Handler Foundation.

LANCE LIEBMAN
Director
The American Law Institute

Introduction

CHAD P. BOWN AND PETROS C. MAVROIDIS

The year 2011 has been a remarkable one for WTO dispute settlement: there were substantially more decisions than the previous year, covering a wide range of issues from anti-dumping and customs matters to consumer and environmental protection. The WTO adjudicating bodies had to confront some issues for the very first time, and this led to noteworthy jurisprudential developments. As customary, we gathered a stellar group of scholars to evaluate from a joint law-and-economics analysis all Reports by the Appellate Body (AB) issued during the calendar year 2011, as well as all Panel Reports that were not appealed and could no longer be appealed (at our cutoff date, 31 December 2011). We made only one exception to our rule, we invited Rob Howse and Phil Levy to write a report on the three TBT (Technical Barriers to Trade) Panel Reports issued during 2011, although all three of them were appealed and AB Reports have been issued in 2012; the reason for disregarding custom has to do with the immense interest that these Reports provoked, the first Reports in the TBT area since *EC–Sardines* (2002). Here we proceed with a short presentation of the Reports in the hope that the reader will find the analyses provided insightful and stimulating.

Hahn and **Mehta** discuss the AB Report on *EC and Certain Member States – Large Civil Aircraft* (DS316), a case involving the subsidization of the Airbus industry by the EU (European Union) and its member states. The authors note that the emergence of Airbus transformed the market structure of the LCA (Large Civil Aircraft) industry into a duopoly of similar-sized full-range manufacturers. The financing of Airbus's upfront investment expenditures came in a significant proportion from public funds. The United States alleged that this violated the SCM Agreement. The United States prevailed before the Panel, and the EU appealed the Report. While the AB followed the US view to a great extent, it did so in a measured way: the category of *per se* illegal export subsidies was interpreted with a view to the manipulation of normal market conditions. In the AB's view, what matters is the distortion on competitive conditions and not the increase of exports. Other aspects of the SCM Agreement were also clarified. For example, the relationship between the effect of the subsidy and the granting of the subsidy itself are closely related but not identical concepts. The Report operates from the premise that the SCM Agreement's regime focuses on the effect, and not on the subsidy as such, which is a manifestation of a political choice by a sovereign Member State. The AB affirmed that a subsidy has a 'life', shorthand for a beginning and an end; in this view, the effect of a subsidy is not bound to be permanent but is bound to terminate. The authors note, with regret, some omissions in the AB Report and most notably the fact that the AB did not clarify to what extent partial privatization, that is sale of assets at market prices to private investors, 'extinguishes' subsidies.

Davey and **Maskus** analyze the AB report on *Thailand – Cigarettes (Philippines)* (DS371). This case evolved around the question whether Thailand was affording to foreign cigarettes less favourable treatment than that reserved for its domestic cigarettes through a host of internal measures (policies). Their paper suggests two improvements that could be made to Panel procedures. It supports the AB's interpretation of Article XX(d) GATT in the present case, which seems to discard an earlier mistaken approach to this provision. It further examines, in some detail, whether the AB's application of the 'less favourable treatment' component of Article III:4 GATT in this and other cases is consistent with the jurisprudence under Article III:2 GATT, and Article 2.1 TBT. From an economics perspective, the case is straightforward on its face. However, the AB's rigorous application of the 'less favourable treatment' principle might not survive a fuller market analysis in terms of policy impacts on conditions of competition. Further, while the authors agree with the rejection of Thailand's claim under Art. XX GATT, they raise the question of whether a strict national-treatment rule may be an unwarranted constraint on policy where there is a clear trade-related external cost to address.

Prusa and **Vermulst** analyze the AB Report on *US–Anti-Dumping and Countervailing Duties (China)* (DS379). In 2007, the United States reversed its longstanding policy prohibiting the simultaneous imposition of anti-dumping duties (ADDs) and countervailing duties (CVDs) against nonmarket economies (NMEs). Subsequently, the United States has imposed concurrent ADDs and CVDs in numerous cases against China. China challenged a number of aspects of the US practice, most notably the double-remedies issue, which occurs when a domestic subsidy is offset by both an ADD and a CVD. The AB correctly ruled, the authors note, that double remedies are inconsistent with the SCM Agreement and that the burden was on the investigating authorities to ensure that double remedies were not being imposed; however, the AB largely limited its discussion to measurement concerns, an approach that may have inadvertently opened the door to future double-remedies disputes involving other methods for computing normal value. Two other issues that are likely to have significant long-term ramifications, in the authors' view, are: (a) the scope of the term 'public body'; and (b) the appropriate use of out-of-country benchmarks. On both issues, the authors believe the AB's conclusions and analysis were correct.

Bown and **Mavroidis** discuss the AB Report on *EC–Fasteners* (DS397). The AB dealt with a number of issues for the first time in this Report. Importantly, it discussed the consistency of the EU regulation on the conditions for deviating from the obligation to calculate individual dumping margins with the multilateral rules. Although China formally won the argument, the AB may have opened the door to treat China as an NME even beyond 2016 when China's NME status was thought to expire under the terms of China's 2001 WTO Accession Protocol. The AB further dealt with numerous other issues ranging from statistical sampling to the treatment of confidential information. In handling its investigation, the EU authorities made a number of questionable decisions regarding the collection of information, and this aspect of the process was central to China's legal challenges.

Hoekman and **Charnovitz** analyze the AB Report on *US–Tyres (China)* (DS399). In 2009, the United States imposed additional tariffs for a three-year period on imports of automotive tires from China under a special safeguard provision included in China's 2001 WTO Accession Protocol. China challenged the measure in the WTO. The case marked the first WTO dispute in which a challenged safeguard was upheld by the AB, the first in which an accession protocol was used successfully as a defense, and the first that China lost as a complaining party. It also was noteworthy, the authors note, in that the safeguard was sought by a labour union and not the domestic industry.

Neven and **Trachtman** assess the AB Report on *Philippines–Distilled Spirits* (DS396). In this case, the AB reconsidered its case law on 'like products' and 'DCS' (directly competitive or substitutable) products (Art. III:2 GATT). The authors note that the AB focused on the effect of differential taxation on domestic products ignoring the degree of substitution across products, a finding that they find hard to reconcile with the overarching purpose of Art. III GATT. They are unhappy with the treatment of evidence by the Panel and the AB since, in their view, foreign and domestic products are distant substitutes for the bulk of the market examined. Putting aside the jurisprudence, a methodologically sound finding regarding substitution (and competition) seems necessary, but not sufficient, for a finding of inefficient discrimination. In order to find inefficient discrimination, there must also be a finding that the nonprotectionist benefits that may arise from the national regulation are not sufficient to justify the discriminatory action. Otherwise, rational regulation that is globally efficient might be invalidated and inappropriately restrict the national right to regulate. In the present case, the Philippines articulated no nonprotectionist rationale for its distinctions. Existing WTO jurisprudence in this area, prior to the AB decision in *US–Clove Cigarettes*, has only hinted at the additional focus on the justificatory role of nonprotectionist regulatory benefits, yet an explicit and appropriately contextualized reference to the nonprotectionist rationale, if any, of regulation seems to be a necessary part of decisionmaking.

Howse and **Levy** authored a paper that examines the basic issues in the three TBT Panel Reports issued in 2011: *US–Clove Cigarettes* (DS406), *US–COOL* (DS386), and *US–Tuna II (Mexico)* (DS381). In a series of controversial decisions, the WTO Panels sought to reconcile legitimate regulatory interests of the state with various obligations to treat imported products in an even-handed and not unnecessarily trade-restrictive manner. Among the key points of contention were which obligation pertained in each case, e.g. national treatment, limits on technical regulations, or rules governing standards. In each case, the Panel imposed significant restrictions on national regulatory practices, and in each case Panel reasoning was challenged by the AB. The authors address some of the key legal and economic issues raised in the original Panel decisions, leaving the late-breaking AB decisions for future analysis. Given the unsettled nature of the terrain, the economic analysis focuses primarily on the question of national treatment, while the legal analysis deals with other interesting points that emerge from these rulings, such as the appropriate level of deference to international standards and the legitimacy of labeling requirements.

Saggi and **Wu** review the Panel Report on *US–Orange Juice (Brazil)* (DS382). Their paper analyzes Brazil's WTO challenge to the methods undertaken by the United States in calculating anti-dumping duties in administrative reviews and other investigations of Brazilian orange juice. The dispute resulted in a Panel ruling that conforms with earlier AB decisions outlawing the use of 'weighted average to transaction' zeroing in such reviews. However, the Panel's stance was driven largely from a desire to preserve 'stability and predictability' within the system, suggesting a practical recognition of the shadow of past AB decisions on the same legal question. In addition, the authors argue that to understand fully the effects of zeroing, it is important to account for the underlying reasons behind observed price changes in the market. They show that zeroing is more likely to convert a negative dumping determination into a positive one when price changes are driven by variations in demand relative to when they are driven by variations in the cost of exporting. In the present case, Brazilian exporters of orange juice experienced an increase in (residual) demand for their product, since, by reducing the local supply of round oranges, adverse weather conditions in the United States made it difficult for US orange-juice producers to meet local demand.

Prusa and **Rubini** scrutinize the Panel Report on *US–Zeroing (Korea)* (DS402) regarding the method of calculating anti-dumping duties. The case mirrors other recent WTO disputes involving zeroing. Even though the United States ceased zeroing in original investigations in December 2006, it implemented the policy change only prospectively. As a result, the margins applied to the products in this dispute remained unchanged because they had been calculated prior to the policy change. The United States did not contest Korea's claims. The Panel confirmed that zeroing was used and, following the long line of Panel and AB rulings, found the practice inconsistent with the Anti-Dumping Agreement. After the Panel Report was adopted, the United States recalculated the margins without zeroing. Nevertheless, it refused to refund unliquidated cash deposits that were based on zeroing, highlighting the United States's continued lukewarm compliance with WTO rulings on zeroing. This dispute offers an opportunity to ponder the weaknesses of the WTO Dispute Settlement and the ability of one Member to take advantage of it. The authors go on to ask two questions: since the facts and their legal assessment were undisputed, why was litigation necessary? Can compliance with WTO law be improved with broader findings and more incisive remedies? In their contribution, the authors offer tentative responses.

Finally, **Broude** and **Moore** analyze the Panel Report on *US–Shrimp (Viet Nam)* (DS404). This unappealed Panel Report not only deals with now-standard controversies involving US zeroing practices, but it also involves a number of novel problems in administrative reviews of US anti-dumping orders that transcend zeroing issues. Most importantly, this dispute highlights the economic, legal, and statistical importance of sample-selection bias when calculating 'all others' rates for exporters that were not queried during dumping investigations. Sampling is particularly problematic in this dispute, since US investigators found only zero and *de minimis* margins in the administrative reviews, a situation in which the relevant provision of the Anti-Dumping Agreement appears to provide no guidance (an apparent '*lacuna*'). The Panel did not directly deal with the key sample-selection issues in the case, and so the authors provide an alternative legal and statistical analysis. Because these issues are likely to become more important as the United States phases out the practice of zeroing, the authors query whether sampling may indeed become the new zeroing.

We would like to thank The American Law Institute (ALI) for its support over the years, without which this project would have never taken off, and especially Marianne Walker and Todd Feldman who yet again provided excellent editorial assistance. We would also like to extend our gratitude to the European University Institute (EUI), and more specifically, to the Global Governance Programme (GGP) of the Robert Schuman Centre (RSC) for cohosting this year's conference and organizing the event in Florence on 4 June 2012: Miguel Maduro, the Director of the GGP, as well as Carlo Maria Cantore (EUI), Silvia Dell'Acqua, and Angelika Lanfranchi (both GGP staff) should be credited with the successful organization.

Our discussants, both those who published their comments as well as those who did not, helped our authors improve the quality of their drafts: Geoff Carlson, Jorge Huerta-Goldman, Fernando González-Rojas, Mark Koulen, Joost Pauwelyn, Michele Ruta, Mark Sanctuary, Simon Schropp, Jasper-Martijn Wauters, and Erik Wijkström did a remarkable job in this respect.

Finally, this is the year that Henrik Horn decided to step down as co-organizer of this enterprise, and Chad P. Bown graciously accepted the invitation to take over his role. This project will always have the footprint of Henrik's idea to organize a permanent law-and-economics forum to seriously scrutinize the output of the WTO adjudicating bodies. We can only endeavor to hope that future editions live up to his dream.

It's a Bird, It's a Plane: Some Remarks on the *Airbus* Appellate Body Report (*EC and Certain Member States – Large Civil Aircraft*, WT/DS316/AB/R)

MICHAEL HAHN

Université de Lausanne, Centre for Comparative, European and International Law, Chair of European Law, Lausanne, Switzerland; University of Waikato School of Law, Hamilton, New Zealand

KIRTIKUMAR MEHTA

Visiting Professor, Fribourg University Law School, Fribourg, Switzerland

Abstract: The emergence of Airbus transformed the market structure of the LCA industry into a duopoly of similar-sized full-range manufacturers. The financing of Airbus's upfront investment expenditures came in a significant proportion from public funds, which violated, in the US's opinion the SCM Agreement. While the Appellate Body follows this view of things to a large extent, it does so in a measured way: the category of *per se* illegal export subsidies is interpreted with a view to the manipulation of normal market conditions; the distortion on competitive conditions matters, not the increase of exports as such. Other aspects of subsidies law clarified are the relationship between effect and subsidy. They are closely related but not identical; rightly, the report operates from the premise that the SCM Agreement's regime focuses on the effect, and not on the subsidy as such, which is a manifestation of a political choice by a sovereign Member state. The Appellate Body affirms that a subsidy has a 'life', a shorthand for a beginning and an end: it follows that the effect of a subsidy is not bound to be permanent but is bound to terminate. It is to be regretted that the Appellate Body avoided clarifying to what extent partial privatization, hence sale of assets at market prices to private investors, 'extinguish' subsidies.

1. Introduction

A comprehensive analysis of this seminal Report ('the *Airbus Report*') will require more than one Ph.D. thesis: After all, we are talking of a Report that was more than nine months in the making (after a Panel had toiled on the case for five years), with three distinguished Appellate Body Members (*Unterhalter, Bautista, Van den Bossche*) and the Secretariat lawyers[1] authoring some 650 pages, with the operative

1 The notice of appeal is dated 12 August 2010, and the Report was circulated on 18 May 2011. However, it is a fair assumption that the Appellate Body Secretariat was starting to work on this Report significantly earlier.

part of the Report starting at page 270. For an institution that prides itself of its Swiss-watch precision (and distinguishes it from some panels) this is, if not a record, then at least one of the longer periods spent on an appeal. We shall not undertake, in the framework of this paper, to analyze in-depth all major issues addressed in the Report. Rather, we understand this small piece as an *amuse bouche* that is supposed to whet the appetite for more. Hence, we will limit ourselves to highlight certain aspects of the decision we consider particularly interesting and worthy of discussion.

It is to be reminded that the *Airbus Report* is part of the on-going *Airbus–Boeing* saga[2], which also led, in 2012, to the Appellate Body Report *United States – Measures Affecting Trade in Large Civil Aircraft – Second Complaint* (WT/DS353) that will be reported next year: the United States and the European Union, respectively, claim that the other partner is unfairly subsidizing its producer of large civil aircrafts ('LCA').

The emergence of Airbus transformed the market structure of the LCA industry from that of a dominant incumbent with two fringe producers with a narrow product range into a duopoly of similar-sized full-range manufacturers. The financing of Airbus's important upfront investment expenditures came in a significant proportion from public funds. The rivalry between Boeing and Airbus on the global market has resulted in new product launches which, together with competition between the LCA manufacturers for orders, significantly increased global demand, but which has shown a relative decline in the preponderant position of Boeing.

The *Airbus* case was initiated by the United States in late 2004;[3] the Panel was established on 20 July 2005 and issued its Report some five years later on 30 June 2010, exceeding considerably the nine months allocated to the Panel phase by the DSU.[4] The European Union appealed, and the Appellate Body Report was adopted on 1 June 2011.

At issue were more than 300 instances of alleged support measures by France, Germany, Spain, the United Kingdom, and by the EC itself over almost four decades. The measures included: the provision of financing for design and development to Airbus companies ('launch aid'); the provision of grants and government-provided goods and services to develop, expand, and upgrade Airbus manufacturing sites for the development and production of the Airbus A380; the provision of loans on preferential terms; the assumption and forgiveness of debt resulting from launch and other large-civil-aircraft production and development

2 See Douglas A. Irwin and Nina Pavcnik (December 2001), 'Airbus versus Boeing Revisited: International Competition in the Aircraft Market', NBER Working Paper No. 8648.

3 *European Communities and Certain Member States – Measures Affecting Trade in Large Civil Aircraft* – Request for Consultations by the United States, WT/DS316/1.

4 Cf. Brendan McGivern (2010), 'Aircraft Subsidies and WTO Rules: The Airbus Decision', 35:4/5 *Air and Space Law*, 305–315.

financing; the provision of equity infusions and grants; the provision of research and development loans and grants in support of large-civil-aircraft development, directly for the benefit of Airbus, and any other measures involving a financial contribution to the Airbus companies. The alleged subsidies relate to the entire family of Airbus planes (A300 through the A380).

Whereas all these measures were, in the US view, subsidies pursuant to Articles 1 and 2 of the WTO Agreement on Subsidies and Countervailing Measures ('SCM Agreement' or 'SCM') causing adverse effects (Articles 5, 6 SCM), the United States further alleged that certain launch aid provided for the A340 and A380 violated the absolute prohibition of Article 3 SCM Agreement to make subsidies contingent on export performance.

2. Claims before the Appellate Body[5]

The main issues that were presented to the AB related to:

(i) the temporal scope and life of a subsidy in application of Article 5 SCM,
(ii) the interpretation of *extinguishment, extraction*, and *pass-through* of subsidies under the provisions of Articles 1, 4.7, 5, 6, and 7.8 SCM,
(iii) the appropriate calculation of benefit of certain subsidies ('Launch Aids') according to the market-investor principle in line with Articles 1 and 14(b) SCM,
(iv) the determination of what is a *de facto* export subsidy pursuant to Article 3.1 (a) SCM,
(v) the weight to be given to a realistic product and geographic-market definition in a case involving Article 6.3(a) and (b) SCM, and
(vi) the assessment of product displacement and lost sales under Article 6.3(a) and (b) SCM.

3. Issues of particular interest

I.

1. The WTO's subsidy's regime is not about prohibiting subsidies *per se* (the lone exception, export subsidies, will be discussed immediately, Subsection II). Rather, it is merely imposing the obligation to do no harm to fellow Members through the granting of state aid.[6] Maybe clearer than ever before, the Appellate Body explains that subsidy and caused effect are two different issues, and that the former is – from

5 Appellate Body Report, *Airbus*, paras. 571 (issues raised by the European Union) and 572 (issues raised by the United States).

6 For a timely and comprehensive overview, cf. Petros C. Mavroidis, Patrick A. Messerlin, and Jasper M. Wauters (eds.) (2008), *The Law and Economics of Contingent Protection in the WTO*, Cheltenham, UK: Edward Elgar Publishing; Marc Bacchetta and Michele Ruta (eds.) (2011), *The WTO, Subsidies and*

a substantive perspective[7] – of interest to Article 5 SCM only as a cause to the latter (unless it is not a priori *verboten*, pursuant to Article 3 SCM).[8]

2. Several consequences arise from this. Firstly, as the SCM focuses on effect and not on cause, the EU argument that subsidies granted – and, possibly, subsidy programs started – before the entry into force of the SCM were immune from its disciplines was a non-starter.[9]

Secondly, this constellation gives occasion to rethink the issue of the 'life of a subsidy' and the Appellate Body takes this invitation up with almost palpable *gusto*. While it flatly rejects the European Union's proposition 'that there must be "present benefit" during the reference period',[10] the proposition that a subsidy has a 'life' is explicitly recognized:

> [It] may come to an end, either through the removal of the financial contribution and/or the expiration of the benefit . . . where it is so argued, a panel must assess whether there are 'intervening events' that occurred after the grant of the subsidy that may affect the projected value of the subsidy as determined under the ex ante analysis. Such events may be relevant to an adverse effects analysis because they may affect the link that a complaining party is seeking to establish between the subsidy and its alleged effects.[11]

Countervailing Measures, Cheltenham, UK: Edward Elgar Publishing; Luca Rubini (2010), *The Definition of Subsidy and State Aid: WTO and EC Law in Comparative Perspective*, New York: Oxford University Press; Pietro Poretti (2009), *The Regulation of Subsidies within the General Agreement on Trade in Services of the WTO: Problems and Prospects*, Alphen aan den Rijn, The Netherlands: Kluwer Law International; Kostantinos Adamantopoulos and Maria Jesus Pereyra-Friedrichsen (2007), *EU Anti-subsidy Law and Practice*, London: Sweet & Maxwell; Marc Benitah (2001), *The Law of Subsidies under the GATT/WTO System*, Alphen aan den Rijn, The Netherlands: Kluwer Law International; Fabian Böhm (2007), *Strukturen internationalen Subventionsrechts: EG-Beihilfenrecht und WTO-Subventionsrecht aus rechtsvergleichender Perspektive*, Frankfurt: Peter Lang. For valuable context cf. Andrew L. Stoler (2010), 'The Evolution of Subsidies Disciplines in GATT and the WTO', 44:4 *Journal of World Trade*, 797–808; Debra P. Steger (2010), 'The Subsidies and Countervailing Measures Agreement: Ahead of Its Time or Time for Reform?', 44:4 *Journal of World Trade*, 779–796.

7 Procedurally, it is of great interest to determine whether the decision of the Appellate Body only covers specific subsidies or, rather, a subsidy program. If the latter is the case, new manifestations of that program are covered by the pertinent decision of the DSB and thus allow the complainant to resort to procedures under Article 21.5 DSU, and thus to speedier resolutions. If the former is the case, any dissatisfaction caused due to harm incurred will have to be resolved by a new complaint: see para. 7.514 et seq. of the Panel Report and para. 471 et seq. of the Appellate Body Report.

8 See the wording of Article 5 SCM: 'No Member should cause, through the use of any subsidy referred to in paragraphs 1 and 2 of Article 1, adverse effects to the interests of other Members, i.e.: (a) injury to the domestic industry of another Member; (b) nullification or impairment of benefits accruing directly or indirectly to other Members under GATT 1994 in particular the benefits of concessions bound under Article II of GATT 1994; (c) serious prejudice to the interests of another Member.'

9 Appellate Body Report, *Airbus*, para. 655 et seq., in particular 681–690.

10 Ibid., para. 711. As a consequence of the European Union's mistaken interpretation of Article 5 (and 6) SCM, it 'conflate[d] present adverse effects, which must be demonstrated under Article 6.3, with present subsidization, which need not' (ibid., para. 712).

11 Ibid., para. 709.

Focusing on the nexus between subsidy and its alleged effect, the Appellate Body explained:

> At the time of the grant of a subsidy, the subsidy will necessarily be projected to have a finite life and to be utilized over that finite period. In order properly to assess a complaint under Article 5 that a subsidy causes adverse effects, a panel must take into account that a subsidy provided accrues and diminishes over time, and will have a finite life. The adverse effects analysis under Article 5 is distinct from the 'benefit' analysis under Article 1.1(b) of the SCM Agreement and there is consequently no need to re-evaluate under Article 5 the amount of the benefit conferred pursuant to Article 1.1(b). Rather, an adverse effects analysis under Article 5 must consider the trajectory of the subsidy as it was projected to materialize over a certain period at the time of the grant.[12]
>
> In sum, a panel's analysis of the adverse effects must take into account how the subsidy has materialized over time. As part of this analysis, a panel must assess how the subsidy is affected, both by the depreciation of the subsidy that was projected ex ante and the 'intervening events' referred to by a party that may have occurred following its grant.[13]

Thus, one may visualize the life-span of the subsidy *as such* and its effects as parallel curve graphs, which are not identical but rather in a sequencing order and may be partially overlapping.

3. Of course, it is one thing to embrace the concept that a subsidy must have an end, and another one to officially determine the 'time of death' – and the effect on the adverse-effect analysis under Article 5 SCM. The European Union had argued that 'sales of shares between private entities, and sales conducted in the context of partial privatizations' had eliminated all or part of past subsidies.[14] In support of this proposition, it had invoked the Appellate Body Reports in *US–Lead and Bismuth II*[15] and *US–Countervailing Measures on Certain EC Products*.[16]

12 Ibid.

13 *[Footnote in the original]* For this reason, we disagree with the Panel, at paragraphs 7.224, 7.225, and 7.266 of the Panel Report, insofar as it suggests that a consideration of 'intervening events', such as the 'extinction' and 'extraction' of subsidies, are not relevant under an adverse-effects analysis.

14 Appellate Body Report, *Airbus*, para. 724.

15 Appellate Body Report, *United States – Imposition of Countervailing Duties on Certain Hot-Rolled Lead and Bismuth Carbon Steel Products Originating in the United Kingdom*, WT/DS138/AB/R; see Gene M. Grossman and Petros C. Mavroidis (2003), 'United States – Imposition of Countervailing Duties on Certain Hot-Rolled Lead and Bismuth Carbon Steel Products Originating in the United Kingdom: Here Today, Gone Tomorrow? Privatization and the Injury Caused by Non-Recurring Subsidies', in Henrik Horn and Petros C. Mavroidis (eds.), *The WTO Case Law of 2001*, Cambridge: Cambridge University Press, pp. 170–200; see also Sherzod Shadikhodjaev (2012), 'How to Pass a Pass-Through Test: The Case of Input Subsidies', 15:2 *Journal of International Economic Law*, 621–646.

16 Appellate Body Report, *United States – Countervailing Measures Concerning Certain Products from the European Communities*, WT/DS212/AB/R.

Rightly, the Appellate Body highlights that both Reports only 'stand for the proposition that a presumption of *extinction*[17] arises where there is a full privatization' which involves sales at fair market value, at arm's length, and a subsequent full transfer of ownership and control. In *Airbus*, the Appellate Body had to examine to what extent a partial privatization and private-to-private sales had an equivalent effect on the lifespan of the subsidies in question. However, the three Appellate Body members tasked with DS316 could not agree on one consolidated position and chose to offer insights into their personal thinking:

(a) Noting that the Appellate Body has previously ruled in privatization cases that a full privatization, conducted at arm's length and for fair market value involving a complete or substantial transfer of ownership and control, 'extinguishes' prior subsidies, one Member is of the view that this rule does not apply to partial privatizations or to private-to-private sales.

(b) One Member noted that, as discussed above, the Appellate Body ruled in *US–Countervailing Measures on Certain EC Products* that ... full privatization at arm's length and for fair market value *may* result in extinguishing the benefit received from the nonrecurring financial contribution bestowed upon a state-owned firm[18] ... This Member considers the *rationale* underlying the Appellate Body's case law on full privatization in the context of Part V of the *SCM Agreement* equally to apply in situations of partial privatization and private-to-private transactions and in the context of Part III of the *SCM Agreement*. However, this Member also notes that, as the Appellate Body emphasized in *US–Countervailing Measures on Certain EC Products*, there is 'no inflexible rule' that a 'benefit' derived from pre-privatization financial contributions expires following privatization at arm's length and for fair market value.[19] Rather ... '[i]t depends on the facts of each case'.[20] An important question in this context is to what extent the partial privatization or private-to-private transactions resulted in a transfer of control to new owners who paid fair market value for shares in the company.

(c) One Member of the Division, though affirming the general test that an extinction of benefit is to be determined upon a consideration of all relevant facts, entertains no small measure of doubt that an acquisition of shares, concluded at arm's length and for fair market value, constitutes relevant circumstances warranting the conclusion that an extinction of benefit has taken place. A subsidy granted to a recipient company contributes to the net asset value of that company. The value of that asset permits the recipient to enjoy an enhanced stream of future earnings over the life of the asset. The asset is the property of the recipient. The recipient's shareholders enjoy the right to the dividends that may

17 Emphasis added.

18 Appellate Body Report, *US–Countervailing Measures on Certain EC Products*, para. 127.

19 Ibid.

20 Ibid.

> be declared by the recipient and to any capital gains that arise from the enhanced earnings attributable to the recipient. When shares change hands on an arm's-length basis and for fair market value, the buyer pays a price that, in the estimation of the buyer, places a proper value on the future earnings of the recipient. Those earnings derive from all the assets of the recipient, including the benefit of any subsidy paid to the recipient. One shareholder may not accurately value or properly manage the assets of the recipient. Precisely for this reason, sales of shares take place: the buyer believes that the assets, properly managed, will be worth more over time than the price paid, and the seller believes the opposite. Time will tell who is correct. The central point is that a sale of shares, whether or not it conveys control, transfers rights in the shares to a new owner. The assets of the company, to which the shares attach, do not change at all. Nor could it be otherwise, because the buyer would then not acquire the full benefit of the bargain: the buyer would pay for an asset (the subsidy) that had in the very sales transaction been 'extinguished'. Shares in listed companies are traded on stock exchanges with great frequency and without any fear that sales on the market diminish the underlying value of the assets owned by these companies. The changing price of listed securities reflects the different valuations that buyers and sellers place upon companies and their underlying assets. However, nothing about these trades extracts the value of any asset, including the benefit of any subsidy granted. That subsidy continues to benefit the recipient, even if the ownership of the recipient's shares changes from one day to another. Given that the Appellate Body in this case does not need to come to any final view on the issue of extinction in the context of a partial privatization or private-to-private sales, these matters do not require more definitive determination.

The Appellate Body had the luxury to not decide the issue as it was of the opinion that the Panel's analysis had drastically fallen short of what was required in the matter: arguments of the European Union with regard to the quality of the transactions in question had, in the Appellate Body's view, not received due attention, both with regard to factual findings and the care with which the arguments of the European Union had been dealt with. This reluctance of the Appellate Body is to be regretted; more clarity on this point would have been most welcome.

4. In addition, the Appellate Body rejected the European Union's proposition that the removal of cash from two Airbus partners constituted an '*extraction*' of subsidies. Recognizing this possibility in principle, it decided that the transactions brought forward by the European Union were not 'of such a nature, kind, and amount as to be relevant to its adverse effects analysis'. In particular, it doubted the existence of a specific relationship between subsidy and cash removal:

> we do consider that, at a *minimum*, the European Communities was required to explain how the specific subsidies received by Dasa and CASA were reflected in

> the balance sheets of those companies, and how the cash removed or 'extracted' represented the remaining or unused value of these subsidies. The mere assertion by the European Communities, without more, that subsidies to Dasa and CASA increased the value of those companies and that *therefore* any cash taken out represents the subsidy or its 'incremental value', does not in our view satisfy the requirement of establishing a 'causal relationship' between the 'cash extraction' and the subsidy.[21]

A second criterion, namely 'whether it had been demonstrated that the extracted cash permanently left or moved beyond the reach of the "company-shareholder unit"' could be left to be analyzed on another day.

5. How to calculate the benefit provided by Launch finance from the four EU Member states concerned? When answering this question, the Appellate Body had the benefit of having had been exposed to numerous arguments from the parties to the dispute on how to define the relevant benchmark for the *ex-ante*-rate-of-return that would have been the threshold for market investors to undertake investment. For all practical purposes, the question focuses on the risk premium a rational private investor would demand in order to engage financially with regard to the different LCA product launches. Emphasizing that point, the Appellate Body's Report[22] stresses that the assessment has to take place on an *ex ante* perspective, i.e. as if it was taken when the profit-maximizing lender and cost-averse borrower commit to the transaction. How the loan actually performed over time is irrelevant: the benefit of hindsight is denied even to the most astute private investors.

6. The central issue analyzed by the Appellate Body in regard to assessing whether the challenged financing measures confer benefit concerns can be separated into two questions: firstly, whether a single fixed project specific-risk premium for all LCA product launches (derived from a 2004 study of venture capital investments) represents an appropriate quantification or whether a more accurate estimate is that obtained from anticipated returns of a sample of risk-sharing suppliers to A 380. In its assessment, the Appellate Body identifies[23] technical problems and inconsistencies in both alternatives. Nevertheless, as both attempts to quantify the appropriate risk premium come to the conclusion that the challenged Launch Aid/Member States' Financing measures do not fully reflect market conditions at the time, the Appellate Body accepts that the LA/MSF measures confer a benefit within the meaning of Article 1.1(b) SCM Agreement. A significant missing element is, however, the lack of a quantitative estimate of the subsidy element represented by LA/MSF measures, thus impeding a realistic and

21 Appellate Body Report, *Airbus*, para. 746.
22 Ibid., paras. 836 and 837.
23 Ibid., paras. 923–928.

robust analysis of the actual displacement orders data when considering that Boeing was receiving subsidies over much of the same period.

II.

1. To the extent they entail the damaging effects on fellow WTO members, enumerated in Article 5 SCM Agreement, subsidies stop being a purely internal method of states influencing the behavior of their economic operators and turn into a matter of interest for WTO law. If a state can show that another state's subsidy has the negative impact described in Article 5 SCM Agreement, it can react, either by attacking the subsidy in the multilateral DSU procedure, or unilaterally by offsetting the harming consequences through countervailing duties.

However, there is a mortal sin that is so wrong (according to the contracting parties to the SCM Agreement) that no concrete adverse-effect damage needs to be shown: a subsidy is, pursuant to Articles 3 and 4 SCM, *per se* prohibited (and thus: attackable and countervailable in a particularly swift and sharp manner) if it is (*de iure* or *de facto*) conditional upon either *export performance* or upon the use of domestic over-imported goods.[24] Article 3 SCM reads in its relevant parts:

> [T]he following subsidies . . . shall be prohibited:
>
> (a) subsidies contingent, in law or in fact[4], whether solely or as one of several other conditions, upon export performance, including those illustrated in Annex I; []
>
> Original Footnote 4 reads:
>
> This standard is met when the facts demonstrate that the granting of a subsidy, without having been made legally contingent upon export performance, is in fact tied to actual or anticipated exportation or export earnings. The mere fact that a subsidy is granted to enterprises which export shall not for that reason alone be considered to be an export subsidy within the meaning of this provision.

2. The measures attacked by the US complaint were not contingent *in law*: none of the legal documents forming the legal basis for the support measures established that the benefit granted was conditional upon Airbus exports.

3. Of course, Airbus operates in a global market (see infra, Subsection III.2). If it was to be a commercial success, it had to acquire market share in the global and (provided they really exist) in regional markets. And while many details about the future champions of the global commercial airline industry were not foreseeable at the time when decisions were made, it was crystal clear that without export markets the project would, quite literally, not fly: how could, for example, the A 380 *not* be

24 Mavroidis *et al.* (2008), above note 6, p. 293.

an economic debacle, unless it acquired significant market share in the Gulf and in the Asia-Pacific region? Despite the US suspicion that EU states subsidize no matter what, European taxpayers expected, given the amounts at stake, at least a significant part of their money back. And that was only to happen if non-EU orders would fill Airbus books.

Relying on detail-rich and not necessarily always completely clear prior Appellate Body case law, the United States could hence make a plausible claim that what the Europeans had done amounted to an *a priori* illegal export subsidy, and should be subjected to the most far-reaching sanctions[25] in WTO law: wasn't the grant of subsidies based on the expectation that Airbus would be an export success? The link between subsidy and export expectation fulfilled, in the complainant's view, the essence of what an export subsidy is: pay-outs tied to export performance. The Panel bought into that narrative: without reasonable expectation of export performance, no business case for Airbus; without a business case, no subsidies; *de facto* thus, the Panel opined, the subsidies were tied to export performance, contingent *in fact* upon exports. In doing so, it relied heavily on the fact that sometimes the documentations of the financing included specific references to exports while this was not the case in others. In the latter case, the Panel accepted that these were actionable subsidies whereas in the former the *rough justice*[26] of the SCM's Part II applied.

4. Prior case law with regard to *de facto* contingency may be summarized as follows: the Appellate Body Report on *Brazil–Aircraft (Article 21.5–Canada)*[27] clarified that a subsidy coming under the purview of the *Illustrative List*[28] was *ipso facto* prohibited; a complainant need not show in detail that the general requirements of Article 3.1 SCM are met. To the contrary, if a support measure does not appear on the *Illustrative List*, the complainant will have to demonstrate that the subsidizing state 'either in law or in fact' made payment conditional on either exports or the use of domestic goods.

In *Canada – Measures Affecting the Export of Civilian Aircraft* ('*Canada–Aircraft*'),[29] the Appellate Body, paying particular attention to the SCM's footnote 4, decided that mere knowledge of the beneficiary's exporting activities

25 For prohibited subsidies, the normal rules of the DSU do not apply. Given that they are ranked at the highest order of WTO violation, deadlines are shortened significantly; cf. Andrew Green and Michael Trebilcock (2007), 'Enforcing WTO Obligations: What Can We Learn from Export Subsidies?', 10:3 *Journal of International Economic Law*, 653–683.

26 Cf. *Reid* v. *Covert*, 354 US 1, at 35–36: 'military justice has been a rough form of justice emphasizing summary procedures, speedy convictions and stern penalties'.

27 *Brazil – Export Financing Programme for Aircraft, Second recourse by Canada to Article 21.5 of the DSU* (WT/DS46/RW/2) 26 July 2001 (*Brazil–Aircraft (Article 21.5–Canada)*).

28 An Illustrative List to the SCM (Annex I) offers a nonexhaustive list of prohibited *export subsidies* which indicates 12 types of support measures.

29 Appellate Body Report, *Canada – Measures Affecting the Export of Civilian Aircraft*, WT/DS70/AB/R (*Canada–Aircraft*).

would not suffice for the *de facto* threshold to be met. Something more is required, the Appellate Body explained:

> The second substantive element in footnote 4 is 'tied to'. The ordinary meaning of 'tied to' confirms the linkage of 'contingency' with 'conditionality' in Article 3.1(a). Among the many meanings of the verb 'tie', we believe that, in this instance, because the word 'tie' is immediately followed by the word 'to' in footnote 4, the relevant ordinary meaning of 'tie' must be to 'limit or restrict as to ... conditions'. This element of the standard set forth in footnote 4, therefore, emphasizes that a relationship of conditionality or dependence must be demonstrated ... In any given case, the facts must 'demonstrate' that the granting of a subsidy is *tied to* or *contingent upon* actual or anticipated exports. It does *not* suffice to demonstrate solely that a government granting a subsidy *anticipated* that exports would result.

Canada–Aircraft then cautioned:

> The second sentence of footnote 4 precludes a panel from making a finding of *de facto* export contingency for the sole reason that the subsidy is 'granted to enterprises which export' ... The second sentence of footnote 4 is, therefore, a specific expression of the requirement in the first sentence to demonstrate the 'tied to' requirement.[30]
>
> ... *De jure* export contingency is demonstrated on the basis of the words of the relevant legislation, regulation or legal instrument. Proving *de facto* export contingency is a much more difficult task. There is no single legal document which will demonstrate, on its face, that a subsidy is 'contingent ... in fact ... upon export performance'. Instead, the existence of this relationship of contingency, between the subsidy and the export performance, must be inferred from the total configuration of the facts constituting and surrounding the granting of the subsidy, none of which on its own is likely to be decisive in any given case ... We note that satisfaction of the standard for determining *de facto* export contingency set out in footnote 4 requires proof of three different substantive elements: first, 'the granting of a subsidy'; second, 'is ... tied to ...'; and third, 'actual or anticipated exportation or export earnings.'[31]

30 Ibid., para. 174 (italics and emphasis in the original).

31 Ibid., paras. 169 and 175. The Appellate Body Report on *United States – Tax Treatment for 'Foreign Sales Corporations' – Recourse to Article 21.5 of the DSU by the European Communities*, WT/DS108/AB/RW, adopted 29 January 2002, DSR 2002:I, 55 (*US–FSC (Article 21.5–EC)*), citing prior relevant case law, provided its understanding of the evidentiary standard associated with a proof that a *de jure* export subsidy indeed occurred: 'We recall that in *Canada–Autos*, we stated: ... a subsidy is contingent "in law" upon export performance when the existence of that condition can be demonstrated on the basis of the very words of the relevant legislation, regulation or other legal instrument constituting the measure ... [F]or a subsidy to be *de jure* export contingent, the underlying legal instrument does not always have to provide *expressis verbis* that the subsidy is available only upon fulfilment of the condition of export performance. Such conditionality can also be derived by necessary implication from the words actually used in the measure.' *US–FSC (Article 21.5–EC II)*, para. 112; see also *Australia – Subsidies Provided to Producers and Exporters of Automotive Leather (Article 21.5 – US)*, WT/DS126/RW and Corr. 1, adopted 11 February 2000 (*Australia–Automotive Leather II (Article 21.5–US)*), paras. 9.36–9.66.

5. The *Airbus Report* develops that body of law:[32] far from breaking with prior precedents, it clearly adds new elements to the definition of an export subsidy under Article 3 SCM. Whereas the Panel had 'equated the standard of export contingency with the reasons(s) for granting a subsidy'[33] – and probably could do so reasonably expecting to be in line with prior Appellate Body jurisprudence – the Appellate Body, this time in no uncertain terms, rejects a 'standard that requires anticipated exportation to be the reason for the granting of the subsidy'.[34] It explicitly states that 'the standard for *de facto* export contingency is [neither] met . . . by showing that anticipated exportation is the reason for granting the subsidy . . . [nor by showing] the subjective motivation of the granting government to promote the future export performance of the recipient'.[35]

Rather, building on its prior jurisprudence, the Appellate Body developes the notion that a subsidy must be 'geared to the promotion of exports':

> Because anticipated exportation 'alone is not proof that the granting of the subsidy is *tied to* the anticipation of exportation',[36] the legal standard for *de facto* export contingency under Article 3.1(a) and footnote 4 of the *SCM Agreement* further requires that there exists a relationship of conditionality between the granting of the subsidy and anticipated exportation. Where a subsidy is alleged to be 'in fact tied to . . . anticipated exportation', the relationship of conditionality is, unlike in the case of *de jure* export contingency, not expressly or by necessary implication . . . can be established by recourse to the following test: *is the granting of the subsidy geared to induce the promotion of future export performance by the recipient?*[37]

The new operative word for describing the special nexus between export performance and the granting of a subsidy is the term *geared*. The Report uses it 20 times, indicating that its drafters wanted to let the world know that a new concept has been added to pre-existing case law. What does it mean, then? The Appellate Body answers this question in para. 1045 of its Report:

> Rather . . . the standard for *de facto* export contingency under Article 3.1(a) and footnote 4 of the *SCM Agreement* would be met when the subsidy is granted so as to provide an *incentive* to the recipient to *export in a way that is not simply reflective of the conditions of supply and demand* in the domestic and export markets undistorted by the granting of the subsidy.

32 For an understandably partial *and* excellent analysis see James Flett (2012), 'From Political Pre-occupation to Legitimate Rule against Market Partitioning: Export Subsidies in WTO Law after the Appellate Body Ruling in the *Airbus* Case', 7:2 *Global Trade and Customs Journal*, 50–58.

33 Appellate Body Report, *Airbus*, para. 1063.

34 Ibid.

35 Ibid., para. 1064.

36 [Original Footnote 2342] Appellate Body Report, *Canada–Aircraft*, para. 172 (original emphasis).

37 Appellate Body Report, *Airbus*, para. 1044 (emphasis added).

In line with other tests established by the Appellate Body that are supposed to avoid the appearance to examine, *horibile dictu*, intent,[38] the Appellate Body establishes *pro forma* objective criteria that are, nevertheless, not free from highly subjective connotations:

> The standard for determining whether the granting of a subsidy is 'in fact tied to . . . the existence of *de facto* export contingency . . . 'must be *inferred* from the total configuration of the facts constituting and surrounding the granting of the subsidy', which may include the following factors: (i) the design and structure of the measure granting the subsidy; (ii) the modalities of operation set out in such a measure; and (iii) the relevant factual circumstances surrounding the granting of the subsidy that provide the context for understanding the measure's design, structure, and modalities of operation.[39] . . . [This] is an objective standard . . . Indeed, the conditional relationship between the granting of the subsidy and export performance must be objectively observable on the basis of such evidence in order for the subsidy to be geared to induce the promotion of future export performance by the recipient.[40]

To what extent does that test establish a standard that deviates from *de jure* export subsidies? After all, it may be imaginable that an *explicit* linkage between export performance and the granting of a subsidy would not qualify as an 'incentive to the recipient to export in a way that is not simply reflective of the conditions of supply and demand in the domestic and export markets undistorted by the granting of the subsidy'. An explicit reference in (domestic) law or in an executive act would then suffice to render a previously as such perfectly legal subsidy – subject only to the limitation to not create the consequences described in Article 5 SCM – into one of the rare instances where the WTO Agreement explicitly states that a state measure is *prohibited*, and thus utterly illegal, subject to the harshest procedural treatment dispended by the WTO Agreement.[41] So could there be a difference between the standard applicable to *de jure* export subsidies and those applicable to *de facto* export subsidies?

Upon closer inspection – and absent laboratory conditions that the Appellate Body does not view as the appropriate test environment[42] – it seems difficult to

38 Appellate Body Report, *Airbus*, para. 1050: 'The standard for *de facto* export contingency is therefore not satisfied by the subjective motivation of the granting government to promote the future export performance of the recipient.'

39 Ibid., para. 1046.

40 Ibid., para. 1050.

41 See the analysis by Konstantinos Adamantopoulos and Vassilis Akritidis (2008), 'Article 3 SCMA', in Rüdiger Wolfrum, Peter-Tobias Stoll, and Michael Koebele (eds.), *Max-Planck Commentaries on World Trade Law, Vol. IV (WTO–Trade Remedies)*, Leiden, The Netherlands: Martinus Nijhoff Publishers, pp. 471–486.

42 The Appellate Body subscribes to the notion that assessments should be made in the 'real world where people live, work and die': Appellate Body Report, *EC – Measures Concerning Meat and Meat Products (Hormones)*, WT/DS26 and WT/DS48, para. 187.

imagine an explicit conditionality between the granting of public funds and export performance that would not constitute an incentive to export *more*, both in absolute and relative terms, than would have been the case under exposure to normal market influences. That would meet the standard established in *Airbus* – it should be recalled: an evidentiary standard! – for *de facto* export subsidies. Because the difference between the WTO regimes for *a priori* illegal export subsidies and for normal state aid are so stark (in both theory and procedural practice), *some* nexus between subsidy and export performance does not suffice to declare measures of a sovereign Member *a priori* illegal. In the case of the *de iure* export subsidy, the support measure is explicitly and manifestly contingent on export performance.[43] Of course, the interpretation of the wording of a text allegedly establishing *de iure* contingency may prove difficult, and in that case the interpreter will take guidance from the *Airbus Report.*

To sum up this point: in line with the general rules, it behooves the complainant to show (and to the adjudicatory bodies of the WTO to establish) that the state measure in question skews market conditions in order to view support measures as per se illegal export subsidies; if it cannot be shown that a subsidy is geared to induce more exports, contrary to market conditions, then it qualifies as a regular subsidy, actionable pursuant to part III of the SCM Agreement, but not one that merits summary justice and *a priori* condemnation.

It is in that light that the test whether a subsidy has been geared to induce the promotion of future export performance by the recipient has to be administered. Firstly, hindsight must not come into play: the test 'must be assessed on the basis of the information available to the granting authority at the time the subsidy is granted'.[44] The Appellate Body defines high thresholds:

> [W]here relevant evidence exists, the assessment could be based on a comparison between, on the one hand, the ratio of *anticipated* export and domestic sales of the subsidized product that would come about in consequence of the granting of the subsidy, and, on the other hand, the situation in the absence of the subsidy. The situation in the absence of the subsidy may be understood on the basis of historical sales of the same product by the recipient in the domestic and export markets before the subsidy was granted. *In the event that there are no historical data untainted by the subsidy*,[45] or the subsidized product is a new product for which no historical data exists, the comparison could be made with the performance that a profit-maximizing firm would hypothetically be expected to achieve in the export and domestic markets in the absence of the subsidy. Where the evidence shows, all other things being equal, that the granting of the subsidy

43 '*De jure* export contingency is demonstrated on the basis of the words of the relevant legislation, regulation or legal instrument. Proving *de facto* export contingency is a much more difficult task': *Canada–Aircraft*, para. 169 et seq.

44 Appellate Body Report, *Airbus*, para. 1049.

45 Emphasis added.

provides an incentive to skew anticipated sales towards exports, in comparison with the historical performance of the recipient or the hypothetical performance of a profit-maximizing firm in the absence of the subsidy, this would be an indication that the granting of the subsidy is in fact tied to anticipated exportation within the meaning of Article 3.1(a) and footnote 4 of the *SCM Agreement.*

6. The Appellate Body's Report in *EC and Certain Member States–Large Civil Aircraft* is certainly a welcome concretization of previously developed concepts. Building on previous jurisprudence, it explains for the first time in such a clear fashion that the decisive criterion for *de facto* export subsidies is the *favoring* of exports contrary to market conditions 'over products destined for domestic consumption'.[46] Only such a restrictive interpretation avoids the absurdity that, say, most Singaporean subsidies would *a priori* fall into the category of prohibited subsidies, as subsidies in a small country with an export-oriented economy will more often than not be granted in expectation of export performance and in order to increase such performance.

It would seem that the Appellate Body, in order to avoid pronouncing itself too firmly on questions that were either not asked or can, in the Appellate Body's opinion, await an answer on another day, refrained from establishing truly operational standards. In fact, it seems that the Appellate Body is even keen to get academic feedback, in particular from economists, to incrementally develop this jurisprudence.

Therefore, the Appellate Body limits itself to establishing some outer parameters of a new export subsidy definition, and illustrates it with an example that shows both the practicability (in the case at hand) but also the remaining, possibly intended, imprecision.

> 1048. The following numerical examples illustrate when the granting of a subsidy may, or may not, be geared to induce promotion of future export performance by a recipient. Assume that a subsidy is designed to allow a recipient to increase its future production by five units. Assume further that the existing ratio of the recipient's export sales to domestic sales, at the time the subsidy is granted, is 2:3. The granting of the subsidy will *not* be tied to anticipated exportation if, all other things being equal, the anticipated ratio of export sales to domestic sales is not greater than the existing ratio. In other words, if, under the measure granting the subsidy, the recipient would not be expected to export more than two of the additional five units to be produced, then this is indicative of the absence of a tie. By contrast, the granting of the subsidy would be tied to anticipated exportation if, all other things equal, the recipient is expected to export at least three of the five additional units to be produced. In other words, the subsidy is

46 Appellate Body Report, *Airbus*, para. 1053.

> designed in such a way that it is expected to skew the recipient's future sales in favour of export sales, even though the recipient may also be expected to increase its domestic sales.

Export subsidies are *per se* illegal, because they represent, in the mercantilist worldview underlying the GATT 1947 and to a large extent the WTO Agreements, an attack (our French colleagues still write on and teach *la guerre commerciale*) of a sovereign state on the (commercial) homeland of another state. Such a scenario, no doubt, would be caught by the standard offered by the Appellate Body.

The new test, however, deals with more complex and realistic constellations: imagine a scenario where the home market is saturated (yet) inexistent, or a scenario where the market is really a world market. If, in that case, a producer wants to expand, the expansion will unavoidably take place not in the domestic market. While the numerical example suggested by the Appellate Body would, at first glance, be cold comfort for such enterprises and the states subsidizing them, the test still reduces drastically the coverage of prohibited subsidies pursuant to Article 3 SCM: this is so because the determinative criterion is, according to the Appellate Body, *whether the subsidy would change the export–import ratio that would normally have developed as a consequence of unfettered supply and demand.*

It would seem that in many instances of state support, measures would be far too complex to be adequately addressed by the complete prohibition of Article 3 SCM. In the *Airbus* constellation that was arguably the case: *Airbus* was also an effort to be less dependent on a foreign quasi-monopoly, closely related with the military-industrial complex of that foreign state;[47] an effort to create incentives for further technological leadership, preserve and create professional jobs, and the like. In those constellations, the regular subsidies regime seems to offer a more appropriate instrument than part II of the SCM. Arguably these constellations often reflect market situations that cannot be assimilated to the *Ceteris Paribus* clause (referred to in paragraph 1047) 'all other things being equal'. The performance of a profit-maximizing entrant into a global market dominated by an incumbent with significant market power is likely to be the result of strategic interactions particularly in regard to product launches, resulting in important and persistent differentials in the margins on sales to customers depending on the degree to which the product ranges of the entrant and incumbent are substitutable. Such market situations can be expected to pose problems for the test proposed since they demand rigorous definitions of the geographic and product markets at issue so as to interpret reliably the trends in domestic and export sales.

Many of the challenges humankind faces in the next century – access to freshwater, transition to a post-carbon energy environment, global warming, food security, nano-technology, fight against multi-resistant pathogenic agents,

47 Public Papers of the Presidents, Dwight D. Eisenhower, 1960, pp. 1035–1040, quoted after http://www.h-net.org/~hst306/documents/indust.html (last visited 13 August 2012).

exploration of outer space and deep-water zones, development and containment of artificial intelligence, to give just a few examples – may benefit from launching aids that will inevitably benefit projects that target the world (i.e., the global market); in this context the distinction between domestic versus foreign consumption seems irrelevant. The potential competitive dangers of such state engagements are obvious, and the SCM offers in its part III et seq. appropriate and timely antidotes. The 'nuclear option' of part II, however, would not seem the appropriate avenue to control abuses of such subsidies.

III.

The Appellate Body upheld the Panel's view that certain launch-aid and other support measures caused serious prejudice to the interests of the United States within the meaning of Article 5(c) SCM. However, it comes as a great relief that the Appellate Body rejects the position of the Panel that in a case involving Article 6.3(a) and (b) SCM it is bound by the complainant's definition of the market at stake.

1. This is what the Appellate Body had to say in this regard:

> 1128 ... [I]n its analysis, the Panel deferred to the United States' subsidized product allegations [that there was – contrary to what the EC had said – only one subsidized product at issue in this dispute, consisting of all models of Airbus LCA] rather than making its own independent assessment of whether all Airbus LCA should be treated as a single subsidized product. In so doing, the Panel failed to make an objective assessment of the matter, including the 'applicability of and conformity with the relevant covered agreements', as required under Article 1 of the DSU ... [T]he Panel's failure to comply with its duties under Article 11 appears to flow directly from its erroneous interpretation of the requirements of Articles 6.3(a) and 6.3(b) of the SCM Agreement, which led it to believe that it lacked the power and was under no obligation to assess independently the 'subsidized product' and the relevant product market. In the absence of such a determination, the Panel did not have a proper basis for assessing whether the alleged subsidized and like products compete in the same market or multiple markets, which is a prerequisite for assessing whether displacement within the meaning of Articles 6.3(a) and 6.3(b) could be found to exist as alleged by the United States ...
>
> 1131. Clearly, there is no inhibition on how a complainant may choose to formulate its claim as to the scope of the 'subsidized product' ... This does not mean, however, that a panel has no duty to review the complainant's formulation of the scope of the 'subsidized product'. Rather, the panel has a duty to ascertain the relevant product market or markets in which the complainant's and respondent's products compete. The notion of 'subsidized product' and 'like product' is, in each case, to be analysed as an integral part of a panel's duty objectively to assess a particular claim of serious prejudice and its obligation to assess the relevant market under Articles 6.3(a) and 6.3(b).

This clarification is to be applauded. It is, of course, the duty of the Panel to define whether in reality pain was inflicted on other Members by subsidies. That requires competitive relationships, real ones, and not just the claim of a party to the dispute. The duty of the Panel to examine what the complaining party presents as the factual basis for its claims seems a self-evident proposition. The Panel is supposed to make an 'objective assessment'[48] of both facts and law; that seems hardly possible with a boilerplate internalization the position of one of the parties to the dispute. On the basis of the available empirical literature on the LCA industry, the benefits of a more refined definition of the product market would not have been theoretical, but, on the contrary, quite operational for the displacement analysis. Empirical studies of LCA industry[49] suggest that LCA models within the industry show quite different degrees of substitution between product ranges: LCA products in the same cluster (defined for example in terms of passenger capacity and range) compete closely with one another but the degree of substitution between the LCA models in different clusters vary widely. The importance of defining correctly the relevant product market is to enable a robust evaluation of displacement of a product by a product that exercises on it a competitive constraint. As noted by the Appellate Body[50] '[a]n assessment of the competitive relationship between products in the market is required in order to determine whether and to what extent one product may displace another. Thus, while a complaining Member may identify a subsidized product and like product by reference to footnote 46, the products thereby identified must be analyzed under the discipline of the product market so as to be able to determine whether displacement is occurring.' A similar reasoning extends to the notion of the geographic scope of the relevant product market. Where the market is cross-border or even global, the distinction between sales to the domestic 'market' and sales to the export 'market' disappear, and so do the terms domestic or export market shares. It follows that any conclusions on discernible displacement of a like product by a subsidized product have to be made on the basis of an objective determination of the relevant product market.

2. Of course, what irritates at first glance is the geographic compartmentalization of markets (e.g., Taiwan, Australia, India) whereas one would have believed that LCAs are exposed to competition in a global market. The key to the Appellate Body's approach is the wording of Article 6.3 SCM.[51] Its subparagraphs (a) and (b)

48 Article 11 DSU.

49 John Sutton (1998), *Technology and Market Structure: Theory and History*, in particular Chapter 16, 'A Complex Case', on civil aircraft, Cambridge, MA: MIT Press, pp. 415–471.

50 Appellate Body Report, *Airbus*, para. 1119.

51 6.3 Serious prejudice in the sense of paragraph (c) of Article 5 may arise in any case where one or several of the following apply: (a) the effect of the subsidy is to displace or impede the imports of a like product of another Member into the market of the subsidizing Member; (b) the effect of the subsidy is to

both concern effects of state aid in a geographically well-defined market: on the one hand 'the market of the subsidizing Member' and, on the other hand, 'a third country market'.

The Appellate Body, as any applier of the law, has to recognize the normative starting point, even though it may not represent a categorization current economic thinking would subscribe to.

> 1117. ... A plain reading of Articles 6.3(a) and 6.3(b) therefore reveals that an analysis of displacement or impedance under those provisions is limited to the territory of the 'subsidizing Member' or the territory of any third country at issue. The manner in which the geographic dimension of a market is determined will depend on a number of factors: in some cases, the geographic market may extend to cover the entire country concerned; in others, an analysis of the conditions of competition for sales of the product in question may provide an appropriate foundation for a finding that a geographic market exists *within* that area, for example, a region. There may also be cases where the geographic dimension of a particular market exceeds national boundaries or could be the world market, even though Articles 6.3(a) and 6.3(b) would focus the analysis of displacement and impedance on the territory of the subsidizing Member or third countries involved.

The Appellate Body however mentions, almost in passing in footnote 2462, that 'in terms of the geographic dimension of markets under Article 6.3(c) of the *SCM Agreement*, it may be appropriate to examine the "world market" and the conditions of competition as they exist in that market'. This, however, is the only occasion to do so, as the first two subparagraphs determine a territorial approach.

IV

1. An interesting economic and quantitative analysis of displacement of orders of Boeing that could be attributed to subsidies to Airbus is attempted by the Appellate Body Report in section IX.C.[52] The analysis is predicated on defining the relevant product market as consisting of three submarkets – *Single-aisle LCA, Twin-aisle LCA*, and *Very Large LCA*. This provisional definition of LCA was selected as it was not contested by either party. The method of analysis adopted by the Appellate Body was to examine the trends in the volume of sales and relative shares of the

displace or impede the exports of a like product of another Member from a third country market; (c) the effect of the subsidy is a significant price undercutting by the subsidized product as compared with the price of a like product of another Member in the same market or significant price suppression, price depression or lost sales in the same market; (d) the effect of the subsidy is an increase in the world market share of the subsidizing Member in a particular subsidized primary product or commodity as compared to the average share it had during the previous period of three years and this increase follows a consistent trend over a period when subsidies have been granted.

52 Appellate Body Report, *Airbus*, para. 1158 et seq.

orders of each of the manufacturers to specific countries, over a six-year reference period. The analysis is therefore very much along the lines outlined in paragraph 1048 of the Report. The analysis of the orders data over 2001–2006 leads the Appellate Body to confirm displacement of Boeing sales to half of the specific countries put forward by the complainant:[53] in terms of unit sales over the period to these countries this amounted to 70% of total orders. This can be regarded as significant, if attention is limited to just these countries, but much less significant in relation to global LCA orders over the reference period.

2. In regard to lost sales, the Appellate Body Report is careful to define the term and the approach needed to identify lost sales 'caused' by the challenged measures. As noted by the Appellate Body Report, this case was the first instance when the issue had been examined by it, under Article 6.3(c) of the SCM Agreement. The Report underlines that the analysis compare the sales actually made by the competing firm(s) of the complaining Member with the sales resulting from a counterfactual scenario in which the firm(s) of respondent Member would not have received the challenged subsidies.[54] The central element in the counterfactual underlying the Appellate Body's Report is that displaced and lost sales for Boeing to certain geographic destinations occurred because the challenged subsidies made it possible for Airbus to launch rival offerings at the time it did. But for the subsidies, there would not have been the availability of competitive alternatives and wider choice of LCA specifications, and hence no loss or displacement of Boeing sales over the reference period would have taken place.

3. In order to fine-tune displaced and lost sales of Boeing during 2001–2006, alternative counterfactual scenarios including the 'no-subsidy' case for Airbus are considered in the Report. For a consistent approach, it would have been necessary to develop a global demand growth evolution corresponding to delayed development of product families by Airbus. Such a counterfactual would have highlighted greatly reduced pressure on Boeing to undertake expensive development expenditure of its own product range. The *Airbus Report* does not consider that there would be a different evolution of global LCA demand-growth under the scenario of a reduced Airbus operation. The common assumptions under the counterfactual scenarios considered are that the development of LCAs by Boeing over the whole period and the global demand for all types of LCAs would be as it actually was during the whole period. An incumbent, dominant or not, has no profit incentives and faces no price pressures from captive customers to escalate developmental spending so as to meet or create prospective demand. On the assumption that Boeing's product development over the period did not benefit from

53 Ibid., para. 1203.
54 Ibid., para. 1216.

subsidies, the basic analytical framework is certainly correct, but simulations reported equate the time pattern of global LCA growth development and product launches by the incumbent in the 'no subsidy' case to the realized development over the reference period of global LCA demand growth and product launches. The core dynamics of LCA industry in the form of strategic interactions between competitors regarding developmental expenditures leading to product launches that simultaneously drive demand growth, as well as react to that demand growth, are not adequately incorporated in the counterfactual simulations.

4. The conclusions[55] drawn in the Appellate Body Report on displacement of sales and lost sales favor, based on the evidential record before the Panel, the counterfactual scenarios that assume that without subsidies there would not have been the same development pace of LCA products of Airbus.

4. Conclusions

1. It is a mixed blessing for the WTO dispute-settlement mechanism that the *Airbus* and *Boeing* cases have been brought. If there ever was a constellation ill-suited for being 'battled out in court', it was this dispute between two close trading partners and military allies, sharing for the moment the lead with regard to large civil aircrafts. While this is not apparent when reading the *Airbus Report* – whereas in the sister Boeing Report[56] the strong involvement of the military is obvious, as the granting authorities are the Pentagon and NASA – it is clear that the European public authorities granting the subsidies in question did so not the least in order to avoid a complete dependency on US aerospace technology that would have had the potential to be crippling on many levels. Regardless of whether these vital interest connotations would have sufficed to reach the threshold necessary for an invocation of Article XXI GATT, they were (and are) real nonetheless. Certainly, the United States has a history of active avoidance of having independent adjudicators look at issues that are of security relevance, and the European Union has never pushed too hard in this respect, as the last-minute compromise in the Helms–Burton dispute illustrates.[57]

Because of the economic significance of this dispute, the strong position of Boeing as a lobbyist, and the rather obvious violation of WTO and EU state-aid law

55 Ibid., paras. 1297–1300.

56 *United States – Measures Affecting Trade in Large Civil Aircraft* (Second Complaint), WT/DS353/AB/R (the *Boeing* Report), for which the same Appellate Body Members were responsible that had been in charge of the *Airbus Report*.

57 Cf. Stefaan Smis and Kim Van der Borght (1999), 'The EU–U.S. Compromise on the Helms-Burton and D'Amato Acts', **93**:1 *American Journal of International Law*, 227–236.

by the Europeans, low priority was given to the arguments advanced by those who preferred a noncontentious negotiated settlement. The result is, of course, far from satisfactory for the US interests pushing that agenda, given that both the European Union and the United States were held to be not in conformity with their obligations under the SCM. Now a dispute that is utterly limited to two trade superpowers and military allies will feed another generation of lawyers' children (maybe even cover their expensive graduate education . . .) and keep academics busy. While *these* results may allow us to rejoice, they would seem not to suffice to tip the balance in favor of an overall positive assessment: a good opportunity to *not* use the multilateral mechanism was missed.

That aside, and apart from some of the desiderata mentioned above, this is a well-crafted Report, in particular given the time constraints: for the United States, speedy justice in the WTO is of constitutional importance, as is illustrated by its threat to propose the application of (regular) consensus rule in the *COOL* case; given the completely different profile of the *Airbus* case, the right timing was very important.[58]

The dispute DS316 is far from over: the European Union, on 5 December 2011,[59] notified the DSB that it had taken appropriate steps to bring its measures fully into conformity with its WTO obligations:

> [T]he European Union took note of all elements of the DSB's recommendations and rulings, including, in particular, the . . . guidance on the way in which subsidies and adverse effects expire, dissipate, terminate or are otherwise removed or withdrawn. In undertaking this review, we consulted, among others, independent experts in: financial economics; investor behaviour; financial and cost auditing, accounting and controlling; product engineering; and Large Civil Aircraft (LCA) fleet management. We have also closely monitored and assessed LCA product and market developments . . . following the period covered by the Panel's review.
>
> As a result of this review, the European Union has adopted a course of action that addresses <u>all</u> forms of adverse effects, <u>all</u> categories of subsidies, and <u>all</u> models of Airbus aircraft covered by the DSB's recommendations and rulings.
>
> Specifically, in bringing its measures into conformity with its WTO obligations, the European Union has addressed all categories of subsidy covered by the DSB's recommendations and rulings: Member State Financing (MSF) loans, capital contributions, infrastructure support and regional aid. Amongst others, the European Union has secured repayment of MSF loans and terminated MSF agreements, increased fees and lease payments on infrastructure support to accord with market principles, and ensured that capital contributions and regional aid subsidies have, in the Appellate Body's words, 'come to an end' and are no longer capable of causing adverse effects. Additionally, the course of action

58 Cf. above note 43.

59 *EC and Certain Member States – Large Civil Aircraft*, WT/DS316/17.

> adopted by the European Union affects Airbus' A300, A310, A320, A330, A340 and A380 aircraft, as well as derivatives thereof, as implicated by the DSB's recommendations and rulings. Finally, as a result of these steps and other intervening market events, the European Union has addressed the forms of adverse effects covered by the DSB's rulings.

In the meantime, the United States had requested, on 9 December 2011, authorization to take countermeasures pursuant to Article 22 DSU and Article 7.9 SCM. Due to a sequencing arrangement, the matter is now before the original Panel: it is interesting, though, that the United States quoted para. 1264 of the Appellate Body Report:

> Without the subsidies, Airbus would not have existed under these scenarios and there would be no Airbus aircraft on the market. None of the sales that the subsidized Airbus made would have occurred. As Boeing (or the other US manufacturer envisaged by the Panel) would be the only supplier(s) of LCA, it (or they) would have made the sales instead.

That seems to indicate a willingness on the side of the complainant to give a broad reading to the European Union's obligation to remove the adverse effects of the subsidy: the line of reasoning would be that as long as there is Airbus, the harmful effects of the subsidies can be felt. It will be interesting to see how this argumentation plays out: the allegedly *wrongful birth* of Airbus did not hinder the Appellate Body to accept in *United States – Measures Affecting Trade in Large Civil Aircraft (Second Complaint)* (DS 353) that the European Union was capable of suffering, pursuant to Article 5(c) SCM, serious prejudice, as a consequence of the lost sales that Airbus had to digest as a consequence of US subsidies.

Thailand–Cigarettes (Philippines): A More Serious Role for the 'Less Favourable Treatment' Standard of Article III:4

WILLIAM J. DAVEY
College of Law, University of Illinois
KEITH E. MASKUS
Department of Economics, University of Colorado, Boulder

Abstract: This paper analyzes a number of economic and legal issues raised by the Appellate Body Report in the *Thai–Cigarettes* case. The paper suggests two improvements that could be made to Panel procedures; supports the Appellate Body's interpretation of Article XX(d) in the present case, which seems to discard an earlier mistaken approach to Article XX; and examines, in some detail, whether the Appellate Body's application of the 'less favourable treatment' component of GATT Article III:4 in this and other cases is consistent with its jurisprudence under GATT Article III:2 and TBT Article 2.1. From an economics perspective, the case is straightforward on its face. However, the Appellate Body's rigorous application of the 'less favourable treatment' principle might not survive a fuller market analysis in terms of policy impacts on conditions of competition. Further, while we agree with the rejection of Thailand's Article XX claim, we raise the question of whether a strict national-treatment rule may be an unwarranted constraint on policy where there is a clear trade-related external cost to address.

1. Introduction

Thailand – Customs and Fiscal Measures on Cigarettes from the Philippines (DS371),[1] hereafter labelled *Thai–Cigarettes*, has at its heart a number of questions surrounding national treatment in Article III:2 of GATT 1994 and the concept of 'less favourable treatment' in Article III:4. In particular, Thailand was charged with engaging in practices that resulted in excessive customs duties on imported cigarettes and excessive value-added taxes charged to imported cigarettes in

1 The Panel and Appellate Body Reports were adopted on 15 July 2011. The reasonable period of time for implementation was set at ten months (expiring 15 May 2012), except in respect of the VAT exemption for resellers of domestic cigarettes, in which case it was set at 15 months (expiring 15 October 2012). WT/DS371/14 (27 September 2011). It appeared that, as of June 2012, Thailand had not completed implementation. WT/DS371/15/Add.2 (15 June 2012).

comparison with domestic competing brands. Moreover, the structure of the Thai VAT placed more onerous administrative burdens on resellers of imported cigarettes than on resellers of domestic like products, suggesting that imports were treated less favourably. In principle, this system could alter the conditions of competition in favour of Thai's monopoly producer and restrain sales of imported brands.

The dispute arose from issues of customs valuation, with the Philippines claiming that Thai Customs had, in the period 2006–2007, systematically rejected the import values declared by Philip Morris Thailand (PMT) in favour of a deductive method that was outside its own procedures and improper under the rules of the WTO Customs Valuation Agreement (CVA). This method was alleged to establish higher cif (cost, insurance, and freight) import prices than would exist had PMT's declared values been accepted. The import price was the foundation for a constructed maximum retail-selling price (MRSP) for imported brands set by Thailand's Directorate General of Excise (DG Excise). The corresponding MRSP for domestic brands was built up from the ex-factory prices of the Thailand Tobacco Monopoly (TTM). The customs-valuation problem, along with added customs duties (for imports only) and a reserve for marketing costs (for both domestic and imported goods, but calculated differently), implied that the MRSPs for PMT's brands were systematically higher than those for TTM's brands.

The tax significance was that the MRSPs were the prices on which VAT collection was based. Because the MRSPs on imports were higher, they faced higher taxes in absolute terms. Thailand countered that its system was consistent with national treatment because the VAT rate was the same between domestic and imported cigarettes and the tax base was being established in the same manner for domestic and imported cigarettes in most instances.[2] However, a further significant issue was that resellers of domestic brands were fully exempted from collecting and paying VAT, while resellers of foreign brands were not. This imposed a stiffer administrative burden on the latter, the basis for a charge that the system offered less favourable treatment to imports.

After seeking consultations, in 2008 the Philippines requested a WTO Panel to investigate these issues. The Panel was established on 17 November 2008 and the Panel Report was circulated to WTO members two years later on 15 November 2010, much beyond the DSU's suggested time frame of nine months between Panel establishment and Report circulation. The Panel found that Thai Customs had acted inconsistently with its obligations under the CVA by: (i) rejecting PMT's declared values in 2006 and 2007 in violation of Articles 1.1 and 1.2; (ii) failing to communicate the grounds for this rejection in violation of Article 1.2(a); (iii) failing

2 In three instances, Thailand in effect did not contest that a different methodology was used for imports, and, in one further instance, the Panel found a difference in how the tax base for imports was calculated. These findings were not appealed.

to provide an adequate explanation for how it determined customs values for imported cigarettes in violation of Article 16; (iv) assessing improperly the deductive value of imported cigarettes in violation of Article 7.1; (v) failing to properly inform PMT of the customs value determined under Article 7.1 and the method used to calculate that value in violation of Article 7.3; and (vi) revealing certain confidential business information to the media in violation of Article 10. These findings, though contested by Thailand in the Panel hearings, were not appealed to the Appellate Body.

The Panel also found Thailand had violated its national-treatment obligations in three ways. First, DG Excise violated GATT Article III:2, first sentence, by discriminating against imported cigarettes in the calculation of MRSPs, on which VAT was based, by using a less favourable method of calculating marketing costs for imported cigarettes than it used for calculating such costs for domestic cigarettes. Second, the VAT exemption for resellers of domestic cigarettes subjected imported brands to a VAT liability in excess of that facing like domestic cigarettes, a policy also inconsistent with Article III:2, first sentence. Third, the exemption subjected imported brands to less favourable treatment in violation of Article III:4 by imposing more burdensome administrative requirements on resellers of such brands as compared to resellers of domestic cigarettes. The Panel rejected Thailand's defense that the administrative burdens were necessary to safeguard against tax evasion, fraud, and counterfeiting of imported cigarettes. The defense was offered both as a claim that the discrimination did not violate Article III:4 and that it was permitted under the general exception found in Article XX(d). Thailand appealed all of these findings except for the first-described Article III:2 violation relating to the calculation of MRSPs.

The Panel also found that Thailand had violated a number of provisions of GATT Article X in connection with its imposition of customs duties and VAT on imported cigarettes. In particular, the Panel found that Thailand violated the publication requirements of Article X:1 by failing to publish (i) the methodology used to determine the price on which value-added tax would be levied on imported cigarettes and (ii) the general rules pertaining to the release of customs guarantees. The Panel also found that Thailand violated the reasonable administration requirement of Article X:3(a) in respect of delays in the [Customs] Board of Assessment process. In respect of Article X:3(b), which requires that WTO members must maintain judicial, arbitral, or administrative tribunals or procedures for the prompt review and correction of administrative action relating to customs matters, the Panel found that Thailand violated that obligation in respect of (i) customs valuation decisions and (ii) appeals of guarantee decisions. Only the latter finding regarding guarantee decisions was appealed.

Thailand appealed the various rulings indicated above in March 2011 and the oral hearing took place in April of that year, with both disputants and several third-party participants, including the United States, Australia, and the European Union, making representations about aspects of the case. In its Report, issued on 17 June 2011,[3] the Appellate Body upheld the Panel's finding that Thailand had acted inconsistently with the national-treatment requirement in Article III:2 by subjecting resellers of imported cigarettes to a higher tax liability. It also upheld the Panel ruling that the VAT exemption subjected imported cigarettes to less favourable treatment than domestic cigarettes, in violation of Article III:4. Further, while recognizing that tax systems may be defended under Article XX(d), the Appellate Body ruled that Thailand had not justified the necessity of its measure in that regard. Finally, it agreed with the Panel that Thailand had failed to provide the requisite independent review tribunals or processes to oversee decisions regarding guarantee charges.

On paper, this case seems rather straightforward and it is hard to fault either the Panel or the Appellate Body Reports. However, the case does raise a number of interesting legal and economic questions, which are the subject of the remainder of this paper. In Section 2, a brief review of trade data is offered to set an economic context. Section 3 presents the legal analysis, focused closely on the meaning of 'less favourable treatment'. In Section 4, we turn to the economics of this situation, raising specific questions. For example, if tax evasion is a problem more endemic to imported than domestic cigarettes, as Thailand claims, is a strict application of national treatment actually optimal? Another question worth asking is how such differential administrative burdens might change competitive market conditions, particularly in the presence of a domestic monopoly supplier. A further wrinkle here arises from the interdependence of the importer with its Philippines supplier and the determination of customs value, when that determination directly affects relative VAT charges. Finally, there is the question of how such administrative uncertainty in tax collections may influence competitive behaviour. We wrap up in a final section.

2. The international trade context

Thailand is a reasonably large market for cigarette consumption. According to the World Health Organization, around 24% of the country's 68 million people smoked cigarettes in 2009, though this proportion has been declining for some time because of active attempts to discourage this behaviour.[4] Indeed, survey data suggests that reported consumption fell from 1.26 billion packs in 1999 to 862 million packs in 2009.[5] At the same time, there appear to be significant amounts of counterfeit or smuggled cigarettes in circulation.

3 The notice of appeal was delayed by 40 days and the Appellate Body report was delayed 20 days beyond its normal 90-day deadline because of the Appellate Body's workload. WT/DS371/7 (7 December 2010); WT/DS371/9 (26 April 2011).

4 World Health Organization, *Report on the Global Tobacco Epidemic 2011*, Geneva.

5 Pavananunt, Pirudee (2009), 'Empirical Analysis of Cigarette Tax Avoidance in Thailand', research report to Tobacco Control Research and Knowledge Management Center, Mahidol University, November.

Table 1. Trade data in cigarettes, Thailand and the Philippines

	Thai imports ($ millions)			Philippine exports ($ millions)	
Year	World	Philippines	% Philippines	World	% Thailand
2005	95.6	66.8	69.8	102.7	64.9
2006	93.1	66.9	71.9	90.3	65.0
2007	92.7	78.2	84.3	89.5	70.9
2008	94.5	72.6	76.8	90.5	63.4
2009	80.8	59.9	74.2	79.7	60.4
2010	107.1	79.2	73.9	107.2	67.7

Source: United Nations COMTRADE database, category 240220.

Domestic manufacture of cigarettes is undertaken solely by the Thailand Tobacco Monopoly (TTM), which is a branch of the Ministry of Finance. Domestic production is monopolized, in principle, to help the government raise revenue from excise taxes, avoid tax evasion, control retail prices, and engage in deterrence campaigns. These objectives seem somewhat at odds with the mandate for TTM to maximize its profits.[6]

While Thailand prevents entry of domestic and international firms into local production for the market, imports have been successively liberalized, largely as a result of tariff cuts under the ASEAN Free Trade Agreement (signed in 1992). Thus, the share of imported brands of total legal cigarette sales rose rapidly from 3% in 1996 to 22% in 2006 (Pavananunt, 2009). Over the same period, the tariff rate faced by ASEAN partners, such as the Philippines, fell from 20% to 5% in three discrete stages. In contrast, the excise tax on tobacco products, levied on both imports and domestic goods, rose from 68% to 79%, attesting to the relatively high taxation of this commodity.

The Philippines is, by far, the largest source of imports of cigarettes into Thailand. Table 1 shows the value and quantities in recent years of Thai imports from the Philippines in 'cigarettes containing tobacco', category 240220 in the 2002 HS system. It also shows the share of Philippine exports in this category going to Thailand. Thus, Thailand's total imports were stable at around $93 million in this period, though they fell off to $81 million in 2009 before rebounding to over $100 million in 2010. On average, Philippine exporters had about 67–75% of the imports in Thailand. Looking at export data, the Philippines has averaged around $90 million to $100 million in total exports, with Thailand taking about 65–70%. Clearly, the Thai market is quite important for cigarette exporters in the

6 Thailand Tobacco Monopoly, *Annual Report 2009*, Bangkok.

Philippines. In that context, there are certainly political-economy reasons for the Philippines to be concerned about Thai restrictions on trade in this sector.

However, the dispute in question surrounds actions taken against a particular importer, Philip Morris Thailand (PMT), in the years 2006 and 2007. As may be seen, Thailand's recorded imports from the Philippines rose in these years, especially in 2007. Thus, there seems little reason to think that the Philippines request for a Panel was motivated by a marked reduction in aggregate trade. Rather, it was aimed at correcting what it saw as improper customs actions raised specifically against PMT and the associated impacts on value-added tax liabilities under Thailand's internal tax regulations.

3. Legal issues: a role for the 'less favourable treatment' standard of Article III:4?

As described above, the *Thai–Cigarettes* case involved a broad-based challenge by the Philippines to the treatment of imported cigarettes by Thailand. At the Panel level, the case was noteworthy from the legal perspective because of the extensive consideration given to the Customs Valuation Agreement (CVA), which has not often been the subject of dispute settlement.[7] However, the Panel's findings of several violations of the CVA were not appealed, nor was its basic finding of tax discrimination arising through the calculation of MRSPs under Article III:2 appealed. This, in itself, is striking because it appears that the genesis of the case was a perception on the part of PMT that Thailand had decided to increase significantly the customs duties and taxes payable on imported cigarettes through manipulation of the customs value of those cigarettes and their MRSP on which value-added taxes were based. Instead, the appeal was limited to rather narrow legal issues related to certain of the Panel's findings under GATT Article III (and an Article XX defense) and GATT Article X. In particular, the Appellate Body Report is noteworthy, if at all, because (i) it confirmed the Appellate Body's practice of giving a quite broad reading to Article III:2 and III:4; (ii) it seemed to restrict the coverage of the Article XX(d) defense compared to one past precedent; and (iii) it gave an expansive reading to Article X's obligation to provide review of customs decisions. In addition, there were two procedural issues of note discussed by the Appellate Body. The most interesting issue in the case was probably the Appellate Body's consideration of the less favourable treatment issue that arises in GATT Article III:4 claims, where it continued its practice of requiring little to be shown by a complainant to establish such treatment.

7 The only other WTO Panel Report ruling on the Customs Valuation Agreement was Panel Report, *Colombia – Indicative Prices and Restrictions on Ports of Entry*, WT/DS366/R, adopted 20 May 2009. The Appellate Body has yet to consider the agreement.

3.1 *Procedural issues*

There were two interesting procedural issues that should be mentioned in passing that arose in *Thai–Cigarettes.*

1. *Typographical errors*

First, on appeal of the Panel's findings on Article XX, it appeared that the Panel may have made an error in a cross-reference that was key to its conclusion on the inapplicability of the Article XX(d) defense raised by Thailand.[8] In defending the Panel's rejection of that defense, the Philippines argued that the cross-reference was a mere clerical error and that the Appellate Body should correct it. Since only the Panel could definitively answer the question of whether there was such an error, it would seem that the Panel could have been asked to correct or confirm the error (if it agreed that there was an error), but the Panel was not asked. Instead, the Appellate Body concluded that while the cross-reference was an 'obvious error', it was not clear what the correct cross-reference would have been, given that the Panel's analysis of the Article XX(d) defense was 'extremely brief', suggesting perhaps that more than a mere typographical error may have been involved.[9] Accordingly, the Appellate Body reversed the Panel's finding that Thailand had failed to establish a valid Article XX(d) defense.[10] It then proceeded to 'complete the analysis' of the issue and concluded that the defense was not established for reasons that are discussed below.[11]

As noted, it appears that the Panel was never asked to clarify the cross-reference. Assuming that the cross-reference was an error, it is unclear why the Panel was not asked. Perhaps it was felt that since the issue was first raised on appeal, the Panel was somehow incapable of responding to a request for clarification. It is not clear why this would be so. While it could be argued that a Panel ceases to exist, and therefore can no longer act on any issue, once it has issued its Report to the parties (or, at least, at the point when the Report is circulated to the WTO membership), it would seem that there is no inherent reason why a Panel could not correct typographical errors after its Report is issued and circulated. Indeed, corrigenda are routinely issued by the Secretariat, although not necessarily with the participation of the Panel. Moreover, unlike the days of GATT dispute settlement when the Panel had no further involvement with a case once the Report was issued, under the WTO Dispute Settlement Understanding the original Panel may be called upon to serve as a compliance Panel under DSU Article 21.5 or as the arbitrator of the level of suspension of concessions under DSU Article 22. Thus, Panels seem to have a

8 Appellate Body Report, *Thai–Cigarettes*, paras. 164–171.
9 Ibid., para. 170.
10 Ibid., para. 171.
11 See Section 3.3 infra.

continuing existence and could be asked by the Appellate Body to correct a typographical error if one is suspected.[12]

In this regard, it is noteworthy that judicial and arbitral bodies typically have such authority. For example, under the US Federal Rules of Civil Procedure, a federal district court may correct a clerical mistake or a mistake arising from oversight or omission whenever one is found in a judgment, on motion or on its own, with or without notice.[13] Similar provisions are found in the UNCITRAL and ICSID arbitration rules.[14] Such a procedure should be available at the WTO, as it would seem to be the best and most efficient way to deal with the sort of typographical error that arose in this case. While the WTO does not have detailed procedural rules like those of UNCITRAL and ICSID to which an appropriate provision could be added, in our opinion the power to correct errors in findings should be viewed as an inherent power of a tribunal.

2. *Right to respond to late-filed evidence*

In response to a question from the Panel following the second meeting with the parties that is at the very end of the typical Panel proceeding, Thailand presented evidence on one aspect of the VAT issue. This evidence essentially rebutted evidence offered at the second meeting by the Philippines. As provided for by the Panel, the Philippines were allowed to comment on Thailand's answer. In its comment, the Philippines submitted an additional piece of rebuttal evidence. Thailand did not ask to comment and did not comment on the new piece of evidence, although at the interim-review stage, Thailand argued that the Panel should not have relied on the new piece of evidence. In its final Report, the Panel ruled that it could rely on the evidence and noted that, as rebuttal evidence, it was not filed in an untimely manner under the Panel's rules.[15] On appeal, Thailand argued that its due-process rights were violated by the Panel's acceptance of the evidence and that the Panel had accordingly violated DSU Article 11.[16] The Appellate Body rejected the appeal, noting that the piece of evidence in question was only one of several pieces on the VAT issue that the Panel considered and that the contested piece of evidence did not

12 To the extent that having the Appellate Body ask a Panel a question might suggest that it was engaged in some sort of remand procedure not authorized by the DSU, the Appellate Body could take the position that it is incumbent on the party claiming that a typographical error is involved in a case to ask the Panel to correct the Report.

13 US Federal Rules of Civil Procedure, Rule 60(a). When an appeal is pending, such a mistake may be corrected only with the appellate court's leave.

14 UNICITRAL Arbitration Rules, Article 38, published by the United Nations Commission on International Trade Law, UNCITRAL Arbitration Rules as revised in 2010, at 24 (2011); ICSID Arbitration Rules, Rule 49, published by the International Centre for the Settlement of Investment Disputes, ICSID Convention, Regulations and Rules, ICSID/15, at 123 (April 2006); American Arbitration Association, Commercial Arbitration Rules, Rule 46 (2009).

15 Panel Report, *Thai–Cigarettes*, paras. 6.122–6.128.

16 Appellate Body Report, *Thai–Cigarettes*, paras. 141–161.

seem to be the principal basis for the Panel's ruling in any event.[17] It also noted that Thailand did not request an opportunity to respond.[18] This seems to be the correct result. One of the authors has served as a panelist on several occasions, and it would seem that Panels are generally open to allowing parties to comment on new evidence, whenever presented. However, the Panel's rules of procedure, which seem fairly standard, provided as follows:[19]

> The parties shall submit all factual evidence to the Panel no later than the first substantive meeting, except with respect to factual evidence necessary for the purposes of rebuttals, answers to questions or comments on answers provided by each other. Exceptions to this procedure will be granted where good cause is shown. In such cases, the other party shall be accorded a period of time for comment, as appropriate.

It would seem that the last sentence should be revised to make it clear that there is always a right to comment on evidence presented. For example, it could be rewritten to read:

> In **all** cases, the other party, **on request**, shall be accorded a period of time for comment, as appropriate.

Normally, there would only be a need for such a request in the situation that arose here, since typically there will in fact be an opportunity for the other party to comment on any evidence that is presented to the Panel. While it is possible, under such a rule, that parties will continue to trade counterevidence and counter-comments for some weeks after what was intended to be the end of the proceedings, the experience of the author who has been a panelist suggests that the parties run out of things to say rather quickly. Thus, adoption of such a rule should satisfy legitimate due-process concerns and should not in any way delay the issuance of the Panel Report.[20]

3.2 *Article III*

Under the applicable Thai tax regime, resellers of domestic cigarettes, which must be obtained from the government-owned tobacco monopoly, were not subject to value-added tax on their sales of cigarettes.[21] As a consequence, they were also not subject to any of the applicable administrative requirements connected with the tax.

17 Ibid., para. 159.

18 Ibid., para. 160.

19 Panel Report, *Thai–Cigarettes*, Annex A-1, para. 15.

20 An alternative approach would be to adopt working procedures that specify that no new evidence may be submitted in comments on the answers to Panel questions. This would ensure that parties have a last chance to comment on any evidence offered in a case, although it might prove to be unnecessarily constraining in some situations.

21 The Thai tax regime is described in detail in Section 4 and in the Appellate Body Report, *Thai–Cigarettes*, paras. 83–103.

Resellers of foreign cigarettes were subject to value-added tax on their sales of foreign cigarettes and the related administrative requirements. However, under Thai law, the amount of VAT collected on the sale of cigarettes at each stage of the resale chain from the manufacturer or importer to the ultimate seller to consumers is based on the maximum retail selling price set by the government for each brand, which means the tax due is the same on each sale. Thus, as is typical in a VAT system, since those subject to VAT are allowed to deduct the VAT paid by them to the seller of the cigarettes from the VAT they receive from their purchaser, the net VAT liability for those selling imported cigarettes is zero, assuming they comply with the applicable administrative requirements in respect of filing VAT returns and of keeping records. In other words, resellers of both domestic and imported cigarettes would normally have no liability for value-added tax on those products – the former because they were exempt from the tax and the latter because the net tax due would be zero given the use of a single price for calculating VAT liability at all stages of the distribution of cigarettes.

Given these circumstances, the Panel found a violation of Article III:2 since sellers of domestic cigarettes were exempt from the value-added tax, while resellers of imported cigarettes were subject to the tax. In the view of the Panel, while resellers of domestic cigarettes could never be subject to VAT on their sales of domestic cigarettes, resellers of foreign cigarettes were subject to VAT and might incur liability if certain conditions were not met (i.e., they failed to file the proper tax forms, retain the proper tax invoices, and meet other administrative requirements for obtaining a VAT refund).[22] Similarly, the Panel found a violation of Article III:4 in that resellers of foreign cigarettes were subject to various administrative requirements – filing tax returns, maintaining certain records, and filing certain reports, and penalties for failure to comply with these requirements – in connection with the VAT regime, while resellers of domestic cigarettes were not.[23]

1. *Article III:2*

On appeal of the finding of a violation in respect of Article III:2, Thailand essentially argued that there was no difference in tax liability because resellers of imported cigarettes could, by filing the proper forms and obtaining and keeping the necessary records, avoid any tax liability. The Appellate Body rejected this argument:[24]

> [W]e do not consider that Thailand's measure precludes a finding of inconsistency with Article III:2 due to the fact that resellers of imported cigarettes may take action to avoid imposition of VAT liability. In our view, the availability of such a course of action does not alter the legal assessment of whether, under Thai law,

22 Panel Report, *Thai–Cigarettes*, paras. 7.568–7.644.

23 Ibid., paras. 7.645–7.738.

24 Appellate Body Report, *Thai–Cigarettes*, paras. 117–118.

> imported cigarettes are subject to internal taxes or other internal charges in excess of those applied to domestic cigarettes. As we have explained, Thailand's measure provides for circumstances in which resellers of imported cigarettes will be subject to VAT liability, to which resellers of domestic cigarettes will never be subject.
>
> ... Imposing legal requirements that result in tax liability on imported products when resellers do not satisfy prescribed conditions necessary to avoid that liability, but which never result in tax liability on like domestic goods, is inconsistent with the requirements of Article III:2, first sentence.

In light of past precedents, this result is not at all surprising. For like products, ***no*** tax differential is permitted.[25] Here, such a differential could have occurred because of the structure of the Thai system. Ergo, that system is not consistent with Article III:2 under past case law. While one could question the significance of this differential treatment, there seemed to be no justification at all for treating resellers of domestic cigarettes and imported cigarettes differently. Requiring Thailand to treat both types of resellers the same way for tax purposes certainly does not seem to infringe in any meaningful way on Thailand's ability to tax and regulate cigarettes.

2. *Article III:4*

The appeal of the finding of a violation of Article III:4 presented a somewhat more difficult issue in that, unlike Article III:2, first sentence, which permits no differential treatment in respect of taxation, Article III:4 does permit different treatment of imported products, so long as the treatment is not less favourable than that accorded to domestic like products. Thus, origin-based discrimination is in theory permitted under Article III:4. Indeed, in *Korea–Beef*, where the Panel found that discrimination between domestic and imported products explicitly based on origin violated Article III:4, the Appellate Body reversed the Panel and stated:[26]

> A formal difference in treatment between imported and like domestic products is thus neither necessary, nor sufficient, to show a violation of Article III:4. Whether or not imported products are treated 'less favourably' than like domestic products should be assessed instead by examining whether a measure modifies the *conditions of competition* in the relevant market to the detriment of the imported products.

25 Appellate Body Report, *Japan – Taxes on Alcoholic Beverages*, WT/DS8/AB/R, WT/DS10/AB/R, WT/DS11/AB/R, adopted 1 November 1996, DSR 1996:I, 97, p. 23. If the products at issue were not like products, but rather were competitive products, there would be a possibility that a relatively minor difference in tax liability would not violate Article III:2, since the test would be whether the competing products were taxed similarly or not. Ibid., pp. 26–27.

26 Appellate Body Report, *Korea – Measures Affecting Imports of Fresh, Chilled and Frozen Beef*, WT/DS161/AB/R, WT/DS169/AB/R, adopted 10 January 2001, DSR 2001:I, 5, paras. 137–138, relying on GATT Panel Report, *US–Section 337*.

> We conclude that the Panel erred in its general interpretation that '[a]ny regulatory distinction that is based exclusively on criteria relating to the nationality or the origin of the product is incompatible with Article III'.

Although the Appellate Body quoted the foregoing in part in the *Thai–Cigarettes* case, as we will see, it arguably did not require a very rigorous demonstration that the conditions of competition between Thai and imported cigarettes had been modified.

The Panel in the *Thai–Cigarettes* case had reasoned that the additional administrative requirements to which resellers of imported cigarettes were subject 'could potentially affect' the conditions of competition between domestic and imported cigarettes because the burden associated with the additional administrative requirements could increase the operating costs of resellers of imported cigarettes, which could cause some potential resellers of imported cigarettes to not sell them so as to avoid incurring those additional costs. The Panel found support for its position in evidence that showed that there was a degree of switching and cross-price elasticity between certain domestic and imported brands, which the Panel felt indicated that the market for those cigarettes was very competitive.[27] In such a market, the increased costs involved in selling imported cigarettes might well deter some resellers from handling such cigarettes. The Panel did not consider how much it would cost to comply with the additional administrative burdens, nor did it ascertain how prevalent this situation would be since the potential cost difference would largely apply only where the reseller of domestic cigarettes did not sell other products subject to VAT (since if it did sell such products, the added administrative structures would have already been in place). Moreover, the Panel did not consider the extent to which a reseller would view these minor costs to be worth incurring by the competitive imperative to offer a full range of cigarettes to its clients.[28]

In its approach to the less favourable treatment issue in *Thai–Cigarettes*, the Appellate Body began by stressing that its resolution in specific cases requires a 'careful examination "grounded in close scrutiny of the 'fundamental thrust and effect of the measure'"', although such scrutiny need not involve empirical evidence[29] and that '[t]he implications of the contested measure for the equality of competitive conditions are, first and foremost, those discernible from the design, structure, and expected operation of the measure'.[30]

27 This evidence had been presented to show that certain imported and domestic brands of cigarettes were like products.

28 There was also a question of whether any administrative costs might be offset by a VAT registrant's ability to take additional credits for other VAT it had paid, such as for utilities and other services. These financial advantages could effectively reduce or negate any additional administrative costs. The Appellate Body ruled that Thailand had failed to produce evidence to support this argument, which it noted arose only in response to the Panel's questions. Appellate Body Report, *Thai–Cigarettes*, para. 139.

29 Ibid., para. 129.

30 Ibid., para. 130.

It then considered Thailand's arguments that the 'could potentially affect' standard used by the Panel was insufficiently rigorous and that the Panel had failed to consider sufficiently the implications of the challenged measure in the marketplace. The Appellate Body rejected this appeal since in its view:[31]

> an analysis of less favourable treatment should not be anchored in an assessment of the degree of likelihood that an adverse impact on competitive conditions will materialize. Rather, an analysis under Article III:4 must begin with careful scrutiny of the measure, including consideration of the design, structure, and expected operation of the measure at issue. Such scrutiny may well involve – but does not require – an assessment of the contested measure in the light of evidence regarding the actual effects of that measure in the market. In any event, there must be in every case a genuine relationship between the measure at issue and its adverse impact on competitive opportunities for imported versus like domestic products to support a finding that imported products are treated less favourably.

The Appellate Body also noted that the Panel's use of the word 'potentially' did not suggest that the Panel had found less favourable treatment based on a 'remote, unsubstantial or 'theoretical possibility'' that competitive conditions might be modified. Rather, it interpreted the Panel's use of the word to reflect the fact that the Panel believed that it was not required to enquire into the actual effects of the Thai measure in order to establish less favourable treatment.[32]

Having said all that, the Appellate Body accepted the Panel's view that the additional administrative burdens imposed on resellers of imported cigarettes would affect their costs and would, in turn, modify the conditions of competition to the detriment of imported cigarettes. While the Appellate Body noted that the Panel could have enquired further into market implications of the Thai measure, 'the mere fact the additional administrative requirements are imposed on imported cigarettes, and not on like domestic cigarettes, provides, in itself, a significant indication that the conditions of competition are adversely modified to the detriment of imported cigarettes.'[33] Thus, in essence, the case stands for the proposition that differential treatment is less favourable for purposes of Article III:4 if it seems to impose any conceivable (even if speculative) additional burden on imported products.

The Appellate Body's interpretation of the less favourable treatment component of GATT Article III:4 has always seemed incomplete and not completely consistent with its national-treatment case law overall. In its first Article III case – *Japan–Alcoholic Beverages II* – the Appellate Body emphasized that Article III:1, which provides that internal taxes and regulations should not be used 'so as to afford protection to domestic production', was the motivating

31 Ibid., para. 134.
32 Ibid., para. 135.
33 Ibid., para. 139.

principle of Article III.[34] Indeed, in its view any differential taxation of like products implied that the taxation was so as to afford protection, although it required that a separate enquiry be made under the second sentence of Article III:2, which governs directly competitive and substitutable products, to determine if the tax measure was applied so as to afford protection.[35] Nonetheless, after having emphasized the importance of the language of Article III:1 and required it as a separate component of establishing a violation of Article III:2, second sentence, the Appellate Body found, in *EC–Bananas III*, that in the case of Article III:4 in deciding whether there was 'less favourable treatment', it was not necessary to consider whether a measure was applied so as to afford protection.[36] This decision was always difficult to understand since it would seem that a natural way of interpreting 'less favourable treatment' in Article III would consider whether the treatment was protectionist, given the important contextual role played by Article III:1.

In the cases following *Bananas*, the Appellate Body seemed to suggest that the less favourable treatment requirement would be given meaningful content. The next Article III:4 case was *Korea–Beef*, where, in the passage quoted above, the Appellate Body emphasized that a mere distinction based on origin was not sufficient to establish less favourable treatment, but rather that an effect on the conditions of competition between the imported and domestic products had to be shown. The next occasion for the Appellate Body to discourse on the concept of less favourable treatment was in the *EC–Asbestos* case. Since the Appellate Body had found that the products involved in the case were not like, there was no need to consider the less favourable treatment issue. However, the Appellate Body had given a broad reading to the concept of like products under Article III:4 – it was held to cover like products as that term was used in Article III:2, first sentence, plus at least some portion of the directly competitive and substitutable products subject to Article III:2, second sentence. The principal justification for an expanded view of like products in Article III:4 was that otherwise the ban on the use of discriminatory taxes on directly competitive and substitutable products could easily be evaded if there was not a similar restraint on the use of discriminatory internal regulations in respect of such products.[37] However, in order to allay concerns that giving a broad scope to 'like products' under Article III:4 would lead to many findings of an Article III:4 violation, the Appellate Body recalled that a violation of Article III:4 also required a showing that the imported product received less favourable treatment, suggesting that likeness was only part of the relevant analysis of an Article III:4

34 Appellate Body Report, *Japan–Alcoholic Beverages II*, pp. 15–18.

35 Ibid., pp. 18–31.

36 Appellate Body Report, *European Communities – Regime for the Importation, Sale and Distribution of Bananas*, WT/DS27/AB/R, adopted 25 September 1997, DSR 1997:II, 591, para. 216.

37 Appellate Body Report, *European Communities – Measures Affecting Asbestos and Asbestos-Containing Products*, WT/DS135/AB/R, adopted 5 April 2001, DSR 2001:VII, 3243, para. 99.

violation. Indeed, it specifically stated that '[t]he term "less favourable treatment' expresses the general principle, in Article III:1, that internal regulations 'should not be applied . . . so as to afford protection to domestic production"'.[38]

Since *Korea–Beef* and *EC–Asbestos*, however, Panels have generally not required much to establish less favourable treatment through modification of the conditions of competition. Where there has been origin-based discrimination, less favourable treatment has been found without much analysis. Any difference in treatment has been viewed as modifying the conditions of competition. Indeed, in *China–Publications and Audio Visual Products*, the Panel noted that:[39]

> the phrase 'treatment no less favourable' is not qualified by a *de minimis* standard. Accordingly, *any* less favourable treatment of imported products . . . is contrary to the obligation in Article III:4, provided such treatment modifies the conditions of competition to the detriment of imported products.

In the *Thai–Cigarettes* case, the Panel noted that 'additional administrative requirements, albeit slight, imposed only on imported products can potentially have a negative impact on the competitive position of [those products]'.[40]

The only exception to this tendency to require little to establish less favourable treatment is the 2005 *Dominican Republic–Import and Sale of Cigarettes* case, where there were two non-origin-based rules challenged – one required the affixing of tax stamps in the Dominican Republic; the other required the posting of a bond to ensure tax payments. In the case of the bond requirement, the Appellate Body upheld the Panel's rejection of the Article III:4 claim. In doing so, it noted that while imported cigarettes bore a higher cost on a per capita basis, that was due to the fact that they had a small market share (and thus the cost of the bond on a per cigarette basis was higher), not because the cigarettes were imported. Accordingly, it found that there was not less favourable treatment for purposes of Article III:4.[41] While the Appellate Body upheld the Panel decision, the case has not played a significant role in subsequent national-treatment decisions, such as the instant case.[42] Indeed, quite recently, the Appellate Body has specifically stated that the *Dominican Republic–Import and Sale of Cigarettes* case does not require an inquiry as to

38 Ibid., para. 100.

39 Panel Report, *China – Measures Affecting Trading Rights and Distribution Services for Certain Publications and Audiovisual Entertainment Products*, WT/DS363/R and Corr.1, adopted 19 January 2010, as modified by Appellate Body Report WT/DS363/AB/R, DSR 2010:II, 261, para. 7.1537.

40 Panel Report, *Thai–Cigarettes*, para. 7.735.

41 Appellate Body Report, *Dominican Republic – Measures Affecting the Importation and Internal Sale of Cigarettes*, WT/DS302/AB/R, adopted 19 May 2005, DSR 2005:XV, 7367, para. 96.

42 Relying on *Dominican Republic–Import and Sale of Cigarettes*, Thailand tried to argue before the Panel that the additional administrative requirements served the legitimate purpose of combating tax evasion, fraud, and counterfeiting of foreign cigarettes, but the Panel ruled that the purpose of the measure was irrelevant under Article III:4 and should be considered, if at all, under Article XX. Panel Report, para. 7.746. This instant case differed from *Dominican Republic–Import and Sale of Cigarettes* in that the measure at issue was not origin-neutral on its face.

whether the detrimental impact of a measure is related to its foreign origin or is explained by other facts or circumstances, but rather only requires consideration of whether the conditions of competition have been modified to the detriment of imported products.[43] From this, one can speculate that the Appellate Body would have upheld a Panel conclusion that the bond requirement modified the conditions of competition to the detriment of importers if the Panel had found that importers are typically smaller firms than domestic suppliers, and that, accordingly, a bond requirement would impose heavier costs on them on a per-item basis.

Thus, the state of the WTO jurisprudence today on Article III:4 seems to be that *any* difference in treatment between imported and domestic goods – no matter how minor – will suffice to modify the conditions of competition between them and violate Article III:4. This result does not sit easily with the Appellate Body's Article III:2 jurisprudence, or its recent TBT Agreement jurisprudence.

The inconsistency in approach between Article III:2 and Article III:4 can be seen by slightly modifying the facts of *Thai–Cigarettes*. Suppose, in the instant case, that cigarettes were found to be directly competitive and substitutable products (not like products) for purposes of Article III:2.[44] (They, of course, would still be like products for purposes of Article III:4 and TBT Article 2.1.) With this change in facts, the Article III:2 issue would not be so clear since the Philippines would have to establish that the taxation was dissimilar. Since the difference would normally be zero, assuming a VAT return was filed, this might be difficult. Moreover, it would be necessary to establish that the dissimilar taxation – normally zero – was applied so as to afford protection to the domestic industry, which would probably be even more difficult to establish. Thus, it is quite possible that there would be a finding of no violation of Article III:2, second sentence. But the same analysis as occurred in the instant case would apply in respect of Article III:4. Thus, there would be no tax discrimination, but the related administrative requirements would violate Article III:4. This highlights the problem of having Article III:4 apply to products that would be treated as directly competitive or substitutable under Article III:2, when 'so as to afford protection' is an element of the Article III:2 claim but not the Article III:4 claim. This, of course, undermines the rationale in *EC–Asbestos* for giving a broad reading to like products for purposes of Article III:4 since it ultimately leads to disparity in – not harmonization of – the respective coverages of Article III:2 and III:4.

The Appellate Body's Article III:4 jurisprudence is also in tension with its 2012 Reports dealing with the TBT Agreement, where the Appellate Body has given

43 Appellate Body Report, *United States – Measures Affecting the Production and Sale of Clove Cigarettes*, WT/DS406/AB/R, adopted 24 April 2012 (*US–Clove Cigarettes*), para. 179 and n.372.

44 This is quite plausible given the differences in taste between competing brands and the jurisprudence that has developed in alcohol-tax cases.

considerable prominence to the 'treatment no less favourable' language of TBT Article 2.1. Article 2.1 provides:

> Members shall ensure that in respect of technical regulations, products imported from the territory of any Member shall be accorded treatment no less favourable than that accorded to like products of national origin and to like products originating in any other country.

This language is obviously quite similar to Article III:4, although an important difference between GATT and the TBT Agreement is that, while the obligations of Article III:4 are moderated by the exceptions in Article XX, the coverage of TBT Article 2.1 is not subject to any exceptions (although the preamble to the TBT Agreement contains language to the effect that Members should not be prevented from taking certain actions for the protection, inter alia, of health, the environment, and consumers).

The Appellate Body has emphasized the similarities between the language of TBT Article 2.1 and GATT Article III, particularly insofar as determining like products. More significantly, in trying to reconcile the effective coverage of GATT Article III, with exceptions, and TBT Article 2.1, without exceptions, and to prevent Article 2.2 from being rendered inutile by Article 2.1, the Appellate Body in *US–Clove Cigarettes* has decided that for purposes of TBT Article 2.1:[45]

> Although we are mindful that the meaning of the term 'treatment no less favourable' in Article 2.1 of the TBT Agreement is to be interpreted in the light of the specific context provided by the TBT Agreement, we nonetheless consider these previous findings by the Appellate Body in the context of Article III:4 of the GATT 1994 to be instructive in assessing the meaning of 'treatment no less favourable', provided that the specific context in which the term appears in Article 2.1 of the TBT Agreement is taken into account. Similarly to Article III:4 of the GATT 1994, Article 2.1 of the TBT Agreement requires WTO Members to accord to the group of imported products treatment no less favourable than that accorded to the group of like domestic products. Article 2.1 prescribes such treatment specifically in respect of technical regulations. For this reason, a panel examining a claim of violation under Article 2.1 should seek to ascertain whether the technical regulation at issue modifies the conditions of competition in the market of the regulating Member to the detriment of the group of imported products vis-à-vis the group of like domestic products.
>
> However, as noted earlier, the context and object and purpose of the TBT Agreement weigh in favour of interpreting the 'treatment no less favourable' requirement of Article 2.1 as not prohibiting detrimental impact on imports that stems exclusively from a legitimate regulatory distinction. Rather, for the aforementioned reasons, the 'treatment no less favourable' requirement of

45 Appellate Body Report, *US–Clove Cigarettes*, paras. 180–182.

> Article 2.1 only prohibits *de jure* and *de facto* discrimination against the group of imported products.
>
> Accordingly, where the technical regulation at issue does not *de jure* discriminate against imports, the existence of a detrimental impact on competitive opportunities for the group of imported vis-à-vis the group of domestic like products is not dispositive of less favourable treatment under Article 2.1. Instead, a panel must further analyze whether the detrimental impact on imports stems exclusively from a legitimate regulatory distinction rather than reflecting discrimination against the group of imported products. In making this determination, a panel must carefully scrutinize the particular circumstances of the case, that is, the design, architecture, revealing structure, operation, and application of the technical regulation at issue, and, in particular, whether that technical regulation is even-handed, in order to determine whether it discriminates against the group of imported products.

Thus, on the one hand, the Appellate Body seems to suggest that the less favourable treatment language of GATT Article III:4 and TBT Article 2.1 should be interpreted similarly, while, on the other hand, it gives real content to the language in Article 2.1 by permitting a modification of the conditions of competition if it stems from a 'legitimate regulatory distinction' (at least in cases of *de facto* discrimination[46]), even though there is no such consideration of that issue under Article III:4. Of course, the justification is that the context of TBT Article 2.1 requires this result, but it is hard to see why the context of Article III:4 – and specifically the context supplied by Article 3.1 – should not also require such a result.

It remains to be seen whether this distinction announced by the Appellate Body can survive. In a very recent case – *US–Tuna II (Mexico)* – the Appellate Body stated that the Panel, which found a violation of the TBT Agreement, should have also analysed the case under Article III:4.[47] The reason given by the Appellate Body for criticizing the Panel's exercise of judicial economy was that it was contested whether the measure at issue was a technical regulation and thus the Panel's findings on the TBT Agreement could have been nullified if the Appellate Body had ruled that the measure was not a technical regulation. It also noted that the scope of the two provisions was different. In the future, it is likely that Panels will feel compelled to consider both TBT and Article III:4 claims, at least so long as the respondent argues that its measure is not a technical regulation. One can easily imagine the situation where a measure will be found to distinguish *de facto* between imported and domestic like products and accord less favourable treatment to the imported products. The measure will not violate Article 2.1 of the TBT Agreement

46 The Appellate Body did not distinguish between *de facto* and *de jure* discrimination in its recent Report in *United States – Measures Concerning the Importation, Marketing and Sale of Tuna and Tuna Products*, WT/DS381/AB/R, adopted 13 June 2012 (US–*Tuna II (Mexico)*).

47 Appellate Body Report, *US–Tuna II (Mexico)*, paras. 403–405.

if a legitimate regulatory distinction is established, but it will violate Article III:4. Since the coverage of Article XX is not as broad as the 'exception' that the Appellate Body has read into the TBT Agreement, one could imagine a measure found to violate GATT Article III:4, but not TBT Article 2.1. Given that the TBT Agreement is the more specialized agreement and the one that would prevail in the event of a conflict with Article III, this result – which probably could not be called a conflict under existing jurisprudence – would seem incongruous. In any event, complainants may again decide to shy away from the TBT Agreement when a measure can be challenged under Article III:4 since the TBT Agreement may afford respondents more scope to argue that a measure is justified than does Article XX.

All in all, one can understand why the Appellate Body has taken the position it has in respect of Article 2.1 of the TBT Agreement. It needed to harmonize the TBT Agreement and GATT Articles III:4 and XX, and it needed to give effect somehow to the preamble of the TBT Agreement. Its approach in *US–Clove Cigarettes*, however, highlights the problems with the way it has largely read the less favourable treatment requirement out of Article III:4. As outlined in the foregoing paragraphs, there are potential inconsistencies between its jurisprudence under GATT Article III:4 and its jurisprudence under GATT Article III:2, second sentence, and TBT Article 2.1. Eventually, some reconciliation will be required. If the Appellate Body is unwilling to import the 'so as to afford protection' test into the less favourable treatment analysis under Article III:4, perhaps it will give more prominence to the discrimination involved, i.e. whether it is *de jure* or *de facto*, and require a more rigorous showing of a modification of the conditions of competition in *de facto* discrimination cases, such as arguably occurred in the *Dominican Republic–Import and Sale of Cigarettes* case.[48]

3.3 Article XX(d)

The Article XX issue was the one that may have involved a typographical error. Article XX(d) provides an exception for measures that are 'necessary to secure compliance with laws or regulations which are not inconsistent with [GATT]'. Thailand claimed that the administrative requirements found to violate Article III:4 were necessary to secure compliance with its VAT regime. The Panel ruled that Article XX(d) did not apply because it had already ruled that the laws or

48 There have long been calls for giving more prominence to the 'less favourable treatment' language of Article III:4 and interpreting it in light of Article III:1. See William J. Davey and Joost Pauwelyn (2000), 'MFN Unconditionality: A Legal Analysis of the Concept in View of its Evolution in the GATT/WTO Jurisprudence with Particular Reference to the Issue of "Like Product"', in Thomas Cottier and Petros C. Mavroidis (eds.), *Regulatory Barriers and the Principle of Non-discrimination in World Trade Law: Past, Present and Future*, Ann Arbor, MI: The University of Michigan Press, chapter 1, pp. 38–41. For a recent review of literature critical of the Appellate Body's Article III:4 jurisprudence, see The American Law Institute (2012), *Legal and Economic Principles of World Trade Law: The Genesis of the GATT, the Economics of Trade Agreements, Border Instruments, and National Treatment*, Report to ALI, Philadelphia, PA: ALI, at pp. 300–309.

regulations with which compliance was sought were not GATT consistent and cross-referenced its finding that the administrative requirements violated Article III:4. The Philippines argued that the cross-reference was a typo, that the Panel intended to refer to its finding that the differential VAT treatment was inconsistent with Article III:2, and that the administrative requirements could therefore not be justified given that the underlying tax provision was invalid. However, the Panel's reasoning on the Article XX(d) issue was so brief it was not clear to the Appellate Body what the Panel had meant, so the Appellate Body itself examined whether Thailand had established the elements of an Article XX(d) defense.[49]

In setting the elements of an Article XX(d) defense, the Appellate Body noted that:[50]

> when an Article XX(d) is invoked to justify an inconsistency with Article III:4, what must be shown to be 'necessary' is the treatment giving rise to the finding of less favourable treatment. [The Appellate Body cited the GATT Panel Report, *US–Section 337* for this proposition, where it is clearly stated.] Thus, when less favourable treatment is found based on differences in the regulation of imports and of like domestic products, the analysis of an Article XX(d) defense should focus on whether those regulatory differences are 'necessary' to secure compliance with 'laws or regulations' that are not GATT-inconsistent.

Having set out this standard, the Appellate Body found four 'critical flaws' in Thailand's defense, the first of which was that 'Thailand sought to justify administrative requirements relating to VAT liability generally, rather than to justify the *differential treatment* afforded to imported versus domestic cigarettes under its measure'.[51] The Appellate Body also recalled that Thailand had not discussed in any detail several other matters essential to a successful Article XX(d) defense.[52]

As noted, the Appellate Body's approach is completely consistent with the approach of the *US–Section 337* case, which the Appellate Body has often cited with approval in respect of other issues, especially involving Article XX. It does, however, appear to be inconsistent with the first Appellate Body case – *US–Gasoline*, where the Appellate Body stated in considering an Article XX(g) defense that the Panel had erred because:[53]

> the Panel asked itself whether the 'less favourable treatment' of imported gasoline was 'primarily aimed at 'the conservation of natural resources [i.e., whether the refusal to provide individualized baselines to foreign refiners was primarily

49 Appellate Body Report, *Thai–Cigarettes*, para. 170.

50 Ibid., para. 177.

51 Ibid., para. 179.

52 Ibid.

53 Appellate Body Report, *United States – Standards for Reformulated and Conventional Gasoline*, WT/DS2/AB/R, adopted 20 May 1996, DSR 1996:I, 3 (*US–Gasoline*), p. 16.

> aimed at the conservation of natural resources], rather than whether the 'measure', i.e. the baseline establishment rules, were 'primarily aimed at' conservation of clean air.

When it analyzed the Article XX(g) defense itself, the Appellate Body started by looking at '[t]he baseline establishment rules, taken as a whole (that is, the provisions relating to establishment of baselines for domestic refiners, along with the provisions relating to baselines for blenders and importers of gasoline).'[54] Had it followed the approach taken in the instant case, the Appellate Body would have only looked at the aspect of the baseline establishment rules found to violate Article III:4.

The Appellate Body's analysis of the Article XX(d) defense was quite cursory, and it gave no indication that it was changing the approach taken in *Gasoline*. Thus, it is not clear whether it intended to make a change or simply overlooked the *Gasoline* case. Hopefully, it intended the change since the *Gasoline* approach has always seemed to be the wrong approach. Indeed, when the Appellate Body did what it did in *Gasoline*, it made no reference to past GATT cases, such as the *US–Section 337*, which followed the approach it has now adopted in the instant case. In any event, by accident or design, it appears that the Appellate Body has reached the right result. It makes no sense to ask if a general law falls within the exceptions of Article XX. The issue is whether a GATT violation is excused, so the issue must be whether the violation is necessary (or, in the case of XX(g), is related to conservation). This can be seen in the extensive discussion of the issue in the *Section 337* case, where the Panel noted that GATT parties must use more GATT-consistent alternatives where such alternatives are reasonably available. It should be noted that the Appellate Body's position in the *Gasoline* case in fact does not seem to have been discussed in other Article XX cases, so the instant case may simply be restating what the rule has always been considered to be (notwithstanding the Appellate Body's position in *Gasoline*).[55]

3.4 Article X:3

The Philippines raised a number of GATT Article X claims in respect of the Thai regime for taxing imported cigarettes. In that regard, the Panel found that Thailand violated the publication requirements of Article X:1 by failing to publish (i) the methodology used to determine the price on which value-added tax would be levied on imported cigarettes and (ii) the general rules pertaining to the release of customs guarantees. The Panel also found that Thailand violated the reasonable-administration requirement of Article X:3(a) in respect of delays in the [Customs]

54 Appellate Body Report, *US–Gasoline*, p. 19.

55 See generally W. Davey (2012), 'Non-Discrimination in the World Trade Organization: The Rules and Exceptions', *Recueil des Cours*, vol. 354, Leiden, The Netherlands: Martinus Nijhoff Publishers, pp. 368–408, also published in 2012, by the same publisher, in book form, under the same title.

Board of Assessment process. In respect of Article X:3(b), which requires that WTO members must maintain judicial, arbitral, or administrative tribunals or procedures for the prompt review and correction of administrative action relating to customs matters, the Panel found that Thailand violated that obligation in respect of (i) customs valuation decisions and (ii) guarantee decisions. Only the latter finding regarding guarantee decisions was appealed.

Under Thai law, when there is doubt as to the applicable duty owed on an import, Thai customs officials may undertake a more in-depth examination of the matter. The goods at issue may be released from customs pending this further examination if the importer pays the uncontested amount due and provides a guarantee that covers the maximum duty that might be payable. The guarantee may be in the form of a cash deposit or a bank (or some sort of government) guarantee. Thailand appealed two aspects of the Panel's decision: (i) whether the decision to require a guarantee constitutes administrative action relating to customs matters as used in Article X:3(b) and (ii) whether the right to appeal the guarantee decision upon the final assessment of duties satisfies Thailand's Article X:3(b) obligations.

On the first issue, the Appellate Body considered the meaning of the components of the phrase 'administrative action relating to customs matters'. It seems clear that the decision to require a guarantee is an administrative action and that it relates to customs matters. The only real issue is whether the decision should be treated as a preliminary one that is reviewable at a later point of time, which raises the question of whether that later review would meet the promptness requirement of Article X:3(b). As to the preliminary nature of the decision, the Appellate Body noted that the Customs Valuation Agreement only specifically requires review of customs-valuation decisions and that the Anti-Dumping Agreement only requires review of 'final' anti-dumping action. However, the Appellate Body was of the view that this context was not all that relevant, particularly since Article X:3(b) was not qualified by any limitation to 'final' action.[56] The Appellate Body was of the view that the decision on the guarantee was a final decision with content of its own, as there was no further action contemplated insofar as securing payment of customs duties was concerned.[57]

As to the question of whether the 'prompt review' requirement was satisfied if an appeal was permitted once the final assessment was issued, the Appellate Body noted that once a final assessment has been issued, the guarantee ceases to have any purpose since the amount due will then be collected. That implies that during the effective or useful life of the guarantee, there is no possibility of review, which means that the prompt-review requirement is not met.[58]

56 Appellate Body Report, *Thai–Cigarettes*, paras. 197, 199.
57 Ibid., para. 215.
58 Ibid., para. 221.

On a first look, this decision seems rather intrusive. While the Appellate Body correctly parses Article X:3(b), it seems to require rather early review of an arguably minor, preliminary matter.[59] However, on reflection, it is worth noting that guarantee decisions can be abused, and customs authorities can delay decisions for a long time. In fact, there were examples of such behaviour being threatened by Thai customs presented to the Panel.[60] Thus, there may be a real problem here. Moreover, the actual requirements to implement this decision may be rather minor. A review of a guarantee decision would not necessarily require the correct valuation of the goods to be established, but rather only whether customs officials had reason to conduct a further investigation and whether the amount of the guarantee was reasonable. At this early stage of the valuation process, presumably Thailand could implement the decision without much effort and the new review process could afford considerable discretion to customs authorities. Thus, in the end, this broad reading of Article X:3(b) may make eminent sense to the extent that it requires little action by WTO members, but may prevent occasional abuses by individual customs officials. Indeed, the preferred course might be to have a general-review provision allowing the challenge of preliminary-type decisions on some sort of gross abuse of discretion grounds.

3.5 *Conclusion*

The Appellate Body Report in the *Thai–Cigarettes* case is consistent with past Appellate Body jurisprudence (except as noted in respect of Article XX) and does not raise significant issues, except insofar as one can question whether the Appellate Body has given adequate consideration to Article III:4's requirement that imported products must be shown to have been accorded treatment no less favourable than that accorded to like products of national origin.

4. Economic analysis

The circumstances underlying the complaint brought by the Philippines against Thailand were described above. However, it is useful to place them into an economic-policy context in order to offer some commentary about interesting issues they raise.

59 The rejection of the relevance of (i) the lack of such a provision in the only detailed WTO agreement dealing with customs valuation – the CVA, which only requires review of valuation decisions, and (ii) the fact that preliminary anti-dumping decisions, which can have a very large trade impact, need not be appealable, was somewhat arbitrary, but it is true that Article X:3 does not refer to 'final' decisions.

60 See discussion in Panel Report, *Thai–Cigarettes*, paras. 1084–1087.

4.1 *Market structure, customs, and taxes*

As noted, there is one domestic manufacturer of tobacco products, including cigarettes, in Thailand. TTM is an agency of the Ministry of Finance, though it is enjoined to maximize profits. TTM has been the sole domestic supplier for decades and until the market was opened to imports, beginning in 1991, had a virtually complete monopoly. Currently, TTM commands about 75% of the market, with imports taking up the rest. According to the Panel Report, TTM produces 19 brands. TTM sells its brands at its chosen ex-factory prices to wholesalers and retailers (called resellers in the case). These brands come in essentially three quality classes, with retail prices (pre-VAT) ranging from 37 baht per pack at the low end to 58 baht per pack at the medium level and 75 baht per pack for deluxe brands. A key factor is that retail prices of TTM's cigarettes invariably equal the 'maximum retail selling prices' (MRSPs), which are set by the government based on a constructed formula reviewed below. TTM may petition the authorities to permit retailers to set lower prices on its brands but, as a branch of the government, never does so.

At the time of the Panel Report, there were 86 imported brands of cigarettes, coming from a large group of countries. As noted, however, the Philippines is the primary source of imports and a major producer is Philip Morris Philippines (PMP), which manufactures and sells them directly to an importing firm called Philip Morris Thailand (PMT), which declares the cost-inclusive cif price it pays and also must pay a 5% duty. Because these entities both exist under the same parent company, there is a risk that the declared price will not really reflect actual production and transactions costs and will instead be a transfer price. PMT then sells these imports to wholesalers and retailers. These resellers may also sell TTM's brands. Like those brands, each imported brand is assigned an MRSP, which is the basis for VAT calculations. However, because these imported products are procured from private firms it is more likely that those firms may wish to petition the authorities to sell at retail prices below the MRSPs.

Part of the dispute revolves around the Thai Department of Customs' treatment of two brands sold by PMT: Marlboro, which competes in the premium market, and L&M, a mid-level brand. On certain occasions in 2006 and 2007, Thai Customs refused to accept the declared customs value put forward by PMT for these cigarettes. Customs officials argued that, despite having accepted such valuations before, in these cases the agency had serious doubts about the legitimacy of those prices. The only grounds offered were that PMT and PMP were closely related and could not be trusted to declare a price approximating an arm's-length valuation. Moreover, Thai Customs argued that similar types of cigarettes were imported at those times at declared prices three to four times higher, a characterization disputed by PMT. The authorities issued a preliminary customs valuation based on a 'deductive valuation' method that resulted in a substantially higher cif value and also required PMT to post a fiscal guarantee against the final valuation. The Panel found these procedures to be inappropriate under terms of the CVA.

For our purposes, the interesting feature is that Thai Customs' decision to raise the cif valuation directly increased the VAT basis (MRSP) for PMT's cigarettes. The reason is that DG Excise uses a mechanical formula for determining MRSPs, as follows.

For TTM cigarettes:

$$\text{MRSP} = \text{ex-factory price} + \text{excise tax} + \text{health tax} + \text{television tax} \\ + \text{local provincial tax} + \text{VAT} + \text{marketing costs.}$$

For imports:

$$\text{MRSP} = \text{cif value} + \text{customs duties} + \text{excise tax} + \text{health tax} + \text{television tax} \\ + \text{local provincial tax} + \text{VAT} + \text{marketing costs.}$$

In these equations, the excise tax is 79% of either the ex-factory price (for TTM) or of the sum of cif value + duties paid (for imports). The health tax is 2% of the excise tax, and the television tax is 1.5% of the excise tax. The local provincial tax is a fixed amount (1.86 baht per pack), and marketing costs could be computed by DG Excise either as a residual or from direct market information. VAT is the value-added tax collected from resellers on domestically produced or imported cigarettes, and is 7% of the associated price (ex-factory or cif, respectively).

It is evident from these expressions that the MRSP on domestic cigarettes is likely to be lower than that on imported brands in the same price category because the former calculation does not include customs duties paid. Further, when Customs assigns a high deductive value to the cif value the relative increase carries through via the excise tax and other tax components. There is a further degree of freedom for DG Excise in the designation of marketing costs for domestic and imported brands. Indeed, the Panel Report noted that the MRSPs were commonly higher for imports than for competing TTM goods, including during the period of deductive valuation. In turn, the absolute value of VAT paid on imports was higher, due to this higher tax basis, which the Panel Report found inappropriate.

Despite that fact, Thailand argued that there was no effective discrimination because the ad valorem VAT rates were the same on both imported and domestic goods. Moreover, the initial VAT payment could be deducted by resellers at each stage (wholesalers, retailers) as they collected VAT at those stages. Ultimately, final consumers would pay the tax, which was assessed at 7% on all cigarettes, despite the different tax bases. The problem here, as discussed above, was the significant difference in administrative burdens. Resellers of TTM products were exempt from collecting and claiming VAT and, therefore, did not have to keep the corresponding books and tax records. Resellers of imported cigarettes, however, had to engage in such accounting, with monthly reporting to the government, a burdensome element in terms of time costs at least.

Thailand's justification for this difference is that domestic cigarettes are produced by a government-owned monopoly and the initial VAT would automatically be posted as government revenue. There is no possibility of evading such a tax (in principle). However, because imports were sold by private firms across borders, it was thought that tax evasion was more likely. Thus, Thailand's Directorate General of Excise essentially argued that the difference in record keeping, despite its burdensome nature, was justifiable as a necessary policy to safeguard internal taxation under Article XX(d). As discussed earlier, both the Panel and Appellate Body rejected this claim.

4.2 *Economic issues*

We turn next to two interesting economic issues this situation raises about which more may be said.

1. *Conditions of competition*

First, consider the question of how the policy scenario described above would affect market competition. One way to think about this is to trace through impacts in retail markets, assuming that domestic brands and imported brands are close, but imperfect, substitutes within similar quality bands. For now, set aside how the domestic manufacturer (TTM) sets its ex-factory price and the importer (PMT) declares its cif value. As noted above, these prices, along with added taxes and costs, determine the MRSPs, which are the VAT tax bases. Retailers may sell domestic, imported, or both brands. Assume (strongly) that retailers are able to order the quantities that would clear demand at these MRSPs. (Recall that the MRSP for domestic brands are essentially equivalent to retail prices in all cases. This is generally true for imports as well, although retailers may choose to sell at a lower price, even if the MRSP remains fixed.) Finally, assume initially that resellers face the same (zero) reporting requirements for VAT on both goods.

In this simple framework, the following results may be readily shown in competition between an imported brand and a domestic brand. First, in any initial equilibrium the MRSP is higher for the import due to the differentially higher add-on factors noted above. At this point, suppose Customs denies the declared cif value for PMT and imposes a higher value. This will carry through into a higher MRSP and VAT liability for that product, essentially an increase in costs of retailing it. The quantity sold will fall at the higher MRSP, reducing PMT's profit. Further, this higher price for the import will raise demand for TTM's brand at the given MRSP, expanding sales and raising TTM's profit. Second, the extent of these impacts depends on market parameters, including own-price elasticities and the cross-price elasticity of the two brands. For example, if we assume a high cross-elasticity (significant demand shift) the derived demand increase for TTM would be relatively large. Third, welfare effects would depend on these elasticities, initial market shares, and the VAT tax rate.[61] Welfare impacts in Thailand would depend on the loss of consumer benefits in the import segment in comparison with the higher TTM profits and the net change in tax revenues, which could be positive or negative.

Now consider some complications to this basic story. First, although the changes in customs values (setting cif value above the declared value) ordered by Thai Customs happened only during the time period in question, in principle a Customs authority could act intermittently over time, generating uncertainty in the importer's cif value without similar uncertainty in the domestic ex-factory price, a possibility exacerbated by the lack of transparency in setting the higher import price. Similarly, decisions by DG Excise to use constructed marketing costs for imports but a residual balancing item for TTM raises more cost uncertainty. In this context, an intermittent uncertainty would appear in retail prices (MRSPs) for resellers of imported goods. However, the uncertainty would be one-way, in that it seems unlikely that Customs would choose to reduce cif value given its resort to deductive computations. To the extent that consumers prefer to avoid such uncertainty, we may anticipate a reduced average demand for the PMT product and, again, a rise in demand for the TTM product. Indeed, it is conceivable (depending on parameters) that for some imported brands this uncertainty would reduce demand sufficiently to deter some resellers from carrying them. An interesting feature here is that, in order to safeguard its tax collections, DG Excise is generally unwilling to permit a reduction in the MRSP (which is based on the cif value). Of course, PMT could attempt to offset the reduction in demand by encouraging its resellers to lower retail price, suggesting that the potential for 'pass through' is an interesting issue here and perhaps should be considered in any future competitive analysis of similar disputes regarding unequal treatment. Even if it did so, however, the MRSP would remain at a higher level, and consumers would pay VAT on an artificially high price. In this context, both the uncertainty in customs and the policy-based stickiness in the MRSPs seem anticompetitive.

Second, Thailand might still argue that the procedures considered to this point are not discriminatory in the law, as opposed to outcomes. However, the key element of national treatment in this case is the exemption from bookkeeping and reporting requirements for sellers of domestic brands. Sellers of imported brands are not given the same advantage and, as a result, face both these administrative costs and the potential for undergoing audits and paying fines if they report inadequately. Despite the fact that resellers pass along the VAT on imported cigarettes to consumers, these relatively higher costs and risks presumably diminish the willingness of some resellers to carry imported brands. In economic terms, the

61 Denise Eby Konan and Keith E. Maskus (2012), 'Preferential Trade and Welfare with Differentiated Products', 20:5, *Review of International Economics*, 884–892.

supply curves of import resellers would shift upward, raising price and cutting the derived demand for imports. It would also expand demand for the domestic competing brands. Note also that resellers may well transact in both domestic and imported goods. Thailand argued that, for these firms, the need to fill out forms for imported brands meant they were saddled with the same costs, implying they would not limit their foreign sales. This seems a dubious claim on its face. It is probably noteworthy that essentially all large retailers sell both imports and domestic products; it is only small retailers that opt out of the foreign brands.

Third, it is surely relevant for competition that the domestic manufacturer, TTM, is a government-owned monopoly. In that context, thinking of TTM and PMT as passive suppliers could be highly misleading. Rather, what matters is how they compete strategically against each other. There is little in the Panel Report to shed light on this issue, so we are left to speculate. The fact that TTM sets an ex-factory price and PMT reports a declared cif value might support a model of price competition. In that case, the cost-increasing factors on the import side discussed here would effectively shift upward the reaction curve of the importer in price space. The result would be higher prices and lower outputs of both goods. However, the impacts would be smaller for the domestic monopolist, raising its market share and profits. Profits of the importer would likely fall. At the retail level, both MRSPs (and retail prices) would be pushed up and consumers would be worse off. Competition would be diminished.

It is possible, however, that these firms compete in quantities. In that event, these policies would shift the foreign reaction curve downward, cutting import sales but expanding sales of the domestic monopolist. Welfare calculations would be more complicated but qualitatively like those in the basic analysis above.

In all of these cases, the competitive conditions would seem to be changed by the policies of Thai Customs and DG Excise in favour of TTM, the domestic monopoly. In that context, it is possible to agree in principle with the Panel and Appellate Body in their findings of inconsistency with Article III.2. Thailand's policies also do not comport with the requirement in Article III.4 that imported products shall be accorded treatment no less favourable than that accorded to like products of national origin.

All that said, return to the legal analysis offered earlier in the paper regarding the meaning of 'no less favourable' in Article III.4. That analysis pointed out that the Panel's rigorous interpretation of this principle is somewhat at odds with the finding in *Korea–Beef* that a measure must actually alter the conditions of competition to be a violation. Jurisprudence under the TBT agreement also points to the need for careful scrutiny of the circumstances of individual cases, at least where there is *de facto* discrimination, to identify modifications of these conditions. If these standards were to be applied, a careful economic and market analysis would be needed to score Thailand's policies, rather than having them rejected directly on grounds of differences in treatment. In this context, both the VAT calculations and the differential reporting requirements presumably generated both *de jure* and *de facto* discrimination. The latter could be disputed on grounds of zero net VAT liability for import resellers and the fact that many retailers sell both domestic and imported cigarettes. However, while the economic factors listed above point to the likelihood of favouritism on behalf of TTM's products, it is ultimately an empirical question.

2. *The Article XX(d) claim*

Working somewhat against the straightforward conclusion that Thailand's policies were discriminatory and ran afoul of Articles III.2 and III.4 is that country's claim that it imposed these differentially higher VAT reporting requirements on resellers of imported cigarettes in order to avoid tax evasion, and this policy was acceptable under the general-exceptions clause. It is worth reproducing XX(d):

> Subject to the requirement that such measures are not applied in a manner which would constitute a means of arbitrary or unjustifiable discrimination between countries where the same conditions prevail, or a disguised restriction on international trade, nothing in this Agreement shall be construed to prevent the adoption or enforcement by any contracting party of measures:
>
> (d) necessary to secure compliance with laws or regulations which are not inconsistent with the provisions of this Agreement, including those relating to customs enforcement, the enforcement of monopolies operated under paragraph 4 of Article II and Article XVII, the protection of patents, trademarks and copyrights, and the prevention of deceptive practices.

Thailand in essence argued that resellers of imported goods had to be required to account for VAT liability and reporting requirements in order to ensure compliance of imported cigarettes with the tax laws. In contrast, because TTM is a government agency (indeed, a component of the Ministry of Finance) there is no question about VAT collection on its sales.

The Panel and Appellate Body took a straightforward view of this matter. In this regard, it was not 'necessary' to have differential reporting requirements to safeguard tax compliance. One obvious alternative to achieve this would be a nondiscriminatory reporting requirement applied to resellers of all cigarettes. Further, as discussed earlier, since the policies in question were ruled inconsistent with GATT rules, they would seem to fail to qualify for XX(d) protection. It is hard to disagree with this interpretation.

At the same time, one might wonder whether a strict national-treatment principle serves as a straightjacket here. A literature has emerged recently on the economics of national treatment (NT). As Saggi and Sera point out, there are conditions under which NT can be harmful to at least one country if products are heterogeneous in quality and markets differ in size. Arguably, those factors are not much in play in the present case, though a careful study of quality differentiation in the cigarette market might find otherwise.[62]

More relevant, however, is Horn's observation that NT constrains national-policy sovereignty in cases where imports generate a larger negative externality than does domestic production.[63] For example, if consumption of imported goods generates greater external costs, such as environmental damage or loss of biodiversity, a country might reasonably prefer to establish a higher consumption tax on it than on the domestic competing good. It is prevented from doing so and, indeed, the 'no less favourable treatment' provision permits only differentiating policy with a lower (not higher) tax on imports.

Arguably, this kind of situation may exist in *Thai–Cigarettes*, though one has to think through it carefully. There is no obvious reason why smoking imported cigarettes generates more health damage than does smoking domestic brands. In this case, the relatively higher VAT burden on imports in Thailand surely fails Horn's test for relief. However, suppose we conceive of tax evasion on imports as a negative externality, perhaps because it shifts the tax burden onto consumers of domestic goods. In the circumstances of this case, it seems evident that tax evasion is impossible for TTM but possible for imports, perhaps through an invalid declared customs valuation. In this context, a higher 'tax' (in the form of reporting requirements) on imports may, indeed, solve this problem, while a similar 'tax' on domestic brands would be just a nuisance.

In the present case, we agree with the Appellate Body that this situation does not satisfy the conditions of Article XX(d), because the differential administrative burden is not necessary to resolve the problem and could be construed as a disguised restriction on trade. Moreover, the CVA already offers a useful tool for dealing with evasion through customs valuation, if not other methods. At the same time, there is room for debate about whether future dispute-settlement cases might recast Article XX as a means of getting beyond the restrictions posed by NT in episodes where a differential tax or treatment of imports really would be necessary to correct a trade-related market externality. At the same time, a word of caution is in order because such an interpretation presumably would run the risk of inviting countries to label an unacceptably wide range of discriminatory policies as needed treatments for external costs.

5. Concluding remarks

On its face, *Thai–Cigarettes* is a straightforward case of discrimination against like imported products arising from differential means of calculating the basis for the

62 Kamal Saggi and Nese Sara (2008), 'National Treatment at the WTO: The Roles of Product and Country Heterogeneity', 49:4, *International Economic Review*, 1365–1394.

63 Henrik Horn (2006), 'National Treatment in the GATT', 96:1, *The American Economic Review*, 394–404.

VAT tax and the additional and burdensome reporting requirements imposed on resellers of imported cigarettes. Both the Panel and the Appellate Body took a strict approach to the meaning of discrimination in finding Thailand's VAT regime for this product a violation of both Articles III.2 and III.4. At the basic level, it is difficult to disagree with these findings. We registered the caution, however, that this rigour seems at odds with the more permissive approach to 'less than favourable treatment' underscored by other recent WTO jurisprudence. In this regard, the Panel might have been better advised to undertake a fuller economic and market analysis to determine whether, in fact, the differential rules really did have a noticeable impact on conditions of competition.

Comment on '*Thailand–Cigarettes (Philippines)*: A More Serious Role for the 'Less Favourable Treatment' Standard of Article III:4'

GEOFFREY S. CARLSON
Attorney-Advisor, US International Trade Commission

Professors William Davey and Keith Maskus provide an excellent and succinct analysis of the legal and economic significance of the Report of the Appellate Body (AB) of the World Trade Organization (WTO) in *Thailand – Customs and Fiscal Measures on Cigarettes from the Philippines*[1] (*Thai–Cigarettes*). The modest aim of this brief comment is to further explore the distinction that the AB appeared to draw between final and provisional decisions *vis-à-vis* GATT Article X:3(b).

As discussed in *Thai–Cigarettes*, the Philippines claimed that Thailand violated Article X:3(b) by failing to provide a means to appeal promptly guarantee decisions relating to customs valuations. GATT Article X:3(b) states, in relevant part:

> Each contracting party shall maintain, or institute as soon as practicable, judicial, arbitral or administrative tribunals or procedures for the purpose, *inter alia*, of the *prompt review* and correction of *administrative action relating to customs matters*. (first italics in original)

There were thus two relevant issues in play regarding guarantee decisions in *Thai–Cigarettes*: (1) if Article X:3(b) provided a right to appeal them, and if so (2) when the appeal should be available. This comment addresses the former.

As a strict textual matter, the AB had little choice but to interpret the phrase 'administrative action relating to customs matters' expansively, as 'acts or decisions of the executive branch of a government'[2] regarding any 'thing'[3] 'hav[ing] some [rational] connection with'[4] 'customs'.[5] Indeed, nothing in the text itself

The views presented in this paper are solely the author's and do not represent the views of the U.S. International Trade Commission or the US government.

1 Appellate Body Report, *Thailand – Customs and Fiscal Measures on Cigarettes from the Philippines*, WT/DS371/AB/R, adopted 15 July 2011 (hereinafter the AB Report).

2 Ibid., para. 192.

3 Ibid., para. 193.

4 Ibid., para. 194.

5 Ibid., para. 193.

meaningfully cabins its scope. But the AB also stated that this language should be interpreted in light of the object and purpose of the GATT, including in light of the principles of due process, transparency, and procedural fairness.[6] The AB gave little substantive content to these principles, but did quote the Panel Report from *EC – Selected Customs Matters* for the proposition that GATT Article X:3(b) 'ensure[s] that a trader who has been adversely affected by a decision . . . has the ability to have that adverse decision reviewed'.[7] However, in uttering this statement, *EC – Selected Customs Matters* was deciding a different issue *vis-à-vis* GATT Article X:3(b).

The AB did, however, appear to potentially limit the article's scope in its application of the law to the facts,[8] rather than in its legal analysis.[9] In that section, the AB appeared to draw a distinction between 'provisional' and 'final' decisions in that the AB found guarantee decisions 'final' and therefore appealable.[10] The AB, however, did not explicitly address the question of whether guarantee decisions could still have fallen within the scope of GATT Article X:3(b) if such decisions were 'provisional'. Nor did it either disavow or adopt the Panel's reasoning that 'the term "administrative action relating to customs matters" . . . is not necessarily limited to *final* administrative determinations.'[11]

Therefore, it is unclear to what extent the AB Report in *Thai–Cigarettes* stands for the proposition that a legal distinction between provisional and final decisions exists in this context. Indeed, as discussed above, nothing in the text as interpreted by the AB in its legal analysis required the distinction, nor did the AB borrow such a distinction from any other WTO agreement. Thus, the issue appears open to interpretation. Further, the AB does not explicitly invoke the principles of due process, procedural fairness, or transparency in its relevant factual analysis to decide the case.[12]

6 Ibid., para. 202. See also Vienna Convention on the Law of Treaties, Article 31(1), 23 May 1969, S. Exec. Doc. L, 92-1, 1155 U.N.T.S. 331 ('A treaty shall be interpreted in good faith in accordance with the ordinary meaning to be given to the terms of the treaty in their context and in the light of its object and purpose.') (hereinafter the Vienna Convention).

7 AB Report, para. 202, quoting Panel Report, *European Communities – Selected Customs Matters*, para. 7.536, WT/DS315/R, adopted 11 December 2006, as modified by Appellate Body Report, WT/DS315/AB/R, DSR 2006:IX-X, 3915.

8 Ibid., part V.B.2.a.

9 Ibid., part V.B.1.

10 Ibid., para. 215 ('It is a *final*, and *not an intermediate*, administrative act . . . The fact that a guarantee provides security for a claim stemming from another administrative action does not change the fact that the imposition of a guarantee *is an administrative action in its own right*.') (emphasis added).

11 Panel Report, *Thailand – Customs and Fiscal Measures on Cigarettes from the Philippines*, para. 7.1035, WT/DS371/R, adopted 15 July 2011, as modified by Appellate Body Report, WT/DS371/AB/R (emphasis in original).

12 The AB does, however, reject Thailand's argument that due process *did not* compel the conclusion that there must be a right of appeal against guarantee decisions. AB Report, para. 214. But the AB draws on prior analysis to do so, not by affirmatively invoking principles of due process to decide the case against Thailand. Ibid., para. 215.

United States – Definitive Anti-Dumping and Countervailing Duties on Certain Products from China: Passing the Buck on Pass-Through

THOMAS J. PRUSA

Rutgers University and NBER

EDWIN VERMULST

VVGB Advocaten

Abstract: In 2007, the United States reversed its long-standing policy prohibiting the simultaneous imposition of anti-dumping duties (ADDs) and countervailing duties (CVDs) against nonmarket economies. Subsequently, the United States has imposed concurrent ADDs and CVDs in numerous cases against China. China challenged a number of aspects of the US practice, most notably the double-remedies issue, which occurs when a domestic subsidy is offset by both an ADD and CVD. The Appellate Body (AB) correctly ruled that double remedies are inconsistent with the Agreement on Subsidies and Countervailing Measures and that the burden was on the investigating authorities to ensure that double remedies were not being imposed; however, the AB largely limited its discussion to measurement concerns, an approach that may have inadvertently opened the door to future double-remedies disputes involving other methods for computing normal value. Two other issues that are likely to have significant long-term ramifications are (i) the scope of the term 'public body' and (ii) the appropriate use of out-of-country benchmarks. On both issues, we believe the AB's conclusions and analysis were correct.

1. Introduction

In the 1980s, the US Department of Commerce (USDOC) determined that, in Soviet-style nonmarket economies (NMEs), the agency could neither identify nor measure grants or subsidies. The reasoning was that subsidies to producers in an NME country were not countervailable within the meaning of the countervailing-duty statute because the purpose of the law was to offset the unfair competitive advantage that foreign producers receive from government subsidies. Yet, in an

The views expressed in this paper are those of the authors and all omissions and errors are also of the authors. We would like to thank Brian Gatta for helpful comments.

NME, the state itself owns or controls most businesses and assets. Consequently, to label government payments as 'subsidies' in such situations would mean that the NME government would be subsidizing itself.

In March 2007, the USDOC reversed this policy for evolved NMEs such as China and Vietnam. Since the policy change, the USDOC still treats both of these countries as NMEs for anti-dumping (AD) purposes, but it also identifies, measures, and countervails subsidies. In the last few years, the United States has imposed simultaneous anti-dumping duties (ADDs) and countervailing duties (CVDs) in more than 20 cases, all but one involving China.[1]

In *United States – Definitive Anti-Dumping and Countervailing Duties on Certain Products from China*,[2] China challenged the United States's new policy and claimed the United States was ignoring its obligations under the Agreement on Subsidies and Countervailing Measures (SCM Agreement). The headline-grabbing claim involved 'double remedies', sometimes referred to as 'double counting'. In this claim, China argued that in various investigations the application of both ADDs and CVDs on the same products from China created a situation where the same instance(s) of subsidization was offset twice. The US made a two-fold rebuttal. First, the WTO distinguishes between export subsidies – where double remedies are presumed and where offsets are provided by the United States (in either market or nonmarket-economy situations) – and domestic subsidies – where no such analysis is required. In other words, the United States argued there was no legal basis for a double-remedies claim. Second, even if there were a basis for a claim, no evidence existed that such double remedies in fact were occurring.

The Panel, citing studies undertaken by the US Government and parallel US court decisions, rejected the latter argument and found that double counting was 'likely'. However, the Panel agreed with the United States on the former and determined that the WTO Agreement did not prohibit the practice.[3]

The WTO Appellate Body (AB) overturned the Panel on this second finding and found that Article 19.3 of the SCM Agreement did contain a requirement to not impose double remedies. However, in a missed opportunity the AB failed to recognize that the *economic rationale* for banning simultaneous AD and CVD for

1 Since the policy change, more than two-thirds of all Chinese and Vietnamese products subject to AD scrutiny have also been simultaneously subject to a CVD investigation, a remarkable statistic given that there had been very little use of CVD by the United States during the preceding decade. See Brian D. Kelly (2011), 'The Offsetting Duty Norm and the Simultaneous Application of Countervailing and Antidumping Duties', **11**:2 *Global Economy Journal*, 1–31; Brian D. Kelly (2008), 'The Law and Economics of Simultaneous Countervailing Duty and Antidumping Duty Proceedings', **3**:1 *Global Trade and Customs Journal*, 41–50; and Chad P. Bown (2010), *Global Antidumping Database*, available at http://econ.worldbank.org/ttbd/gad/.

2 *United States – Definitive Anti-Dumping and Countervailing Duties on Certain Products from China*, Panel Report, WT/DS379/R, adopted 25 March 2011, modified by Appellate Body Report, WT/DS379/AB/R, adopted 25 March 2011 (hereinafter *US–AD and CVD (China)*).

3 Panel Report, *US–AD and CVD (China)*, paras. 14.67–14.75.

an export subsidy applies equally well to domestic subsidies when the United States's NME methodology is used to compute normal value. The AB only concluded that double remedies are 'likely' to occur and refrained from putting 'likely' into context. The AB recommended investigating authorities focus on the extent to which domestic subsidies have lowered the export price of a product (which according to the AB captures the impact of the domestic subsidies). Once the price impact is measured, the investigating authorities then need to take the necessary corrective steps to adjust for the double counting.

Our critique of the AB's decision is nuanced. On the one hand, due to particulars of US AD and CVD methods (discussed below), we believe the AB's determination misses the mark with respect to the specific cases and methods underlying this dispute. On the other hand, we believe the AB's measured position is more appropriate when the double-remedies issue is interpreted in the context of WTO NME rules.

While somewhat overshadowed by the double-remedies issue, we believe at least two other claims will likely have significant long-term consequences for the use of AD and CVD against China. One key question is what constitutes a 'public body'. Given the nature of China's economy, this question will be relevant for most future CVD cases. The United States's position was that any entity controlled by a government via majority state ownership can be considered a 'public body'. The AB found this interpretation too broad and instead determined that whether an entity is a 'public body' hinges on whether the entity is vested with or exercises 'governmental authority', a formulation that presumably envisages scenarios in which a state-owned corporation acting under commercial conditions would not necessarily be considered a public body.

A second key question is the permissibility and propriety of out-of-country benchmarks. Is the Chinese government sufficiently involved in the relevant industries to preclude the use of domestic commercial markets as a benchmark in order to determine the benefit of the subsidy provided to the recipient? If so, then how should out-of-country benchmarks be chosen and calculated? The AB, leaning heavily on findings in *US–Softwood Lumber IV*,[4] concluded that the fact that the Chinese government is the predominant supplier makes it likely that private prices will be distorted; nonetheless, the AB indicated that a case-by-case analysis is still required.

The AB clearly had difficulties with the cavalier Panel review of the USDOC's findings on appropriate out-of-country benchmarks. It considered that the Panel did not review the methodology employed by the USDOC in constructing an out-of-country benchmark for China's local-currency interest rates with the rigor

4 *United States – Final Countervailing Duty Determination with Respect to Certain Softwood Lumber from Canada*, WT/DS257/AB/R, adopted 17 February 2004, DSR 2004:II, 571 (*US–Softwood Lumber IV*).

required to satisfy the 'objective assessment' standard. While the AB made this ruling on the basis of Article 11 of the WTO Dispute Settlement Understanding (DSU), which is normally characterized as a 'procedural' provision, the practical effect of the ruling should be to impose a level of discipline on the use of out-of-country benchmarks that investigating authorities might not have otherwise considered to exist.

2. Background to the dispute

In 2007, the US Department of Commerce (USDOC), in its dual anti-dumping and anti-subsidy investigation of *Coated Free Sheet Paper* (CFSP) from China, reversed its longstanding policy against applying the countervailing-duty law to countries it deemed to have 'non-market economies'.[5] That policy, first adopted by the USDOC in 1984 and affirmed in 1986 by the US Court of Appeals for the Federal Circuit in the *Georgetown Steel* case,[6] was based on the view that, given the highly distortionary nature of the role played by the governments of centrally planned economies with no discernible private sector, it would not be appropriate to apply the countervailing-duty legislation to NMEs because a 'non-market economy would in effect be subsidizing [itself]'.[7]

In CFSP, the USDOC reconciled the *Georgetown Steel* case – which the Supreme Court did not hear and remains 'good law' in the United States as of the time of this writing – with its decision to apply countervailing duties against China by distinguishing the 'Soviet-style economies of the 1980s',[8] which were the subject of the *Georgetown Steel* case,[9] with present-day China. The USDOC considered that, while China should remain 'an NME for purposes of the US anti-dumping law'[10] in light of the continued perceived distortion in China's domestic sales prices and costs and thus their inability to produce reliable 'normal values', China's economy had nevertheless changed in fundamental ways such that it was no longer considered to resemble the 'traditional Soviet-style command economy'[11] that was the subject of the *Georgetown Steel* case.

> Pricing committees, or similar state agencies, administratively set nearly all prices in the Soviet-style economies of the 1980s. Moreover, prices were not fixed with

5 First formalized in the 29 March 2007 USDOC Memorandum '*Countervailing Duty Investigation of Coated Free Sheet Paper from the People's Republic of China – Whether the Analytical Elements of the Georgetown Steel Opinion are Applicable to China's Present-Day Economy*' (hereinafter '*Georgetown Steel* Memo'), available at http://ia.ita.doc.gov/download/prc-cfsp/CFS%20China.Georgetown%20applicability.pdf (last visited 10 December 2012).

6 *Georgetown Steel* v. *United States*, 801 F.2d 1308 (Fed. Cir. 1986).

7 Ibid., at 1316.

8 *Georgetown Steel* Memo, p. 2.

9 Poland and Czechoslovakia were the subjects of the *Georgetown Steel* case.

10 *Georgetown Steel* Memo, p. 2.

11 Ibid.

> any deference to the forces of supply and demand, but rather served as an accounting device between supplier and consumer enterprises. In contrast, although price controls and guidance remain on certain 'essential' goods and services in China, the PRC Government has eliminated price controls on most products; '*market forces now determine the prices of more than 90 percent of products traded in China*'.[12] (Emphasis added)

Beyond the issue of whether, given its NME status in the AD context, the USDOC could apply its CVD legislation to China in *any* manner, the USDOC's change of course on China raised a key issue that would go on to be the focus of this WTO dispute.[13] This concerned what is commonly termed the 'double-remedies' issue, where double remedies are considered to occur in situations in which the concurrent imposition of CVDs and ADDs has the effect of offsetting twice the same instance(s) of subsidization. Although the CFSP investigation itself did not actually result in the concurrent imposition of CVDs and ADDs, the four subsequently initiated dual investigations against Chinese goods did, and thus they, together, served as the basis for China's requests for the establishment of a WTO Panel.[14]

In CFSP as well as the four subsequent investigations, the Chinese producers had argued before the USDOC that because China was designated an NME in the parallel AD investigations and thus subject to the United States's surrogate-country 'NME methodology' for the calculation of normal values, any ADD calculated on the basis of that methodology would necessarily reflect any instances of subsidization, thereby rendering CVDs duplicative. The basis for this argument stems from the fact that, under US law, normal values based on surrogate countries are presumed to be unsubsidized, and thus not 'depressed' or affected in any way by subsidies granted by the government that is the target of the investigation. Where that is the case, the dumping margin on which the eventual duty is based would be higher than it would be if the normal value were depressed by the subsidies. This assumes, of course, that the subsidies countervailed in the parallel CVD investigation would have, in fact, depressed the normal value in the AD investigation *pro rata* (or 'dollar for dollar') if Chinese domestic costs/prices were actually used to derive the normal value used in the comparison between export price and normal value.

12 Ibid., p. 5.

13 As we discuss in section 5, a series of US domestic-court challenges to the USDOC's change of practice were pursued concurrently with this WTO dispute. These challenges ultimately forced the US Congress to revise the United States's CVD statute in order to allow its use against NMEs. The revisions to the statute were also aimed to address the AB's adverse findings in this dispute.

14 Namely, (i) *Circular Welded Carbon Quality Steel Pipe*; (ii) *Certain New Pneumatic Off-the-Road Tires*; (iii) *Light–Walled Rectangular Pipe and Tube*; and (iv) *Laminated Woven Sacks*. See Panel Report, *US–AD and CVD (China)*, para. 2.1.

In response to the argument that double remedies were impermissible under US law and that it was incumbent upon the USDOC to adopt a methodology that would ensure that they not be imposed, the USDOC considered that absent an explicit statutory directive to address the issue, US CVD legislation does not permit any adjustment – the full value of the benefit must be offset by the CVD (regardless of how much of the benefit is passed through to prices). The USDOC also considered the assumption on which the argument was based, i.e. that non-export-contingent subsidies[15] lower domestic prices *pro rata*, to be flawed in any event,[16] and went on to impose concurrent CVD and ADD in the four investigations underlying the WTO complaint, as well as several others initiated afterwards.

Apart from the double-remedies issue, the USDOC's decision to apply the US CVD legislation to China also raised a host of issues relating to how the substantive provisions of the CVD legislation – mostly relating to the identification and quantification of subsidies – could be applied to a country still considered, at least by the United States, to be in transition from its 'command-economy past'.[17] Examples of this include the relevance of China's 'Five Year Guidelines' and other planning documents in the determination of *de jure* specificity of subsidies; the scope of the meaning of the term 'public body' as it relates to the question of whether China's state-owned commercial banks (SOCBs) and other state-owned enterprises (SOEs) can be considered to be providing goods and services as government actors; and the circumstances in which it is appropriate to consider SOEs' involvement in an industry sufficient to render any domestic price in that industry incapable of providing an 'undistorted' benchmark for the purposes of calculating the amount of the benefit received, and then how to construct an out-of-country benchmark.

While most of the more contentious aspects of the underlying investigations and WTO dispute relate to topics that are common in many CVD investigations, such as the determination of specificity and the calculation of benefit amounts, the legally relevant facts of this dispute tend to relate more to issues that are germane to China's economy in particular and as a whole (as well as certain other NMEs perhaps), rather than the specific producers or even the specific industries targeted by the investigations. It is for that reason that this dispute, while only targeting the first four USDOC investigations resulting in concurrent ADDs and CVDs, should

15 It is normally taken for granted that export subsidies, i.e. subsidies contingent on export performance, do reduce export sales prices *pro rata*. This view is reflected in GATT Article VI:5, which provides that '[n]o product shall be subject to both anti-dumping and countervailing duties for the purpose of dealing with one and the same situation arising from dumping or from export subsidization'.

16 The arguments made before the USDOC by both China and the interested producers on double remedies can be found in the 17 October 2007 *Issues and Decision Memorandum for the Final Determination in the Less-Than-Fair-Value Investigation of Coated Free Sheet Paper from the People's Republic of China*, pp. 10–12 (hereinafter '*CFS Paper Decisions Memo*').

17 See *CFS Paper Decisions Memo*, p. 19 et seq.

nevertheless have wide-reaching consequences for all of the investigations conducted against China up to the point of the issuance of the AB Report, as well as those to be initiated in the future.

3. Key issues examined in the Panel and AB reports

3.1 Double remedies

The Panel in this dispute ruled in favor of the United States on most issues of systemic importance. With regard to the double-remedies issue, the arguments put before the Panel by China were significantly different from the arguments treated by the USDOC at the investigation stage, and later the US Court of International Trade (CIT), because of the differences between the US CVD law and the text and substantive provisions of the GATT and the SCM Agreement. Though China cited no less than eight different articles of the GATT and the SCM Agreement[18] in support of its contention that the USDOC's imposition of double remedies in the underlying investigations was impermissible, the Panel rejected the arguments made in connection with each. Hence, even though the Panel found that double remedies were likely to occur, the articles cited by China simply did not address the issue of double remedies.[19]

The AB disagreed and considered that, when read in light of various other articles for context, Article 19.3 of the SCM Agreement, which requires that duties be collected 'in appropriate amounts',[20] forbids the imposition of concurrent duties which offset the same subsidization twice. In addition to finding the concept of the collection of duties constituting double remedies to be incompatible with the notion of 'appropriateness',[21] the AB went a step further and placed the burden of proof on the investigating authority to rebut the presumption that there is, in fact, double counting in cases in which a parallel AD/CVD investigation makes use of an AD NME methodology. The AB considered that while it did not necessarily agree with the *pro rata* argument advanced by China, and the accompanying conclusion that CVDs in dual investigations using NME methodologies were entirely accounted for in the dumping investigations, double remedies were nevertheless 'likely' to occur in such dual investigations.[22] This likelihood seemed to be the impetus for the AB's shifting of the burden onto the investigating authorities.

18 Namely, Articles VI:3 and 1:1 of the GATT 1994 and Articles 10, 12.1, 12.8, 19.3, 19.4, and 32.1 of the SCM Agreement.

19 Panel Report, *US–AD and CVD (China)*, para. 14.120 (Article 19.4 of the SCM Agreement), 14.130 (Article 19.3 of the SCM Agreement), 14.136 (Article VI:3 of the GATT 1994), 14.138 (Article 10 of the SCM Agreement), 14.139 (Article 32.1 of the SCM Agreement), 14.147 (Article 12.1 of the SCM Agreement), 14.148 (Article 12.8 of the SCM Agreement), 14.182 (Article I:1 of the GATT 1994).

20 It is noted that Article 9.2 of the WTO Anti-Dumping Agreement contains very similar wording.

21 AB Report, *US–AD and CVD (China)*, para. 547 et seq.

22 Ibid., paras. 596–604.

3.2 *The 'public body' determination*

With regard to the issues concerning the identification of subsidies pursuant to Articles 1 and 2 of the SCM Agreement, the Panel first treated the issue of whether the USDOC acted in a manner inconsistent with Article 1.1(a)(1) of the SCM Agreement in considering that China's SOCBs and SOEs were 'public bodies'. Considering the term 'public body' to encompass 'any entity controlled by a government',[23] where 'majority government ownership is clear and highly indicative evidence of government control',[24] the Panel went on to find with relative ease, in light of the fact that the SOEs were majority owned by the Chinese government, that the USDOC did not act inconsistently with Article 1.1(a)(1) by 'giving primacy to evidence of majority government-ownership'. The Panel reached a similar conclusion in the context of the SOCBs in light of the majority government ownership of the banks, and considered it relevant that the USDOC concluded that, in addition to simple ownership, 'there was extensive government involvement in and control over [the SOCBs'] operations'.[25]

The AB overruled the Panel on this issue as well, finding its interpretation of the term 'public body' too broad. As opposed to the Panel's focus on 'control', the AB considered that:

> the determination of whether a particular conduct is that of a public body must be made by evaluating the core features of the entity and its relationship to government in the narrow sense. That assessment must focus on evidence relevant to the question of whether the entity is vested with or exercises governmental authority.[26]

It was on this basis that the AB overruled the Panel's acceptance of the USDOC's decision considering certain of China's SOE input suppliers to be public bodies. Instead of performing an analysis on the basis of the sort of factors listed by the AB, the USDOC 'appl[ied] a rule of majority government-ownership',[27] which the AB found unacceptable. The AB did, however, consider the approach of the USDOC with regard to the SOCBs to be acceptable under its new formulation. In the case of the banks, the USDOC did not apply the 'simple ownership' test, but rather took into account various other considerations which the AB considered to, as a factual matter, not be incompatible with the conclusion that the entities in question exercised governmental authority.

23 Panel Report, *US–AD and CVD (China)*, para. 8.94.
24 Ibid., paras. 8.133–8.136.
25 Ibid., paras. 8.139–8.143.
26 AB Report, *US–AD and CVD (China)*, para. 345.
27 Panel Report, *US–AD and CVD (China)*, para. 8.99.

3.3 De jure specificity in lending and regional specificity in land-use rights

China's claims concerning specificity determinations pursuant to Article 2 of the SCM Agreement consisted of one attacking the determination of *de jure* specificity in the context of SOCB lending to the tire industry under Article 2.1(a) of the SCM Agreement, and another attacking the determination of regional specificity in the context of the provision of land-use rights under Article 2.2.

With regard to the first, the Panel reviewed the evidence considered by the USDOC in making its specificity determination in the *Certain New Pneumatic Off-the-Road Tires* investigation, including but not limited to: 'central government planning documents' which singled out the tire industry as 'encouraged'; 'provincial and municipal government planning documents' considered to implement the centrally mandated plan; provisions of those documents relating to the financing of that industry, and China's Commercial Banking Law, which was considered to require the SOCBs to consider government macroeconomic policies in making lending decisions.[28] The Panel then concluded, on the basis of the totality of the evidence and affording the USDOC due deference as a trier of fact, that 'a reasonable and objective investigating authority could have determined ... [that China] explicitly identified "certain enterprises" in the sense of Article 2.1(a) of the SCM Agreement for encouragement and development'.[29]

On appeal, the AB understood China to be focusing its challenge more on the relationship between the Panel's analysis and the USDOC's analysis than the specificity conclusion itself. On that point, the AB did acknowledge a disconnect between 'certain elements of the Panel's reasoning [and] the rationale employed by the USDOC in its specificity determination' but did not consider that to amount to legal error given the facts of the case.[30] The AB therefore upheld the Panel on this issue.

China's other specificity-related claim, that the USDOC acted inconsistently with Article 2.2 of the SCM Agreement in considering the land-use rights granted to one of the companies in the *Laminated Woven Sacks* (LWS) investigation to be 'regionally specific', marked what was probably the most substantial of China's few wins at the Panel stage. In a decision that was not appealed by the United States, the Panel considered that even though the industrial park in which the allegedly subsidized land was located could constitute a 'geographical region' within the meaning of Article 2.2,[31] the USDOC nevertheless erred in considering

28 Panel Report, *US–AD and CVD (China)*, paras. 9.80–9.94.

29 Ibid., para. 9.106.

30 AB Report, *US–AD and CVD (China)*, paras. 398–400.

31 Although China argued that geographical regions 'must necessarily have some sort of formal administrative or economic identity' in the manner of political subdivisions, which the industrial park was not, the Panel considered that the term 'geographical region' could 'encompass any identified tract of land within the jurisdiction of a granting authority'. Panel Report, *US–AD and CVD (China)*, paras. 9.140–9.144.

that location within the park could, in itself, constitute the grant of a regionally specific subsidy. The Panel noted that such an analysis, combined with the USDOC's finding that the government was the ultimate owner of *all* land in China, led to the problem of 'land-use rights, wherever in China they were provided, [being] regionally specific' on account of their necessarily being located *somewhere*.

Thus, the Panel considered that a proper finding of regional specificity in such circumstances would require the land to have been provided pursuant to some sort of distinct regime, such that evidence would point to a fundamental difference between the provision of land-use rights within the geographical region and that located outside of it.[32] While the United States did not appeal this decision, China did, citing the systemic implications that the Panel's reasoning could have, but the AB did not consider the Panel to have erred.[33]

3.4 Out-of-country benchmarking

3.4.1 The permissibility of out-of-country benchmarking

With regard to the provision of (1) land-use rights, (2) financing through preferential lending, and (3) steel inputs sold by entities considered to be public bodies, the USDOC had considered that the Chinese Government's involvement in the relevant markets was so pervasive that there was effectively no domestic 'commercial' (i.e., undistorted by government intervention) market that could serve as a benchmark against which to compare the price of the good or service provided in order to determine the benefit of the subsidy provided to the recipient. Accordingly, the USDOC resorted to the construction of 'out-of-country benchmarks' in order to calculate the amount of benefit of the subsidies to their recipients.

With respect to all three broad benefit categories, the Panel held that the USDOC was justified under Article 14 of the SCM Agreement in its determinations that the relevant industries were distorted to the point that they precluded the selection of a domestic benchmark. In each case, the Panel afforded the USDOC relatively wide discretion with regard to its factual conclusions, focusing primarily on the quality of the evidence examined in each case. With regard to SOE-produced steel inputs, the Panel upheld the USDOC's determination that the Chinese steel industry was incapable of producing a reliable domestic benchmark principally, but not solely, on account of the SOEs' market share and very dominant position in the market

32 It should be noted that the Panel's holding on regional specificity, and the United States's decision to not appeal it, has not disposed of the question of whether and how China's provisions of land-use rights might be considered 'sectorally' specific pursuant to Article 2.1 of the SCM Agreement. For a critique of the methodology of the European Commission in its attempt to do just that in the *Coated Fine Paper* from China investigation, see Edwin Vermulst and Brian Gatta (2012), 'Concurrent Trade Defense Investigations in the EU, the EU's New Anti-Subsidy Practice against China, and the Future of Both', 11:3 *World Trade Review*, 527–553.

33 AB Report, *US–AD and CVD (China)*, para. 424.

(96.1%). With regard to the land-use rights, the Panel upheld the USDOC's determination that because of the prohibition of private land ownership in China such that 'all land [is] owned by some level of government', there is essentially no commercial market for land in China.[34] The Panel analyzed both the steel input and land-use right questions under Article 14(d) of the SCM Agreement, and relied heavily on the AB Report in *US–Softwood Lumber IV*, which first established the possibility of resorting to an out-of-country benchmark.

The Panel's analysis of China's claim relating to the decision to use out-of-country interest-rate benchmarks for the purposes of determining the benefits provided by China's 'policy-lending program' was similar to that in the land and steel contexts, except in that loans are treated under Article 14(b) of the SCM Agreement, and likewise the Panel seemed to rely heavily on the deferential 'adequate and reasoned conclusion' standard. In concluding that 'a reasonable and objective investigating authority *could* have concluded that the government played a predominant role in the Chinese commercial lending market... such that the observed rates were not suitable as benchmarks',[35] the Panel did not give much of an indication on what it thought about the USDOC's conclusions on the substance, but clearly found particularly persuasive the 'extensive reference to publications by outside institutions (OECD and IMF)'[36] as well as the thoroughness of the USDOC's investigation on this question.

The AB upheld the Panel's conclusions with regard to the two benefit categories challenged in this regard (China did not challenge the land-use rights' determination), clarifying and expanding its interpretation of the *US–Softwood Lumber IV* Report which formed the basis for the Panel's holdings. With regard to the steel inputs and the importance of the government being the 'predominant supplier' in the industry, the AB noted that it considered *US–Softwood Lumber IV* to indicate that 'if the government is a *significant* supplier, this fact alone cannot justify a finding that prices are distorted'.[37] However, 'where the government is the *predominant* supplier, it is likely that private prices will be distorted, but a case-by-case analysis is still required'.[38] Because of the overwhelming predominance of the

34 Panel Report, *US–AD and CVD (China)*, para. 10.76.

35 Ibid., paras. 10.144–10.148, emphasis added. The reader may make what it will of the unexplained difference between articulation of the standard of review employed by the Panels in the *US–AD and CVD (China)* case, on one hand, and the *China – Countervailing and Anti-Dumping Duties on Grain Oriented Flat-Rolled Electrical Steel from the United States* case, WT/DS414/R, circulated to WTO Members 15 June 2012 (appeal in progress), on the other. In the former case, in which the Panel upheld substantially all of the US practice *vis-à-vis* China, the Panel applied the '*could have* found' formulation, whereas in the latter, in which the Panel rejected substantially all of the challenged elements of the Chinese CVD practice *vis-à-vis* the United States, the Panel consistently framed its inquiries in terms of what an 'unbiased and objective investigating authority *would have* found'. See paras. 7.51, 7.112.

36 Ibid., paras. 10.144–10.148.

37 AB Report, *US–AD and CVD (China)*, para. 441.

38 Ibid.

Chinese SOEs in the steel market (relevant to the two pipe and tube cases), along with what the Panel considered to be the USDOC's consideration of 'other factors' thus eschewing the application of the forbidden '*per se* rule' with respect to market share, the AB upheld the Panel's decision.

The AB similarly upheld the USDOC's rejection of in-country interest rates for RMB-denominated loans, first noting that 'inherent in Article 14(b), as in Article 14(d), is sufficient flexibility to permit the use of a proxy in place of observed rates in the country in question where no "commercial" benchmark can be found'.[39] Having officially expanded the *US–Softwood Lumber IV* reasoning with regard to Article 14(d) of the SCM Agreement (goods and services) to Article 14(b) (loans), the AB went on to consider that the USDOC's analysis was in fact sufficient to conclude that 'the Chinese Government, by participating in the RMB-lending market and by intervening in that market (beyond its monetary policy role), is able to and does in fact distort interest rates'.[40] The analysis to be made in the lending context is thus markedly different from the analysis in the goods-and-services context in that the government being a substantial or predominant supplier of loans is not necessarily a relevant inquiry, especially when the government interference is such that even foreign banks are affected in their lending practices such that their rates must be deemed 'non-commercial'.

3.4.2 The propriety of the actual benchmarks selected

Pursuant to its determination that the Chinese land and lending industries, the latter with regard to both Chinese RMB- and USD-denominated loans, were distorted such that they required out-of-country benchmarks for the purpose of the benefit quantification, the USDOC went on to select as proxies Thai land prices, an interest rate based on a 'regression analysis of inflation-adjusted interest rates in 33 lower-middle-income countries',[41] and 'an annual average LIBOR-based interest rate', respectively.[42]

In its evaluation of the consistency of the benchmarks with Article 14 of the SCM Agreement, the Panel determined that, just as a finding of a certain level of distortion is the fact that permits an authority to resort to an out-of-country benchmark in the first place, the benchmark construction process requires an 'investigating authority to do its best to identify a benchmark that approximates the market conditions that would prevail in the absence of the distortion'.[43]

39 Ibid., para. 490.

40 Ibid., para. 501.

41 Panel Report, *US–AD and CVD (China)*, paras. 10.192–10.194.

42 Ibid., para. 10.210.

43 Ibid., para. 10.187 (footnotes omitted). It was also noted that in *US–Softwood Lumber IV*, the Appellate Body cautioned that: '[w]hen an investigating authority resorts ... to a benchmark other than private prices in the country of provision, the benchmark chosen must, nevertheless, relate or refer to, or be connected with, the prevailing market conditions in that country, and must reflect price, quality,

The Panel also considered that its task in this regard was essentially limited to the evaluation of 'the internal logic of the methodology employed, and the soundness and appropriateness of the data relied upon'[44] for the construction of the proxy benchmark. As was the case with the review of the USDOC's initial distortional analyses, the Panel considered itself similarly constrained by its standard of review, which dictates that it only seek to determine whether the selected benchmarks are such that 'a reasonable and objective investigating authority *could* use'[45] them.

In a holding not appealed by China, the Panel considered itself satisfied that the method adopted in order to determine the land benchmark was consistent with Article 14(d), primarily because of the range and variety of factors that the USDOC took into account in determining the likeness between the Thai and Chinese land markets. In a holding not appealed by the United States, the Panel rejected the LIBOR-based benchmark used for benchmarking USD-denominated loans, though only on the basis of the fact that the USDOC used yearly average rates to construct the benchmark, as opposed to the actual LIBOR rates prevailing at the time that the loans countervailed were granted.[46] This detail, therefore, would not hinder in any meaningful way the United States's ability to countervail USD-denominated loans using a LIBOR-based benchmark, but it would require the USDOC to employ slightly more labor in matching each loan with the prevailing benchmark at the time of the loan, as opposed to using the rejected 'one size fits all' approach.

Finally, in a holding that was appealed by China, the Panel held with regard to the United States's benchmark for RMB-denominated loans that the benchmark selected passed muster under the standard of review discussed above. Similar to its analysis in the land context, the Panel looked at the methodology employed by the USDOC, as opposed to the result of the application of the benchmark, and considered the various aspects of the methodology to be 'appropriate' and 'not unreasonable'. These included the decision to rely on a basket of other countries' currencies as the basis for the proxy, the selection of that basket according to a preexisting World Bank grouping of countries in the same income category as China, an inflation adjustment, and various other factors 'related to the quality of the countries' institutions',[47] such as 'political stability, government effectiveness and rule of law.'[48] The Panel concluded by noting that it did not consider the benchmark to be 'perfect', but only that a 'reasonable and objective investigating

availability, marketability, transportation and other conditions of purchase or sale, as required by Article 14(d)'. Ibid., para. 10.181.

44 Ibid., para. 10.206.

45 Ibid., paras. 10.187, 10.205 (emphasis added).

46 Ibid., paras. 10.217–10.219.

47 Ibid., para. 10.207.

48 Ibid.

authority could have used the methodology used by the USDOC', and that it did not appear arbitrary or biased.[49]

In a holding of uncertain practical effect in light of its procedural nature, the AB nullified the Panel's holding on the benchmark used for RMB-denominated loans not on substantive grounds, but rather because the AB considered the Panel's analysis so cursory as to violate its obligation under Article 11 of the DSU to perform an 'objective assessment of the matter'.[50] The AB considered, in a passage characteristic of its general view on the Panel's analysis, that the Panel 'appear[ed] to have simply accepted the USDOC's determinations and relevant supporting evidence without engaging in a critical and searching analysis, or testing the adequacy and reasonableness of the USDOC's determinations in the light of other plausible alternative explanations',[51] and that it 'rather passively accepted the reasons provided by the USDOC for its determinations, without engaging in a critical and searching analysis and without considering the USDOC's determinations in the light of plausible alternative explanations'.[52]

While the AB did not go on to complete the analysis because of what it considered to be insufficient undisputed facts on the record that would permit such completion, the AB did go beyond merely criticizing the cursory nature of the Panel's analysis. Indeed, it effectively overruled the Panel's interpretation of its standard of review in the context of the evaluation of the consistency of out-of-country benchmarks with Article 14 of the SCM Agreement. The clearest example of this comes in the form of the AB's holding the Panel's description of its own mandate – as being limited to the examination of the 'internal logic of the methodology' and 'soundness of the data' used – to be in itself incapable of discharge of the 'objective assessment' obligation.[53]

In addition, the AB's explanation that the Panel had an obligation to review 'whether the reasons put forth by the USDOC justified the proxy that it constructed, *including in the light of other plausible alternatives*',[54] indicates that it views the level of deference to be afforded to investigating authorities to be one which requires that the benchmark selected *was*, given the circumstances of the investigation, reasonable, and not merely that it *could have* been reasonable. To the extent that the AB suggests that the benchmark selected must be reasonable in comparison to other potential candidates, and not simply unreasonable on its face, as the Panel's analysis suggested, this would seem to imply the imposition of a substantive obligation on authorities to adequately examine the various potential benchmarks.

49 Ibid., para. 10.208.
50 AB Report, *US–AD and CVD (China)*, para. 518.
51 Ibid., para. 525.
52 Ibid., para. 526.
53 Ibid., para. 519.
54 Ibid., para. 523 (emphasis added).

4. Legal and economic analysis

US–AD and CVD (China) presents four issues of systemic interest[55] pertaining basically to the conduct of AD and CVD investigations against perceived nonmarket economies[56] such as China. These are:

(1) double remedies;
(2) qualification as 'public bodies' within the meaning of Article 1.1(a)(1) of the SCM Agreement of SOCBs and SOEs;
(3) *de jure* specificity of loans granted by SOCBs and regional specificity of land-use rights; and
(4) the decision to use and selection of out-of-country benchmarks within the meaning of Article 14(b) and 14(d) of the SCM Agreement.

Before delving into the analysis of these issues, it seems useful to provide a brief recap of the notion of nonmarket economies and its consequences in the trade remedies' context in the GATT/WTO.

4.1 Nonmarket economies in the GATT/WTO

The second interpretative note Ad Article VI(1) GATT 1947 (hereinafter: second Ad note) provides that:

> It is recognized that, in the case of imports from a country which has a complete or substantially complete monopoly of its trade and where all domestic prices are fixed by the State, special difficulties may exist in determining price comparability for the purposes of paragraph 1, and in such cases importing contracting parties may find it necessary to take into account the possibility that a strict comparison with domestic prices in such a country may not always be appropriate.

Thus, this note gives GATT members carte blanche to determine normal value in AD investigations involving countries meeting these criteria.[57] In practice, members developed the surrogate- or analogue-country concept for this purpose, meaning that they would use prices or costs in a market-economy country as the basis for normal value.[58]

55 As we will see below, some of these issues may be relevant in market-economy cases, too.

56 The decision whether to treat certain countries as nonmarket economies lies with the investigating authorities, at least until 2016 in case of China and until 2019 in case of Vietnam. Even though more and more countries treat China as a market economy these days for purposes of application of their anti-dumping law, key trading partners of China, such as the EU, the United States, and Brazil, still treat it as a nonmarket economy for that purpose.

57 This note still applies as Article 2(7) of the current Anti-Dumping Agreement explicitly provides that 'this Article is without prejudice to the second Supplementary Provision to paragraph 1 of Article VI in Annex I to GATT 1994'.

58 In a variation of the surrogate-country concept, the United States uses the so-called factors-of-production test, taking the quantities of inputs used in the production process by the nonmarket economy producer, but valuing them at their prices in a market economy.

Furthermore, as neither this note nor any other provision in the GATT (or the WTO) provides a listing of countries that have a 'complete or substantially complete monopoly of their trade and where all domestic prices are fixed by the State' (colloquially and in various instances of WTO members' domestic-trade-remedies legislation referred to as nonmarket economies), it was left to GATT members to unilaterally determine which countries met these requirements. While a GATT member holding that *another* GATT member met the requirements might have quickly found itself the subject of a dispute-settlement proceeding that it probably would have lost – after all, it is hard to find a country that has a *complete or substantially complete monopoly of its trade* and where *all domestic prices are fixed by the State* – non-GATT members of course did not have this possibility, as a result of which countries such as China, Russia, Ukraine, and Vietnam were routinely treated as nonmarket economies and subjected to the surrogate-country methodology, which in light of, among others, the incomparable nature of the surrogates chosen and their lack of incentive to cooperate (except to obtain a competitive advantage over their 'nonmarket economy' competitors) almost invariably led to findings of high dumping margins.

While Russia and Ukraine, over time, managed to be treated as market economies by countries such as the United States and the EU, ostensibly because they met the technical criteria unilaterally established by the latter, but in reality arguably because of political considerations, China (and Vietnam) had to agree to special provisions in their Protocols of Accession to the WTO effectively allowing other WTO members to continue to treat them as nonmarket economies until 2016 and 2019, respectively, whether or not the conditions of the second Ad note are actually met. Indeed, in the case of China, a recognition among the negotiating members that its economy as of 2001 could not reasonably be characterized as the sort referred to in the Ad note is what prompted the inclusion of the special provision in the first place.

Thus, paragraph 15 of China's Accession Protocol states that:

> **15. Price Comparability in Determining Subsidies and Dumping**
> Article VI of the GATT 1994, the ... Anti-Dumping Agreement and the SCM Agreement shall apply in proceedings involving imports of Chinese origin into a WTO Member consistent with the following:
>
> (a) In determining price comparability under Article VI of the GATT 1994 and the Anti-Dumping Agreement, the importing WTO Member shall use either Chinese prices or costs for the industry under investigation or a methodology that is not based on a strict comparison with domestic prices or costs in China based on the following rules:
>
> (i) If the producers under investigation can clearly show that market economy conditions prevail in the industry producing the like product with regard to the manufacture, production and sale of that product, the importing WTO

Member shall use Chinese prices or costs for the industry under investigation in determining price comparability;

(ii) The importing WTO Member may use a methodology that is not based on a strict comparison with domestic prices or costs in China if the producers under investigation cannot clearly show that market economy conditions prevail in the industry producing the like product with regard to manufacture, production and sale of that product.

(b) In proceedings under Parts II, III and V of the SCM Agreement, when addressing subsidies described in Articles 14(a), 14(b), 14(c) and 14(d), relevant provisions of the SCM Agreement shall apply; however, if there are special difficulties in that application, the importing WTO Member may then use methodologies for identifying and measuring the subsidy benefit which take into account the possibility that prevailing terms and conditions in China may not always be available as appropriate benchmarks. In applying such methodologies, where practicable, the importing WTO Member should adjust such prevailing terms and conditions before considering the use of terms and conditions prevailing outside China.

...

(d) Once China has established, under the national law of the importing WTO Member, that it is a market economy, the provisions of subparagraph (a) shall be terminated provided that the importing Member's national law contains market economy criteria as of the date of accession. In any event, the provisions of subparagraph (a)(ii) shall expire 15 years after the date of accession. In addition, should China establish, pursuant to the national law of the importing WTO Member, that market economy conditions prevail in a particular industry or sector, the non-market economy provisions of subparagraph (a) shall no longer apply to that industry or sector.

Until 11 December 2016 therefore, WTO members may use the surrogate-country methodology for China on the basis of paragraph 15(a)(ii) of the Protocol. On that date, paragraph 15(a)(ii) will expire and the special rules for normal-value determination applicable to China can no longer be applied as explicitly clarified by the AB in *EC–Fasteners*:

> Paragraph 15(d) of China's Accession Protocol establishes that the provisions of paragraph 15(a) expire 15 years after the date of China's accession (that is, 11 December 2016). It also provides that other WTO Members shall grant before that date the early termination of paragraph 15(a) with respect to China's entire economy or specific sectors or industries if China demonstrates under the law of the importing WTO Member 'that it is a market economy' or that 'market economy conditions prevail in a particular industry or sector'. Since paragraph 15(d) provides for rules on the termination of paragraph 15(a), its scope of application cannot be wider than that of paragraph 15(a). Both paragraphs concern exclusively the determination of normal value. *In other words, paragraph 15(a) contains special rules for the determination of normal value in*

> *anti-dumping investigations involving China. Paragraph 15(d) in turn establishes that these special rules will expire in 2016 and sets out certain conditions that may lead to the early termination of these special rules before 2016.*[59]

Therefore, from 11 December 2016, Section 15 of the Accession Protocol can no longer be relied upon to use the surrogate-country methodology as regards Chinese imports in AD investigations.

This still leaves open the question whether post-2016 WTO members could possibly rely on the second Ad note to effectively continue use of the surrogate-country methodology. However, per the AB in *EC–Fasteners* this appears unlikely:

> The second Ad Note to Article VI:1 refers to a 'country which has a complete or substantially complete monopoly of its trade' and 'where all domestic prices are fixed by the State'. This appears to describe a certain type of NME, where the State monopolizes trade and sets all domestic prices. *The second Ad Note to Article VI:1 would thus not on its face be applicable to lesser forms of NMEs that do not fulfill both conditions, that is, the complete or substantially complete monopoly of trade and the fixing of all prices by the State.*[60]

Last, it is noted at this stage that the various Protocols of Accession[61] do foresee the imposition of countervailing duties against NMEs, though – supposedly in light of the then-prevailing practice among the principal trade defence users of not applying their CVD laws to NMEs – there was no provision explicitly accounting for the possibility of double remedies in concurrent AD/CVD investigations against NMEs. In this respect, one may draw a parallel with model zeroing, which did not exist as a practice as long as WTO members were free to apply simple zeroing.

4.2 *Double remedies*

4.2.1 *Pass-through*

The fact that simultaneous imposition of ADD and CVD may lead to double remedies has been recognized by the GATT signatories from the outset. Article VI:5 GATT provides that 'no product ... shall be subject to both anti-dumping and countervailing duties to compensate for the same situation of dumping or export subsidization'. The fact that Article VI:5 GATT notes the impermissibility of double remedies in the context of export subsidies but not domestic subsidies was a key element of the United States's legal argument.

The following two examples clarify why the GATT distinguishes between export and domestic subsidies. First, consider an example where a producer receives an export subsidy of US$5/unit; she sells in her domestic market at US$100 and for

59 AB Report, *European Communities – Definitive Anti-Dumping Measures on Certain Iron or Steel Fasteners from China*, WT/DS397/AB/R, adopted 28 July 2011, para. 289 ('*EC–Fasteners*') (emphasis added).

60 Ibid., n.460 (emphasis added).

61 See, e.g., paragraph 15(b) of the Protocol of Accession of China quoted above.

export at US$95; the effect of the export subsidy is to lower the export price by US $5. Article VI:5 implies that the investigating authorities could either impose an ADD of US$5 or a CVD of US$5; however, it could not impose both because that would amount to double remedies.

One can criticize Article VI:5 on the grounds that it abstracts from what the recipient of the subsidy actually does with the money and/or, more generally, that it ignores the fungibility of money. More formally, Article VI:5 embodies two very specific assumptions about the pass-through of the export subsidy: (i) the export subsidy is completely passed through to the export price and (ii) none of the export subsidy is passed through to the home-market price. Despite the questionable empirical validity of the pass-through assumptions, the explicit link between the act of exporting and the receipt of an export subsidy appears to be the basis for limiting the scope of Article VI:5 to export subsidies.

Now contrast this example with the following, which involves a countervailable domestic subsidy of US$7. Suppose investigating authorities observe a domestic market price of US$93 and an export price of US$89. In addition, suppose investigating authorities (could) determine that without the domestic subsidy the domestic market price would have been US$100 and the export price would have been US$96. Under these circumstances, the proper trade remedy would involve both an ADD of US$4, which would eliminate the price differential, and a CVD of US$7, which would restore the prices to what they would be without the domestic subsidies. Like the previous example, this example embodies very specific (and again perhaps empirically invalid) assumptions about pass-through of the subsidy; notably, the domestic subsidy is assumed to symmetrically and completely pass through to both the export price and the home-market price.[62]

These examples make it clear that the economic logic behind Article VI:5 GATT hinges on the pass-through effects of domestic and export subsidies being different. One type of subsidy (export subsidy) is presumed to affect the export price (after all, it is contingent on export) and have little impact on the normal value, while the other type of subsidy (domestic subsidy) is believed to affect the export price and normal value comparably.

In practice, however, the economic effects of export and domestic subsidies are likely to be far murkier. Export subsidies may well affect home-market prices. Similarly, it is not hard to imagine a situation where, for example, a domestic subsidy has a large effect on the home-market price but a small impact on the export price. An enormous economics literature has examined pass-through both theoretically and empirically over the past two decades, and there is overwhelming

62 The United States's CVD statute requires the USDOC to treat the <u>entire</u> subsidy as a benefit, even if it is not fully passed through to the prices. Said differently, US CVD rules *assume* complete pass-through of the subsidy and do not require the USDOC to measure pass-through in a typical CVD investigation.

evidence that pass-through is neither complete nor symmetric.[63] Even weak forms of the 'law of one price', which follows from an assumption of symmetric pass-through, are rejected in empirical study after empirical study.[64] Economists have repeatedly found that pass-through will not typically be symmetric across destination markets. The robust empirical finding is that a cost shock will result in a price change of x% to one market but of y% to another market. Market structure, technology, upstream and downstream cost conditions, market share, the nature and duration of cost shocks, and product differentiation have all been found to affect pass-through.

This discussion is at the heart of our assessment of the AB's decision. On the one hand, we believe the AB failed to appreciate that specific provisions in US statutes imply that the *calculated* pass-through will be essentially the same as the pass-through *assumed* in Article VI:5 GATT. Specifically, the United States's methods result in a *domestic* subsidy having price pass-through effects similar to that which Article VI:5 GATT implicitly assumes occurs with an *export* subsidy. US AD NME methods entirely eliminate the impact of domestic distortions (including any subsidization) on the normal value side; hence subsidies can only pass through to the export price. Therefore, double remedies will definitely occur under US procedures.[65]

If the AB had recognized and embraced this economic logic, it could have narrowly crafted its report by using the underlying logic of Article VI:5 GATT in support of a finding that the simultaneous use of AD and CVD under US methods is always inconsistent under the NME method. This strong but narrow approach would have allowed the AB to make a definitive statement about double

63 See Kenneth A. Froot and Paul D. Klemperer (1989), 'Exchange Rate Pass-Through When Market Share Matters', 79:4 *The American Economic Review*, 637–654; Michael M. Knetter (1993), 'International Comparisons of Pricing-to-Market Behavior', 83:3 *The American Economic Review*, 473–486; Michael M. Knetter (1994), 'Is Export Price Adjustment Asymmetric?: Evaluating the Market Share and Marketing Bottlenecks Hypotheses', 13:1 *Journal of International Money and Finance*, 55–70; Pinelopi K. Goldberg and Michael M. Knetter (1997), 'Goods Prices and Exchange Rates: What Have We Learned?', 35:3 *Journal of Economic Literature*, 1243–1272; Steve McCorriston, C. W. Morgan, and Anthony J. Rayner (1998), 'Processing Technology, Market Power and Price Transmission', 49:2 *Journal of Agricultural Economics*, 185–201; Larry S. Karp and Jeffrey M. Perloff (1989), 'Estimating Market Structure and Tax Incidence: The Japanese Television Market', 37:3 *The Journal of Industrial Economics*, 225–239; Steve McCorriston, C. W. Morgan, and Anthony J. Rayner (2001), 'Price Transmission: The Interaction between Market Power and Returns to Scale', 28:2 *European Review of Agricultural Economics*, 143–159; José Manuel Campa and Linda S. Goldberg (2005), 'Exchange Rate Pass-Through into Import Prices', 87:4 *The Review of Economics and Statistics*, 679–690.

64 See Kenneth Rogoff (1996), 'The Purchasing Power Parity Puzzle', 34:2 *Journal of Economic Literature*, 647–668; Kenneth A. Froot, Michael Kim, and Kenneth Rogoff (2001), 'The Law of One Price Over 700 Years', International Monetary Fund Working Paper, WP/01/174.

65 At the time of this WTO proceeding, US statutes prohibited the USDOC from making any adjustments to its calculated CVD to account for pass-through issues. Whether the statutory changes enacted subsequent to this case are sufficient to satisfy the WTO AB will likely be the subject of future WTO disputes.

remedies but to limit the scope of the determination to just the US NME methodology.

On the other hand, the AB may have made a deliberate decision to craft a broader decision. The AB seemed to recognize that, in general, double remedies and pass-through are fundamentally empirical questions. The empirical literature has shown that pass-through is rarely 100% and rarely 0%. How much of a domestic subsidy passes through to the home-market price and how much passes through to the export price is something an investigating authority should measure and then make adjustments for. We believe this latter interpretation is the most logical way to interpret the AB's decision and explanation.

Even though the AB supposedly opted for a broader interpretation, it was incumbent upon the AB to have considered how domestic subsidies pass through to normal value under NME methods as compared with other methods for computing normal value. Had it done so, it would have been able to comment on the specifics of US procedures that generate double remedies.

4.2.2 *Methods for calculating normal value*

The pass-through issue is complicated by the fact that the ADA provides for four alternative methods for calculating the normal value in a dumping determination: the home-market method, the constructed-value method, the third-market method, and the NME method. Pass-through of a domestic subsidy may vary depending on the method used. Moreover, at the time when a firm sets its prices, it does not know what method would be used if it were to later find itself subject to an anti-dumping investigation. This uncertainty further dims the prospect of empirically observing symmetric pass-through.

In broad terms, the dumping margin is calculated as

$$ADD = P_{normal\_value} - P^{US}_{exp}(C_{Home}(s), s)$$

where home-market costs are denoted as C_{Home} and the subsidy is denoted s. The computation of P_{normal_value} varies by the specific method used. That is

$$\begin{aligned}
ADD &= P_{Home}(C_{Home}(s), s) - P^{US}_{exp}(C_{Home}(s), s) && \text{if home market method}\\
ADD &= P^{CV}_{Home}(C_{Home}(s), s) - P^{US}_{exp}(C_{Home}(s), s) && \text{if constructed value method}\\
ADD &= P^{3rd_mkt}_{exp}(C_{Home}(s), s) - P^{US}_{exp}(C_{Home}(s), s) && \text{if third country method}\\
ADD &= P^{CV}_{Home}(C_{surrogate}) - P^{US}_{exp}(C_{Home}(s), s) && \text{if NME method}
\end{aligned}$$

The domestic subsidy may take the form of direct cash support by the government or subsidized-loan terms. The subsidy can also affect the costs of production, say by offering the firm(s) lower electricity rates, lower input costs, etc. This latter type of subsidy is referred to as the provision of goods or services at less than adequate remuneration (LTAR) and was an important form of subsidization in several of the investigations that were the basis for this dispute.

Under the home-market method for determining normal value, an investigating authority would compare the home-market price (P_{Home}) with the export price (P_{exp}^{US}). The examples in the preceding subsection were based on this method. Economic theory implies that both prices depend on the costs and therefore both prices should experience some pass-through of the subsidy.

Under the United States's constructed-value approach, the normal-value home-market price (P_{Home}^{CV}) is calculated using a cost-plus approach. The USDOC first determines how much of each factor of production is needed to produce the good and then values each input using information on prices in the home market. For example, if a case involved a product from Japan, the United States would use Japanese home-market prices for labor, the raw materials needed to produce the product, electricity, etc., of the producer concerned when constructing the cost of the product. In addition, the USDOC will add a markup for selling, general, and administrative expenses and profits. However, the constructed-value method will not necessarily fully purge the subsidy distortion from either the normal value or the export prices, because home-market costs can be affected by the domestic subsidy, which in turn can affect both prices. Moreover, we expect asymmetric pass-through with the constructed-value approach. The reasoning is that the pass-through of the subsidy to the normal value is via a fixed-coefficient function that imposes a specific relationship between the subsidized inputs and the price. The pass-through to the normal value will not depend on other factors that economic theory tells us affects pass-through (e.g., the elasticity of demand). By contrast, pass-through of the subsidy to the export price will depend on pass-through elasticity, which depends on many factors such as market structure, the firm's share in the export market, technology, etc. We would not expect two such very different approaches to produce the same pass-through elasticity.

Under the third-country method, the export price of the like product to an appropriate third country is used for the normal value. As with the home-market method, standard microeconomic theory predicts that both prices – the export price to the third country ($P_{exp}^{3rd\_mkt}$) and to the complaining market (P_{exp}^{US}) – will be affected by pass-through of the domestic subsidy via distorted input costs and/or direct subsidization.

The nonmarket-economy method is the final approach. The ADA gives importing countries significant discretion in the calculation of normal value of products exported from NMEs. As with the constructed-value method, the USDOC gathers information on the company's 'factors of production' – the physical quantities of all the inputs used in producing the merchandise. However, in the NME method, the USDOC values those inputs on the basis of prices in a *surrogate* country. The normal value ($P_{Home}^{CV,\ surrogate}$) is therefore a cost-based normal value derived from company-specific factors of production combined with *surrogate-country prices* of those factors. At least in the United States, surrogate countries are market economies judged to be at a level of economic development similar to that of the NME country in question.[66] The USDOC only chooses surrogate costs that are deemed to be fairly traded. Thus, under the United States's NME procedures, a nonmarket economy's domestic subsidization program should have no effect on the constructed normal value. However, we acknowledge that subtle nuances in the precise constructed costs and specific input-pricing data might mean the NME constructed value is not fully neutered of the domestic subsidies. Even so, there can be no doubt that the US approach results in a considerably muted (if any) impact of the subsidies on the normal value. By contrast, NME's domestic-subsidization programs will have a more direct effect on the export price (P^{US}_{exp}) via distorted input costs and direct subsidization.

4.2.3 *Pass-through and normal value*

The double-remedies problem hinges on whether the impact of a domestic subsidy (which is being offset by a CVD) is also partially or fully captured by the ADD. For the home-market and third-country methods, if the subsidized firm passes through the subsidy symmetrically to all measured prices, then double counting will *not* occur, and the imposition of concurrent AD and CVD duties will not offset the subsidization twice. For these methods, double remedies do not depend on full pass-through but symmetric pass-through.

This, however, is not the case for AD margins using the NME method. The USDOC's NME approach means the main avenue, and in all likelihood the only avenue,[67] for the subsidy to influence the dumping margin is the export price. Therefore, double remedies are inevitable to some extent unless a given export subsidy has had zero impact on the export price – any difference between the NME normal value and the export price is already corrected by the ADD, at least to the extent that there has been pass-through to the export price. The objective of the United States's surrogate-country methodology is to calculate the price of the product, as if it would have been produced and/or sold unsubsidized by a producer in a market economy, i.e. under normal market conditions without government interference, the resulting normal value would normally be an unsubsidized price. The process of constructing the normal value for an NME should therefore purge all subsidies. Given that the subsidy has already been taken into account when calculating the dumping margin, a concurrent CVD will generate double remedies. USDOC NME procedures therefore virtually guarantee that double remedies will occur.

Article VI:5 GATT disallows simultaneous use of AD and CVD for export subsidies based on a presumption that the export subsidy will only affect the export price – when in fact within the firm money is fungible and hence it is possible

66 Other WTO members, such as the EU, do not require the surrogate country to be at a level of economic development similar to the NME under investigation.

67 But see the caveats in Section 4.2.5, infra.

an export subsidy could affect the home-market price too. We believe the economic basis for Article VI:5 GATT applies equally to the US NME methodology because domestic subsidies are essentially purged from the first term of the AD duty, $P^{CV}_{Home}(C_{surrogate})$, and are allowed to fully pass through to the second term, $P^{US}_{exp}(C_{Home}(s), s)$

$$ADD = P^{CV}_{Home}(C_{surrogate}) - P^{US}_{exp}(C_{Home}(s), s).$$

The implicit assumption of Article VI:5 GATT is the attenuated ability of an export subsidy to pass through to the normal value. Likewise, by selecting a 'market economy' surrogate country, the logic of the US NME methodology is designed to result in little or no ability for domestic subsidies in the NME to pass through to the normal value. Moreover, the United States's countervailing-duty statute required the CVD duty to be equal to the full value of the calculated benefit (i.e. prohibited any adjustment in light of pass-through or other considerations).[68]

Therefore, the economic logic behind Article VI:5 GATT and the economic implications of US NME methods are the same. Given the particulars of US procedure, we believe Article VI:5 GATT could have been the basis for a strong definitive finding that the US practice was inconsistent. The AB instead opted for a more cautious approach. The AB concluded that 'double remedies were "likely" to occur in cases where NME methodology is used to calculate the margin of dumping' and permitted the United States to pursue implementation by focusing on *how much* double counting occurs.[69] The AB seemed to understand that if an investigating authority were to make adjustments to account for such double counting, then the two remedies could be used simultaneously. Depending on the specific procedures, such adjustments may resolve the double-remedies issue.

Nevertheless, by focusing on measurement the AB may have inadvertently opened the door to additional double-remedy challenges. What if affected countries can measure and document the extent of double remedies under other methods for calculating normal value? It seems improbable that the WTO would allow double remedies under some methods for calculating normal value but not under the NME method.

4.2.4 *Examples of double remedy*

The AB's Report does not clearly address (i) the pass-through implications of Article VI:5 GATT and (ii) the applicability of that logic for the current dispute, especially given the specifics of US AD and CVD rules. The AB's determination has resulted in the dispute being viewed as a measurement issue. Even the United States

68 The US Congress recently changed the statute to allow USDOC to make adjustments.

69 AB Report, *US–AD and CVD (China)*, para. 541.

acknowledges that measurement is extremely messy and complicated.[70] Going forward, it will be very difficult for future Panels to ascertain whether the measurement was in fact done correctly.

We now present two examples of the implementation approach proposed by the AB. In the first example, the subsidies are of the form of lower (LTAR) input costs. In the second example, we consider the situation where market-benchmark prices (used in the CVD calculations) differ from the surrogate-country prices (used in the AD calculations).

Example 1 – subsidized inputs. We begin with a simple example where the subsidies only affect the 'materials, labor, and electricity' costs of the firm (see Table 1).

AD duty calculation. To keep the example as simple as possible, we assume other factors in the USDOC's factors-of-production analysis (overhead, SG&A, and profit) are not affected by the subsidies. In this example, we assume that (i) the material inputs are subsidized by US$150 less than their surrogate cost (US$300 versus US$450), (ii) labor costs are subsidized by US$5 (US$40 versus US$45), and (iii) electricity costs are subsidized by US$5 (US$20 versus US$25). As a result, the cost of the firms' 'material, labor, and electricity' (or MLE) is US$160 less than their comparable surrogate values (US$360 versus US$520).

We assume the Chinese firm's home-market price is US$535 and the export price is US$500.[71] If China were considered a market economy and the home-market method were used to compute normal value, then the dumping amount would be US$35 (US$535 less US$500), implying an AD margin of 7%.[72]

Under US NME rules, however, the home-market prices for materials, labor, and electricity would be replaced by those in the surrogate country. For instance, the USDOC might use Thai costs. In our example, we have an NME normal value of US$695, which implies a dumping amount of US$195 (or 39%). Of the dumping amount obtained using NME methods, 32% is due to using the NME methodology (39% less 7%).

CVD duty calculation. Under US CVD rules, the subsidy benefit is based on a USDOC 'market benchmark' valuation. As we have discussed at length elsewhere

70 The USDOC's response to the Section 129 proceeding highlights the complications in attempting to measure the extent of double remedy. See USDOC memo 'Section 129 Proceeding Pursuant to the WTO Appellate Body's Findings in WTO DS379 Regarding the Antidumping Duty Investigation of Circular Welded Carbon Quality Steel Pipe (CWP) from the People's Republic of China: Preliminary Determination of Adjustments to the Antidumping Duty Cash Deposit Rates', 31 May 2012.

71 For simplicity, in these examples we assume the firm's home-market price is equivalent to a price obtained using the constructed-value method. This is not necessarily the case, and we do so only to be explicit how the dumping amount and countervailing duty would be calculated.

72 The United States does not have a lesser-duty rule so the dumping amount would be the dumping duty.

Table 1. Double remedy–subsidized inputs

	NME AD calculation		CVD calculation
	Actual costs (China)	Surrogate costs	Market benchmark
Raw material (M)	$300	$450	$450
Labor (L)	$40	$45	$45
Electricity (E)	$20	$25	$25
-->MLE	$360	$520	$520
Overhead (O)	$100	$100	$100
SG&A (S)	$40	$40	$40
Profit (R)	$35	$35	$35
Normal value (MLE+O+S+R)	$535	$695	
Mkt benchmark price			$695
US export price	$500		
Dumping amount ($)	$35	$195	
Dumping amount (%)	7%	39%	
Dumping amount attributable to NME	32%		
Destination price with NME dumping amount	$695		
Benefit from subsidies			$160
CVD (%)			32%
Dumping amount (%) + CVD duties	71%		
Destination price with simultaneous AD & CVD	$855		

in this paper, the choice of the market benchmark is a matter of considerable importance in CVD cases. The USDOC attempts to ascertain what the market prices were at the time the Chinese firms purchased the inputs. Given that it was investigating both AD and CVD allegations, it would seem sensible (and simplest) if the USDOC just used the prices in the surrogate country (which were determined during the AD part of the investigation). However, that is not what the USDOC does. Instead, it creates what it believes is a representative market price. This market-benchmark price could be the average of prices in 'comparable' countries, be based on another country's price, or be based on reliable and verifiable market information. In some cases, the market-benchmark price is the same as the surrogate-country price. Often it is not.

To keep this first example as simple as possible, we assume that the market benchmark is the same as the surrogate cost. This means that the USDOC would determine that the subsidy benefit is US$160 (US$695 less US$535), implying a CVD of 32%. This is precisely the dumping amount that is due to NME methods. In other words, in this example the CVD is exactly equal to the dumping amount attributable to NME methodology. The full amount of the CVD is a double remedy.

Table 2. Double remedy–subsidized inputs and market-benchmark complications

	NME AD calculation		CVD calculation
	Actual costs (China)	Surrogate costs	Market benchmark
Raw material (M)	$300	$450	$495
Labor (L)	$40	$45	$50
Electricity (E)	$20	$25	$30
--> MLE	$360	$520	$575
Overhead (O)	$100	$100	$100
SG&A (S)	$40	$40	$40
Profit (R)	$35	$35	$35
Normal value (MLE+O+S+R)	$535	$695	
Mkt benchmark price			$750
US export price	$500		
Dumping amount ($)	$35	$195	
Dumping amount (%)	7%	39%	
Dumping amount attributable to NME	32%		
Destination price with NME dumping amount	$695		
Benefit from subsidies			$215
CVD (%)			43%
CVD attributable to mkt/surrogate difference			11%
Dumping amount (%) + CVD duties	82%		
Destination price with simultaneous AD & CVD	$910		

If there is any doubt that double remedies have a large effect, the normal-value calculation is US$695. This, in fact, would be the destination price with the NME AD duty levied. However, if the unadjusted CVD is also levied, the destination price is US$855.

Example 2 – Subsidized inputs combined with mismatch of market benchmarks and surrogate-country valuations. We again assume that the subsidy only affects material, labor, and electricity costs (see Table 2). The additional complication in this example is due to the difference between the market-benchmark and surrogate-country valuations.

AD duty calculation. The AD duty calculation, in this second example, is the same as in the previous example. Due to the subsidy, the firms' MLE is US$160 less than the surrogate values (US$360 versus US$520).

We again assume the Chinese firm's home-market price is US$535 and the export price is US$500. If China were considered a market economy and the home-market method were used to compute normal value, then the dumping amount would be US$35 (US$535 less US$500), implying an AD margin of 7%.

As in the previous example under US NME rules, the home-market prices for materials, labor, and electricity would be replaced by those in the surrogate country. In our example, we have an NME normal value of US$695, which implies a dumping amount of US$195 (or 39%). Once again, of the dumping amount obtained using NME methods 32% is due to using the NME methodology (39% less 7%).

CVD duty calculation. We now consider a complication stemming from the United States's use of 'market benchmarks' in its CVD analysis. We now allow the market-benchmark valuation to deviate from the surrogate-country values. Given that the USDOC basis for determining the 'market benchmark' is entirely different from the basis for picking a surrogate country, this mismatch often occurs. For example, while the surrogate country might value the raw materials at US$520 (used for the AD calculation), the market benchmark might value those same raw materials at US$575 (used for the CVD calculation).

In this example, the subsidies are determined to have produced a benefit of US$215 (as compared to US$160 in the first example). As a result, the CVD margin is larger (43%) than the dumping amount. Despite this mismatch, double remedies occur. The CVD margin can be decomposed into the part that is due to the use of NME methods when computing the dumping amount (32%) and the part that is due to the mismatch between the surrogate-country and benchmark valuation (11%).

In this example, the AD remedy alone is sufficient to make the destination price equal to the normal value (US$695). When the unadjusted CVD is also levied, the destination price rises to US$910.

4.2.5 Caveats

The intention of the US NME method and US CVD is the same – to purge the effects of government involvement on prices. We believe the AB could have used Article 19.3 of the SCM Agreement to definitively find the US practice inconsistent. Given the United States's NME methodology, we believe that some form of double remedies are automatic. The real issue is not *if* double remedies will occur under the NME method but rather *how much* occurs.

There are three possible qualifications to this conclusion. First, one might be concerned that surrogate-country producers are also benefiting from subsidies. While this might be a valid concern for NME methods used by other WTO members, we do not believe it is relevant for the United States. According to USDOC procedures, the surrogate country(ies) is (are) chosen because (i) they are comparable with the NME and (ii) because they are unsubsidized. Under USDOC procedures, a country with subsidization in the relevant input market would not be selected as a surrogate country.

Second, one might be concerned that the Chinese producers have such a dominant role on the world market of the product concerned that their (subsidized) prices have depressed prices on the world market or, at least, in the surrogate country. Again, we believe this concern is generally not applicable to the US situation given USDOC procedures which construct normal value using surrogate costs. We stress, however, that this conclusion hinges on the fact that the United States uses the factors-of-production methodology. While the NME's subsidy does not affect surrogate-country values because of the United States's factors-of-production approach, it *could* affect NME surrogate-country normal values used by other WTO members. For example, the EU will choose a surrogate country and then normally use the prices in that country. In such cases, the concern about the possibility of China's subsidized prices depressing prices in the surrogate country might be legitimate.

Third, there is a concern that the profit margin used by the USDOC might be affected by the subsidy. That is, the subsidies might allow the export prices charged by the Chinese firms to be lower than they would otherwise be, which in turn might lower the profit rate in the surrogate country. Thus, even though surrogate values are used, the ADD might not fully capture the effects of the subsidy. This is a valid concern; however, it was not part of the United States's argument to the AB.

4.2.6 Concluding thoughts on double remedies

Based on the foregoing analysis, we agree with the AB's conclusion that Article 19.3 of the SCM Agreement prohibits the imposition of concurrent AD and CVD duties which offset the same subsidization twice. However, we feel the AB could have relied on this Article to find the United States's simultaneous use of AD and CVD remedies (when the United States's NME methodology is used) illegal *tout court*. Instead, the AB opted for a broader determination and concluded that double remedies are 'likely' to occur and refrained from putting 'likely' into context. This leaves open the possibility for the United States to establish that, in other NME cases, concurrent duties in fact will not offset the same subsidization twice.

We believe the AB's approach will likely open the door to additional double-remedies disputes in future years. The AB failed to adequately characterize when or if double remedies would occur, and the AB's measurement concerns are in fact not limited to the NME method. The AB focused on the issue 'whether and to what extent domestic subsidies have lowered the export price of a product and… whether the investigating authority has taken the necessary corrective steps to adjust its methodology to take account of this factual situation'.[73] It seems to us that this focus is misplaced because the same question could then be raised with regard to Article VI:5, thereby creating a significant loophole in the applicability of that provision. Similarly, the question now exists why investigating authorities are

73 AB Report, *US–AD and CVD (China)*, para. 599.

not measuring double remedies when other methods are used to compute normal value. Where domestic prices are not used as the benchmark for calculating normal value and the impact of the subsidies is therefore effectively ignored, in principle there will be double remedies unless the investigating authority can show that the alternative normal value (whether surrogate country or constructed value-based) is also subsidized or influenced by subsidization.

As an aside, it is noted that the AB did not address the issue whether double remedies must be taken into account when calculating the dumping/subsidies *margin*, and indeed Article 19.3 SCM Agreement would not provide a legal basis for that as it deals with the levy of countervailing duties. As *US–AD and CVD (China)* targeted US cases and the United States does not use the lesser-duty rule, ADDs are based on the dumping margins and therefore the margins found and duties are the same. The distinction is therefore irrelevant. However, the difference may be material in cases involving countries that do use a lesser-duty rule, such as the EU.[74] This is all the more so where the target of the investigations is China, and ADDs then often are based on the (lower) injury margins. The EU practice is to deduct the CVD from the ADD and, in cases where the duties are based on the injury margin,[75] to deduct the CVD from the injury margin that forms the basis for the imposition of the ADD. Therefore, at the stage of the duty collection, there are no double remedies. On the other hand, the EU does not make any adjustment at the stage of calculating the dumping and subsidy margins. This means that at least one inflated margin will be presented to the public, thereby feeding the perception in some quarters that Chinese producers benefit from high subsidies allowing them to dump their products in other markets.

4.3 The 'public body' determination

Contrary to dumping, which is a practice of private parties, subsidization always involves not only the private sector, which will benefit from the subsidization, but also the government, which makes a financial contribution to confer that benefit. Indeed, this is clear from the very start of the SCM Agreement, which provides in Article 1.1(a)(1) that a subsidy shall be deemed to exist if 'there is a financial contribution by a government or any public body within the territory of a member (referred to in this Agreement as "government")'. The dispute on this point involved the question whether the USDOC had appropriately determined that Chinese SOEs and SOCBs constituted public bodies within the meaning of this Article. Because of the pervasiveness of SOEs and SOCBs in the Chinese economic

74 See, for more detail, Edwin Vermulst and Brian Gatta (2012), 'Concurrent Trade Defense Investigations in the EU, the EU's New Anti-Subsidy Practice against China, and the Future of Both', **11**:3 *World Trade Review*, 527–553.

75 See for EU practice on calculating injury margins, Edwin Vermulst (2010), *EU Anti-Dumping Law and Practice*, 2nd edition, London, UK: Sweet & Maxwell, pp. 461–486.

system, this finding is of significant importance not only as a matter of substance but also on purely procedural grounds, as it allows investigating authorities to solicit information on a wide range of Chinese entities in a CVD investigation, thereby significantly increasing the workload for the respondents, i.e. not only the producers under investigation but also the Chinese government itself, as well as the likelihood of findings based on facts available, particularly in cases where investigating authorities treat noncooperation by SOCBs and SOEs, which are legally independent from the government, as 'non-cooperation' on the part of the government. Not surprisingly, therefore, China challenged the approach of the USDOC, which had tended to focus principally on majority ownership by the government of the entities involved and which was essentially condoned by the Panel, which had defined a public body as any entity controlled by the government.

The AB considered this approach too simplistic and held that a public body within the meaning of the SCM Agreement must be an entity that possesses, exercises, or is vested with governmental authority. Whether the government 'controlled' an entity might be a relevant consideration, but it could not be a dispositive one. In completing the analysis, the AB then considered that the USDOC had improperly determined that the SOE input suppliers (producers of steel, rubber, and petrochemical inputs) constituted public bodies, but upheld the USDOC's findings with respect to the SOCBs on the ground that such findings were based on evidence not only of government control, but also of the SOCBs having effectively exercised certain governmental functions.

Thus, as reported by the AB, the USDOC had considered the following elements with regard to the SOCBs:

> (i) 'near complete state-ownership of the banking sector in China'; (ii) Article 34 of the Commercial Banking Law, which states that banks are required to 'carry out their loan business upon the needs of [the] national economy and the social development and under the guidance of State industrial policies'; (iii) record evidence indicating that SOCBs still lack adequate risk management and analytical skills; and (iv) the fact that 'during [that] investigation the [USDOC] did not receive the evidence necessary to document in a comprehensive manner the process by which loans were requested, granted and evaluated to the paper industry'.[76]

As regards the SOE input suppliers, it must be highlighted that the AB ruled against the United States essentially on evidentiary grounds. Therefore, the ruling does not preclude the United States from qualifying SOEs as public bodies in the future; it merely requires the United States to shift the focus of its analysis to whether the SOEs possess, exercise, or are vested with governmental authority. The United States in fact might comply with this by examining the five factors that it

76 AB Report, *US–AD and CVD (China)*, para. 349, citing the *CFS Paper Decisions Memo*, pp. 58–60.

normally analyses in order to determine whether an entity qualifies as a public body[77] and which are:

(i) government ownership;
(ii) government presence on the board of directors;
(iii) government control over activities;
(iv) pursuit of governmental policies or interests; and
(v) whether the entity was created by statute.[78]

Ahn has rightly drawn attention to the AB explaining that 'whether the functions or conduct are of a kind that are ordinarily classified as governmental in the legal order of the relevant member may be a relevant consideration for determining whether or not a specific entity is a public body'.[79] He considers that this may complicate a finding of 'public body' 'since the governmental roles "in the legal order" of China tend to be more intrusive'.[80]

4.4 *De jure specificity in lending and regional specificity in land-use rights*

In order for subsidies to be countervailable, they must be specific. Article 2 SCM Agreement, titled 'specificity', contemplates two types of specificity: sectoral specificity in Article 2.1 and regional specificity in Article 2.2. Sectoral specificity, in turn, can be found to exist *de jure* (Article 2.1(a) and (b))[81] or *de facto* (Article 2.1(c)).

De jure specificity. The AB considered that *de jure* specificity within the meaning of Article 2.1(a) can be found only 'if the limitation on access to the subsidy to certain enterprises is express, unambiguous, or clear from the content of the relevant instrument, and not merely "implied" or "suggested"'.[82] On the other hand, the AB considered that the limitation on access could relate to the financial contribution, the benefit, or both.[83]

For purposes of implementation of the 11th Five-Year Plan, which ran from 2006 to 2010, the Chinese State Council distinguished between four categories of projects/industries, i.e. encouraged, restricted, eliminated, and permitted. The projects/industries falling within the first three categories were further described in the Guiding Catalogue of the Industrial Restructuring, while all other

77 As China had argued before the USDOC during the administrative proceedings.

78 AB Report, *US–AD and CVD (China)*, para. 343.

79 Dukgeun Ahn (2011), 'United States – Definitive Anti-Dumping and Countervailing Duties on Certain Products from China', 105:4 *American Journal of International Law*, available at SSRN: http://ssrn.com/abstract=1864025; SSRN version at 3.

80 Ibid., at 4.

81 AB Report, *US–AD and CVD (China)*, para. 369.

82 Ibid., para. 372.

83 Ibid., paras. 374–378.

projects/industries were considered to belong to the permitted category, provided that they were legal. The permitted category is therefore a residual category. China argued that SOCBs provided financing not only to the 539 projects/industries in the encouraged category but also to the vast permitted category. The AB rejected this argument on evidentiary grounds,[84] thereby perhaps leaving open the door for a future revisit of this issue.

China had also argued that the encouraged category was so wide as to preclude a finding of subsidization to 'certain enterprises', but the AB found that neither the USDOC nor the Panel had decided the specificity issue on this basis alone, but rather on the basis of the totality of the evidence available at the central, the provincial, and the municipal levels.[85]

It seems relatively clear from the cases that the off-the-road tire industry at issue was targeted by various governmental levels, but – abstracting from the case – we wonder whether the approach taken by the United States and condoned by the Panel and the AB does not run the risk of becoming a self-fulfilling prophecy. Assume, for the sake of argument, that legal instruments cover a sector of the country's economy that as a whole is not specific. In the course of a CVD investigation, the investigating authorities then find that the product under investigation is included in this sector and that a producer of the product concerned is considered eligible for and in fact receives subsidies. It seems to us that this does not necessarily indicate specificity, and thus whether or not there is documentary evidence at various governmental levels (central, provincial, and municipal) that identify the product and/or the producer as being eligible for support appears irrelevant. This is because it seems perfectly possible that producers of other covered products may be eligible for similar support. Thus, the focus of the query should then be whether the producers under investigation receive more subsidies than other sectors covered by the instruments.

Regional specificity. We recall that the Panel had ruled that the USDOC had violated Article 2.2 of the SCM Agreement by determining in the LWS investigation that the government provision of land-use rights was regionally specific. More specifically, the Panel found that the USDOC had failed to assess whether the provision of land-use rights by the granting authority Huantai County in the New Century Industrial Park constituted a 'distinct regime' – for instance, by virtue of price differences – compared with the land-use rights outside the Industrial Park in the same County.

On appeal by China, the AB repeated that a limitation on access to the financial contribution was sufficient.[86]

84 There was no Panel finding on loans to the permitted category. Ibid., para. 385.
85 Ibid., paras. 386–395.
86 Ibid., paras. 413–414.

China had also appealed certain statements by the Panel that, according to China, suggested that a subsidy would be regionally specific if it were provided as part of a 'distinct regime' even if the identical subsidy were also available elsewhere. The AB rejected this appeal basically on the grounds that China was reading too much into the statements of the Panel and that they were *obiter* in any event.[87] However, in rejecting the appeal, the AB has left open the question whether and, if so, under what circumstances the provision of land-use rights may constitute a countervailable subsidy. This is a missed opportunity because the issue will undoubtedly come up again as various countries continue to countervail land-use rights.

4.5 *Out-of-country benchmarking*

As we have seen, the USDOC had, in various cases, resorted to out-of-country benchmarking with regard to provision of inputs (hot-rolled steel) by SOEs, land-use rights, and loans provided by SOCBs (both RMB-denominated and USD-denominated). The legal basis for the first two was Article 14(d)[88] while the legal basis for the latter was Article 14(b)[89] SCM Agreement.[90] The fact that Article 14(d) allows for out-of-country benchmarking was already established in *US–Softwood Lumber IV*. However, the finding of the AB that Article 14(b) similarly allows resort to out-of-country benchmarking with regard to loans was a first.

In *US–Softwood Lumber IV*, the Appellate Body had emphasized that the circumstances under which investigating authorities may resort to out-of-country benchmarking are 'very limited'[91] and found that:

> an investigating authority may use a benchmark other than private prices of the goods in question in the country of provision, when it has been established that those private prices are distorted, because of the predominant role of the government in the market as a provider of the same or similar goods.[92]

87 Ibid., paras. 421–422.

88 Article 14(d) SCM Agreement provides that the provision of goods or services or purchase of goods by a government shall not be considered as conferring a benefit unless the provision is made for less than adequate remuneration, or the purchase is made for more than adequate remuneration. The adequacy of remuneration shall be determined in relation to prevailing market conditions for the good or service in question in the country of provision or purchase (including price, quality, availability, marketability, transportation, and other conditions of purchase or sale).

89 Article 14(b) SCM Agreement provides that a loan by a government shall not be considered as conferring a benefit, unless there is a difference between the amount that the firm receiving the loan pays on the government loan and the amount the firm would pay on a comparable commercial loan which the firm could actually obtain on the market. In this case, the benefit shall be the difference between these two amounts.

90 Interestingly, China had initially pursued claims under Paragraph 15 of its Accession Protocol before the Panel, but later decided not to pursue those, see AB Report, *US–AD and CVD (China)*, n.401.

91 Appellate Body Report, *US–Softwood Lumber IV*, para. 102.

92 Ibid., para. 103.

The AB clarified that in *US–Softwood Lumber IV* it had distinguished between the government being a *significant supplier* and the government being the *predominant supplier*, and that the key focus of the enquiry should be on the likelihood of the prices being distorted as a result. Clearly, where the government is the predominant supplier, the likelihood of resulting distortion is greater. Building on this, the AB considered that if the government is a significant supplier, this alone cannot justify a finding that prices are distorted, and therefore further evidence would be necessary. However, where the government is the predominant supplier, as was the case for hot-rolled steel, resulting distortion is *likely*, but even then a case-by-case analysis is still required, although it might be less rigorous than if the finding of distortion is based on the government merely being a significant supplier.[93]

This means that in the course of an investigation, other evidence must be considered by the investigating authorities – even where the government is the predominant supplier – although it may be (cursorily) rejected ultimately.[94]

As regards the possibility of out-of-country benchmarking under Article 14(b), the AB considered that:

> a benchmark loan under Article 14(b) must be a 'loan which the firm could actually obtain on the market'. The use of the conditional tense, 'could', suggests that a benchmark loan under Article 14(b) need not in every case be a loan that exists or that can *in fact* be obtained in the market. In this respect, we agree with the Panel that this refers 'first and foremost' to the borrower's risk profile, that is, whether the benchmark loan is one that could be obtained by the borrower receiving the investigated government loan. Thus, we consider that Article 14(b) does not preclude the possibility of using as benchmarks interest rates on commercial loans that are not actually available in the market where the firm is located, such as, for instance, loans in other markets or constructed proxies.[95]

The AB also agreed with the Panel that it would be possible to use loans denominated in other currencies, where the currency in which the loans is denominated is distorted.[96]

The AB further agreed with the Panel that there is a difference between the government as the setter and implementer of the general monetary policy of a country (e.g., by establishing discount rates)[97] and 'the government participating as a lender and/or otherwise intervening in the lending market as such, in a way and to an extent that effectively it is the government, and not the market, that establishes

93 AB Report, *US–AD and CVD (China)*, para. 441.
94 Ibid., para. 454.
95 Ibid., para. 480.
96 Ibid., paras. 484–487.
97 Interest rates charged by the Central bank on loans made to banks.

the lending rates'[98] and that, on the basis of the evidence before it, the USDOC could have decided not to use interest rates in China.

However, the AB then agreed with China that the Panel had violated Article 11 DSU by failing to critically and searchingly review whether the reasons advanced by the USDOC justified the proxy that it constructed, including in the light of other plausible alternatives (e.g., proxies based on countries selected according to national saving rates rather than GNI, or in the light of a benchmark based on interest rates from a third, surrogate country, as China had suggested during the administrative proceedings).[99] Thus, the AB did not necessarily find that the USDOC methodology was wrong, but rather that the Panel had not sufficiently analyzed whether other – better – methodologies could have been used.

5. Concluding comments

This dispute involves several important issues, and with respect to most of these matters we think the AB made sensible and well-grounded legal rulings. On the 'public body' question, the issue of the appropriate use of out-of-country benchmarks, and on the matter of *de jure* specificity of loans granted by SOCBs and regional specificity of land-use rights, we believe the AB legal arguments are well-reasoned and properly based on WTO provisions.

The 'public body' issue will almost surely be an important issue going forward. How much government ownership and how much government involvement/influence suffices for a SOE/SOCB to be treated as a public body? The answer to that question will affect Chinese CVD cases for perhaps the next couple of decades. Interestingly, one unanticipated consequence of this Report is what it might mean for countries other than China, particularly the United States and the EU Member States, in light of post-financial-crisis bank bailouts. The ramifications for EU and US banks, which are being supported by EU and US governments as a result of the financial crisis, will become clearer in a few years.

The appropriateness of out-of-country benchmarks will also have significant long-run consequences for WTO members. China will be subject to market-economy AD rules within four years. At that point, the double-remedies issue may well diminish in importance, but the out-of-country benchmarks likely will not. What country is comparable with China? There are few countries that can match China's huge economies of scale. India could be a possibility, but supposedly it would depend on the product under consideration.

A thematic undercurrent of the dispute was the need for WTO Members to base determinations on actual data and analysis. For example, when the United States was able to document that it based its market benchmarks on respected third-party

98 AB Report, *US–AD and CVD (China)*, para. 494.
99 Ibid., para. 523.

data and formal technical analysis, the AB deferred to the United States's judgment even though it acknowledged that a different and perhaps equally acceptable analysis may have given a different result. On the other hand, when the United States was unable to provide any evidence for its judgments (e.g., simply asserting that state ownership means public body and not even contemplating measuring double remedies), the AB rejected the approach. Ironically, one of the shortcomings the AB suffered from in this case was the same lack of effort by the Panel. In many ways, the lackluster effort of the Panel made the AB's job in this case considerably harder. For instance, had the Panel asked the United States to produce evidence that double remedies did not occur, the AB might have had a chance to craft its determination with specific reference to the actual methods in this dispute. Without such information, the AB instead resorted to justifying its condemnation of double remedies with an overly vague discussion of pass-through.

The most widely discussed part of the AB's decision involves the most widely discussed aspect of the dispute – double remedies. At one level, focusing on measurement seems like a reasonable compromise. It suggests that the AB was unhappy with the United States's overly simplistic approach and also that it was cautiously deferring to the possibility of a need for both remedies (maybe because the measurement exercise is so complex). In this regard, we believe the AB was particularly sensitive to other Member countries' AD/CVD procedures and the possibility that double remedies would not occur under different rules. We believe, however, that the AB would have been much more on point if it had clearly explained why there might still be a need for CVD when the United States's NME method fully purges the constructed normal value of all domestic distortions, including domestic subsidies, at least under the United States's factors-of-production test. The most obvious approach would have been to base its judgment on the lack of pass-through to the NME normal value.

Further, the AB may have inadvertently set the stage for a slew of new double-remedies claims. What if affected countries can measure and document the extent of double remedies under other methods for calculating normal value? It seems improbable that the WTO would allow double remedies under some methods for calculating normal value but not under the NME method. This dispute establishes that the burden is on the investigating authorities to ensure that double remedies are not being imposed regardless of the method for calculating normal value. However, as far as we are aware, neither the United States nor any other WTO member has ever measured and offset double remedies in any simultaneous AD and CVD proceeding. A reasonable interpretation of this Report is that there is a need to do so.

Finally, it should be noted that in addition to the WTO dispute, the USDOC's decision on double remedies was also brought by one of the parties to one of the four underlying disputes before the US Court of International Trade, which ruled against the USDOC on the double-remedies issue and ordered it to either somehow account for the possibility of double remedies, or else abandon the practice of the concurrent imposition of duties against China altogether.[100] On appeal, the US Court of Appeals for the Federal Circuit went a step further and declared the practice of applying the CVD law to NMEs to be impermissible altogether, with or without a potential double-counting issue, on a point of US law unrelated to any of the provisions of the WTO agreements.[101]

As a result of this Federal Court decision, on 13 March 2012 the United States amended its countervailing-duty statute to allow CVD law to be applied against imports from NMEs.[102] The new law applies retroactively covering all proceedings since November 2006.[103] This amendment also purportedly resolves the double-remedies problem, allowing USDOC to reduce the ADD to the extent the CVD has inflated the dumping margin. However, the double-remedies offset only applies to investigations and administrative reviews initiated on or after the date of enactment of the statute, and to any redeterminations that the USDOC is required to make pursuant to WTO dispute-settlement decisions. This limited fix raises the very real specter of a series of similar double-remedies disputes somewhat akin to the burdensome zeroing cases that finally seem to be coming to a conclusion, a development unlikely to be good for the political support for the WTO DSU.

100 See *GPX Int'l Tire Corp.* v. *United States*, 645 F. Supp. 2d 1231 (Court of International Trade 2009) and *GPX Int'l Tire Corp.* v. *United States*, 715 F. Supp. 2d 1337 (Court of International Trade 2010).

101 See *GPX International Tire Corp. et al.* v. *United States*, 666 F.3d 732 (Fed. Cir. 2011), reh'g granted, 678 F.3d 1308 (Fed. Cir. 2012).

102 H.R. 4105, 112th Congress, 2nd Session, Pub. L. No. 112–99, 126 Stat. 265 (2012).

103 GPX Int'l appealed the constitutionality of the new legislation. The issue of constitutionality first arose in the immediate aftermath of the legislation, when the Court of Appeals asked the parties for briefs on the implications of the new legislation for the pending case. GPX raised the constitutional issues. The Court of Appeals decided to send the case back to the Court of International Trade to hear the constitutional issues in the first instance. GPX's brief raised three constitutional issues concerning the retroactivity provisions of the new law: (1) that they impermissibly impose punishment in violation of the Ex Post Facto Clause; (2) that they fail the requirements for a retroactive tax to be consistent with the Due Process Clause; and (3) that they apply only to certain importers, in violation of the Equal Protection Clause. As of this writing, the Court has not yet ruled on these constitutional-law arguments.

Treaty Interpretation or Activism? Comment on the AB Report on *United States – ADs and CVDs on Certain Products from China*

JOOST PAUWELYN
Graduate Institute, Geneva

This comment is limited to the 'public body' issue and the question of so-called 'double remedies'. It ends with a few tentative explanations as to why the Appellate Body in this dispute opted for a rather restrictive interpretation or, depending on one's viewpoint, activist approach as compared to the Panel in the same case.

1. Public body

On 'public body', Prusa and Vermulst write that the Appellate Body's (AB) 'conclusions and analysis were correct' (see abstract), unfortunately, without further explanation. Unless tweaked in future refinements, the AB's test of 'governmental authority/function' is highly questionable as a matter of law, and unlikely to work as a matter of practice.

The applicable SCM provision refers to 'a financial contribution by a government or any public body within the territory of a Member' (underlining added). By defining 'public body' as limited to entities that are exercising 'governmental authority', the AB has essentially read out of the SCM Agreement the words 'or any public body'. If the drafters only wanted to cover what is usually understood as 'government', they would not have added these words. When the AB refers to the Articles on State Responsibility of the International Law Commission (ILC) on the subject of when (wrongful) conduct can be 'attributed' to a 'state', the ILC defines what is meant by 'government' or 'state'. Yet, the SCM Agreement went beyond this and expanded coverage to include not only 'government' but also 'any public body'. The ILC Articles say nothing on the meaning of 'public bodies', a term that does not even appear in those Articles. The AB relies ultimately on ILC Article 5. Yet, the reasoning is circular: The only thing that Article 5 says is that 'conduct of a person or entity... which is empowered by the law of that State to exercise elements of the governmental authority' shall be considered 'an act of the State'. So all that Article 5 says is the obvious and was not contested, namely that entities 'exercising elements of governmental authority' are, indeed, part of the 'government'. It says nothing on what a 'public body' is, let alone does it limit the definition of 'public body' to the entities covered under Article 5. Again, Article 5 and the entire ILC Articles do not even mention the words 'public body'.

A better approach would have been (i) to consider the SCM Agreement as *lex specialis* (after all, SCM Article 1 sets out primary rules on what is a subsidy – ILC Articles 4–8 elaborate on secondary rules in respect of attribution of wrongful conduct); (ii) to examine the ordinary/dictionary meaning of 'public body' which, the AB conceded, includes bodies *controlled by the state*; and (iii) to then assess whether anything in the surrounding context of the SCM Agreement should lead the AB to *exclude* from this 'ordinary meaning' entities controlled by the government. No such excluding language exists: not in the SCM Agreement or anywhere else in the WTO treaty or in the ILC Articles. If anything, when it comes to China, China's Working Party Report confirmed that state-owned enterprises are 'government actors' for purposes of SCM Article 1.1(a).[1]

Instead, we are now left with what could turn out to be a very unclear and subjective test of 'governmental authority/function': When does an entity have governmental authority? What is a governmental function? How can any of this be proven? Will governments not find ways to hide delegation of power or instructions, especially if they control the board of a company anyhow? An informal phone call or discussion should suffice, without leaving any trace, so how is a competitor supposed to find evidence of this – as the Panel in this dispute put it, this would amount to finding 'evidence that the government directed itself'.

The test of 'control' by the government (e.g. through ownership or the right to appoint directors), that is, the test upheld by the Panel in this dispute (and previous Panels before it) is a more objective test and more workable, even though it does remain a proxy. After all, at this stage ('financial contribution by a government or any public body'), the question is only about *who* gives the financial contribution, what is the *nature* of the body or entity providing the loan or goods, not *why* the loan or goods are provided (e.g. for this or that governmental or other purpose).

1 Paragraph 172 of China's Working Party Report, confirmed as a binding part of China's accession through China's Accession Protocol, provides: 'Some members of the Working Party, in view of the special characteristics of China's economy, sought to clarify that when state-owned enterprises (including banks) provided financial contributions, they were doing so as government actors within the scope of Article 1.1(a) of the SCM Agreement. The representative of China noted, however, that such financial contributions would not necessarily give rise to a benefit... The Working Party took note of this commitment' (underlining added).

The question of *what* is done or *why*, comes up only later, under 'benefit'. For example, a loan is provided by the government or a public body, which in itself is not a problem or wrongful. It becomes a problem or 'subsidy' only if the loan is provided below market terms, that is, so as to 'benefit' the one receiving the loan and is specific. This noncommercial nature of the loan is then seen as a proxy for the loan being awarded for noncommercial purposes, if you wish, in pursuit of one or the other 'governmental function'. As Cartland *et al.* put it: 'the question of whether a particular entity can be considered a public body . . . has simply to do with whether the entity can be used as a conduit for providing a subsidy . . . being vested with or exercising [governmental] authority is unnecessary for an entity to be a conduit for subsidies.[2]

The best way out of this conundrum may already be indicated by the AB itself, when it found that proof of 'meaningful control' by the government can be sufficient evidence of exercise of governmental authority.[3] Ultimately, the AB already found that Chinese state-owned commercial banks are 'public bodies', even under its newly announced test of 'governmental authority/function', and this on relatively little, additional evidence of these banks operating under the influence of, and in pursuit of, governmental objectives. If further tweaked in this direction, the test may be clarified and become more workable, by essentially moving back to evidence of 'meaningful control' by the government (not just majority ownership) which can then work as a proxy of governmental authority/function (unless rebutted by the government in question who will, in most cases, be the only party in possession of the relevant evidence anyhow).

2. Double remedies

In respect of 'double remedies', Prusa and Vermulst offer an insightful analysis of the economics of cumulative application of countervailing (CVD) and anti-dumping (AD) duties. They show that in many, if not most, scenarios (export subsidies, domestic subsidies in nonmarket economies as well as domestic subsidies in market economies) some overlap or 'double remedy' is possible, depending on a number of factors, in particular, the degree of pass-through of the subsidy on domestic prices, export prices, and/or surrogate values in a third country. Overlap is, in other words, a matter of degree and calculation. However, what they overlook is that the drafters of the WTO treaty were aware of this and to simplify matters set up a number of 'legal fictions'. In GATT Article VI:5, they did outlaw cumulative application of CVD and AD duties in respect of *export subsidies*, based on the

2 M. Cartland, G. Depayre, and J. Woznowski (2012), 'Is Something Going Wrong in the WTO Dispute Settlement?', 46:5 *Journal of World Trade*, 979, at 1000 and 1001.

3 AB Report, para. 318: 'evidence that a government exercises meaningful control over an entity and its conduct may serve, in certain circumstances, as evidence that the relevant entity possesses governmental authority and exercises such authority in the performance of governmental functions'.

simplifying assumptions or 'legal fiction' that an export subsidy will have no impact on domestic prices and fully pass through into lower export prices.[4] The drafters of GATT (in 1947) and later the SCM Agreement (in 1994) and, later still, China's Accession Protocol (in 2001) did *not* impose a similar prohibition in respect of other (domestic) subsidies. They could have done so, and based on GATT Article VI:5 knew how to do this, but did *not* do so. Instead, for domestic subsidies they 'assumed' something different and, to simplify complex economic effects, worked on the basis of another 'legal fiction', namely that domestic subsidies pass through to the same extent into both domestic and export prices so that a prohibition on cumulation is *not* warranted. For domestic subsidies in a nonmarket economy (NME), such as (in US eyes) China, where surrogate values in a third country may be used, this 'legal fiction' may be more tenuous than in a market-economy scenario (although, as Prusa and Vermulst admit, also surrogate values may be affected by subsidies). Yet the drafters maintained the fiction also for nonmarket economies. Indeed, in Rule 15 of China's Protocol of Accession they elaborated in quite some detail how AD and CVD can be imposed against Chinese imports without, at any stage, even hinting at the fact that, when it comes to China as an NME, a choice must be made between either AD or CVD.

Many of these 'legal fictions' may be inaccurate from an economic perspective as they may not capture the exact economic effects in all scenarios. Yet, for negotiators, lawyers, and investigators, these 'legal fictions' were considered necessary to simplify matters. That these 'fictions', and the legal rules that are built on them, make limited economic sense is no reason to change the rules or to make a finding of violation. Yet, that is exactly what Prusa and Vermulst call for. That 'the economic rationale for banning simultaneous AD and CVD for export subsidies applies equally well (or perhaps even better) to domestic subsidies when the NME method is used to compute normal value' may well be correct. Yet, this is no excuse for the AB, as an adjudicator (not a legislator), to change the explicit text of the one rule where cumulation is prohibited, that is, to amend GATT Art. VI:5 for it to outlaw not only cumulation in respect of export subsidies but also in respect of (some) domestic subsidies. Many WTO rules do not make full economic sense. Applying the same logic, GATT Art. XI:1, which only prohibits *quantitative* export restrictions (not export *taxes*), would then also need to be 'judicially revised' as, in economic terms, one can achieve the same effect with a (permitted) export tax as the effect stemming from a (prohibited) export quota. There as well, in Prusa and Vermulst's words, 'the *economic rationale* for banning [quantitative export restrictions] applies equally well to [export taxes]'.

4 GATT Article VI:5 reads as follows: 'No product of the territory of any contracting party imported into the territory of any other contracting party shall be subject to both anti-dumping and countervailing duties to compensate for the same situation of dumping or export subsidization.'

Prusa and Vermulst use the analogous economic rationale for export subsidies and the cumulation of CVD and AD duties in an NME scenario to conclude that, in the latter scenario as well, the AB should simply have prohibited any cumulation (as GATT Art. VI:5 does in respect of export subsidies) rather than calling upon US investigating authorities to measure the actual extent of overlap and to then limit CVD duties accordingly. Since 'measurement [of double remedies] is extremely messy and complicated', Prusa and Vermulst suggest to impose the same simplifying 'legal fiction' as the fiction imposed for export subsidies in GATT Art. VI:5 and to outrightly prohibit any cumulation of CVD and AD duties in an NME scenario. Measuring the exact degree of cumulation will, indeed, be messy. However, WTO drafters realized this and, as pointed out earlier, did opt for a number of simplifying 'legal fictions': for export subsidies they prohibited cumulation; for other subsidies they did not. Prusa and Vermulst may be correct that one better turns to a 'legal fiction' instead of opening Pandora's box of trying to measure the exact degree of pass-through and resulting overlap. However, the legal fiction they then turn to is not the one currently written in the WTO rule book, but the legal fiction they would opt for if they had to redraft the WTO treaty. This is not the role of an adjudicator, but the task normally bestowed on treaty negotiators.

Prusa and Vermulst do not even address the ultimate legal hook on which the AB hung its prohibition on double remedies in the NME scenario, namely SCM Article 19:3. It seems beyond doubt that the drafters of this provision did not even think of this scenario, let alone the prohibition that the AB read into Article 19:3.[5] Article 19:3, in relevant parts, simply reads that 'when a countervailing duty is imposed ... such countervailing duty shall be levied, in the appropriate amounts in each case, on a non-discriminatory basis on imports of such products from all sources found to be subsidized'. By its very terms, this provision addresses not the calculation of a subsidy or a CVD duty, nor the imposition of a CVD, but only the subsequent and technical step of actually 'levying' the CVD duty set in earlier steps. Moreover, it has nothing to do with adjusting the CVD duty in view of certain circumstances (e.g. cumulation with an AD duty) but only with ensuring that the correct or 'appropriate' CVD duty is imposed on the relevant product, on a 'non-discriminatory basis' (e.g. if one Chinese producer got subsidies of 10 per unit, and another subsidies of only 5, the CVD levied on imports of the first should, appropriately, be 10 and those of the second 5). Finally, Article 19:3 explicitly lists those scenarios where a CVD can no longer be imposed (renunciation of the subsidy or where an undertaking has been accepted), and this list does not include nor even remotely refer to the question of AD or cumulation.

5 Cartland *et al.*, supra note 2, at 995 ('The effect of the AB's analysis ... is to render the lesser-duty rule essentially mandatory in the context of simultaneous application of AD and CVD to non-market economies ... One does not to be a researcher in the history of the negotiations of Article 19 ... to know that such a linkage between the amount of a subsidy and injury has never been agreed.').

3. Treaty interpretation or activism?

In conclusion, both in respect of 'public body' and 'double remedies', the AB has opted for an approach that limits the scope for investigating authorities to impose countervailing duties: a financial contribution can only amount to a 'subsidy' when provided by an entity exercising governmental authority; the amount of a CVD, in the NME scenario where also AD duties are imposed, must be adjusted and limited to avoid 'double remedies'. It is notoriously difficult to decide whether this is an instance of AB activism (reading 'any public body' out of the SCM Agreement and reading a prohibition on cumulation into Art. 19:3 where the drafters provided none) or whether this is merely an instance where the AB interpreted the WTO treaty restrictively following the steps of treaty interpretation set out in the Vienna Convention on the Law of Treaties. This is a matter that, more often than not, lies in the eye of the beholder.

What can, in any event, be said is that compared to the Panel in this case (who interpreted public body as including entities controlled by the government, and did not see a prohibition on cumulative application of AD and CVD duties other than in the scenario of export subsidies), the AB has taken a considerably more restrictive approach. What could possibly explain this rather drastic move, and dramatic reversal of the Panel Report? Is this proof of the AB slowly removing itself from a predominantly textual approach to treaty interpretation? Did the AB decide these matters as questions of first impression, inspired by elements of common sense, general principles, or analogies more than the actual rules agreed upon? In the face of deadlock in the Doha Round of negotiations for more than ten years now, is the AB hereby more willing to update the rules itself to newly emerging circumstances, even though the original drafters most probably never thought of these new scenarios?

One puzzling element, in this respect, is the AB's almost complete neglect of China's Accession Protocol (in particular Rule 15 on AD and CVD) as well as China's Working Party Report (quoted earlier). These documents postdate the conclusion of the WTO treaty and provide a more updated expression of intent, one that is, in addition, focused on the peculiar situation of China. They could and did provide additional insights into what WTO negotiators had in mind. Yet, partly because of how the parties argued the case, the AB did not seek to benefit from them and instead opted for a more inward looking, judicial approach.

Writing in 2004, Richard Steinberg was not all that worried about the imbalance between the (automatic) judicial branch and the (consensus-blocked) legislative branch of the WTO, pointing out correctly that there are multiple, informal ways in which WTO members (as principals) can steer or influence Panels and the AB (as agents).[6] Yet, principal–agent literature teaches us that the existence of multiple

6 Richard H. Steinberg (2004), 'Judicial Lawmaking at the WTO: Discursive, Constitutional, and Political Constraints', 98:2 *American Journal of International Law*, 247–275.

principals affects overall discretion of the agents (or interpretation space in our case).[7] If divergence of interests among principals increases, new autonomy will open up for judicial agents or, as John Ferejohn put it, 'Courts and agencies are capable of independent or autonomous action where the constitutional legislature is too fragmented to react.'[8] This is a crucial insight which may explain the AB's restrictive interpretation or, if you wish, activism, in this and some other more recently decided disputes.[9] Whereas at the time of its creation in 1994, the WTO was controlled by a handful of countries (especially the EU and the US), in more recent years multiple powerful actors have emerged (including China, Brazil, India, and South Africa and, most recently, Russia). This interest divergence increases the AB's interpretation space, and, in turn, enables the AB to be more activist, knowing that its rulings may upset some powerful countries but please others. Steinberg pointed out, in 2004, that 'WTO dispute settlement could assume a new form as a result of fundamental changes in the political environment, such as the dispersion of power at the WTO or a divergence of interests of powerful states. If either shift were to occur, the strategic space for judicial lawmaking at the WTO would expand, as it would become more difficult to establish and sustain the political cooperation necessary to check or correct AB action.'[10] The 2011 AB Report on *US–China ADs and CVDs* may well be evidence of a move in exactly this direction.

7 Daniel L. Nielson, and Michael J. Tierney (2003), 'Delegation to International Organizations: Agency Theory and World Bank Environmental Reform', 57:2 *International Organization*, 241–276.

8 John Ferejohn (2002), 'Judicializing Politics, Politicizing Law', 65:3 *Law and Contemporary Problems*, 41–68 at p. 63.

9 See Manfred Elsig and Joost Pauwelyn (forthcoming 2013), 'The Politics of Treaty Interpretation: Variations and Explanations Across International Tribunals', in Jeffrey L. Dunoff and Mark A. Pollack (eds.), *Interdisciplinary Perspectives on International Law and International Relations: The State of the Art*, Cambridge: Cambridge University Press.

10 Richard H. Steinberg (2004), 'Judicial Lawmaking at the WTO: Discursive, Constitutional, and Political Constraints', 98:2 *American Journal of International Law*, 247–275, at p. 275.

One (Firm) Is Not Enough: A Legal–Economic Analysis of *EC–Fasteners*

CHAD P. BOWN

DECTI, The World Bank, Washington, DC, USA

PETROS C. MAVROIDIS

EUI, Firenze, Italy

Abstract: The WTO's Appellate Body (AB) dealt with a number of issues for the first time in this Report. Importantly, it discussed the consistency of the European Union (EU) regulation with the multilateral rules on the conditions for deviating from the obligation to calculate individual dumping margins. Although China formally won the argument, the AB may have opened the door to treat China as a nonmarket economy (NME) even beyond 2016 when China's NME status was thought to expire under the terms of China's 2001 WTO Accession Protocol. The AB further dealt with numerous other issues ranging from statistical sampling to the treatment of confidential information. In handling its investigation, the EU authorities made a number of questionable decisions regarding the collection of information, and this aspect of the process was central to China's legal challenges.

1. The legal facts

China complained against an imposition of antidumping (AD) duties by the European Union (EU)[1] concerning various classes of fasteners. China advanced a series of claims before the Panel and prevailed in the most significant ones, chief among them the claim that China's treatment as a nonmarket economy (NME) entailed specific consequences, and did not amount to a licence to impose AD duties on presumptions rather than on hard facts.

The Panel had found that the EU had violated its obligations under Articles 6.10 and 9.5 AD by imposing countrywide AD duties against Chinese exporters solely

Thanks to Jasper-Martijn Wauters and Mark Koulen for excellent comments during the conference organized at EUI on 4 June 2012, and to Aksel Erbahar for providing outstanding research assistance. Any opinions expressed in this paper are the authors' and should not be attributed to the World Bank. All remaining errors are our own.

1 Throughout this paper, we use the acronym EU to refer to the defendant. In fact, this acronym has already been substituted for the term EC (European Community) in the WTO glossary. The official name of the Report we discuss here is, of course, *EC–Fasteners* since the Panel had been established before the Treaty of Lisbon, which provoked the change from EC to EU, entered into force.

because China was considered to be an NME; in particular, the Panel found that specific provisions of the EU legislation[2] (the Market Economy Test, MET, and the Individual Treatment, IT) were in violation of the above-mentioned provisions. Importantly, the Panel found that the EU measure was at odds with the AD Agreement both 'as such' (that is, irrespective of its application in particular cases) and 'as applied' in the present dispute.

Here is how the EU system works: the EU will subject all imports from NMEs to countrywide dumping margins, except for the following instances (quoted from paras. 7.49–7.50 of the Panel Report):

> 7.49. Article 9(5) provides for an exception to the specification of a country-wide duty rate. It provides:
> 'Where Article 2(7)(a) applies, an individual duty shall, however, be specified for the exporters which can demonstrate, on the basis of properly substantiated claims that:
> '(a) in the case of wholly or partly foreign owned firms or joint ventures, exporters are free to repatriate capital and profits;
> (b) export prices and quantities, and conditions and terms of sale are freely determined;
> (c) the majority of the shares belong to private persons; state officials appearing on the board of directors or holding key management positions shall either be in minority or it must be demonstrated that the company is nonetheless sufficiently independent from State interference;
> (d) exchange rate conversions are carried out at the market rate; and
> (e) State interference is not such as to permit circumvention of measures if individual exporters are given different rates of duty.'
>
> These criteria are generally referred to as the 'individual treatment ('IT')' test. If a producer demonstrates that it meets these conditions and is thus entitled to IT, the EU authorities will specify an individual duty rate for that producer. Exporters who do not satisfy the IT test will be subject to the country-wide duty rate.
>
> 7.50. In sum, when an exporter from a WTO Member that the European Union treats as a NME is subject to an anti-dumping investigation conducted by the European Union, the following possibilities with respect to the determination of normal value and the imposition of duty apply:
>
> (a) If the exporter satisfies the MET, then its normal value will be determined on the same basis as for producers in market economies. A dumping margin for that producer will be calculated by comparing that normal value to the export prices of that producer, and an individual duty rate will be applied to that producer.
> (b) If the exporter fails the MET ('NME exporter'), then its normal value will be determined on the basis of an alternative method (typically based on

2 Council Regulation (EC) 1225/2009 (hereinafter the EU Regulation).

prices in an analogue third country). Whether the export price used in calculating the dumping margin will be based on the exporter's own export sales will depend on whether the exporter requests and is granted IT.

(i) If the NME exporter makes such a request and demonstrates that it meets the criteria in Article 9(5) of the Basic AD Regulation, the NME exporter will have an individual duty rate applied to it, calculated on the basis of a comparison of the alternative-method normal value with its own export prices.

Otherwise, the non-IT NME exporter will be subject to a country-wide duty rate. The determination of the export price used to calculate that country-wide duty rate will depend on the level of cooperation on the part of the non-IT exporters altogether. If the level of cooperation is high, i.e. if the cooperating non-IT exporters account for close to 100% of all exports, the export price will be based on a weighted average of the actual price of all export transactions effected by these exporters. If, however, the level of cooperation is low, i.e. if the non-IT exporters account for significantly less than 100 percent of all exports, the Commission will resort to facts available to complete the missing information. The selection of the facts available will depend on the gravity of non-cooperation and may include statistical import data.

The Panel found that the EU measure was inconsistent with the EU obligations under Article I GATT, since the EU was treating imports from NMEs worse than imports of like products from market economies.

The Panel upheld China's claims to the effect that the EU measure constituted a violation of Article 6.2 AD and 6.4 AD since the EU based its decision to impose AD duties on facts other than those that it had requested the Chinese exporters to provide. It finally found that the EU had violated its obligations regarding treatment of confidential information since it accepted that the entities supplying similar information did not have to also provide a nonconfidential summary. The Panel rejected the Chinese claims regarding the consistency of the EU practices with Article 2.4 AD, which requests WTO Members to perform a fair comparison between normal value (NV) and export price (EP). It decided to exercise judicial economy and not rule on claims regarding the consistency of the EU measure with Articles 9.3 and 9.4 AD, as well as with Article X.3 GATT.

The parties to the dispute challenged all findings mentioned supra, and the Appellate Body (AB) had its hands full yet again in the context of a dispute coming under the purview of the AD Agreement.[3]

3 WTO Members typically raise the highest number of claims per dispute when litigating the consistency of contingent-protection instruments, see Horn *et al.* (2011), and also www.worldbank.org/trade/wtodisputes (last visited 15 October 2012). The World Bank's *Temporary Trade Barriers Database*

Section 2 provides a brief background of the economic markets involved in this case and a related antidumping investigation and WTO dispute. In Section 3, we briefly discuss the appealed issues and in the immediately following Section 4 we present, in detail, the findings of the AB on each one of them. Section 5 contains our analytical assessment of some of the key areas of the AB Report in which the issue of statistical sampling arose. Section 6 concludes.

2. The economic facts and markets involved

This section briefly describes some of the underlying economic features of the traded products subject to the antidumping measure, WTO dispute, and related policies – all based on publicly available data.

2.1 *The EU import market for steel fasteners*

In November 2007, the European Union initiated an antidumping investigation into imports of certain steel fasteners from China. A fastener is a hardware device that joins two or more objects together. The EU's preliminary investigation was completed in August 2008 without imposition of preliminary measures. The final determination resulted in the imposition of antidumping measures in January of 2009.

Table 1 summarizes some of the key features of the EU steel fasteners import market and policies that affect its imports of those products. The EU's applied MFN tariff on steel fasteners imports was 3.7%, a rate identical to its WTO binding. Domestic petitioners in the European Union's steel fasteners antidumping investigation were represented by the European Industrial Fasteners Institute (EIFI). While the actual number and identity of firms behind the EIFI petition are unknown, in terms of geographic distribution of reported production in the EU's official antidumping announcement, the EU reported verifying the surveyed domestic-producer information of five firms from Italy, one from Poland, and one from Sweden – firms allegedly chosen in part because they represented a large percentage of total community-wide domestic production.[4]

Of the more than 110 Chinese exporting firms that responded to the EU investigation, eight received individual treatment and firm-specific antidumping measures. The result of the investigation led to two of these firms not facing any antidumping measures, whereas the other six firms faced duties ranging from 26.5% to 79.5%. One of the Chinese firms facing a zero rate, Yantai Agrati Fasteners Co. Ltd, was the Chinese subsidiary of one of the EU's surveyed domestic producers headquartered in Italy (Agrati SpA). The other Chinese firm facing a zero

(Bown, 2012) contains detailed data on most WTO members' use of antidumping, safeguards, and countervailing duties and is available at http://econ.worldbank.org/ttbd/ (last visited 15 October 2012).

4 These firms were Agrati SpA (Italy), Finnveden Bulten (Sweden), Fontana Luigi SpA and LOBO SpA (Italy), Growermetal Srl (Italy), Invitea SpA (Italy), Societa Bulloneria Europea SpA (Italy), and Srubex Fabryca Lancut SA (Poland).

Table 1. EU and China steel-fasteners import markets associated with antidumping cases

	European Union	China
Tariff binding levels for named products	3.7%	8.0%–10.0%
Applied MFN tariffs for named products	3.7%	8.0%–10.0%
Total imports of named products, 2008	$2.1 billion	$1.4 billion
Domestic firms	• European Industrial Fasteners Institute (EIFI)	• China's Industrial Association of Mechanical General Parts
Foreign firms (antidumping duty)	• Biao Wu Tensile Fasteners Co. Ltd (69.9%) • Celo Suzhou Precision Fasteners Co. Ltd (0.0%) • Changshu City Standard Parts Factory and Changshu British Shanghai International Fastener Co. Ltd (63.1%) • Golden Horse (Dong Guan) Metal Manufactory Co. Ltd (26.5%) • Kunshan Chenghe Standard Components Co. Ltd (79.5%) • Ningbo Jinding Fastener Co. Ltd (64.4%) • Ningbo Yonghong Fasteners Co. Ltd (78.3%) • Yantai Agrati Fasteners Co. Ltd (0.0%) • Cooperating exporting producers (77.5%) • All other companies (85.0%)	• KAMAX–Werke Rudolf Kellermann GMBH & Co. KG (6.1%) • All other companies (26.0%)

Source: compiled by the authors from Bown (2012), WITS and Eurostat.

rate, Celo Suzhou Precision Fasteners Co. Ltd, was the Chinese subsidiary of Grupo Celo, a Spanish-headquartered company that was not involved in the public report. For more than 100 other Chinese exporters that the EU deemed to have cooperated with the investigation, they faced a common countrywide rate of 77.5%, and the all other (noncooperating) firms faced a rate of 85.0%.

According to trade data that are publicly available at the tariff-line level, the EU steel-fasteners market for the product ultimately subject to its antidumping measures peaked at $2.1 billion in extra EU imports in 2008, having doubled from its 2005 level. As Figure 1(a) illustrates, more than half of the growth in EU imports of this product during this period came from China alone. EU steel-fasteners imports from China peaked at $1.1 billion in 2008, having risen steadily from $100 million less than a decade earlier. China's exports of this product to the

Figure 1. EU import market for certain steel fasteners, 2002–2010

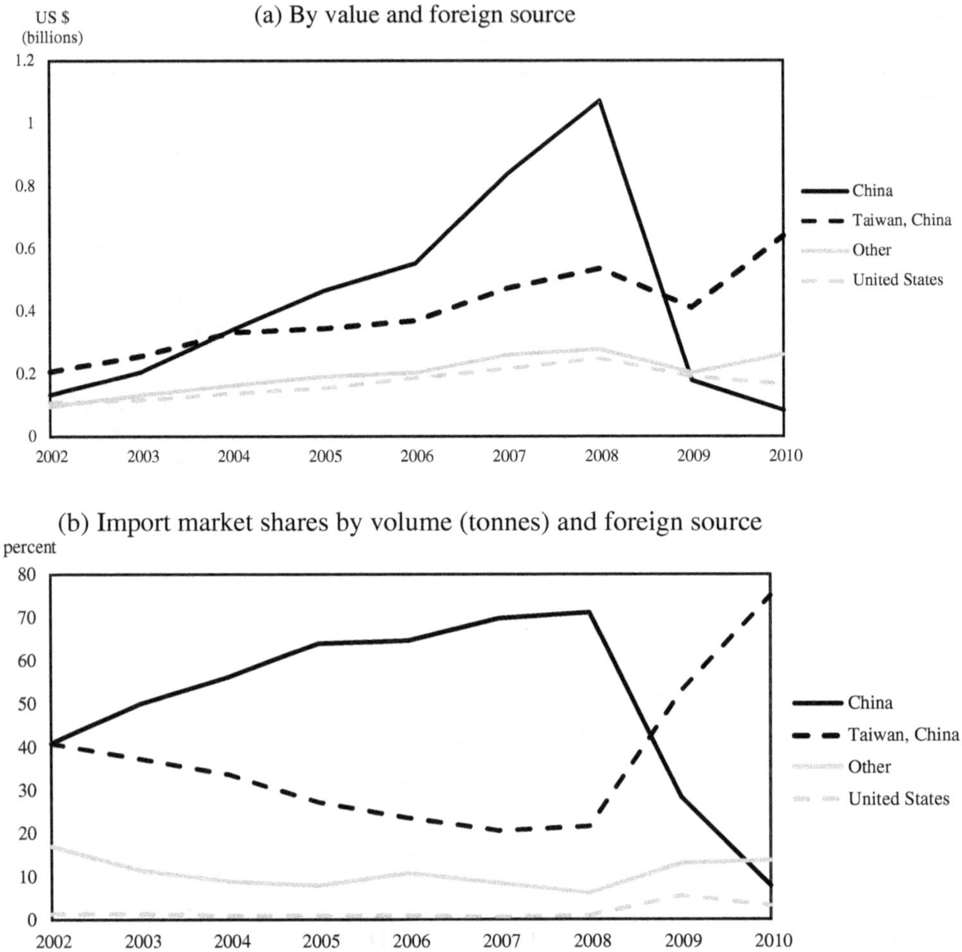

Source: Compiled by the authors with data from Bown (2012) and Eurostat.

EU dropped off considerably after imposition of the antidumping measure, falling by more than $1 billion to $82 million by 2010.

Figure 1(b) illustrates China's share of the EU import market for these products had risen to more than 70% by 2008, falling off to only 8% by 2010 after imposition of the measure. Other major foreign suppliers of the EU market for these particular products included Taiwan, China, and the United States – indeed, most of the EU import market share vacated by China due to the imposed antidumping measure was reallocated toward imports from Taiwan, China – from 22% in 2008 to 75% in 2010. Nevertheless, a combination of the antidumping measure on China and weak overall EU import demand associated with the Great

Recession and the lingering European debt crisis has resulted in the total volume of EU imports of steel fasteners dropping off considerably. While not shown in the figures, the data indicate that by 2010 total EU import volumes were only 40% of their peak level reached in 2007.[5] The value of total EU steel-fasteners imports of $1.1 billion in 2010 was also back to its 2005 level, 54% of its peak level reached in 2008.

Finally, it is also noteworthy that in October 2010, the EU began an anticircumvention investigation examining allegations that the Chinese exporters subject to the EU antidumping order on steel fasteners were shipping their product through Malaysia. As of 2010, Malaysia exported only $12 million in steel fasteners to the EU, 1% of the extra-EU import market by value (2% by volume) – though this had increased from less than 0.5% just two years earlier. In July 2011, the EU extended the antidumping measures imposed on China to at least 11 firms in Malaysia (European Union, 2010, 2011).

2.2 *China's import market for steel fasteners*

While the EU's antidumping case and China's associated WTO challenge were limited to the facts at issue in the EU antidumping case, any discussion of the political–economic background to the dispute would be incomplete if it did not also inform on the related Chinese antidumping investigation and measures imposed on imports from the EU. This is appropriate given the timing of two cases that covered potentially quite similar products and possibly affecting an overlapping set of firms that compete in both markets.

Less than one month before the final decision in the EU's antidumping investigation, China announced it was initiating an antidumping investigation of its own over certain steel fasteners imports from the EU. The antidumping investigation was initiated in December 2008; China imposed provisional antidumping duties in December 2009. In May of 2010, the WTO received a formal DSU request for consultations from the EU regarding the provisional antidumping duties that China had applied. In June 2010, China applied final measures.

Table 1 also summarizes key features of China's steel-fasteners import market and import policies. China's applied MFN tariff on the steel fasteners under its antidumping investigation was either 8.0% or 10.0%, depending on the specific product variety named in the investigation. For each named variety, however, China's applied MFN tariff was identical to its WTO binding; thus, like the EU, it also had no scope to raise applied MFN tariffs. The domestic petitioner in China's steel-fasteners antidumping investigation was China's Industrial Association of

5 According to the 8-digit tariff line Eurostat import data, extra-EU total imports of the steel fasteners at issue in the antidumping investigation totalled 904 thousand tonnes in 2007 and fell to 351 thousand tonnes in 2010.

Figure 2. China's import market for certain steel fasteners, 2002–2010

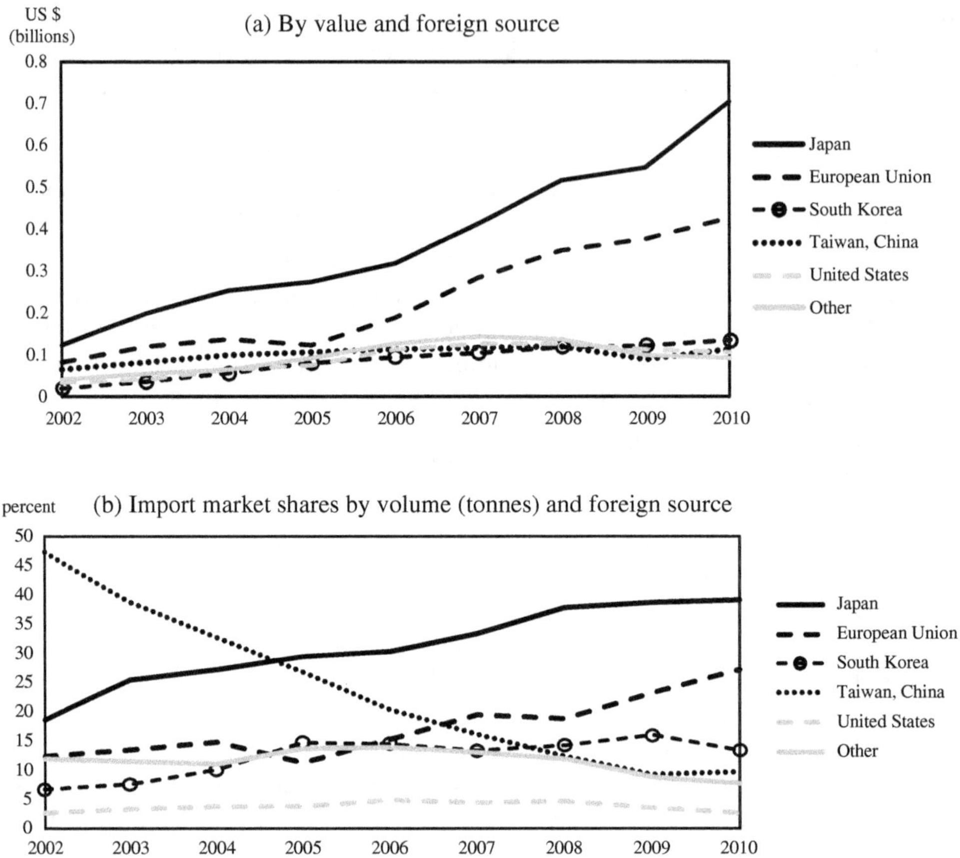

Source: Compiled by the authors with data from Bown (2012) and UN Comtrade made available via WITS.

Mechanical General Parts; the exact set of domestic firms behind the petition is unknown. There was only one European firm named in the antidumping investigation – KAMAX-Werke Rudolf Kellermann GMBH & Co. KG – and China imposed a 6.1% antidumping duty on its exports. The European firm KAMAX was headquartered in Belgium and provided steel fasteners primarily for the auto industry. KAMAX had other subsidiaries across the EU, United States, and Japan, in 2010 it established a trading company in China, and subsequent to China's antidumping decision in 2012 it announced it had begun construction of its first production plant in China (KAMAX, 2012a,b). For all other European exporters, China applied an all-other-firm rate of 26%.

Figure 2(a) illustrates that China's import market for the steel-fasteners product ultimately subject to its antidumping measures was $1.4 billion in 2008, also having doubled from its 2005 level.[6] Steel-fasteners imports from the EU had nearly tripled during this period, from $124 million to $349 million. Figure 2(b) illustrates the EU's share of China's import market for these products had risen to 19% by 2008, accelerating to 27% by 2010 at the time of the imposition of the final antidumping measure, when it was expected to begin to decline. The other major foreign suppliers to China's market for these particular products are Japan; Taiwan, China; South Korea; and the United States. Like the EU, Japan's share of the China import market for these products had also increased considerably during this time period – increasing by nearly 10 percentage points (from 30% to 39%) between 2006 and 2010. In volume terms, Figure 2(b) shows the growth in Japanese and EU share of China's import market during this time period is largely coming at the expense of Taiwan, China, and to a lesser extent from the United States and South Korea.

While not shown in the figures, it is also worth noting that the Great Recession did not result in a substantial, long-run impact on China's total imports of these products, unlike the case for the EU described earlier. China's overall imports of steel fasteners by 2010 were nearly 33% higher than their 2007 levels by value and nearly 40% higher by volume.

2.3 Differentiating between the EU and China certain steel-fasteners markets

While both the EU and China's antidumping cases referred to certain steel fasteners, to what extent are these similar or even substitutable products? The simple fact that there was substantial two-way trade in steel fasteners across long geographic distance suggests that these products are likely to be somewhat differentiated.[7]

One possibility is that these products are differentiated along the dimension of complexity or product quality (Schott, 2008), what has come to be known in economics as occupying different places on the 'quality ladder' (Khandelwal, 2010). Figure 3 provides a first pass at this question by examining the unit values

6 This figure is also derived from publicly available data. However, unlike the EU data which derive from Eurostat, the Chinese import data are not at the tariff-line level but instead the 6-digit HS level from WITS. Nevertheless, according to the available data from China's tariff-line tariff codes, the 8-digit tariff-line codes listed in its antidumping investigation cover all of the sub-products within the more aggregated 6-digit HS product codes, suggesting in this instance that the 6-digit HS data series is identical to summing up the 8-digit HS data.

7 Next, it turns out that one half of the 8-digit product lines in the relevant HS-06 product categories for the EU were left out of the antidumping investigation. The following HS08 lines were included in the EU's antidumping petition: 73181290, 73181491, 73181499, 73181559, 73181569, 73181581, 73181589, 73181590, 73182100, and 73182200. The HS08 lines within the same HS06 product categories that were left out of the petition were 73181210, 73181410, 73181510, 73181520, 73181530, 73181541, 73181549, 73181551, 73181561, and 73181570. As noted above, this is different from China's antidumping case in which all of the 8-digit tariff lines within the HS06 product categories were part of the antidumping investigation.

Figure 3. Import price comparison for EU vs. China's certain steel-fasteners products in AD cases

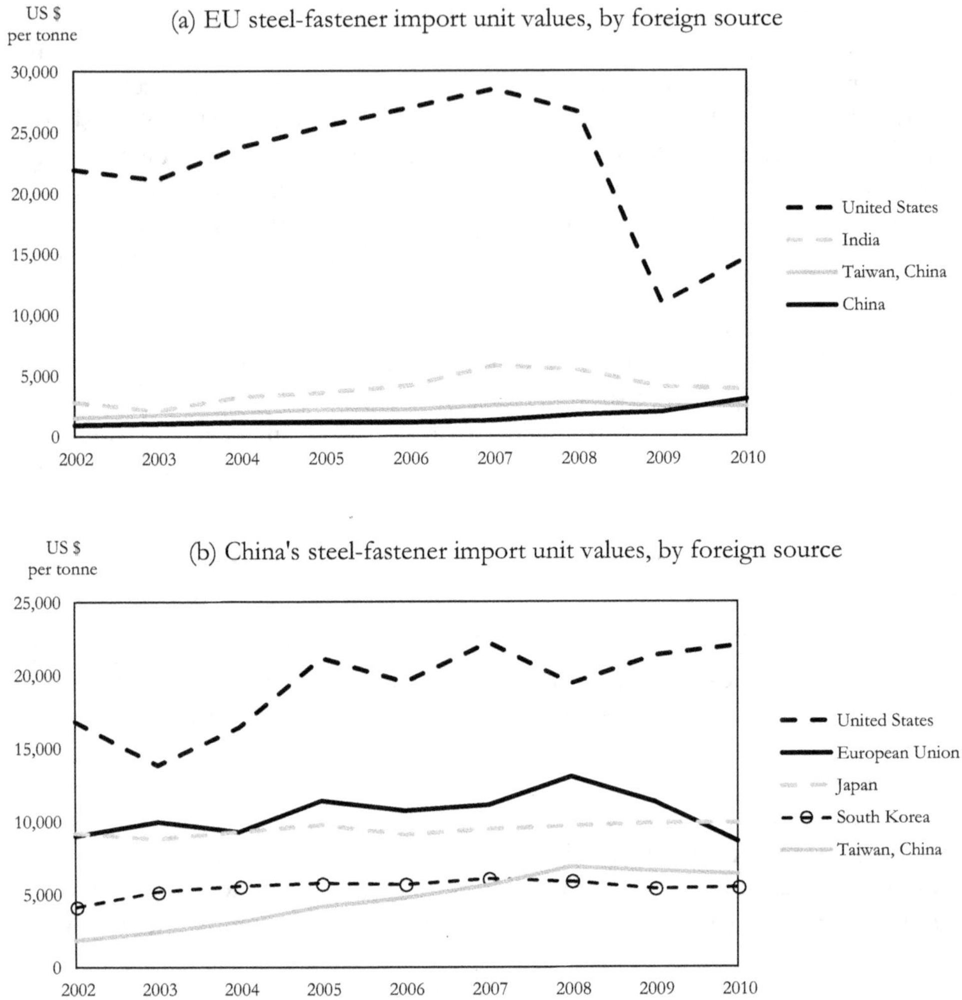

Source: compiled by the authors with data from Bown (2012), Eurostat, and UN Comtrade made available via WITS.

for the certain steel fasteners import products across different foreign-source countries. Figure 3(a) illustrates the EU's unit value for imports across four different foreign sources of the eight-digit HS products named in its antidumping investigation (see again Figure 1) – the United States; China; Taiwan, China; and India. Begin with the EU's imports from the United States. Clearly, there is a substantial distinction between the EU's imports from the United States and the EU's imports from China and Taiwan regarding otherwise identical HS08 product lines. Before the onset of the global trade collapse of 2008–2009, unit values on imports from the United States averaged between $21,000 and $28,000 per tonne each year.[8] During this same period, unit values on imports from China and Taiwan, China averaged only $1,000 to $3,000 per tonne – suggesting a substantially differentiated product compared to imports from the United States. The United States had a very small share of the EU's import market (see again Figure 1(b)); together, these facts suggest that the United States may be supplying European customers with a more highly specialized product, and the Chinese and Taiwanese firms may be supplying a relatively more homogeneous variety likely produced at high scale and low cost.[9]

Next, consider the Chinese import market in Figure 3(b). As a benchmark, begin again with the unit values of China's imports from the United States during this period, which ranged from $14,000 to $22,000 per tonne per year. The fact that these were not as high as the US import unit values in the EU market suggests some level difference in demand for the certain steel fasteners between the EU and China markets. Next, the unit value on Chinese imports of steel fasteners from the EU averaged $9,000 to $13,000 per tonne during 2002–2010. While this was not as high as China's average unit value on steel fasteners imports from the United States, it is much higher than the unit value of EU imports of steel fasteners from China in its antidumping case illustrated in Figure 3(a). The difference is more stark after accounting for the overall difference in price levels, e.g., by comparing unit values of imports from the United States across the two markets. Thus, using the US import values as a benchmark, a comparison of the import unit values from the products covered by the reciprocal antidumping cases is consistent with a model of China exporting relatively low-end varieties of steel fasteners to the EU market and the EU exporting relatively high-end varieties of steel fasteners to the Chinese market.

Finally, preliminary indicators point to two potentially quite different economic outcomes resulting from the EU and Chinese antidumping cases. While overall EU imports have dropped, a second result from the European imposition of antidumping on imports of steel fasteners from China is likely to be substantial trade diversion. The preliminary evidence (see again Figure 1(a)) is an increase in EU imports from nontargeted exporters such as Taiwan, China, that were historical suppliers producing a similarly priced variety of steel-fasteners imports. Ultimately,

8 Unit values on imports from the United States dropped dramatically during the Great Recession, even as the quantity of imports from the United States nearly doubled between 2008 and 2009.

9 Figure 3a also illustrates the unit values on EU imports from India. These unit values – ranging between $2,000 and $6,000 per tonne – were consistently higher than the unit values on imports from China and Taiwan, China – though they were much lower than the unit values on imports from the United States. Even though imports from India of this product were negligible during this period (less than $3 million in 2006), this point is interesting given that India was chosen as the analogue country for China in the normal-value calculation.

this antidumping case results in a relocation of production from China to Taiwan, China, and not necessarily the relocation of substantial production back to the EU. On the other hand, provided KAMAX follows through with the announced production facility in China, China's antidumping duties on imports from the EU of high-end steel fasteners could result in 'tariff-jumping' foreign direct investment (Blonigen, 2002) – that is, a relocation of production from the EU to China.

3. The issues before the AB

The AB faced a number of issues from both parties to the dispute[10] that could, for all practical purposes, be classified as follows:

(a) China's NME status;
(b) the understanding of the term 'major proportion';
(c) the possibility to sample producers in the injury analysis as well (and not only when defining dumping margins);
(d) the attitude of the EU investigating authority (IA) with respect to the 'parallelism' of the subject matter between the requested information and the basis for the EU decision to impose AD duties;
(e) the treatment of confidential information by the EU.

Claims under heading (a) were, in principle, of transitional value as far as China is concerned since, by virtue of the explicit wording of Article 15 of China's Protocol of Accession, China cannot be treated as an NME after 2016, that is 15 years after its succession to the WTO. And yet, in our view, they carry particular weight: the AB response is one of the scarce attempts to shed some light on the NME carveout, an issue that for various reasons had not been comprehensively discussed before this Report was issued; the findings here are of relevance to all WTO Members that are considered NMEs. Moreover, as we will try to demonstrate infra, the findings of the AB in this respect could be viewed as the basis for treating imports from China differently from those originating in market economies beyond 2016 as well. We will address this discussion below.

4 The AB findings

4.1 *Individual treatment (China's nonmarket-economy status)*

We described briefly above the MET and IT tests that appear in Articles 9(5) and 2.7(a)–(c) of the EU Regulation. Recall that successful invocation of MET status confers automatically IT, while a failed attempt is not necessarily prejudicial since interested exporters can still request IT; they can also bypass the MET process and

10 Zang (2011) offers a discussion of the dispute with respect to the claims regarding the NME status of China.

request simply IT. Two questions form the heart of the dispute between China and the EU in this context: first, under what conditions can an IA deviate from its obligations to calculate individual dumping margins? Second, who should carry the burden of proof to demonstrate that an exporter should be considered as originating in an NME?

With respect to the first question, the AB entertained the claim by the EU to the effect that the Panel got it wrong when it held that under Article 6.10 AD sampling is the only exception to the obligation to calculate individual dumping margins.[11] The AB, upholding the Panel's findings in this respect, found that the default obligation for WTO Members is to calculate individual dumping margins, the possibility to impose duties on a countrywide basis being reserved only to the cases referred to in the AD Agreement and not to any other case (para. 320 and para. 329). It rejected a number of scenarios offered by the EU where countrywide duties were in order since, in the AB's view, they were all provided for in the AD Agreement and none of them provided justification for the EU practices to impose countrywide duties when exports originate in NMEs (paras. 321–327). The AB thus established that the EU was in violation of its obligations under Article 6.10 AD when it imposed countrywide duties on Chinese exporters because they originate in an NME: there is no corresponding exception to the obligation to calculate individual dumping margins in the AD Agreement.

Next was the question regarding the allocation of the burden (of production) of proof to show whether an exporter should be considered as originating in an NME or not. Strictly speaking, a finding here was not necessary for the resolution of the dispute: a finding that individual dumping margins could not be lawfully calculated in this case should signal 'game, set and match' for China. The AB nevertheless, facing an appeal to this effect, addressed this issue as well. Recall that according to the EU system described above, it is for the exporter to request MET status (that might lead to IT). Here we care about MET status only. To understand the discussion regarding the conformity of MET with the AD Agreement, we need to place this legal institution in its natural context, that is the NME context.

The AD Agreement does not refer to NMEs at all; they are addressed in Article VI GATT. The AB has consistently held that both the AD Agreement and Article VI GATT are legally relevant to the regulation of antidumping. It is thus through the

11 Sampling can lawfully take place when a statistically valid sample has been chosen or when it is impractical for the IA to calculate individual dumping margins, say, because of the large number of exporters involved. Although the two methods, normatively at least, should not be regarded as equivalent (in the name of impracticality a statistically invalid sample – that is, a sample of producers that does not reproduce the properties of the whole – might be chosen, and thus the investigation might suffer from sample bias), they are recognized as such in Article 6.10 AD. One of the (many) paradoxes of AD is that while dumping is acknowledged to be private business practice, still orders can be applied on countrywide basis without meaningful investigation as to whether the law of one price holds, see on this score the analysis in Mavroidis and Sapir (2008).

case-law door that NMEs entered into the WTO picture.[12] NMEs are defined in the Interpretative Note ad Article VI GATT as:

> a country which has a complete or substantially complete monopoly of its trade and where all domestic prices are fixed by the state.

The Note allows WTO Members to deviate from the obligations imposed in Article VI GATT (as further explicated in the AD Agreement) but does not explain what methodology exactly they should be following in similar cases:

> It is recognized that, in the case of imports from a country which has a complete or substantially complete monopoly of its trade and where all domestic prices are fixed by the State, special difficulties may exist in determining price comparability for the purposes of paragraph 1, and in such cases importing contracting parties may find it necessary to take into account the possibility that a strict comparison with domestic prices in such a country may not always be appropriate.

Normally, an IA, in the absence of legislative guidance as to what to do in such cases, will either use data from third-country producers, or construct the NV. In *EU–Footwear (China)*, the Panel faced a claim by China that, by choosing Brazil as surrogate country for China, the EU had violated its obligations under the AD Agreement; the Panel discarded it, underlining the wide discretion IAs have when choosing surrogate countries for NMEs (paras. 7.253ff.).

Not surprisingly, the NME status of China was an important issue in the Chinese accession process. The Chinese Accession Protocol starts from the principle that WTO Members have a choice either to use Chinese prices or costs for the industry (that is, to treat China as any other market-economy country), or to use a methodology based on the general rule that it is up to the producers under investigation to:

> clearly show that market economy conditions prevail in the industry producing the like product with regard to the manufacture, production and sale of that product.[13]

If this has been the case, the importing WTO Member is obliged to use Chinese prices: in other words, if China is able to establish that it is (either as a whole or with regard to a particular industry) a market economy according to the criteria set forth in the importing WTO Member's national law, China (e.g., the Chinese industry in question) must be treated as a normal market economy/industry. In order to benefit from market-economy status, the criteria conferring it must have existed in the importing WTO Member's law at the time of China's accession in 2001; it is not entirely clear what happens if similar criteria were not in place at the

12 Czako *et al.* (2003) and Mavroidis *et al.* (2010) discuss the relevant case law; Palmeter (1995) and Stewart *et al.* (2009) discuss the negotiating history of the AD Agreement.

13 WTO Doc. WT/L/432 at para. 15.

time of China's accession, and it is an open question whether WTO Members finding themselves in this situation are precluded from treating China as an NME. This will be, if at all, a short-lived situation, since the NME status of China will expire, at the latest, 15 years after accession, that is by 2016.

In the opposite case, a methodology that is not based on a strict comparison with domestic prices or costs in China may be used. If this methodology is applied, the WTO Antidumping Committee has to be notified about it. China's Accession Protocol does not set forth which methodology is to be used in cases where the importing WTO Member does not use Chinese prices and costs; the final report of the Working Party on China's Accession[14] provides some clarification though in this respect: the authority shall normally utilize, to the extent possible, and where cooperation existed, the prices or costs in one or more market-economy countries that are significant producers of comparable merchandise, and that are either at the level of economic development comparable to that of China, or are otherwise an appropriate source for the prices or costs to be utilized in light of the nature of the industry under investigation. Those WTO Members that do not have an established practice in this respect should make best efforts to ensure that their methodology for determining price comparability is along similar lines. In addition, it provides that due-process rights of Chinese exporters be respected.

It is clear from the discussion above that the burden of proof to show that a company should not be regarded as originating in an NME lies with the Chinese company requesting this privilege: paragraph 15 of the Protocol of Accession says as much. Nevertheless, the burden is allocated to the Chinese company only with respect to the NV. Nothing in the Protocol of Accession imposes the burden on Chinese companies to disavow NME status with respect to EP. With respect to EP, hence, the allocation of the burden of proof reverts to the original distribution; that is, it is for the IA to demonstrate NME status and proceed in the consequential calculation of dumping margins. Paragraph 15 of the Protocol of Accession, in other words, is a limited exception and covers NV only; the EU presumption thus goes against the letter and the spirit of Articles 6.10 and 9.2 AD, the two provisions dealing with calculation of dumping margins (paras. 363ff. of the AB Report, and especially 364 and 366). Since, in the eyes of the AB, the EU measure ran afoul of the WTO 'as such'; that is, irrespective whether it had been applied to a particular case, it also ran afoul as applied in the instant case (para. 409).

The consequence of this finding led the AB to two more conclusions: first, since duties had in its view been illegally calculated, the obligation to not discriminate had been violated as well, since other exports to the EU market would not suffer from similar treatment (para. 398); second, since the duties had been illegally

14 WTO Doc. WT/ACC/CHN/49 at para. 151.

imposed, the EU had ipso facto violated its obligations under Article XVI GATT and 18.4 AD (para. 398).

4.2 *Major proportion of the industry*

The question before the AB, in this respect, was whether the EU decision to find that 27% of the EU fasteners producers constituted a major proportion of the domestic industry was consistent with Articles 4.1 and 3.1 AD. The latter requires that the determination of injury be based on 'positive evidence' whereas the former obliges WTO Members to examine injury of the domestic producers as a whole, without nevertheless providing a specific quantitative benchmark, say a fixed percentage of the domestic duty the health of which should be discussed in the context of injury analysis.

It is clear from the discussion in the AB Report (paras. 420ff.) that, in the eyes of the AB, the EU was inspired by Article 5.4 AD when deciding on the percentage of the domestic industry (the 27%) that validly represents the whole. In the AB's view, this is wrong, since the two provisions are designed to address different issues: Article 5.4 AD deals with the percentage of the domestic industry that must anyway back a petition to (eventually) impose AD duties and the WTO legislator decided that a 25% threshold was appropriate in order to avoid flimsy requests;[15] Articles 3.1 and 4.1 AD, on the other hand, are integral parts of the injury analysis where the WTO legislator aims at securing that AD duties will be (eventually) imposed when the industry as a whole has suffered from dumping practices, and not a small, unrepresentative percentage thereof. Indeed, the AB itself, without going the full nine yards and providing a number, did state that the term 'major proportion' points to a 'relatively high proportion' (para. 419). The AB, however, did not give a number here. Actually, it went as far as to state that a major proportion could be less than 50% on occasion and as low as 25% in case of fragmented industries (paras. 415ff.).

Because the EU had inappropriately linked the percentage of the major industry to that in Article 5.4 AD, the AB found that it had violated its WTO obligations in this respect (Article 4.1 AD). Violation of Article 4.1 AD means ipso facto that Article 3.1 AD has also been violated since the major industry has been inappropriately defined and, consequently, AD duties were ultimately imposed in disregard of the requirement to base findings on positive evidence (para. 430). Note, however, that the EU practice has changed and that the link to the standing requirement is no longer EU practice. Finally, in paragraph 460, the AB condoned the EU practice to provide exporters with a 15-day deadline to make themselves

15 It is far from clear that this threshold decisively helps avoid sample bias since the 25% could, for example, correspond to the part of the industry that did not modernize, did not invest in new technologies/ equipments etc., and as a result might have contributed itself to its downfall.

known (in case they do not, the EU can, of course, proceed with the remaining exporters).

4.3 *Do you like sampling too?*

This point deserves an introduction. We are not dealing with a new claim here but merely with an argument[16] in support of the claim discussed immediately supra to the effect that the EU had violated its obligations under Article 3.1 AD: China argued before the Panel and the AB that the EU had violated its obligations under this provision also because it had picked an unrepresentative sample of domestic producers (a statistically invalid sample) to conduct its injury analysis; having defined the major proportion to comprise 27% of the domestic production, the EU picked a number (65% of this sum, that is 45 producers) and went ahead with its investigation.

We dedicate a separate heading to this point because of the novelty of the issue we are confronted with: the AD Agreement allows for sampling when it comes to defining dumping margins; it is silent on sampling for purposes of establishing injury resulting from dumping. Statutory silence was not perceived as an obstacle by the EU authorities to go ahead and sample producers in order to perform the injury analysis.

The AB did not find anything wrong with the EU practice in this respect. In its view, the absence of specific language allowing sampling in injury analysis is no reason in and of itself to disallow a similar practice (para. 436); the percentage chosen by the EU does not run afoul of its obligations under the AD Agreement since, in parallel with the sampling scenario when defining dumping margins, the EU does not have to pick a statistically valid sample (it can also pick the sample of producers that can be investigated); finally, the EU has every right, in accordance with the AB to exclude, from its sample, producers that have not responded within 15 days to its questionnaire, otherwise the whole investigation process risks being unduly long (para. 460).

4.4 *Surprise, surprise (you pay for this, but they give you that)*

The whole investigation was conducted using PCNs (Product Control Numbers). Six elements made up the PCNs identified by the Commission, the type of fasteners, their strength/hardness, coating, the presence of chrome on coating, their diameter, and their length/thickness. The Commission sent questionnaires requesting information on this specification of the 'like product' under investigation to Chinese exporters and to Pooja Forge, an Indian company that was used as a surrogate to define dumping margins by the EU Commission (since Chinese exports

16 A claim, as per constant WTO case law, is the identification of a factual situation and the legal provision that is allegedly violated as a result of its existence. One or more arguments can be raised in support of specific claims.

originated in an NME, as noted supra). The questionnaires even provided for an example of the product under investigation, namely:

> Self-tapping screw, case hardening, not coated, diameter 4,2 millimeters, length 13 millimeters.

So much is clear (paras. 469–470). Pooja Forge, nonetheless, had not provided information on the PCNs requested. The Commission thus based its estimation on product types defined by two factors, strength class and the distinction between standard and special fasteners. The Panel found that the Chinese producers were informed very late in the process about the quality of the information provided by the Indian company, and the ensuing discrepancy with the information they had provided themselves (paras. 461–462). The late notification had as a consequence the impossibility for the Chinese producers to request adjustments. This fact, in and of itself, sufficed for the AB to find that the EU had violated its obligations under Article 6.4 AD (para. 505). A violation of Article 6.4 AD entails ipso facto a violation of Article 6.2 AD since the two provisions are related, one being specific law to the other (para. 506). Due to the Commission's failure to indicate what information was relevant, the Chinese exporters could not exercise their rights under Article 2.4 AD, the provision obliging WTO Members to make fair comparison between NV and EP making due allowances whenever warranted. And here comes the trick: the Panel accepted and the AB confirmed that because of the discrepancy mentioned so far (because of the Commission's attitude), Chinese exporters were not in a position to exercise their rights under this provision (para. 515). But the Panel found no evidence supporting that there were differences affecting price comparability and hence did not find against the EU with respect to China's claim that Article 2.4 AD had been violated. Hence, the AB, upholding the Panel's findings in this respect, found that the EU did not act inconsistently with its obligations under Article 2.4 AD (para. 528, but all paragraphs from para. 519 onwards are relevant to this discussion).

4.5 *Private investigations and confidential information*

Some EU economic operators had provided confidential information without also providing a nonconfidential summary, and, in China's and the Panel's view, the EU, by not insisting that they do so, had violated its obligations under various paragraphs of Article 6 AD. The legal regime regarding supply of confidential information is a bit convoluted, and some explanation, albeit brief, is in order.

According to the AD Agreement, information is confidential either by its very nature or because it has been provided on a confidential basis. The Agreement contains an illustrative list of information that is confidential by its very nature.[17]

17 An Illustrative List helps the parties to a contract and/or the judge to avoid a Type II error (a false negative): armed with some specific examples, it will not overlook the application of a law when confronted with cases reflecting similar factual situations.

A party that provides similar information must show good cause why it should be treated as confidential information, irrespective of whether the information provided is by nature confidential or has been supplied as such.[18] Additionally, a nonconfidential summary should be provided as well, unless there are exceptional circumstances where its supply is not possible (Article 6.5 AD). The Chinese claim concerns this last point: the EU producers did not provide a nonconfidential summary, and the EU did not insist that they do. As a result, of course, the right of defense of the Chinese companies was negatively affected since they were deprived of information probably crucial to their eventual success before the European IA.

Agrati, an EU producer, for example, had provided a nonconfidential summary of information concerning some injury factors, but not for others. For the latter, the following statement had been included:

> The information cannot be summarized without disclosing confidential information which can cause damage to our company. The information has been provided as limited (para. 550).

Fontana Luigi, another EU producer, did not supply a nonconfidential summary with regard to distribution systems and price setting. The reason for doing so was presented in the following terms:

> The information is by nature confidential because its disclosure would be of significant competitive advantage to a Competitor (para. 551).

In the AB's view, none of the information provided met the 'exceptional circumstance' standard established in Article 6.5 AD that must be met for the obligation to provide a nonconfidential summary to be waived (para. 553). Consequently, the AB, upholding the Panel, found that the EU had violated its obligations under Article 6.5 AD by accepting the justification of the two companies as valid reasons to waive their obligation to provide a nonconfidential summary.

5. A critique

From an economics perspective, the existence of the Antidumping Agreement is difficult to rationalize, given the number of ways in which its language regarding impermissible behaviour by firms competing across borders is inconsistent with permissible profit-maximizing behaviour by firms competing within one country. Thus, in our analysis, we take the Antidumping Agreement as given and focus our critique exclusively on the legal and economic implications of how it is being interpreted and applied in this particular instance.

18 On past case law regarding the 'good cause' requirement, see Mavroidis *et al.* (2010).

The first issue that we address is statistical sampling. If antidumping authorities use statistical sampling, how it is used can play a critical role, influencing the outcome of the antidumping investigation. In this particular application, our analysis focuses on three different instances in which the sampling issue arose: (i) in the selection of Chinese exporting firms from which the EU gathered information to make its initial MET decision, (ii) in the use of the Indian firm, Pooja Forge, as an analogue that was used to construct dumping margins for the Chinese exporters who were deemed in an earlier decision to be from a nonmarket economy, and (iii) in the selection of firms in the domestic industry from which the EU gathered information to make its injury determination.[19]

It is worth stepping back and thinking through the likely economic and statistical goals of the statistical-sampling exercise before turning to a critical examination of the EU's applications in this instance. Most importantly, there is no guidance from the Antidumping Agreement or the EU's antidumping provisions to suggest any other goal of the exercise but simply characterizing 'average' behaviour – that is, that which is typically represented by the mean or median of the statistical distribution.

Note that it is not necessary for the Antidumping Agreement or the EU's antidumping provisions to have remained silent about this issue; that is, either could have been written so as to focus the antidumping authority's analysis and attention on something *other than* 'average' behaviour. For example, one hypothetical possibility would be to explicitly dictate that the antidumping authority's analysis should reflect concern not for the average but for the 'highest' performers – e.g., say, the highest decile or quartile of the distribution – where 'highest' might be based on indicators such as profitability, firm size, a ranking based on the prices of products. Alternatively, or in other settings, provisions might explicitly dictate that the antidumping authority's analysis should reflect Rawlsian-like concern for the 'lowest' performers in the distribution. The main point is that no alternative guidance has been put forward on this issue.

5.1 Initial sampling of Chinese exporting firms for MET

The first question is the process by which the EU sampled Chinese exporting firms to gather information to make its initial market-economy test decision. Table 2 summarizes the results of five key phases of the sampling-selection procedure and

19 As one final aside on the noneconomic rationale for antidumping noted above, the mere existence of both so large a number of Chinese exporting firms and domestic (EU) producing firms – numbers so large that it was necessary for the EU to sample rather than survey them all – again highlights the fact that antidumping is not a policy concerned with identifying and dealing with potential *predation*. The large number of firms suggests few entry barriers, thus making it extremely unlikely that a sufficient number of EU producers would be driven out of business so that Chinese exporting firms would be able to coordinate amongst themselves to then raise prices in a way so as to impose long-run costs on EU consumers due to a lack of market competition.

Table 2. Results of EU sampling procedure of Chinese exporting firms for the market-economy test

Phase of EU investigation	Remaining number of exporting firms in the sample at completion of phase	Share of total China exports of steel fasteners to EU
1. *Initiation of EU investigation*	NA (though inferred as greater than 110)	1.00
2. *EU sends out request for exporters to make themselves known within 15 days*	120	NA
3. *EU eliminates from sample of 120 firms 10 firms that it finds do not produce fasteners or that are firms that export for others*	110	0.64*
4. *EU selects from 110 cooperating firms those to survey that had the largest representative value of exports*	9	0.39
5. *Of the 9 firms chosen to survey, the EU decides that 4 firms refused to cooperate and eliminates them from sample*	5	0.35**

Notes: NA = not available. *Calculated as equal to 0.39/0.61; i.e. = (9's exports as a share of total exports from PRC)/(9's exports as a share of 110 cooperating firms). **Calculated as equal to 0.54/(1/0.64); i.e. = (5's exports as a share of 110 cooperating firms)/(1/110 firm's share of exports in total PRC exports).
Source: Authors' tabulation from data provided in EU (2009).

responses that resulted in the sample of Chinese firms whose data the EU ultimately examined to make the MET determination. Step 1 is the initiation of the investigation and thus begins with the universe of Chinese exporting firms which produce 100% of total fastener exports to the EU, by definition. In Step 2, the EU sent out a general request to Chinese exporters asking to make themselves known; 120 firms came forward as a result. In Step 3, the EU determined that of the 120 firms that revealed themselves as exporting fasteners to the EU, 110 firms were actual exporters, and these firms represented 64% of total Chinese fastener exports to the EU. In Step 4, the EU decided to select 9 of the 110 firms to provide the detailed data necessary to make the MET determination, and these firms represented 39% of the universe of Chinese export sales to the EU. In Step 5, the EU threw out the data of four of the nine firms as being unreliable. The remaining five Chinese firms on which the EU based the MET determination combined to represent slightly less than 35% of the universe of Chinese export sales to the EU.

Is it likely that this sample represented 'average' characteristics of the Chinese exports? In order to address this question, even when focusing on 'average' behaviour, it is important to understand whether the MET should be based on the sampling statistic related to the behaviour of the average 'exporter' (firm) or the behaviour of the firm producing the average 'product'. These two are likely to be quite different. As we will see below, the EU's sampling procedure and the selection issues that arise make the second outcome much more likely than the first.

If the goal of the sampling exercise is to capture the behaviour of the average Chinese firm that exports this product to the EU, it is potentially problematic for the EU to make its decision about the market-economy status of more than 110 firms based on information collected from these particular five firms. These five Chinese firms were not drawn from a random sample; that is, they are the result of a multistage process that could result in sample-selection bias stemming from two distinct influences. On the one hand, the Chinese firms that decided to cooperate at Steps 2 and 5 in the investigation may be quite different from the other, nonsampled Chinese firms that did not choose to cooperate. In other words, the Chinese firms' selection of themselves into or out of the sample could be influenced by strategic considerations such as whether the truthful information that they would provide would be harmful or helpful to the outcome that is in their best interest overall.[20] Furthermore, among the pool of reporting firms, the EU did not randomly sample but instead selected some of the *largest* exporters. There is extensive economic research literature providing evidence that exporting firms are 'different' – that is, more productive with presumably lower costs for a given level of quality – than other firms (Bernard *et al.*, 2012). It could well follow that larger exporters are then systemically different from smaller exporters, along similar dimensions, and thus making a set of observations that had over-sampled from one segment of the statistical distribution particularly biased. The implication is that the EU approach may be closer to capturing the behaviour of the Chinese firm producing the average product being exported to the EU; it is less likely that this sampling procedure is best able capture the behaviour of the average Chinese firm that is exporting.

To what extent does a potentially biased sample matter for this particular case? Interestingly, if the key determinant regarding whether Chinese firms receive market-economy treatment is *not* firm-specific, then the difficulty of how to deal with these sample-selection issues could be moot. For example, suppose the technology to make fasteners is relatively common across all Chinese firms and that most of a firm's costs are simply the cost of the steel-wire-rod input. Furthermore, assume that the price of steel-wire rod is not determined by the market (as the EU alleged in the investigation) and finally that *access* to the subsidized input did not

20 For example, a Chinese exporting firm that is part of a multinational enterprise with production facilities in other countries (that they could reallocate production outside of China) could potentially (and perversely) prefer an outcome in which the EU imposes antidumping duties on all Chinese firms, especially if its main competitors in the EU market are other Chinese firms without production facilities abroad (e.g., Blonigen and Ohno, 1998). Such a firm would presumably make its decision of whether to report at all based on whichever choice led to the greater likelihood of the EU imposing antidumping duties.

vary across firms.[21] Because the impact of the subsidized input is common across all Chinese firms that produce and export fasteners, there is no statistical issue of sample selection potentially misinforming the EU's binary choice for whether the entire set of firms operate in a market economy. This is one alternative way to interpret how the EU proceeded.

From an economics perspective, the relevance of the statistical sampling-issue for the MET determination confronting the Panel and the AB in this case rests on the validity of the EU allegation that the key input of steel-wire rod does not have a price that is determined by the market and that this is enjoyed equally by all Chinese fastener exporting firms. Put differently, the sampling issue is moot if this allegation is correct and if the impact of the nonmarket price for that input is common across all Chinese exporting firms. That is, regardless of whether the EU samples only (any) one firm, collects information from the whole universe of firms, or chooses any option in between, it will always obtain the same result in the MET. Thus, the issue of sampling in this case only becomes relevant if it is incorrect that steel-wire rod is a subsidized input that commonly distorts the costs (and output-pricing decisions) across all Chinese steel-fastener exporting firms.

5.2 'Sampling' one Indian analogue firm to construct normal values

Given that the Chinese firms did not pass the MET, a second statistical-sampling issue arises regarding the analogue firms from which the EU constructs the normal value in the dumping-margin calculation. In this instance, the EU chose India as the analogue country and it requested information from two Indian firms, only one of which provided the information. There are at least two sampling issues that arise in this particular case: the choice of country and the sampling of firms.

First, we have insufficient information to assess the choice of India as an analogue country. Nevertheless, it is worth noting from our examination of the publicly available trade data that India had both an extremely small share of the EU import market (relative to China and Taiwan, China – the latter a potential alternative choice for the analogue country), and India had relatively higher unit values than EU imports from both China and Taiwan, China (see again Figure 3a). To the extent that higher unit values in the EU import market correspond to higher costs and higher prices for domestic sales at home, this would make India an attractive candidate for an analogue country.

The second issue results from the fact that the EU chose to request information from only two Indian firms and only one of which, Pooja Forge, provided information that the EU deemed adequate to use to construct the normal value for

21 Note that it does not necessarily follow that if the steel-wire-rod input is subsidized, then there must be common access to the subsidized input across firms. For example, such heterogeneity of access could arise across firms if government subsidy or tax-rebate programs were based on firm characteristics such as size (or access to policymakers), or if their availability differed geographically across regions.

Table 3. Results of EU sampling procedure of community producers of fasteners for injury test

Phase of EU investigation	Remaining number of firms in the sample at completion of phase	Share of total EU steel-fasteners production
1. *Initiation of EU investigation*	NA (though 'over 300 mostly small and medium-sized enterprises')	1.00
2. *EU sends out request for firms to make themselves known within 15 days*	46	0.30
3. *EU selects from 46 cooperating firms those to survey that had the largest production volume*	7	NA
4. *Of the 7 firms chosen to survey, the EU decides that 1 firm refused to cooperate and eliminates it from sample*	6	0.27

Note: NA = not available.
Source: Authors' tabulation from data provided in EU (2009).

all of the Chinese firms in the dumping-margin calculation. From a statistical perspective, the result of this process is that the information of only one Indian firm is used to construct the normal value for more than 110 Chinese exporting firms. For statistical reasons alone, it is highly remote that this one Indian firm represents the average Chinese exporting 'firm' (or even the Chinese firm producing the average exported 'product') from the universe of Chinese exporting firms ultimately confronted with the antidumping duty.

5.3 Sample of EU producers of fasteners for injury test

A third area of the EU investigation in which the issue of statistical sampling arose is with respect to the injury test for EU producers of the like product. Table 3 illustrates the four-step process by which the EU arrived at the sample of domestic firms by which it collected information so as to determine whether the domestic industry was injured.

Step 1 is the initiation of the investigation and thus begins with the universe of domestic EU firms (producing 100% of EU total fastener sales, by definition), which the EU reported as 'estimated at over 300 mostly small and medium-sized enterprises but including a few larger companies' (EU, 2009, (112)). In Step 2, the EU sent out a general request that EU producers make themselves known; the result was that 46 firms came forward, which the EU reported as representing 30% of domestic production. In Step 3, the EU selected seven of the 46 firms (based on volume) to provide the detailed data necessary to make the injury-test determination; these firms represent an unknown share of the universe of EU production. In Step 4, the EU throws out the data of one of the seven firms; of the remaining six EU firms on which the injury-test determination is based, the EU reported that they combined to represent 27% of the universe of EU production volume of fasteners.

A number of the same sampling issues already described above in the context of sampled Chinese exporting firms also arise in the context of EU producers. It is extremely unlikely that these six EU firms represent the average of the universe of EU steel-fasteners producers given that they are the result of a multistage process; the likely result is sample-selection bias stemming from two main influences. Again, given that response to EU requests for information is not compulsory, EU firms may base on strategic considerations their decision regarding whether to select into the sample by positively responding to the request for information. Second, the sample is also not random due to the fact that the EU used the size of the firm (volume of production) as a selection criterion, conditional on the set of firms that voluntarily responded. Indeed, the EU estimated domestic production to be comprised of more than 300 producers of steel fasteners, and most were small- and medium-sized enterprises and not the large-volume firms that were ultimately part of the sample under analysis. While this decision rule ensures that maximal EU production is covered by the injury investigation, it does not follow that the EU is examining whether the average steel-fasteners-producing firm suffered injury. By selecting based on production volume, it is much more likely that the EU is capturing the behaviour of the firm that produces the average 'product' competing with the imported Chinese fasteners and not the average 'firm'.

5.4 *First, a window, then a door: moving away from the obligation to calculate individual dumping margins*

The AB found that the EU practice to calculate a general (as opposed to individual) rate for Chinese companies because they were considered to belong to an NME was at variance with the EU obligations under the AD Agreement. It did, however, add a passage which allows an IA to deviate from its obligation to calculate individual margins even in cases other than sampling.

The AB Report however, added in paras. 376ff. a passage that offers some additional (to those contemplated by Article 6.10 AD) possibilities to investigating authorities. A small detour to prior case law is necessary: in *Korea–Certain Paper*,[22]

22 Panel Report, *Korea – Anti-Dumping Duties on Imports of Certain Paper from Indonesia*, WT/DS312/R, adopted 28 November 2005. To be sure, the AD Agreement does not explicitly deal with the situation where different offshoots belong to the same economic entity and whether one margin or more (of AD duties) should be calculated in similar cases. This was a total invention of the AB. In theory, the invention is a good one if the entity adopts the same pricing policy, but only under this very strict condition. In theory also, it could very well be the case that offshoots of the same company (say Chrysler, Germany and Chrysler, UK) adopt divergent pricing policies when exporting to Japan; it would be erroneous in similar cases (and indeed, it would defeat the very purpose of the AD Agreement) to calculate one dumping margin for the two Chrysler companies simply because they belong to the same group even though they

the Panel had held that an IA can legitimately calculate the same margin for a group of companies that together constitute one economic entity, a 'single entity' being the term it had explicitly used; what exactly this term refers to was not made crystal clear in that Report, but in all likelihood a 'control'-type of criterion seemed appropriate. In *EC–Fasteners*, the AB went one step further, and in para. 376 it explained how it understood the term:

> These situations may include: (i) the existence of corporate and structural links between the exporters, such as common control, shareholding and management; (ii) the existence of corporate and structural links between the State and the exporters, such as common control, shareholding and management; and (iii) control or material influence by the State in respect of pricing and output.

And later, when discussing the criteria for state control, it noted (para. 381):

> evidence of State control or instruction of, or material influence on, the behaviour of certain exporters in respect of pricing and output. These criteria could show that in the absence of formal structural links between the State and specific exporters, the State in fact determines and materially influences prices and output.

Now what exactly should we make of all that? The AB, on the one hand, cites *Korea–Certain Paper* but, on the other, provides a 'wide' understanding of the term 'single entity'. One cannot thus exclude that, upon demonstration of 'influence' by the State (which does not have to be equated to control as the term 'or' used in the quoted paragraph unambiguously suggests) or 'behaviour' by companies (a very loose term and hence, in principle, an easy-to-meet evidentiary standard) IAs could well impose countrywide dumping margins against Chinese companies in the future as well. The AB closed the door to the possibility for similar calculations for NMEs but opened a huge window through its understanding of 'single entity'. At this stage, the AB paragraphs quoted above are mere obiter dicta, e.g., they were not decisive for the resolution of the present dispute, and we will thus have to await their first application in a future dispute in order to draw definitive conclusions.

Since these paragraphs were obiter dicta with no operational consequences for the resolution of the dispute, the remaining steps were all downhill for the AB: a violation of Article 6.10 AD leads to a violation of Article 9.2 AD: indeed, how could it be that duties will be collected in appropriate amounts (as Article 9.2 AD requires) if, having determined individual dumping margins, the IA imposes countrywide duties (para. 339)? Arithmetically, a similar endeavor would be correct only in the highly unlikely scenario where all individually calculated dumping margins are identical. This was evidently not the case here.

have adopted divergent pricing policies. The AB did not adequately explain itself on this score. It seems that thus the original sin was committed already in *Korea–Certain Paper*. As we will demonstrate in what follows here, in *EC–Fasteners*, the AB went down the sinful road a couple of miles.

5.5 Is 'Major proportion' a major proportion anymore?

Recall that, because the EU had inappropriately linked the percentage of the major industry in Article 4.1 AD to that in Article 5.4 AD, the AB found that it had violated its WTO obligations in this respect. This much is clear. But the AB did not stop here, although it could have done so. It went on to provide its own understanding of what constitutes 'major industry', and when doing so, the AB stated that this term points to a 'relatively high proportion' (para. 419). The AB, however, did not give a number here. Actually, it went as far as to state that a major proportion could be less than 50% on occasion and as low as 25% in case of fragmented industries (paras. 415ff.).

All this is reason enough to be worried as to the manner in which this term will be applied in the future: how low a percentage is still high enough to meet the threshold of major proportion? We do not know. And what does the invented term 'fragmented industries' amount to? We do not know. Did the AB try to borrow from antitrust theory where, in case of large numbers of firms serving 2–4% of the market, a firm with 25% could be held to be in dominant position? We do not know, but in antitrust analysis barriers to entry in the market will be a key criterion to determine whether dominance exists, and nothing in the AB Report is reminiscent of this type of analysis.

Unfortunately, the AB yet again chose to introduce an open-ended term ('fragmented industries') with no statutory underpinnings, the exact parameters of which will be illuminated only in future practice.

6. Concluding remarks

The WTO adjudicating bodies are agents with no authority to question the legitimacy of the law itself. They cannot, for example, put into question whether the discretion allowed to IAs to choose between a statistically valid sample (which will provide information regarding the pricing behaviour of the average exporting firm), and a number of exporting firms that can be reasonably investigated (which will more likely instead provide information regarding the pricing behaviour of the firm producing the average product) is well founded. As a result, our critique of the Report cannot focus on shortcomings of the law itself.

Like other Reports in the area of contingent protection, this Report evidences the rather 'liberal' attitude of the AB when dealing with these issues. For example, the AB could have stopped when finding that the EU cannot calculate an 'all others rate' to products originating in an NME. There was little need to discuss the possibility to do so if there is a particular relationship between the state and its 'national' companies. And yet it did, as the Panel had done before in *Korea–Certain Paper*. By the same token, it could have stopped its analysis when finding that the threshold established in Article 5.4 AD cannot be used 'lock, stock, and barrel' in the context of analysis under Article 4.1 AD. And yet it did not and moved on to provide its understanding of how this term should be understood using 'plastic' terms that we have no idea how they will be molded in the future. In the past, the AB has evidenced a similar attitude when dealing with challenges in the context of sunset reviews.

Surprisingly, it is the AB, a body often accused for being overtly textualist when interpreting WTO law, that has recourse to similar interpretative attitudes. Furthermore, this type of judicial activism has thus far managed to escape the attention of critics. Nevertheless, its consequences could be spectacular: the AB in future case law could hold that Chinese, Vietnamese, etc. companies have particular links with the state, and, hence, there is no obligation for an IA to calculate individual margins. Instead, IAs could stop at determining national rates; the risk for abuses here should not be underestimated. In this respect, the AB may be overconfident if it believes that it can 'tame' exuberant IAs in the future; for one, the AB is no trier of facts, and the question of links between companies and the state is an eminently factual issue. This point alone should give pause to the AB in this area in future practice.

References

Bernard, A. B., J. B. Jensen, S. J. Redding, and P. K. Schott (2012), 'The Empirics of Firm Heterogeneity and International Trade', *Annual Review of Economics*, **4**: 283–313.

Blonigen, B. A. (2002), 'Tariff-Jumping Antidumping Duties', *Journal of International Economics*, **57**(1): 31–49.

Blonigen, B. A. and Y. Ohno (1998), 'Endogenous Protection, Foreign Direct Investment and Protection-building Trade', *Journal of International Economics*, **46**(2): 205–227.

Bown, C. P. (2012), *Temporary Trade Barriers Database*, World Bank, available at http://econ.worldbank.org/ttbd/ (last visited 19 October 2012).

Czako, J., J. Human, and J. Miranda (2003), *A Handbook on Anti-Dumping Investigations*, Cambridge: Cambridge University Press.

European Union (EU) (2009), 'Council Regulation (EC) No. 91/2009: Imposing a Definitive Anti-Dumping Duty on Imports of Certain Iron or Steel Fasteners Originating in the People's Republic of China', *Official Journal of the European Union*, L 29/1, 31 January.

European Union (EU) (2010), 'Commission Regulation (EU) No. 966/2010', *Official Journal of the European Union*, L 282/29, 27 October.

European Union (EU) (2011), 'Regulations: Council Implementing Regulation (EU) No. 723/2011', *Official Journal of the European Union*, 18 July.

Horn, H., L. Johannesson, and P. C. Mavroidis (2011), 'The WTO Dispute Settlement System 1995–2010: Some Descriptive Statistics', *Journal of World Trade*, **45**(6): 1107–1138.

KAMAX (2012a), 'Company', available at http://www.kamax.com/en/company/, last visited 19 October 2012.

KAMAX (2012b), 'Locations', available at http://www.kamax.com/en/company/locations/, last visited 19 October 2012.

Khandelwal, A. K. (2010), 'The Long and Short (of) Quality Ladders', *Review of Economic Studies*, 77(4): 1450–1476.

Mavroidis, P. C., P. A. Messerlin, and J. M. Wauters (2010), *The Law and Economics of Contingent Protection in the WTO*, Cheltenham, UK: Edward Elgar.

Mavroidis, P. C. and A. Sapir (2008), '*Mexico: Antidumping Measures on Rice*: Don't Ask Me no Questions and I won't Tell No Lies', *World Trade Review*, 7(1): 305–323.

Palmeter, N. D. (1995), 'United States Implementation of the Uruguay Round Antidumping Code', *Journal of World Trade*, **29**(3): 39–82.

Schott, P. K. (2008), 'The Relative Sophistication of Chinese Exports', *Economic Policy*, **53**(1): 5–49.

Stewart, T. P., A. S. Dwyer, D. A. Gantz, and T. J. Prusa (2009), 'Antidumping: Overview of the Agreement', in K. W. Bagwell, G. A. Bermann, and P. C. Mavroidis (eds.), *Law and Economics of Contingent Protection in International Trade*, Cambridge: Cambridge University Press, pp. 197–263.

Zang, M. Q. (2011), '*EC–Fasteners*: Opening Pandora's Box of Non-Market Economy Treatment', *Journal of International Economic Law*, **14**(4): 869–892.

US–Tyres: Upholding a WTO Accession Contract – Imposing Pain for Little Gain

STEVE CHARNOVITZ
George Washington University Law School
BERNARD HOEKMAN
World Bank and CEPR

Abstract: In 2009, the United States imposed additional tariffs for a three-year period on imports of automotive tires from China under a special-safeguard provision included in China's Protocol of Accession to the WTO. China challenged the measure in the WTO. The case marked the first WTO dispute in which a challenged safeguard was upheld by the Appellate Body; the first in which an accession protocol was used successfully as a defense; and the first that China lost as a complaining party. It also was noteworthy in that the safeguard was sought by a labor union, not the domestic industry. This paper reviews the WTO Appellate Body's findings and discusses a number of the legal and policy implications regarding China's Accession Protocol, the Safeguards Agreement, and WTO accession law, as well as economic aspects of the case.

Introduction

In *US–Tyres*, the World Trade Organization (WTO) Appellate Body upheld in full the Panel Report which had affirmed a three-year special-safeguard action that the United States imposed in 2009 on certain tire imports from China. The safeguard was a centerpiece of the Obama Administration's early trade policy[1] and proved controversial due to its unusual initiation and its counterproductive economic effects (Eisenstein, 2010–2011; Ikensen, 2009). The legacy of *US–Tyres* includes several distinctions: It marked the first WTO dispute in which a challenged

This paper was prepared for The American Law Institute project *Legal and Economic Principles of World Trade Law* and reviews the WTO Appellate Body Report *United States – Measures Affecting Imports of Certain Passenger Vehicle and Light Truck Tyres from China*, WT/DS399/AB/R, 5 September 2011, adopted 5 October 2011, in conjunction with the Panel Report. The views expressed are those of the authors only. We thank Simon Schropp for helpful comments on an earlier draft as well as participants at the workshop at the European University Institute for their suggestions.

1 In his State of the Union Address on 24 January 2012, President Obama declared, 'We brought trade cases against China at nearly twice the rate as the last administration – and it's made a difference. Over a thousand Americans are working today because we stopped a surge in Chinese tires' (Obama, 2012).

safeguard was upheld (the only previous General Agreement on Tariffs and Trade (GATT) or WTO ruling upholding a challenged safeguard was in 1951); it is the first dispute in which an accession protocol was used successfully as a defense; and it is the first case that China lost as a complaining party.

The special safeguard was part of the contract that enabled China to join the WTO. The Protocol of Accession negotiated between WTO Members and China provides for a Transitional Product-Specific Safeguard Mechanism (TPSSM). This Mechanism (WTO, 2001: para. 16) specifies that in cases where increased imports from China cause or threaten to cause market disruption for domestic producers of like or directly competitive products, WTO Members may request consultations with China 'with a view to seeking a mutually satisfactory solution, including taking measures under the WTO Agreement on Safeguards' (see Appendix for an excerpt from the TPSSM). If China agrees that its exports are causing such market disruption, it may take remedial action (presumably a voluntary export restraint – see Lee, 2002). If consultations do not resolve the matter within 60 days, the importing country may 'withdraw concessions or otherwise limit imports to the extent necessary to prevent or remedy' such market disruption. For market disruption to exist, imports need to 'be increasing rapidly, either absolutely or relatively, so as to be a significant cause of material injury, or threat of material injury to the domestic industry' based on 'objective factors, including the volume of imports, the effect of imports on prices for like or directly competitive articles, and the effect of such imports on the domestic industry'. Measures may be imposed only for such period of time as needed to prevent or remedy market disruption. Prior to imposing such a measure, the importing Member must collect evidence from interested parties and provide a written notice of the decision, including the reasons for imposing a measure. Under the Protocol, a remedy under the TPSSM can only be imposed during the first 12 years following China's accession, i.e., until mid-December 2013.

The negotiation of a transitional safeguard mechanism as part of China's accession protocol appeared to reflect a desire by WTO members to make it easier to take action against China if imports from China following its accession were to rise too fast.[2] The legal standard for import relief under the Accession Protocol is both less stringent (i.e., easier to satisfy) and less clearly defined than the criteria that must be satisfied in order to comply with the rules of the general WTO safeguard mechanism. Moreover, under the WTO Agreement on Safeguards, all exporters of the product concerned are ostensibly affected because safeguard measures are supposed to be applied on an MFN basis. TPSSMs are similar to antidumping or countervailing-duty actions in that they target specific countries, but are subject to fewer detailed procedural requirements and entail no presumption about 'unfair' behaviour by foreign firms or government.

2 For a good analysis of the history of the TPSSM, see Spadi (2002).

By mid-2010, only two WTO Members besides the United States had imposed a TPSSM safeguard: Turkey and India (Ji and Huang, 2011: 11). Several countries had launched such investigations, but they did not eventuate in a safeguard. Before 2009, the same situation had occurred in the United States. Although six petitions for import relief under the relevant US statute (Section 421 of the Trade Act of 1974, as amended) were filed by US industries between 2001 and 2008, four of which resulted in findings of market disruption and material injury by the investigating authority, i.e., the US International Trade Commission (USITC), President George W. Bush decided in all four cases that imposition of trade barriers was not in the national interest.

This changed in 2009 with the imposition of US tariffs on imports of certain passenger and light truck tires from China (Grimmett, 2011). Not only was this the first instance in which the United States took action under the TPSSM, it was also the first instance of a 'China safeguard' being contested by China in the WTO. It thus raised questions that have not yet been dealt with in WTO dispute settlement including the interpretation of the TPSSM and the relationship between 'special safeguard' measures and the global safeguard mechanism that is provided for under the WTO Agreement.

US–Tyres is also of interest because it illustrates the tension between the national 'producer-centric' nature of WTO rules and obligations and the ongoing process of globalization – the geographic fragmentation and 'vertical specialization' of production. The latter reduces the net benefits of trade-policy instruments to multinational companies, which have incentives to undertake production activities in low(er)-cost countries. This process of specialization has implications for workers who are negatively affected by decisions to move production to other countries. A basic policy question raised by the case is whether and how trade policy should be used to address the adjustment costs associated with globalization.

The paper proceeds in five sections: Section 1 introduces the dispute and provides the economic backdrop. Section 2 provides a summary of the four legal decisions in the dispute, the USITC, the WTO Panel, the Appellate Body, and the WTO Dispute Settlement Body (DSB). Section 3 discusses the implications of the *Tyres* decision for WTO jurisprudence. Section 4 offers some economic and policy-related observations. Section 5 concludes.

1. Economic background of the case

The *Tyres* case was brought by the United Steel, Paper and Forestry, Rubber, Manufacturing, Energy, Allied Industrial and Service Workers International Union (USW). The USW argued that imports of Chinese tires – worth some $2 billion in 2008 (about 25% of total imports) – had caused market disruption and materially injured the domestic industry. Upon investigation, the USITC agreed with the USW and recommended the imposition of additional tariffs for a three-year period (at a rate of 55% for the first year, 45% for the second, and 35% in the third). The USITC also suggested that the President 'take such action as is within his authority to direct the US Department of Commerce and the US Department of Labor to expedite the consideration of petitions for trade adjustment assistance filed by domestic firms or workers producing tires' (USITC, 2009: 30).[3] The President authorized the imposition of tariffs, although at lower rates than recommended (35%, 30%, and 25% for years 1, 2, and 3, respectively). These tariffs expired near the end of September 2012.

This case was unusual in being brought by a union (representing workers) rather than by the domestic industry (firms). Indeed, it was even more unusual in that the US industry did not support the case and in some instances opposed the imposition of trade measures. The USW argued that the major increase in imports of tires from China between 2004 and 2008 had contributed to the loss of 4,000 US tire-related jobs and that announced plant closings implied another 3,000 jobs would be lost in 2009 (USITC, 2009: 14). The quantity of imports from China more than tripled during the 2004–2008 period, rising from 14.6 million tires in 2004 to 46.0 million tires in 2008. Imports from other sources fell from 98 to 93 million units during this period. US production of tires fell from 218 to 160 million units between 2004 and 2008. Thus, the ratio of Chinese imports to domestic production rose from 6.7% to 28.7% of US output; imports from other sources grew from 45% to 58%.

While not denying these trends in domestic employment and production, and in imports, the tire industry argued that the tires produced in China were low-cost, relatively low-quality products that could not be economically produced in the US. These so-called 'tier-3' tires constituted only a small share of total output of domestically produced tires. Most production of tires in the US centers on higher-quality branded products (tier 1 and tier 2), which were much less affected by import competition from China or other countries. According to the USITC (2009), only 18.6% of US production involved tier-3 tires. Given the quality differentiation/market segmentation of passenger and light-truck tires, the industry argued that higher trade barriers would raise the prices of the affected low-cost tires without doing much if anything to increase US employment as the relevant production had largely disappeared (Tire Industry Association, 2009).[4] China

3 Trade Adjustment Assistance is available to workers negatively affected by import competition as well as those who have been affected by outsourcing. As discussed below, the latter situation is more relevant to the case at hand. Along with agreeing to a safeguard, President Obama called for an expedited petitioning process.

4 In a 2009 press release, the Association stated its belief that the action was 'a politically motivated decision that will end up costing more jobs than it saves. These tariffs will not bring back the jobs that the union claims have been lost; it will not create any new tire manufacturing jobs, and it will most likely result in the loss of thousands of retail tire industry jobs in the U.S., affecting everyone from the shop that services your tire to the tire wholesalers – many of whom are small businesspeople struggling to stay afloat in this economy ... The tire manufacturers made the decision years ago to shift production of lower-cost tires out of the U.S. All this action will do is force the tire manufacturers to shift production of these lower-cost tires to other countries, such as Brazil and India. The bottom line is that despite what the union and the President believes, these jobs are not coming back ... This tariff will price tires out of reach of many consumers, and will lead to a tightening in the remaining supply of lower-cost tires. Also, given that the lower-cost tires

Table 1. US tire imports (value, 2007–2011, US$ million and percent)

Country	2008	2009	2010	2011	2008–09	2009–10	2010–11	2008–11
Canada	1,444	1,483	1,783	1,942	2.7%	20.2%	8.9%	34.5%
China	1,970	1,742	1,525	1,801	−11.6%	−12.4%	18.0%	−8.6%
Japan	1,160	1,078	1,495	1,469	−7.2%	38.7%	−1.8%	26.5%
Korea	786	639	1,171	1,453	−18.6%	83.1%	24.1%	85.0%
Thailand	332	296	536	803	−10.8%	80.8%	49.8%	141.7%
Mexico	298	275	390	569	−7.9%	41.9%	45.9%	90.8%
Indonesia	175	186	330	455	6.5%	77.3%	37.7%	160.2%
Germany	243	180	229	350	−26.0%	27.4%	52.8%	44.1%
Brazil	298	249	331	340	−16.5%	33.0%	2.8%	14.2%
Taiwan	128	80	188	217	−37.4%	134.0%	15.4%	69.1%
World	7,934	6,890	8,865	10,657	−13.2%	28.7%	20.2%	34.3%

Source: USITC website.

argued these points in the WTO dispute, asserting that the US industry had voluntarily engaged in outsourcing of low-end tires and that 'the reduction in domestic manufacturing of tires and the increase in imports from China were the consequences of deliberate economic decision-making by the US tyre industry' (WTO, 2010: para 7.9).

The US tire industry has experienced major restructuring and change in the last 30 years. It dominated the world market in the early 1970s, accounting for some 60% of global production. Four of the top five producers were US companies (Rajan *et al.*, 1997). By 1991, the US share of global output had fallen to 17% and has remained near that level since; in 2010 it was about 15%. There is only one large US-owned producer in the industry (Goodyear), and only one relatively small company (Cooper) that focuses primarily on tier-3 tires. The lion's share of the global market is taken by foreign-owned firms, with Michelin and Bridgestone accounting for about 35% of the total (Bank of America/Merrill Lynch, 2010). Seven of the ten firms that produce tires in the United States had affiliates or joint ventures in China in 2008 (Bridgestone, Cooper, Goodyear, Michelin, Pirelli, Toyo, and Yokohama) (USITC, 2009: 49).

Although China's exports of tires to the United States grew rapidly in the 2000s, imports from other sources dominate – accounting for some 75% of all imports in 2008 (Table 1). A key feature of the case was that imports from China were concentrated in a specific segment of the market – the unbranded, low-end. This presumably was a major factor motivating the launch by the USW of a Section 421

imported from China help those most vulnerable in this current economy – working-class citizens – we are deeply concerned that many consumers may delay or even defer replacing their tires when necessary, thus creating a potential safety hazard on America's roads.' See Tire Industry Association (2009). A number of these arguments appear to be based on Prusa (2009).

safeguard petition which by definition involves a sole focus on China, ignoring other sources of import competition. However, as pointed out by Prusa (2009) and the industry representatives during the USITC investigation, the effectiveness of a safeguard in preserving US production is degraded by the ease with which other foreign suppliers can enter the market at prices close to those charged by Chinese firms. The evidence suggests that such substitution has occurred and that other suppliers have offset the decline in Chinese exports that was induced by the imposition of tariffs.

2. Summary of the national and international safeguard rulings

2.1 USITC decision

The competent US domestic authority (i.e., the USITC) split on whether the special safeguard was warranted. All commissioners agreed that subject imports from China were 'increasing rapidly' and that these imports were causing 'material injury' to the domestic competing industry. In doing so, the Commission noted that 'material injury' was a lesser degree of injury than 'serious injury' which is the requirement for a normal safeguard (i.e., Section 201). But there was divergence on the issue of causation. The four-commissioner majority found that imports were a 'significant cause' of material injury, and noted that Section 421 (unlike Section 201) did not require a weighing of causes. The dissenters disagreed that there was sufficient causal nexus between the imports and the injury. Rather, the two dissenters explained that the decline in domestic production was the result of the economic recession and a strategic decision by US producers to shift certain production to China as well as other countries. The dissent also noted that some parts of the domestic industry did not support the petition for relief. As is its usual practice, the Commission focused only on Section 421, not the international-law requirement, in this case the Accession Protocol.

In calling for a three-year safeguard, the USITC predicted that it 'would significantly improve the competitive position of the domestic industry' and that non-Chinese imports 'will capture a minority of the reduction in subject imports' (USITC, 2009: 35–37). The USITC also estimated that the safeguard would add 'nearly 1,200 jobs on a full time basis' and that the effect on US welfare would range from a $71 million loss to a $73.3 million gain (USITC, 2009: 37–38).

2.2 Panel decision

Like Section 201 of the Trade Act of 1974 (global safeguards), Section 421 does not provide for judicial review in the United States. Thus, the only way to appeal a safeguard action is by bringing a case to the WTO. The Panel unanimously upheld the US safeguard, which was challenged by China as a violation of Paragraph 16 of the China Protocol. When it needed to apply the various vague terms in the TPSSM, the Panel drew heavily on past WTO safeguard jurisprudence and other case law to fill in gaps in the interpretation of the provisions of the TPSSM. Nevertheless, the Panel avoided importing it all and, in contrast to previous global safeguard disputes, did not go out of its way to find a violation.

Drawing from WTO jurisprudence, the Panel explained that its standard of review was to make an 'objective assessment' of the matter before it and to consider whether the USITC evaluated the 'objective factors' in Paragraph 16 and whether the Commission provided a 'reasoned and adequate explanation of its determination' (WTO, 2010: paras. 7.11, 7.15). Using dictionaries to parse the meanings of the key terms in Paragraph 16, the Panel concluded that USITC did not fail to evaluate properly whether imports from China were increasing rapidly. On causation, the Panel found that Section 421 did not violate the Protocol, as such, nor did it violate it as applied. Drawing from dictionaries, the Panel concluded that a 'significant' cause required more than a mere contribution, but did not require a cause more significant than other causative factors (WTO, 2010: para. 7.158). After reviewing the record, the Panel found that the evidence was sufficient to support the Commission's affirmative finding of causation.

Borrowing from WTO case law on subsidies, the Panel imputed a nonattribution test to the definition of causation (though not a full-blown analysis),[5] but disagreed with China that the USITC had attributed to imports the injury caused by other factors. Although the Panel found fault with the Commission's assessment of one plant closing (WTO, 2010: para. 7.299), the Panel stated that there was not convincing evidence that US producers 'voluntarily' closed US production capacity independent of competition from China, and therefore the Panel upheld the Commission. While noting that the dissenting Commissioners concluded that the outsourcing of production was independent of imports, the Panel held that 'it would be inappropriate for the Panel simply to make a choice between the views of the majority and the dissenting commissioners' (WTO, 2010: para. 7.321). Another 'other' factor considered by the Panel was non-Chinese imports which were over two-thirds of total imports during the entire period of investigation. Nevertheless, the Panel found that 'the dominant feature of the US market was the rise of subject imports from China at the expense of both nonsubject imports and the US industry' (WTO, 2010: para. 7.367).

China also challenged the US safeguard as a violation of GATT Articles I:1 and II:1.[6] The GATT Article I claim was warranted because the US safeguard imposed additional duties solely on tires from China. The Panel's resolution of this claim is deeply mysterious:

> 7.418. China's GATT 1994 claims are entirely dependent on its claims under Paragraph 16 of the Protocol.[557] Since we have not accepted China's claims under

5 WTO (2010, para. 7.394).

6 Notably, China did not lodge a GATT Article XIX claim or argue that its 'unforeseen developments' requirement was incorporated into the Protocol.

> Paragraph 16 of the Protocol, we similarly do not accept China's claims under Article I:1 and II:1 of the GATT 1994.
>
> [557] The dependent nature of China's GATT 1994 claims is shown by China's argument that there is 'also' a GATT 1994 violation because of the additional duties 'not having been justified as emergency action under relevant WTO rules' (*See* China's First Written Submission, paras. 417 and 421).

What does the Panel mean? The parallelism between not accepting China's Protocol claims and its GATT claims suggests that the Panel resolved them both in the same way; namely, by ruling against them. Although the GATT claim was not appealed, support for this explanation can be found in the Appellate Body Report, which stated that the Panel 'rejected consequential claims by China that the United States acted inconsistently' with GATT Articles I and II (WTO, 2011a: para. 6). Moreover, in its Report, the Panel concluded that 'the United States did not fail to comply with its obligations under Paragraph 16 of the Protocol and Articles I:1 and II:1 of the GATT 1994' (WTO, 2010: para. 8.1). So there is considerable support for the thesis that the Panel ruled that the US safeguard was not a violation of GATT Articles I and II. On the other hand, since the US safeguard was not carried out in accordance with the MFN principle, a finding that there was no Article I violation was hardly obvious, and yet here the Panel offered no explanation for why there was no violation.

The rather contorted explanation of the Panel quoted above might be read to suggest that China had predicated its GATT claims on being vindicated on its Protocol claims. Such a condition precedent would be an odd posture for a WTO complainant who would typically want to win the second claim even if it did not win the first claim. Yet perhaps that was China's intention, to claim a GATT violation only if the United States could not raise the Protocol as a defense. But if that were the case, the right outcome would have been to refrain from issuing a ruling on the GATT claim rather than to rule against it.

Unfortunately, there is no way to know exactly what China's GATT claim was. The Panel asserts that the claim was 'dependent' but offers no evidence other than directing the reader to 'see' China's First Written Submission, which the Panel fails to append to its Report. This Submission is not posted on the WTO website, and the WTO Secretariat has confirmed that it is being kept confidential. Based on the Panel's brief characterization of China's claim, it seems that China argued that there was a violation of GATT Articles I and II because the safeguard could not be justified as an emergency measure under GATT Article XIX.[7] If that is what China meant, then it was wrong for the Panel to mischaracterize the GATT claim as being dependent on the Protocol claim. All in all, it is hard to escape the conclusion that the Panel was intentionally nontransparent in addressing the Article I claim.

7 China's Request for Consultations, WT/DS399/1, 16 September 2009, appears quite clear that China was asserting the GATT claims separately from its claims under the Accession Protocol.

2.3 *Appellate body decision*

China appealed the Panel's holding on the issues of increased imports, causation, and on whether the Panel made an objective assessment of the facts. Surprisingly, China did not appeal the Panel's puzzling holding on GATT Article I. Although critical of the Panel on a few specific points,[8] the Appellate Body upheld the Panel's ruling in its entirety on the interpretation and application of the TPSSM. After using a dictionary to parse the meaning of imports 'increasing rapidly', the Appellate Body upheld the Panel on its application of the increasing imports criterion. On the causation test, the Appellate Body parsed the term 'significant cause' in China Protocol Paragraph 16.4 and held that this 'significant cause' requirement is not a more rigorous standard than found in other WTO agreements which require that imports 'cause' injury. Instead, the Appellate Body postulated that the 'object and purpose of the Protocol' leads to an interpretation wherein temporary relief will be available whenever rapidly increasing imports are making an important contribution to material injury of the domestic industry (WTO, 2011a: paras. 181, 184). On the application of the TPSSM causation standard, the Appellate Body found that the TPSSM 'gives investigating authorities a certain degree of discretion in selecting the methodology to assess the existence of a causal link' (WTO, 2011a: para. 190), and therefore the Appellate Body did not agree with China that the TPSSM required the USITC to find a correlation between the year-by-year changes in imports and injury factors. China also appealed on the grounds that competition between its tires and US domestic production was 'highly attenuated' with US production being concentrated in tier-1 tires and China's exports in tiers 2 and 3. In response, the Appellate Body noted that the USITC properly established the presence of both domestic and Chinese tires in tiers 2 and 3 and significant competition between them.

The Appellate Body also agreed with the Panel that the need for nonattribution analysis was 'inherent' in the TPSSM (WTO, 2011a: para. 252). The Appellate Body examined each of the other causes put forward by China, and concluded that none of them negated the Panel's finding that imports were an important cause of injury. Regarding the domestic industry's business strategy, China objected to the Panel's upholding of the USITC conclusion that the closing of the Bridgestone tire plant could be attributed to subject imports. In response, the Appellate Body refused to consider this appeal on the grounds that it was improperly pleaded (WTO, 2011a: para. 273). It is interesting to note that the debate about Bridgestone at the USITC and the WTO was not based on the evaluation of market data but rather on the interpretation of a press release and news article at the time of the plant closing. China also objected to the Panel's refusal to choose between the conclusion of the Commission's majority and dissent regarding the so-called

8 WTO (2011a: paras. 211, 219, 223, 257, 297).

independent business strategy. Here the Appellate Body agreed with the Panel that it was not its role to decide whether the majority or the dissent was actually correct.

China also appealed on the grounds that the Panel sought to buttress the evidence for causation by relying on information not in the USITC determination. The Appellate Body explained that a Panel is not precluded from relying upon evidence in the USITC staff report even though such evidence was not marshaled by the investigating authority in its decision. In addition, the Appellate Body rejected this appeal by China due to a pleading error (WTO, 2011a: paras. 330–331).

2.4 *DSB adoption*

One month after the Appellate Body handed down its Report (which came 99 days after the appeal), the DSB adopted the *US–Tyres* Panel and Appellate Body Reports. China complained that the Appellate Body had rendered the term 'significant' futile (probably meaning inutile) and that by upholding the safeguard, the WTO would be sending the 'wrong signal' about 'protectionist measures' (WTO, 2011b, para. 9). Several other WTO Member governments also spoke out, but mainly to express concern that the Appellate Body had missed the 60- and 90-day deadlines in the WTO Dispute Settlement Understanding (DSU) without sufficient consultation of the parties.

3. Implications of the decision for WTO case law

The *US–Tyres* case demonstrates the use of an accession agreement to justify a protectionist measure that would not have been possible under multilateral WTO law. Although enabling protectionism is not the central purpose of WTO law, protection is certainly one purpose, and in this episode the WTO performed as the WTO community expected that it would. Had WTO judges ruled against the safeguard, such an outcome would have been unexpected (given the facts supporting the USITC ruling), and would have led to criticism of the WTO and perhaps made it more difficult to consummate ongoing accession agreements, such as the negotiations with Russia.

What follows examines the implications of the case for the China Protocol, for WTO Safeguards law, and for WTO Accession law.

3.1 *Interpretation of the TPSSM*

The most positive thing one can say about the Appellate Body decision is that it upheld the contract wherein China paid a higher price than any other country to join the WTO. The price China paid was to agree to a myriad of unique rules that only apply to the China WTO membership. *US–Tyres* will be the leading precedent if there are any future TPSSM cases, but because this special safeguard expires before the end of 2013, it is possible that no additional disputes will arise.

WTO accession agreements are a unique feature of international law because they can require the applicant government to agree to applicant WTO-Plus obligations, whereby the applicant signs on to higher obligations than incumbents, and to incumbent WTO-Minus provisions, whereby the applicant agrees that incumbents will have a diminished level of obligations toward them (see Charnovitz, 2008: 871). The TPSSM is an example of an incumbent WTO-Minus provision that allows the United States to impose a safeguard against China without complying with the usual rules in the WTO Agreement on Safeguards. Note also that the TPSSM is not reciprocal; China cannot impose such measures on the United States.

The TPSSM provided tangible benefits to the United States because, without it, a safeguard might not have been possible. As the USITC noted, lower-price imports from countries other than China were 100–200% higher than those from China (USITC, 2009: I-20), and yet no global safeguard by the United States was attempted. Had the USW filed a petition for a global safeguard under Section 201, it might have been turned down because the petitioner would have had difficulty showing sharply increased imports,[9] serious rather than material injury, and causation under the higher 'substantial cause' standard. As the Appellate Body explained, 'serious injury' is a 'much higher standard' (WTO, 2011a: para. 183).

The question of whether the Protocol was meant to make it easier or harder for WTO Members to impose a temporary safeguard on China should have been answerable by recourse to the fairly recent negotiating history. Oddly, neither party sought to introduce such history. Rather, the Panel decided the key issues through recourse to seven different dictionaries. In doing so, the Panel made no effort to explain how it chose which dictionary it would rely upon for each interpretive exercise.

In our view, China was justified in criticizing the Appellate Body at the DSB meeting.[10] While agreeing that the cause had to demonstrate an 'important contribution' (WTO, 2011a: paras. 185, 195), the Appellate Body explained that merely being one of several contributing causes was sufficient to meet the TPSSM's causation test (WTO, 2011a: para. 318). The Appellate Body justified this position by holding that because Paragraph 16.1 of the Protocol did not use the term 'significant', it would interpret Paragraph 16.4 'harmoniously' to infer less meaning to the term 'significant' in Paragraph 16.4 (WTO, 2011a: para. 182). This was an error by the Appellate Body. Paragraph 16.1 of the Protocol refers to consultations, rather than to the right of action. Paragraph 16.4 of the Protocol clearly requires a 'significant cause' standard, and it was inappropriate for the Appellate Body to characterize Paragraph 16.1 as diluting Paragraph 16.4.

The data show that the China safeguard may have succeeded in lowering tire imports from China to the United States from 45.6 million in 2009 to 29.7 million

9 The Appellate Body has suggested that the increase in imports has to be recent, sudden, and sharp, and in the *Tyres* case total imports rose from 113 million in 2004 to 140 million in 2007 and 139 million in 2008.

10 In addition, the Appellate Body was wrong in arguing that the lower standard for injury in the Protocol was probative in imbuing meaning to the term 'significant cause'. See WTO (2011: paras. 182–184).

in 2011. Yet over the same period, total US tire imports rose from 125 million in 2009 to 150 million in 2011. Such an outcome is not surprising as a partial (country-specific) safeguard is likely to be ineffective in (temporarily) lowering overall imports if there are many competing suppliers. If so, a partial safeguard, such as the TPSSM, is simply an opportunity to discriminate against one country of origin while allowing competing countries to fill the supply gap.

That is what happened in this dispute. As China explained to the DSB:

> It was puzzling that the United States expected to rescue its tyre industry out of the economic crisis by imposing punitive duties on China's tyres through the product-specific safeguard measures. Predictably, the measures did not work. They injured China's legitimate trading interests, but did not help reduce the US imports of tyres ... The US measures merely distorted international trade. (WTO, 2011b: para. 8)

Such distortion of international trade is a byproduct of the one-way discrimination allowed in the TPSSM. China is made to bear the full costs of the protection erected by the United States.[11] The costs to China will far exceed the benefits accruing to the US producers because other foreign suppliers to US markets filled in the gap. As discussed below, the safeguard did lead to trade deflection and a shuffling of import market shares without materially affecting domestic employment in tire production in the United States. The import market outcome from the safeguard turned out to be exactly the opposite of what the USITC predicted.

Of course, China's observation raises the question of what the Obama Administration's intention was in imposing the safeguard. Even if it did not substantially increase domestic production in the US tire industry, the safeguard may have succeeded in the political purpose of gratifying the rubber-workers union (Will, 2009) and/or of appearing to be punishing China without generating significant costs to US households (insofar as replacing China with other sources of low-cost tires meant that a selective safeguard would only have a moderate effect on retail prices). In the last several weeks of the US Presidential campaign, the China tires case became another bone of contention between the two candidates (Hohmann, 2012).

3.2 *WTO Law of Safeguards*

To date, the WTO case law has not been kind to countries using global safeguards; every case that has been contested has been lost by the safeguard-invoking country.[12] In part, this is because key terms such as 'unforeseen developments',

11 If China were able to find third-country markets for those tires, then it could reduce some of those costs. Nevertheless, such exports to third countries could further distort international trade.

12 Of course, most safeguards are not contested in the WTO. A snapshot of WTO data shows 33 global safeguards in effect on 26 October 2011 of which only one has been contested so far. See G/L/972, 1 November 2011.

'serious injury', 'increased quantities', and 'cause' are not defined in the Safeguards Agreement. Without clarity regarding the baseline to be applied to imports, how to assess the link between imports and injury, and what constitutes an 'unforeseeable' event that generates an import surge, governments confront great uncertainty on whether the approaches they follow in determining whether to impose safeguards will pass muster by a WTO Panel and the Appellate Body.

Sykes (2003, 2004) and Grossman and Sykes (2007) have argued that the Appellate Body has made it very difficult for countries to apply safeguards by utilizing the language in Article XIX GATT in reviewing challenged safeguards without clarifying the meaning of the key terms. Particularly problematic has been the insistence on applying the 'unforeseen developments' test to safeguard actions. In practice, this test had ceased to be applied or considered relevant by GATT contracting parties, and for that reason presumably was not included in the Agreement on Safeguards. The re-introduction of this test by the Appellate Body appeared to reverse the intent of those who had negotiated the Safeguards Agreement. Overall, 'Appellate Body decisions since the inception of the WTO have only made matters worse, to the point that the legal requirements for the use of safeguards are largely incoherent, and no nation can employ them without the near certainty of defeat in the dispute resolution process should they be challenged' (Grossman and Sykes, 2007: 91). Sykes (2003) concludes that the incoherence can only be resolved through a re-negotiation of the agreement or through action by the Appellate Body to define key terms.

In negotiating China's Protocol of Accession, WTO Members were apparently unwilling to rely on the global safeguards available under the Agreement on Safeguards. This unwillingness must have reflected a view that the available global safeguards were inadequate. So the TPSSM can be understood as a temporary patch for the WTO's dysfunctional safeguard program. As noted above, the patch dissolves after 2013 when safeguards against China must conform to regular WTO law.

The inadequacy of the WTO global safeguard arose from two problems in WTO dispute settlement. One was that the Appellate Body inserted a requirement to demonstrate 'unforeseen developments' that had not been included in Article 2.1 of the Safeguards Agreement. The other was that WTO adjudicators gave limited deference to the safeguard decisions of domestic authorities.[13]

Neither of these problems occurred in the *US–Tyres* case. As discussed above, the Panel did not require the USITC to demonstrate unforeseen developments, and the

13 For example, see Panel Report, *Dominican Republic – Safeguard Measures on Imports of Polypropylene Bags and Tubular Fabric*, WT/DS415, 416, 417, 418/R, adopted 22 February 2012, paras. 7.314–7.315; Appellate Body Report, *Argentina – Safeguard Measures on Imports of Footwear*, WT/DS121/AB/R, adopted 12 January 2000, paras. 129–131; Appellate Body Report, *United States – Definitive Safeguard Measures on Imports of Circular Welded Carbon Quality Line Pipe from Korea*, WT/DS202/AB/R, adopted 8 March 2002, paras. 218–222.

Panel was very deferential to the USITC on both facts and the application of Accession law. For example, the Panel properly ruled that it was not its role to decide whether the USITC majority or minority were correct. It is probably a vain hope that a deferential stance will be channeled back into regular safeguard cases. In the only safeguard dispute since *Tyres, Dominican Republic–Bags*, the Panel did cite the *US–Tyres* case, but did not show any of the deference of the *Tyres* Panel.

3.3 WTO Law of Accession

An accession protocol is formally an agreement between the WTO and the applicant country, and such protocols are not listed among the covered agreements subject to adjudication under the DSU.[14] So far, no theory of enforceability of accession agreements has emerged in WTO dispute settlement. The Panels and Appellate Body have enforced the agreements in all of the accession cases, but have not explained why, and parties have not questioned such enforceability. In *US–Tyres*, China did not challenge enforceability. The Appellate Body pointed out that the Protocol itself provides that it 'shall be an integral part' of the WTO Agreement (WTO, 2011a: para. 118), but that does not help in explaining enforceability because one would presume that international agreements cannot contract themselves into the WTO merely by self-certifying that they are integral parts of the WTO Agreement. The WTO has provisions for amendments in Article X, but those provisions were not used for the China accession. It may be that an accession agreement has the capacity to implicitly amend the WTO (see Charnovitz, 2008: 893), but even this solution is problematic because there is no obvious constitutional limiting principle for what can be put into the WTO through an accession agreement.

In contrast to the two previous WTO accession cases, the *Tyres* panel and Appellate Body did not tiptoe around some of the knotty doctrinal issues of the law of accession. Indeed, the Panel held that the China Protocol was a 'covered agreement' and the Appellate Body held that it was a 'WTO agreement'.[15] The Panel showed no hesitation in considering the Protocol as a 'covered agreement' for the purpose of using as the interpretive framework the Vienna Convention on the Law of Treaties (WTO, 2010: paras. 7.23, 7.32, 7.149) even though the Vienna Convention does not apply to treaties between states and international organizations.

Besides enforceability, the other key doctrinal challenge in accession is how the rules of the accession agreement relate to the multilateral rules in WTO agreements (Charnovitz, 2008: 905–911). For example, does GATT Article I trump an accession agreement or does the accession agreement trump GATT Article I?

14 See WTO Agreement, Art. XII:1 and DSU Appendix 1.

15 WTO (2010, paras. 7.15, 7.24). WTO (2011, paras. 120, 121, 181, 201). It is interesting to note that the WTO Secretariat now includes accession agreements as 'agreements' in the list of WTO covered agreements. See http://www.wto.org/english/tratop_e/dispu_e/find_dispu_cases_e.htm#results (last visited 1 November 2012).

The relationship of accession law to general WTO law had arisen in the two previous accession cases, but only through the interpretation of terms in the accession agreement. In the *Tyres* case, by contrast, the Panel ruled that the US safeguard did not violate GATT Article I without relying on specific language in the accession agreement. Yet it is hard to know what to make of this precedent because the Panel, unaccountably, did not offer any transparent reasoning to justify its decision.

Although the TPSSM is ostensibly separate from the WTO Agreement,[16] both the Panel and the Appellate Body borrowed copiously from WTO jurisprudence to interpret the TPSSM. Such borrowing occurred in the two previous accession cases and showed a volition by Panels to interpret accession rules in an integrative fashion with general WTO law. Indeed, the Panel cited 23 WTO cases, only five of which were safeguard cases and none of which was previous accession cases. The Appellate Body was even more mimetic in citing 22 additional WTO cases. That WTO adjudicators interpreting the TPSSM would draw upon existing trade-remedy case law was predicted well in advance by thoughtful trade-law analysts (see Andersen and Lau, 2002).

4. Economic observations

4.1 *Material injury*

The TPSSM uses the terms 'domestic producers' and 'domestic industry' but does not define them. Yet the focus of the USITC determination whether the tire industry was materially injured was on productive activity in the United States. It is not clear to us that this is the proper interpretation. Whether there was material injury of the domestic US industry was contested by respondents before the USITC but not by China at the WTO.

The US tire industry is a global industry, dominated by large multinationals. These firms make production-location decisions on the basis of expected demand in the major markets they serve, and balance off differences in production costs across locations against the trade and other transactions costs that are associated with serving a market through exports. While employment, capacity, and output in the United States may fall, the financial returns of the major tire companies were healthy until the global recession struck. Weak economic activity in one market – the United States – need not signal the industry is 'injured'.

4.2 *Causation and definition of like products (relevant market)*

In bringing the case, the USW argued that the decline in US production of tires was due to import competition. US tire producers argued that the decline reflected a decision to exit the tier-3 segment as other varieties and products were more

16 Note, however, that the TPSSM provides for notifications to be given to the WTO Committee on Safeguards.

profitable, and that this was a major reason why imports were not a cause of material injury. Instead, the observed injury reflected the business cycle and other demand factors.

It is difficult empirically to separate these two claims, as deliberately exiting a segment for which there is demand will by definition result in increased imports. One can get a sense of the relationship by determining if Chinese imports began to rise (faster) after US plants producing tier-3 tires were closed. This was not done in the investigation – indeed there is little explicit focus on what the plants that were shut down in the 2004–2008 period were producing, and where and in what type of production tire producers were investing inside and outside the United States.

Two USITC commissioners had a dissenting view on whether imports from China met the required injury–causation standard. This became a key argument for China in the dispute – the question being how imports from China could be a significant cause of material injury when 80% of US production in 2008 was of tier-1 and tier-2 tires, while most Chinese imports were in tier 3. China also raised this question on appeal. The dissenting Commissioners found that imports were not a significant cause of material injury, but rather that the US industry had consciously and deliberately been pursuing a gradual exit from producing low-margin tires.

No effort was made in the USITC report to assess quantitatively the degree of substitutability of Chinese for US tires in general – beyond a qualitative questionnaire – and not at all for substitution across tiers. The Panel and the Appellate Body simply noted their agreement with the USITC in concluding that tires are technically good substitutes – any tire of the right size for any given rim will 'work' and all tires must satisfy specific safety standards, so in that sense 'a tire is a tire is a tire', whether it is tier 1, 2, or 3.

This is questionable from an economic perspective. Tires are differentiated products that vary in quality, with significant investments made by producers in brands and marketing that presumably have a positive rate of return. To argue that such differentiation is not relevant from the perspective of assessing whether imports have a negative effect seems inappropriate.

The question then is whether a more narrow definition of the relevant market would have made a difference. China exports primarily one variety of tires – namely, unbranded, low-end products. If one takes the view that the investigation should have been limited to this segment of the market, it would have been much more likely that the 'correctly defined' domestic industry that produces such tires would have been found to be materially injured, addressing the concerns expressed by the dissenting Commissioners.[17] Conversely, if one sticks with a focus on the tire

17 In the USITC questionnaire, 7 out of 10 US producers stated they had not suffered negative effects from Chinese imports; one indicated its credit rating and capital investment had declined; and only two noted reductions in production. As no information is provided that allows the firms to be identified, it is not

industry as a whole but takes a narrow view of defining like products, it would clearly be much harder to claim that the material injury that is observed across the broader industry (i.e., all three tiers) is due to imports from China. All we would point out here is that the analysis offered by the USITC is not very rigorous, making no effort for example to estimate the relevant substitution elasticities. Conversely, the Panel and Appellate Body make much of the fact that the respondents in the USITC case could not agree on what differentiated tier 3 from tiers 1 and 2.

4.3 *Trade deflection*

According to USITC data, the value of total imports of tires in 2008 was $7.9 billion, of which China accounted for $2 billion (see Table 1). In 2009, as a result of the recession caused by the financial crisis, total imports fell to $6.9 billion (−13%), with Chinese exports dropping by a similar proportion (11.6%). In 2010, the first full year of the special safeguard, the value of imports from China fell by another 12.4%, as compared to growth in the overall value of tire imports, which expanded by almost 29% to $8.9 billion. Virtually all sources of import supply saw growth. Canada became the biggest foreign supplier of tires by value in 2010 ($1.8 billion) as a result of a 20% rise in export value between 2009 and 2010. Countries that saw the largest growth in percentage terms included Japan (40%), Korea (83%), Thailand (81%), Mexico (42%), Indonesia (77%), and Taiwan (134%). Canada and Japan, the number 1 and 3 import sources by trade value, tend to produce high-quality, branded, tier-1 tires. Thus, it appears that the decline in Chinese exports was offset by imports from other countries in East Asia.[18]

A similar pattern is observed if one focuses on developments in the value and destination of China's tire exports. The value of China's reported exports to the United States fell by 8% in 2009 and by another 19% in 2010, and the Chinese share of the US market fell from 39% in 2009 to 19% in 2011. But China's exports to 'the rest of the world' increased 74% between 2009 and 2011, rising from $3.2 billion to $5.6 billion.[19]

The total value of US imports of tires increased 54% between 2009 and 2011 (Table 1). Thus, the safeguard had a large effect on Chinese exports to the United States, but much of the affected tires appear to have been redirected to other markets, with other exporters taking up the slack – i.e., the main effect was to 'shuffle' sources of supply and export market destinations. Such shuffling can also be inferred from developments in the volume of imports from different sources.

possible to determine what share of the industry the adversely affected firms have. But the response by the 'most vocal' respondent (longest reply) to the question of anticipated effects indicates that firm is small.

18 See Lee (2011) for an empirical analysis. Korea and Thailand rank 8th and 9th in global exports of rubber/plastic products; Taiwan ranks 14th. In Thailand and Indonesia, exports are mostly driven by foreign direct investment.

19 These numbers were obtained from United Nations Commodity Trade, accessed through World Integrated Trade Solution.

Table 2. US tire imports (quantities, 2007–2011)

	In 1,000 units of quantity				
Country	2007	2008	2009	2010	2011
China	46,876	49,761	45,570	34,582	29,650
Canada	22,622	20,562	18,842	22,396	22,671
Korea	15,122	14,576	11,961	21,386	22,226
Japan	19,126	17,397	14,036	19,314	16,593
Thailand	3,637	4,927	4,781	8,512	10,805
Indonesia	5,976	5,959	5,392	9,333	10,267
Mexico	4,892	5,350	5,058	7,435	9,827
Taiwan	4,464	3,539	2,277	5,211	5,158
Brazil	6,105	5,850	4,830	5,738	4,551
Germany	4,335	3,253	2,192	2,620	3,553
Total	152,990	148,461	124,978	149,597	150,256

Source: USITC website.

While China remains the largest foreign supplier of tires to the United States, reflecting the low unit values of the tires that are exported to the United States (Table 2), other countries saw a significant increase in shipments to the United States after the safeguard. The countries that appeared to be competing most directly with China on price were Indonesia and Taiwan. Both had average unit values of around $35 in 2009 and 2010. Together these two countries exported an additional 9 million tires in 2010, which was almost equal to the 11-million-unit decline experienced by China. Korea and Mexico, two other countries that saw very large increases in exports to the United States, appeared to be selling somewhat higher-quality tires, with unit values averaging $54 in 2009 and 2010. Note, however, that the overall decline in China's exports to the United States was 20 million tires and that the low-end producers did not come near to filling that gap – indicating that average prices increased after the safeguard was imposed.[20] There was an across-the-board increase in unit values in 2011 that was driven in part by rising costs of rubber and oil (Table 3). Unit values for Indonesia and Taiwan increased to the $42–44 range, but unit values of Chinese exports rose much more proportionately – from $38 in 2009 to $44 in 2010 to $61 in 2011.

20 Hufbauer and Lowry (2012) argue that unit values of tire imports rose in the 4th quarter of 2009 – the period immediately after the imposition of the 35% tariff – by an amount that translates into an $800 million annualized increase in prices paid by US consumers for tires. This may be an over-estimate. Prices certainly increased in 2009 and thereafter, but this appears to be mostly driven by higher input costs and a recovery in demand. There is no mention of the effect of the tariff in industry literature – this seems mostly limited to articles in the popular press (e.g., Bussey, 2012). Account also needs to be taken of the rapid increase in exports from countries at unit values that are similar to those of China before the safeguard.

Table 3. US tire imports (unit values, 2007–2011)

	US dollars/unit of quantity				
Country	2007	2008	2009	2010	2011
China	38.1	39.6	38.2	44.1	60.7
Canada	65.8	70.2	78.7	79.6	85.7
Korea	51.0	53.9	53.5	54.7	65.4
Japan	58.9	66.7	76.8	77.4	88.5
Thailand	74.2	67.4	62.0	63.0	74.3
Indonesia	26.2	29.3	34.5	35.4	44.3
Mexico	52.0	55.7	54.3	52.4	57.9
Taiwan	38.0	36.3	35.3	36.1	42.1
Brazil	45.4	51.0	51.6	57.7	74.8
Germany	59.5	74.6	81.9	87.3	98.4

Source: USITC website.

This may reflect some shift towards higher-quality exports as well as the effect of the tariffs.

4.4 *Effectiveness of tariffs as an instrument to address adjustment costs*

The *US–Tyres* case illuminates a basic flaw in the Safeguards Agreement, which is that its sole instrument, a trade restriction, may have little effectiveness and relevance in helping workers address adjustment problems. In an era of limited economic globalization, there was a greater unity of interest of domestic workers and producers, and so a trade restriction for import-competing producers could reliably help both those producers and their workers. While raising tariffs or other barriers to trade is detrimental to consumers, the interests of the factors of production employed in an import-competing industry were likely to be aligned.

Today, with global supply chains and increasing fragmentation of global production, the situation may be very different. The *Tyres* case illustrates the point. The issue was noted by the *Tyres* Panel in pointing out that there was a 'question of the suitability or relevance of safeguard mechanisms in the context of "outsourcing" and "globalization"' (WTO, 2010, para. 7.9). A cynical view of the *Tyres* dispute might say that it provided protection to the domestic industry that it did not want, and minimal relief to the workers who were never going to regain the jobs that had been purposefully outsourced.

The trade deflection that resulted from the discriminatory nature of the China safeguard measure meant that it achieved little in terms of expanding US-produced output and increasing employment in the tire-building industry. Hufbauer and Lowry (2012) argue that the safeguard at most saved 1,200 jobs, based on the observed rise in industry employment between September 2009 and September 2011. This is exactly what the USITC analysis had suggested (USITC, 2009: 37, n.205).

More realistically, however, the impact on tire-manufacturing jobs was zero. Total employment in the tire industry stood at 52,000 workers in late 2009; in 2011 it was also 52,000.[21] A narrower occupational definition of tire builders and molders indicates total employment of 16,700 workers in 2011, down from 17,800 workers in 2009 and 21,700 in 2008, but up from 15,000 in 2010.[22] This suggests that during 2009–2011 total employment fell. Moreover, any increase in jobs – even if it was 1,200 – needs to be assessed in the context of the 5,000 jobs that the USITC found had been lost during the period of investigation (USITC, 2009: 17), and any jobs lost in related service activities as a result of safeguard-induced higher retail prices for tires – garages, retail outlets, etc. (Prusa, 2009; Hufbauer and Lowry, 2012).

Nearly three years after the imposition of the safeguard, the evidence suggests that the economic returns have been meager at best and more likely negative. The employment numbers illustrate the inefficacy of a tariff to save or create jobs in an industry that is organized globally and that allocates production of different varieties of its product mix to countries that have a comparative advantage to produce them. A tariff instrument is unlikely to be useful in safeguarding a country's competitiveness in a world of vertical specialization and global production. A targeted tariff may provide benefits to a discrete set of workers (see USW, 2012), but it will do so only if a country has an industry that produces the products at issue. If production has largely been shifted to locations in other countries, the efficacy of trade-policy remedies is inherently limited and the cost–benefit ratio of increasing import tariffs for the nation as a whole increases. In the limit, if there is no local production, the only effect of raising tariffs is to tax consumers and workers generally.

These weaknesses may have implications for the operation of the trading system looking forward. One possible consequence of the ineffectiveness of selective protection may be a push towards relaxing the requirements for global safeguards so as to make it easier to raise tariffs on all imports so as to induce greater domestic production. This would clearly be very costly from an economic-efficiency and consumer-welfare perspectives.

What is needed is a greater effort to identify and make available alternative instruments to assist workers who are negatively affected by globalization. Instead of centering the Safeguards Agreement on raising the price of imports, the Agreement should be restructured as a positive mechanism to promote greater competitiveness and job creation in WTO Member countries (Charnovitz, 2006: 140–146). The Safeguards Agreement recognizes the goal of 'facilitating

21 As reported in the Bureau of Labor Statistics (BLS) Current Employment Statistics database for NAICS sector 3236210, which spans all tire production, including heavy trucks and retreading. This is down from 59,000 in 2007–2008. See http://www.bls.gov/ces/ (last visited 1 November 2012).

22 These figures are for Standard Occupational Classification sector 519197 as reported in the BLS Occupational Employment Statistics. See http://www.bls.gov/oes/ (last visited 1 November 2012).

adjustment' (see Article 7.4), but does not contain instruments suitable for that purpose (Horn and Mavroidis, 2003: 405).[23]

4.5 *Other issues*

This case raises a number of political-economy questions and puzzles, some of which have already been mentioned. For example, did the union truly believe that raising import protection would save US jobs in the tire industry or were there other considerations that motivated the case? The likelihood that the measure would only generate trade deflection was clearly identified by analysts at the time (Prusa, 2009). It may be that this was not believed. The USITC analysis that the recommended tariff would expand US production and employment may have played a role here.

Another question is why did the majority of the industry oppose the case given that they were exiting or had already abandoned the tier-3 segment? If the case led to higher prices for low-end tires, this would presumably induce some consumers to upgrade their tires. If it led to deflection, it presumably would not have much of an effect. One factor underpinning the opposition might have been a fear of disruption to the operation of affiliates in China. Of total tire imports of 139 million tires in 2008, 75 million units originated in US-owned plants or joint ventures. While only a little over 10% of this quantity (8 million units) originated in China, it accounted for some 20% of total imports of tires from China. Another factor might have been a concern with possible retaliation by China. The Chinese government did retaliate against a nonautomotive-related sector (chicken parts), using an antidumping measure – see Bradsher (2009).[24]

As noted, US imports of tires in 2008 from most other countries had higher unit values than those from China. This suggests some firms could benefit from restrictions on Chinese imports if a significant share of the expected increase in imports from non-Chinese sources would involve plants in which US firms have a stake – especially if the safeguard led to a significant increase in prices (as the difference between the unit costs of Chinese and non-Chinese tires would be reduced). All non-Chinese imports taken together from other developing countries in 2008 (some 25 million units) were less than total imports from China (46 million), suggesting that a significant trade restriction along the lines of what the USW was looking for (a limit of 21 million units) could have had such effects.

23 Of course, there is no constraint imposed on WTO members to put in place domestic mechanisms to assist workers – as the United States has done. An important policy question is whether the recommendations by the USITC to expedite petitions for trade-adjustment assistance by tire-industry workers were implemented, and to determine what could be done to enhance the effectiveness of such assistance.

24 Under the accession protocol, if a safeguard measure is taken as a result of a relative (absolute) increase in the level of imports, China has the right to suspend the application of substantially equivalent concessions or obligations if the measure remains in effect more than two (three) years (WTO, 2001: para. 16:6).

5. Conclusion

The *US–Tyres* case provides a vivid illustration of an incumbent WTO-Minus accession law in operation. China's Accession Protocol made it easier for other WTO Members to impose a safeguard against China than would have been the case if the regular WTO rules in the Safeguards Agreement had to be used. Moreover, WTO Members were permitted to target the safeguard solely against China, something that is not possible under the Safeguards Agreement.

This was an unusual case in that it was brought by the steelworkers labor union rather than by the industry – which did not think import barriers were justified or useful to it. In our view, the Appellate Body and Panel exhibited a proper level of deference to the decision issued by the competent national authorities (namely, the USITC and the US President). We hope that future Panels in safeguard cases seek to show the same level of deference.

As the only WTO dispute to date to bless the use of a safeguard, the *Tyres* case may suggest either that WTO safeguard law is being interpreted too stringently or that WTO safeguard law needs to be liberalized. Presumably, the labor union that brought the case would have petitioned for a global safeguard if they thought the relevant conditions had been satisfied. The fact that there was no such petition suggests that the TPSSM was seen to provide a path to import relief that would not have otherwise been available in the absence of the special rules in China's accession contract. Rather than relax the criteria for obtaining global safeguards protection, we believe the case illustrates the importance of reconceiving the Safeguards Agreement with more efficient (less costly) and more effective instruments to promote economic adjustment for workers and communities.

Finally, the *Tyres* case is notable in its holding that an accession commitment is a covered agreement to be interpreted in the same manner as regular WTO law, and the Panel ruling that the TPSSM does not violate GATT Article I, even though the safeguard is applied only to China. The Panel did not explain the basis for this ruling despite the duty of a WTO judge to do so.

References

Andersen, Scott and Christian Lau (2002), 'Hedging Hopes with Fears in China's Accession to the World Trade Organization: The Transitional Special-Product Safeguard for Chinese Exports', *The Journal of World Intellectual Property*, 5(3): 405–476.

Bank of America/Merrill Lynch (2010), 'Global Tire Quarterly Review', July.

Bown, Chad P. (2011), 'Taking Stock of Antidumping, Safeguards and Countervailing Duties, 1990–2009', *The World Economy*, **34**(12): 1955–1998.

Bradsher, Keith (2009), 'China Moves to Retaliate against US Tire Tariff', *The New York Times*, 13 September.

Bussey, John (2012), 'Get-Tough Policy on Chinese Tires Falls Flat', *The Wall Street Journal*, 20 January, available at http://online.wsj.com/article/SB10001424052970204301404577171130489514146.html (last visited 2 November 2012).

Charnovitz, Steve (2006), 'The (Neglected) Employment Dimension of the World Trade Organization', in Virginia A. Leary and Daniel Warner (eds.), *Social Issues, Globalisation and International Institutions: Labour Rights and the EU, ILO, OECD and WTO*, Leiden, The Netherlands: Martinus Nijhoff Publishers, pp. 125–155.

Charnovitz, Steve (2008), 'Mapping the Law of WTO Accession', in Merit E. Janow, Victoria Donaldson, and Alan Yanovich (eds.), *The WTO: Governance, Dispute Settlement and Developing Countries*, Huntington, NY: Juris Publishing, pp. 855–920.

Eisenstein, Adam (2010–2011), 'Free Trade, Tires, and Tariffs: Why Imposing Import Duties Against Chinese Goods is the Wrong Course of Action for the United States', *The Federal Circuit Bar Journal*, **20**(2): 305–335.

Grimmett, Jeanne J. (2011), 'Chinese Tire Imports: Section 421 Safeguards and the World Trade Organization (WTO)', CRS Report R40844, July.

Grossman, Gene M. and Alan O. Sykes (2007), 'United States – Definitive Safeguard Measures on Imports of Certain Steel Products', *World Trade Review*, **6**(1): 89–122.

Hohmann, George (2012), 'Cheap Chinese Tires Become Election Issue', *Charleston Daily Mail (West Virginia)*, 29 October.

Horn, Henrik and Petros C. Mavroidis (2003), 'US – Lamb United States – Safeguard Measures on Imports of Fresh, Chilled or Frozen Lamb Meat from New Zealand and Australia: What Should Be Required of a Safeguard Investigation?' *World Trade Review*, **2**(3): 395–430.

Hufbauer, Gary Clyde and Sean Lowry (2012), 'US Tire Tariffs: Saving Few Jobs at High Cost', Policy Brief 12–9 (April), Petersen Institute for International Economics, available at http://www.iie.com/publications/pb/pb12-9.pdf (last visited 2 November 2012).

Ikenson, Daniel (2009), 'Burning Rubber: Proposed Duties on Chinese Tires Whiff of Senseless Protectionism', *Free Trade Bulletin* 39, Center for Trade Policy Studies, available at http://www.cato.org/pubs/ftb/FTB-039.pdf (last visited 2 November 2012).

Ji, Wenhua and Cui Huang (2011), 'China's Experience in Dealing with WTO Dispute Settlement: A Chinese Perspective', *Journal of World Trade*, **45**(1): 1–37.

Lee, Joonhyung (2011), 'Who Benefited from the US Tariffs on the Chinese tires?', MPRA Paper No. 29705, available at http://mpra.ub.uni-muenchen.de/29705/1/MPRA_paper_29705.pdf (last visited 2 November 2012).

Lee, Yong-Shik (2002), 'The Specific Safeguard Mechanism in the Protocol on China's Accession to the WTO: A Serious Step Backward from the Achievement of the Uruguay Round', *The Journal of World Intellectual Property*, **5**(2): 219–231.

Obama, Barack H. (2012), 'Remarks by the President in State of the Union Address', White House, 24 January.

Prusa, Thomas J. (2009), 'Estimated Economic Effects of the Proposed Import Tariff on Passenger Vehicle and Light Truck Tires from China', American Coalition for Free Trade in Tires, July.

Rajan, Raghuram G., Paolo Volpin, and Luigi Zingales (1997), 'The Eclipse of the US Tire Industry', Working Paper No. 97–13, US Census Bureau, Center for Economic Studies.

Spadi, Fabio (2002), 'Discriminatory Safeguards in the Light of the Admission of the People's Republic of China to the World Trade Organization', *Journal of International Economic Law*, **5**(2): 421–443.

Sykes, Alan O. (2003), 'The Safeguards Mess: A Critique of WTO Jurisprudence', *World Trade Review*, **2**(3): 261–295.

Sykes, Alan O. (2004), 'The Persistent Puzzle of Safeguards: Lessons from the Steel Dispute', John M. Olin Law and Economics Working Paper No. 212 (2nd Series), The University of Chicago Law School, available at http://www.law.uchicago.edu/files/files/212.aos_.steel_safeguards.pdf (last visited 2 November 2012).

Tire Industry Association (2009), 'Tire Industry Association Expresses Disappointment With President's Decision Concerning Chinese Tire Tariff', Press release, 14 September, available at http://www.tireindustry.org/pdf/news_archives/pressrelease091409.pdf (last visited 2 November 2012).

US International Trade Commission (USITC) (2009), *Certain Passenger Vehicle and Light Truck Tires from China*, Washington DC: USITC (July), available at http://www.usitc.gov/publications/safeguards/pub4085.pdf (last visited 2 November 2012).

United Steelworkers (USW) (2012), 'Saving Jobs by Fighting Unfair Trade', available at http://www.usw.org/media_center/news_articles?id=1079 (last visited 2 November 2012).

Will, George (2009), 'With China Tire Tariffs, Obama Bows to Labor', *The Seattle Times*, 24 September.

World Trade Organisation (WTO) (2001), 'Accession of the People's Republic of China', WT/L/432, 23 November.

World Trade Organisation (WTO) (2010), *United States – Measures Affecting Imports of Certain Passenger Vehicle and Light Truck Tyres from China*, Panel Report, WT/DS399/R.

World Trade Organisation (WTO) (2011a), *United States – Measures Affecting Imports of Certain Passenger Vehicle and Light Truck Tyres from China*, Appellate Body Report, WT/DS399/AB/R.

World Trade Organisation (WTO) (2011b), 'Minutes of Meeting Held on 5 October 2011', Dispute Settlement Body, WT/DSB/M/304.

Appendix: WTO China-Specific Safeguard (excerpts)

16. Transitional Product-Specific Safeguard Mechanism

1. In cases where products of Chinese origin are being imported into the territory of any WTO Member in such increased quantities or under such conditions as to cause or threaten to cause market disruption to the domestic producers of like or directly competitive products, the WTO Member so affected may request consultations with China with a view to seeking a mutually satisfactory solution, including whether the affected WTO Member should pursue application of a measure under the Agreement on Safeguards. Any such request shall be notified immediately to the Committee on Safeguards.

...

3. If consultations do not lead to an agreement between China and the WTO Member concerned within 60 days of the receipt of a request for consultations, the WTO Member affected shall be free, in respect of such products, to withdraw concessions or otherwise to limit imports only to the extent necessary to prevent or remedy such market disruption. Any such action shall be notified immediately to the Committee on Safeguards.
4. Market disruption shall exist whenever imports of an article, like or directly competitive with an article produced by the domestic industry, are increasing rapidly, either absolutely or relatively, so as to be a significant cause of material injury, or threat of material injury to the domestic industry. In determining if market disruption exists, the affected WTO Member shall consider objective factors, including the volume of imports, the effect of imports on prices for like or directly competitive articles, and the effect of such imports on the domestic industry producing like or directly competitive products.

Philippines – Taxes on Distilled Spirits: Like Products and Market Definition

DAMIEN NEVEN

Graduate Institute of International and Development Studies

JOEL P. TRACHTMAN

Fletcher School of Law and Diplomacy, Tufts University

Abstract: This paper provides a legal–economic analysis of the Appellate Body decision in *Philippines – Taxes on Distilled Spirits* (*Philippines–Spirits*). In *Philippines–Spirits*, the Panel and the Appellate Body had an opportunity to consider again the scope of 'like products' and of 'directly competitive or substitutable products' under Article III:2 of GATT. The Panel and Appellate Body followed the Border Tax Adjustments factors in order to determine whether the products were sufficiently similar. The Appellate Body explicitly extended its jurisprudence from other areas of Article III to a like-products determination under the first sentence of Article III:2: this analysis is to be focused on the degree of competition between the imported and domestic products. We observe that the effect of different taxation on domestic products is affected by the degree of substitution between products as well as competitive conditions, whereas the Appellate Body seems to focus on the former and ignore the latter. We also question some of the Panel and Appellate Body interpretations of the evidence regarding the degree of substitution between products. Overall, we find that even if there may be a segment in which foreign and domestic products compete, the reported evidence in this case would seem to be consistent with the view that for the bulk of the market, foreign and domestic items are distant substitutes.

Putting aside the jurisprudence, a methodologically sound finding regarding substitution (and competition) seems necessary, but not sufficient, for a finding of inefficient discrimination. In order to find inefficient discrimination, there must also be a finding that the nonprotectionist benefits that may arise from the national regulation are not sufficient to justify the discriminatory action, otherwise, rational regulation that is globally efficient might be invalidated, inappropriately restricting the national right to regulate. In the present case, the Philippines articulated no nonprotectionist rationale for its distinctions. Existing WTO jurisprudence in this area prior to the Appellate Body decision in *US–Clove Cigarettes* (in the context of Article 2.1 of the technical barriers to trade agreement) has only hinted at the additional focus on the justificatory role of nonprotectionist regulatory benefits,

We would like to thank J. Wouters, P. Mavroidis, M. Ruta, K. Maskus, and participants in the June 2012 ALI workshop in Florence for useful comments on an earlier draft of this paper.

yet an explicit and appropriately contextualized reference to the nonprotectionist rationale, if any, of regulation seems to be a necessary part of decision-making.

1. Introduction and facts

This appeal related to complaints brought by the European Union (EU) and the United States (US) against the Philippines, claiming that the Philippines's excise-tax regime applicable to distilled spirits was inconsistent with Article III:2 of the General Agreement on Tariffs and Trade 1994 (GATT, 1994).[1] The EU and US claimed that the Philippines violated the national-treatment obligations contained in both the first sentence (First Sentence) and the second sentence (Second Sentence) of Article III:2, by applying different internal tax treatment to distilled spirits produced from certain 'designated raw materials' (sap of the *nipa*, coconut, cassava, *camote*, or *buri* palm, or from juice, syrup, or sugar of the cane), compared to the tax treatment applied to distilled spirits from 'non-designated raw materials' (everything else).

With respect to the US complaint, the Panel found violations of both the First Sentence and the Second Sentence. The Appellate Body confirmed these findings. With respect to the EU complaint, the Panel only examined consistency with the First Sentence, and found violations. The Appellate Body found that the Panel erred in treating the EU's Second Sentence claims as made in the alternative, and completed the analysis to find a violation of the Second Sentence in connection with the EU's claims.

It will be recalled that the First Sentence prohibits internal taxes on imported products in excess of internal taxes on like domestic products, while the Second Sentence, as elaborated by the related ad note, prohibits the application of dissimilar internal taxes on domestic products compared to those applied to directly competitive or substitutable imported products in a manner so as to afford protection to the domestic products.[2] The Appellate Body has repeatedly stated that the object and purpose of Article III is 'to provide equality of competitive conditions for imported products in relation to domestic products'.[3]

The Philippines argued that its measures were not discriminatory in the sense of Article III:2 because its distinctions were not based on national origin, but on different raw materials. Indeed, this was a case of alleged *de facto* discrimination. In connection with the First Sentence claims, the Philippines argued that the Panel

1 Appellate Body Report, *Philippines – Taxes on Distilled Spirits*, WT/DS396/AB/R, WT/DS403/AB/R, adopted 20 January 2012 (hereafter *Philippines–Spirits*).

2 For an excellent legal and economic analysis of the jurisprudence in this area, see Henrik Horn and Petros C. Mavroidis (2004), 'Still Hazy after All These Years: The Interpretation of National Treatment in the GATT/WTO Case-law on Tax Discrimination', 15:1, *European Journal of International Law*, 39.

3 Appellate Body Report, *Japan – Taxes on Alcoholic Beverages*, WT/DS8/AB/R, WT/DS10/AB/R, WT/DS11/AB/R, adopted 1 November 1996, p. 16 (citations omitted) (hereafter *Japan–Alcoholic Beverages*).

erred in its interpretation and application of the term 'like products'. The Philippines argued that any significant physical difference would be sufficient to render two products unlike.[4] The Panel disagreed, finding that sugar-based and non-sugar-based distilled spirits are 'like' despite numerous physical differences. So, the Appellate Body was required to determine whether the Panel erred in finding that each type of imported distilled spirit involved in this dispute made from nondesignated raw materials is 'like' the same type of domestic distilled spirit made from designated raw materials.

With respect to the Second Sentence claims, the Appellate Body was required to determine whether the Panel erred in finding that all the distilled spirits at issue, whether imported or domestic, and irrespective of the raw materials from which they were made, were 'directly competitive or substitutable' (DCOS) products.

All products at issue are distilled spirits of the following types: gin, brandy, rum, vodka, whisky, tequila, and tequila-flavoured spirits. The Panel found that all distilled spirits produced in the Philippines are made from designated raw materials (i.e., sugar), and based on ethyl alcohol processed in the Philippines or in other countries where sugar cane is produced commercially. Therefore, all distilled spirits produced in the Philippines were subject to a flat tax rate of 14.68 Philippine pesos per proof litre. On the other hand, 'the vast majority of' distilled spirits imported into the Philippines are processed from nondesignated raw materials, and are therefore subject to one of three tax rates, depending on their net retail price. These rates are 158.73, 317.44, and 634.90 pesos per proof litre.[5]

2. Legal analysis

The term 'discrimination' is not easily applied in all cases. We may 'know it when we see it', but it is useful to attempt to delineate the components of a finding of discrimination. This case focused on the interpretation and application of Article III:2. Article III:2 contains two prohibitions, designated as First Sentence and Second Sentence, and including the relevant ad note:

> Article III:2. The products of the territory of any contracting party imported into the territory of any other contracting party shall not be subject, directly or indirectly, to internal taxes or other internal charges of any kind in excess of those applied, directly or indirectly, to like domestic products. Moreover, no contracting party shall otherwise apply internal taxes or other internal charges to imported or domestic products in a manner contrary to the principles set forth in paragraph 1.*
>
> Ad note. A tax conforming to the requirements of the first sentence of paragraph 2 would be considered to be inconsistent with the provisions of the second

4 Appellate Body Report, *Philippines–Spirits*, para. 13.
5 Ibid., paras. 100–103.

sentence only in cases where competition was involved between, on the one hand, the taxed product and, on the other hand, a directly competitive or substitutable product which was not similarly taxed.

Provided it is found that the national measure is an internal tax or other internal charge, the substantive questions in Article III:2 discrimination cases are the following:

1. Product competition comparison. The threshold question is whether the relevant imported and domestic products are sufficiently in competition with one another to go on to the next step of considering whether the relevant national measure constitutes discrimination. This is by necessity a question of whether the relevant imported and domestic products are, or potentially can be, in the same market, and can only be answered by establishing first a threshold of competitiveness. Although the Appellate Body has repeatedly said that the product comparison is like an 'accordion' with different breadths in different contexts,[6] it would assist predictability and consistency of decision-making to establish a uniform threshold of competitiveness for purposes of discrimination cases. The Appellate Body has held in the context of the Second Sentence and Article III:4, and in the present case has confirmed in the context of the First Sentence, that the determination of the 'likeness' or direct competition or substitutability (DCOS) of products is to be made by reference to an analysis of product competition. And yet, the Appellate Body has also repeatedly stated that it is reluctant to rely on quantitative analyses of competitive relationships.[7]
2. Treatment comparison. Assuming that there is sufficient competition, is the class of imported products subject to adverse treatment compared to the class of domestic products? Adverse treatment is defined in the Article III:2 context as higher taxation (First Sentence) or dissimilar taxation (Second Sentence).

For First Sentence claims, the product competition comparison and the treatment comparison described above are necessary and sufficient to complete a case for violation. As the Appellate Body stated in *Canada–Periodicals:*

> [T]here are two questions which need to be answered to determine whether there is a violation of Article III:2 of the GATT 1994: (a) whether imported and domestic products are like products; and (b) whether the imported products are taxed in excess of the domestic products. If the answers to both questions are affirmative, there is a violation of Article III:2, First Sentence.[8]

6 *Japan–Alcoholic Beverages*, at 21 ('The width of the accordion in any one of those [provisions] must be determined by the particular provision in which the term 'like' is encountered as well as by the context and the circumstances that prevail in any given case to which that provision may apply.')

7 Appellate Body Report, *Korea – Taxes on Alcoholic Beverages*, WT/DS75/AB/R, WT/DS84/AB/R, adopted 17 February 1999, para. 134 (hereafter *Korea–Alcoholic Beverages*).

8 Appellate Body Report, *Canada – Certain Measures Concerning Periodicals*, WT/DS31/AB/R, adopted 30 July 1997, pp. 22–23 (hereafter *Canada–Periodicals*).

3. So as to afford protection. On the other hand, the Second Sentence includes a reference to 'the principles set forth in paragraph 1'. This has been interpreted to mean a reference to the language of Article III:1 stating that domestic measures should not be applied 'so as to afford protection to domestic production' (SATAP). This language calls for an additional analytical step, which we address in detail below. In short, it focuses on the objective structure of the measure in order to infer whether it is designed so as to afford protection.

2.1 *Like products*

In *Japan–Alcoholic Beverages*, the Appellate Body found that the scope of 'like products' under the First Sentence is to be construed narrowly in order to avoid condemning too broad a class of governmental measures, because the First Sentence lacks the moderating consideration of SATAP.[9]

For the First Sentence claims, the critical question in *Philippines–Spirits* was whether the regulatory categories established under Philippines law – essentially the distinction between designated raw materials and nondesignated raw materials – would be accepted as providing distinct treatment to products that were not like products, or whether, instead, distilled spirits made with designated raw materials are like products by reference to distilled spirits made with nondesignated raw materials. So, the critical question was whether the imported and domestic products at issue were like products. The Panel found that '(i) all distilled spirits at issue in this dispute are "like products", whether imported or domestic, and irrespective of the raw materials from which they are made; and (ii) each type of imported distilled spirit at issue in this dispute made from non-designated raw materials is "like" the same type of domestic distilled spirit made from designated raw materials'.[10]

The Appellate Body first examined the Panel's second finding. The Panel followed the *Border Tax Adjustments*[11] factors, as developed in subsequent jurisprudence, examining (i) the products' properties, nature, and quality, that is their physical characteristics; (ii) the products' end uses in the Philippines; (iii) the Philippine consumers' tastes and habits; and (iv) the products' tariff classification.[12] The Appellate Body also examined the relevant internal regulations of the Philippines. The Appellate Body pointed out that these criteria are not exhaustive, but are tools available for assessing the evidence relating to the competitive relationship between imported and domestic products in order to establish likeness.[13]

9 *Japan–Alcoholic Beverages*, pp. 19–20.

10 Appellate Body Report, *Philippines–Spirits*, para. 110.

11 Report of the Working Party, Border Tax Adjustments, L/3464, adopted 2 December 1970.

12 The original *Border Tax Adjustments* factors did not include tariff classification, but the Appellate Body confirmed that tariff classification is an additional criterion in *Japan–Alcoholic Beverages*, at 23.

13 Appellate Body Report, *Philippines–Spirits*, para. 131.

The Appellate Body thus extended its earlier jurisprudence in which it had already found that the like-products analysis and DCOS analysis is based on an analysis of the competitive relationship between the imported and domestic products in the context of Article III:4[14] and in the context of the Second Sentence, respectively.[15]

But if the *Border Tax Adjustment* factors are simply tools, under what circumstances should a Panel or the Appellate Body adopt a different set of tools, which might be superior? The Appellate Body noted that 'a panel examines these criteria in order to make a determination about the nature and extent of a competitive relationship between and among the products'.[16] As discussed below, the set of factors examined in traditional Article III product comparisons seems less sophisticated, less precise, and less plausible than a modern economic analysis of the extent of competition between two products, which is essentially the question of the definition of the relevant market in which they compete.

And yet in *Korea–Alcoholic Beverages*, the Appellate Body approved the Panel's finding that 'if a particular degree of competition had to be shown in quantitative terms, that would be similar to requiring proof that a tax measure has a particular impact on trade'.[17] The Panel in that case was concerned that 'if a certain *degree* of competition must be shown, it is similar to showing that a certain *amount* of damage was done to that competitive relationship by the tax policies in question'.[18] In the *Japan–Alcohol* case, the Appellate Body had held that no proof of trade effects is required. However, while showing competition in quantitative terms is a necessary predicate to showing trade effects arising from the tax policies in question, the Panel's logic is incorrect because an additional step is required to move from identifying the degree of competition to establishing the effects of the national measure on competition. Nor is it necessarily correct, at least from an economic standpoint, that showing trade effects should not be part of the Article III analysis. We agree with Robert Hudec that any tribunal considering discrimination in the trade context will inevitably be influenced by the aim and effects of the relevant measure.[19] If Hudec's insight is correct, it would be best to make the parameters for these assessments explicit.

14 Appellate Body Report, *European Communities – Measures Affecting Asbestos and Asbestos Containing Products*, WT/DS135/AB/R, adopted 5 April 2001 (hereafter *EC–Asbestos*).

15 *Korea–Alcoholic Beverages.*

16 Appellate Body Report, *Philippines–Spirits*, para. 119, citing *EC–Asbestos.*

17 Appellate Body Report, *Korea–Alcoholic Beverages*, paras. 130–131.

18 Panel Report, *Korea – Taxes on Alcoholic Beverages*, WT/DS75/R, WT/DS84/R, adopted 17 February 1999, as modified by Appellate Body Report WT/DS75/AB/R, WT/DS84/AB/R, para. 10.42.

19 Robert E. Hudec (1998), 'GATT/WTO Constraints on National Regulation: Requiem for an "Aim and Effects" Test', 32:3 *The International Lawyer* 619, 620 [hereafter 'Aim and Effects']; reprinted in R. E. Hudec (1999), *Essays on the Nature of International Trade Law*, London: Cameron May, at 359–395, and at http://www.worldtradelaw.net/articles/hudecrequiem.pdf (last visited 25 July 2012). See also Amelia Porges and Joel P. Trachtman (2003), 'Robert Hudec and Domestic Regulation: The Resurrection of Aim and Effects', 37:4, *Journal of World Trade*, 783–799.

No claims were raised on appeal regarding the Panel's finding that the imported and domestic products share the same end uses.[20] As to physical characteristics, the Philippines argued that 'like products' under the First Sentence is limited to 'identical products'. According to the Philippines, any significant difference in physical characteristics would be sufficient to render the products unlike.[21] This position would certainly limit the scope of application of the First Sentence. However, the Appellate Body disagreed, finding that the simple fact of different raw materials need not have been viewed as disqualifying the imported and domestic spirits from being considered 'like'.[22] Perhaps if the difference in physical characteristics had a nonprotectionist regulatory implication, as the difference between asbestos and fibreglass components of insulation had in the *EC–Asbestos* case, the Appellate Body would have found a way to distinguish the products.

The Appellate Body then turned to the Philippines's argument that because differences in chemical composition resulted in different taste, flavour, and aroma, the imported and domestic spirits were not like. The Panel had found that for each type of distilled spirit – gin, brandy, vodka, whisky, tequila, and tequila-flavoured spirits – there was similarity in physical characteristics despite the differences in raw materials. The Appellate Body accepted the Panel's determination, considering that 'if differences in raw materials leave fundamentally unchanged the competitive relationship among the final products, the existence of these differences would not necessarily negate a finding of "likeness"'.[23] The production process for the Philippines domestic spirits was designed to ensure that the final product is as close as possible in organoleptic properties to the imported products made from raw materials that are more traditional. Again, the Appellate Body examines these factors as qualitative determinants of a competitive relationship, leaving open the question of how the Appellate Body would handle a circumstance in which the competitive relationship is not affected by the differences, but where the differences result in a consumption externality or production externality that government determines to address through regulation.

The next of the *Border Tax Adjustments* factors addressed by the Appellate Body was consumer tastes and habits. The Panel had found what it called a significant degree of competitiveness or substitutability between domestic and imported distilled spirits in the Philippine market.[24] It based its conclusions on two reports on substitutability in consumer preferences by Euromonitor International and by M. J. Abrenica and J. Ducanes (the 'substitutability studies').[25] 'The Panel

20 Appellate Body Report, *Philippines–Spirits*, para. 113.

21 Ibid., para. 115.

22 Ibid., para. 122.

23 Ibid., para. 125.

24 Panel Report, *Philippines–Spirits*, para. 7.62.

25 *Euromonitor International*, 'Consumer Perceptions Regarding Substitutability in the Philippines Distilled Spirits Market' (August 2010) (submitted by complainants); and M. J. Abrenica and J. Ducanes,

considered that both substitutability studies suggest that a simultaneous increase in the price of domestic Philippine distilled spirits and decrease in the price of imported distilled spirits, such as that which would result from an equalization in the respective levels of the excise tax, could result in the substitution of the consumption of domestic distilled spirits for imported distilled spirits in the Philippine market.'[26]

The Appellate Body observed that the degree of competition and substitutability that is required under the First Sentence must be higher than that under the Second Sentence. It referred to its finding in *Canada–Periodicals* that a relationship of 'imperfect substitutability' would still be consistent with DCOS under the Second Sentence, but that a relationship of perfect substitutability would fall under the First Sentence.[27] However, the Appellate Body in the present case observed that perfect substitutability is not *required* for First Sentence cases: 'products that are close to perfectly substitutable can be "like products"'.[28] Furthermore, the Appellate Body found that the fact that domestic and imported distilled spirits in the Philippines do not share all channels of distribution does not establish that they are not like products.[29] Therefore, the Appellate Body did not consider that the Panel erred in determining that the products at issue were like products.

The Philippines had also claimed that the Panel acted inconsistently with Article 11 of the DSU by concluding that there was no evidence of the existence of two separate markets, based on price, in the Philippines. 'The Panel found that "a large proportion of the Philippine population has a limited ability to purchase distilled spirits beyond certain price levels", but that the market is not divided into two segments.'[30] The Appellate Body found that the Panel had taken into account the evidence submitted by the Philippines, but had appreciated it differently.

The third factor addressed by the Appellate Body in determining whether the imported and domestic spirits were like products was tariff classification. The Panel found that all of the distilled spirits at issue in this case fall under Harmonized System (HS) heading 2208, and that the HS six-digit subheadings for gin and vodka make no distinction between distilled spirits on the basis of their raw materials. On the other hand, the six-digit subheadings for brandy and whisky refer to nonsugar raw materials. Thus, for the Panel, the six-digit subheadings did not offer conclusive guidance.[31] The Appellate Body recalled that in *Japan–Alcoholic Beverages*, it found that tariff classification could be a helpful indicator of similarity only if

'On Substitutability Between Imported and Local Distilled Spirits' (University of Philippines School of Economics Foundation, 10 October 2010) (submitted by the Philippines).

26 Appellate Body Report, *Philippines–Spirits*, para. 146, citing Panel Report, para. 7.57.

27 Ibid., para. 148, citing *Canada–Periodicals*.

28 Ibid., para. 149.

29 Ibid., para. 153.

30 Ibid., para. 156, quoting Panel Report, *Philippines–Spirits*, para. 7.59.

31 Panel Report, *Philippines–Spirits*, para. 7.71.

sufficiently detailed. The Appellate Body disagreed with the Panel, finding that these six-digit subheadings, including their explanatory notes, 'would not suggest that domestic brandies and whiskies made from designated raw materials are "like" imported brandies and whiskies made from non-designated raw materials'.[32] However, since tariff classification is only one of the relevant criteria, the Appellate Body did not find that this is an error that rises to the level of a failure by the Panel to comply with its duties under Article 11 of the DSU.[33]

The Philippines argued that the Panel should have considered that the internal regulatory regimes of the EU and the US that prohibit the marketing of whisky and brandy made from sugar as brandy or whisky provided evidence that these were not like products. However, the Appellate Body found that the like-products determination is a market-by-market determination, and that the market to be evaluated in this case is the Philippines market, in which regulation does not make these distinctions.[34]

Consequently, the Appellate Body upheld the Panel's finding that, by imposing on each type of imported distilled spirit at issue in this dispute, because it was not made from designated raw materials, internal taxes in excess of those applied to like domestic distilled spirits of the same types, the Philippines violated the requirements of the First Sentence.[35]

Although the relevant language was not clear, the Panel seemed to add that all distilled spirits at issue in the current dispute were like products. In response, the Appellate Body held that 'to the extent that the Panel found, in paragraph 7.77 of its Reports, that *all* distilled spirits at issue in this dispute, regardless of the different types, are "like products" within the meaning of Article III:2, first sentence, of the GATT 1994, we disagree with this finding by the Panel'.[36] In connection with its analysis, the Appellate Body stated that 'we do not consider that a *significant* degree of competitiveness or substitutability would support a finding of "likeness"'.[37] Thus, a finding of likeness requires a degree of competition that is higher than merely significant.

What do we learn about the definition of 'like products' from this decision? The Appellate Body has elaborated its jurisprudence further, but has not given great guidance from which states may anticipate which products will be 'like' and which will not. Physical differences alone are insufficient to make products 'unlike'. Products 'close to' perfectly substitutable are 'like'. More than a 'significant' degree of competitiveness or substitutability is needed. So, as states formulate taxation,

32 Appellate Body Report, *Philippines–Spirits*, para. 163.
33 Ibid., para. 164.
34 Ibid., paras. 167–168.
35 Ibid., para. 174.
36 Ibid., para. 179 (emphasis in original).
37 Ibid., para. 181 (emphasis in original).

they will have difficulty anticipating whether the categories they establish will withstand WTO scrutiny.

Is it possible to add greater precision? We would conjecture that it is not, so long as nonprotectionist regulatory purpose cannot be considered independently. That is, by reserving to Panels and to itself great discretion to determine 'likeness', the Appellate Body retains room for judgment that can be used to determine products that are in competition with one another to be unlike, where the national regulatory distinction at issue serves a sufficiently significant nonprotectionist purpose. If, alternatively, the nonprotectionist regulatory purpose were considered elsewhere in the analysis – for example in the analysis of SATAP – then the determination of likeness in competitive terms could be made more precise and predictable. Of course, however, SATAP is not currently a relevant analysis under First Sentence claims.

2.2 *Directly competitive or substitutable products*

The Philippines also appealed the Panel's finding that the relevant products were DCOS, and that the tax was applied 'so as to afford protection'. It will be recalled that this Second Sentence analysis is understood as a 'cumulative' obligation; even if a national tax meets the requirements of the First Sentence, it must also meet the requirements of the Second Sentence.

In *Japan–Alcoholic Beverages*, the Appellate Body confirmed that it is appropriate to examine competition in the relevant markets, including cross-price elasticity of demand, as one factor, in addition to the *Border Tax Adjustment* factors, in determining DCOS.[38]

In *Philippines–Spirits*, 'the Panel rejected the Philippines' argument that the price gap between imported and domestic spirits, combined with the income disparity in the Philippines, demonstrates the existence of two distinct segments in the Philippine distilled spirits market'.[39] The Appellate Body agreed with the Philippines that evidence of major price differentials could indicate that imported and domestic products are in separate markets. However, the Panel did not perform a complete analysis to determine the scope of the market. Nevertheless, the Panel found sufficient overlap in prices, and sufficient variation in purchasing power, to demonstrate instances of actual competition that suggest that imported and domestic distilled spirits are '*capable* of being directly competitive or substitutable in the future'.[40] On this basis, the Panel found a direct competitive relationship between domestic and imported distilled spirits.

38 *Japan–Alcoholic Beverages*, at 25.

39 Appellate Body Report, *Philippines–Spirits*, para. 197, citing Panel Report, *Philippines–Spirits*, para. 7.118.

40 Panel Report, *Philippines–Spirits*, para. 7.121 (emphasis in original).

It is important that the Panel based its views on the capability of future competition,[41] and that the Appellate Body accepted this in the present case and in earlier cases. So, it is not just a test of actual competition, but of potential competition. But the textual basis for this extension is uncertain: the text of the ad note to Article III refers to 'directly competitive or substitutable', not to capability of being 'directly competitive or substitutable'. Yet the Appellate Body's focus since *Japan–Alcoholic Beverages* seems to be on potential competition but for the challenged national measure, rather than a broader analysis.

In *Philippines–Spirits*, the Philippines argued that the Panel erroneously focused on the nature and quality of competition between the relevant imported and domestic products, rather than on the degree of competition. The Philippines cited the Appellate Body's decisions in *Korea–Alcoholic Beverages*[42] and in *US–Cotton Yarn*[43] in support of the argument that the correct analysis focuses on the *degree* of competition. In *Korea–Alcoholic Beverages*, the Appellate Body held that imported and domestic products are DCOS when they are 'in competition' in the marketplace.[44] It further held that the term 'directly' suggests 'a degree of proximity in the competitive relationship between the domestic and the imported products'.[45]

However, in *Philippines–Spirits*, the Panel stated that 'the question before us under Article III of the GATT 1994 is not so much what the "degree of competition" between the products at issue is, but what is the "nature" or "quality" of their "competitive relationship" '.[46] In a sense, this is a correct statement of what the Panels and Appellate Body actually do, because they do not seek to quantify the degree of competition.

Nevertheless, the Appellate Body found that the Panel 'appropriately ascertained the extent of the competitive relationship between imported and domestic distilled spirits in the Philippine market'.[47] The Panel found that the Substitutability Studies indicate that there is 'a significant degree of competitiveness or substitutability' in the Philippine market between the imported and domestic distilled spirits at issue.[48]

So, in both *Philippines–Spirits* and in *Korea–Alcoholic Beverages*, the Appellate Body has demanded a sufficient degree of competitiveness. However, the Appellate Body has insisted that this is broadly a qualitative, not a quantitative exercise,

41 Ibid., para. 7.100, citing *Korea–Alcoholic Beverages*, para. 114; *United States – Transitional Safeguard Measure on Combed Cotton Yarn from Pakistan*, WT/DS192/AB/R, adopted 5 November 2001, para. 91 (hereafter *US–Cotton Yarn*).

42 Appellate Body Report, *Philippines–Spirits*, para. 201, citing Philippines' appellant's submission, para. 88, citing *Korea–Alcoholic Beverages*.

43 Ibid., citing *US–Cotton Yarn*.

44 Appellate Body Report, *Korea–Alcoholic Beverages*, para. 114.

45 Ibid., para. 116.

46 Panel Report, *Philippines–Spirits*, para. 7.101.

47 Appellate Body Report, *Philippines–Spirits*, para. 204.

48 Panel Report, *Philippines–Spirits*, para. 7.113.

although it can take some quantitative data relating to cross-price elasticity of demand into account. In the course of approving the Panel's focus on the 'nature and quality' of competition, while examining as part of its analysis the degree of competition, the Appellate Body in *Philippines–Spirits* reiterated its antipathy to quantitative analysis: 'In *Korea–Alcoholic Beverages*, the Appellate Body expressly found that a particular degree of competition need not be shown in quantitative terms, and cautioned panels against placing undue reliance on "quantitative analysis of the competitive relationship", because cross-price elasticity is not "the decisive criterion" in determining whether two products are directly competitive or substitutable.'[49] As discussed below, most economists would wonder what other criteria are relevant, while accepting that it would be inappropriate to find products not competitive where the alleged discriminatory measure is the basis for a price differential that suppresses competition.

In addition, the Philippines appealed on the basis of an argument that the Panel 'erred in finding direct competition on the basis of a "non-representative" segment of its population having "access" to both types of spirits "at least on special occasions"'.[50] Note that this is an argument about the definition of the relevant market for purposes of a finding of discrimination. However, the Appellate Body found that the Panel's finding of price overlap both for high- and low-priced distilled spirits supported the Panel's determination that the market is not segmented.[51] Furthermore, the Appellate Body found that 'instances of *actual* competition are also highly probative in relation to *potential* competition'.[52]

Finally, the Philippines claimed that the Panel failed to comply with the requirement under Article 11 of the DSU because it failed to make an objective assessment of the facts in its examination of the substitutability studies. The Euromonitor International survey had not estimated cross-price elasticity of demand, but had estimated that 'in a tax-neutral environment the market share of imported distilled spirits would increase by between 13% and 24.5%'.[53] On the other hand, the Abrenica and Ducanes study estimated cross-price elasticity of demand for imported and domestic spirits to range between −0.01 and 0.07, considered by the authors to be 'low'. The Appellate Body considered that the weight and significance to be attributed to that estimated cross-price elasticity coefficient falls within the Panel's discretion as trier of facts.[54] It also found important support for the Panel's finding in the Euromonitor International survey, which showed a significant degree of substitutability. It therefore found sufficient support for the Panel's appreciation

49 Appellate Body Report, *Philippines–Spirits*, para. 207, citing Appellate Body Report, *Korea–Alcoholic Beverages*, paras. 130, 131, 134.

50 Appellate Body Report, *Philippines–Spirits*, para. 213.

51 Ibid., para. 215.

52 Ibid., paras. 226, 228.

53 Ibid., para. 232.

54 Ibid., para. 236.

of this evidence to the effect that 'the studies support the proposition that there is a significant degree of competitiveness or substitutability'.[55]

2.3 *So as to afford protection (SATAP)*

The First Sentence does not specifically refer to the principles of Article III:1, including the seemingly nonmandatory language to the effect that domestic measures 'should not be applied to imported or domestic products so as to afford protection to domestic production'. Therefore, the Appellate Body in *Japan–Alcoholic Beverages* found that the First Sentence criteria of 'like products' and 'higher tax' are sufficient, in and of themselves, to instantiate the principles of Article III:1, without a separate analysis of whether the measures are applied 'so as to afford protection'. However, because the Second Sentence specifically invokes these principles, a separate finding of SATAP is required.[56]

Grammatically, 'so as to afford protection' could be understood to direct attention to either of two things: (i) the intent of the measure, or (ii) the effect of the measure. In *Japan–Alcoholic Beverages*, the Appellate Body stated that SATAP is not an issue of subjective intent: a Panel is not required to examine evidence of the actual legislative or regulatory intent.[57] Rather, the Appellate Body in that case referred to the 1987 GATT Panel Report in an earlier iteration of that dispute, and made the following statement:

> As in that case, we believe that an examination in any case of whether dissimilar taxation has been applied so as to afford protection requires a comprehensive and objective analysis of the structure and application of the measure in question on domestic as compared to imported products. We believe it is possible to examine objectively the underlying criteria used in a particular tax measure, its structure, and its overall application to ascertain whether it is applied in a way that affords protection to domestic products.[58]

So, it is not subjective aim that is to be evaluated, but an objective analysis of the structure of the measure is required in order to infer a protective aim.

The injunction against examination of subjective intent has not been followed consistently. In *Canada–Periodicals*, the Appellate Body stated that it was following *Japan–Alcoholic Beverages* in applying the SATAP component of the Second Sentence analysis. It nevertheless proceeded to refer to legislative documents and government statements indicating the 'objective and structure' of the tax in question.[59] *Canada–Periodicals* thus confirms that the Appellate Body can

55 Panel Report, *Philippines–Spirits*, para. 7.113.
56 *Japan–Alcoholic Beverages*, at 18–19.
57 Ibid., at 27–28.
58 Ibid., at 29.
59 *Canada–Periodicals*, at 27–28.

consider both objective and subjective evidence of aims, in connection with the SATAP criterion.

The Philippines alleged that the Panel also erred in its finding that dissimilar taxation of the imported and domestic distilled spirits at issue was applied '*so as to afford protection*' to Philippine distilled spirits. The Panel had rejected the argument made by the Philippines that its tax had no *effect* on competitive conditions because of the combined effect of (i) the low purchasing power of the Philippine population, and (ii) the pre-tax price differences between domestic and imported products. The Panel stated that the Appellate Body had rejected a similar argument in *Korea–Alcoholic Beverages*, because the earlier-stage finding that the products are directly competitive or substitutable precludes a finding of no competitive effect.[60] Interestingly, the Appellate Body agreed with the Panel that 'the assessment of whether the excise tax could affect the competitive relationship between domestic and imported distilled spirits in the Philippine market pertains to the prong of analysis directed at determining whether the products are [DCOS]'.[61]

In the *Korea–Alcoholic Beverages* case, the Appellate Body had already clarified that SATAP is not concerned with trade volumes, or a particular trade effect, but is concerned with the conditions of competition.[62] The Appellate Body in *Philippines–Spirits* quoted the Appellate Body's language in the *Korea–Alcoholic Beverages* case: 'it is . . . not incumbent on a complaining party to prove that tax measures are capable of producing any particular trade effect'.[63]

So, according to the Panel and Appellate Body, there is no need to determine the capability of the different taxation to cause trade effects in connection with the SATAP analysis, as this is already included in the DCOS analysis. However, the Panel and Appellate Body are inappropriately combining two analyses: (i) whether the imported and domestic products are sufficiently in competition with one another, and (ii) whether and to what extent the tax at issue is capable of causing or causes trade effects. Perhaps the Panel and Appellate Body assume that any differential tax, applied to goods sufficiently in competition, causes actionable trade effects, or perhaps they believe that discrimination can be found without a finding of trade effects.

So, the remaining meaning of SATAP has to do with an objective assessment of design or intent. In *Philippines–Spirits*, 'the Panel reviewed "the design, architecture and structure" of the measure in some detail and observed that, while "*[a]ll* designated raw materials are grown in the Philippines and *all* domestic distilled spirits are produced from designated raw materials", the vast majority of imported

60 Appellate Body Report, *Philippines–Spirits*, para. 246.

61 Ibid., para. 256.

62 *Korea–Alcoholic Beverages*, paras. 119, 153.

63 Appellate Body Report, *Philippines–Spirits*, quoting *Korea–Alcoholic Beverages*, para. 153.

distilled spirits "are *not* made from designated raw materials"'.[64] From this, the Panel drew the inference that the Philippines' tax system operated SATAP.

In *Chile–Alcoholic Beverages*, the Appellate Body stressed that the SATAP analysis is completely separate and additional to a finding of dissimilar taxation.[65] This emphasis, and separation, foreshadowed the Appellate Body's approach to the issue of 'less favourable treatment' under Article III:4 in paragraph 100 of *EC–Asbestos*. The Appellate Body referred again to the *Japan–Alcoholic Beverages* decision to the effect that the evaluation must consider objectively the structure of the national measure.

In *Chile–Alcoholic Beverages*, the Appellate Body evaluated the actual incidence of the tax, and found that the design of the tax coincidentally causes it to fall most heavily on imported goods, with imported goods falling largely into the high-tax category.[66] The Panel had found that the structure of the Chilean alcohol tax did not relate to the purposes stated by Chile, and found that this lack of correlation – lack of 'suitability' – confirmed its finding that the Chilean measure was applied SATAP. On appeal, Chile argued that the Panel was wrong to inquire as to the purposes of the regulation. However, the Appellate Body approved this inquiry, stating that a measure's purposes are 'intensely pertinent' to the question of whether the measure is applied SATAP. This is because a plausible purpose – in the Appellate Body's words a 'countervailing explanation'[67] – might have helped to 'explain' a tax structure that otherwise appears to be applied so as to afford protection. So, again, aim may be relevant to a determination of SATAP.

SATAP has also emerged in Article III:4 jurisprudence, despite the lack of any specific invocation of Article III:1. After establishing a 'competitive likeness' test under Article III:4, the Appellate Body in the *EC–Asbestos* decision made clear that formal differences in the treatment of like products are not sufficient to make out a violation of Article III:4. There must also exist 'less favourable treatment'. 'The term "less favourable treatment" expresses the general principle, in Article III:1, that internal regulations "should not be applied ... so as to afford protection to domestic production".'[68]

In *EC–Asbestos*, the Appellate Body states that 'a Member may draw distinctions between products which have been found to be "like", without, for this reason alone, according to the group of "like" *imported* products "less favourable treatment" than that accorded to the group of "like" *domestic* products'.[69]

64 Appellate Body Report, *Philippines–Spirits*, para. 255, quoting Panel Report, *Philippines–Spirits*, para. 7.182 (emphasis in Panel Report).

65 Appellate Body Report, *Chile – Taxes on Alcoholic Beverages*, WT/DS87/AB/R, WT/DS110/AB/R, adopted 12 January 2000, para. 55 (hereafter *Chile–Alcoholic Beverages*).

66 Ibid., para. 66.

67 Ibid., para. 71.

68 *EC–Asbestos*, para. 100.

69 Ibid.

The willingness to examine the class of imported products compared to the class of domestic products (presaged in *Chile–Alcoholic Beverages*), as opposed to examining the best treatment accorded to any domestic like product compared to the worst treatment accorded to any imported like products, is critical. Under *Asbestos*, different treatment alone – based on regulatory categories that distinguish between otherwise like products – is neither sufficient nor necessary to prove less favourable treatment. The Appellate Body seems to expect a substantive additional test to be applied under the rubric of 'less favourable treatment'.

It seems clear that SATAP would not be considered under the First Sentence. Although we do not know the precise relationship between 'like products' under the First Sentence and 'like products' under Article III:4, it seems safe under *EC–Asbestos* to say that the former is narrower. Thus, if 'like products' under the First Sentence is understood as dealing with products that are more or less identical, including features that implicate regulation, perhaps there is no need for a SATAP analysis under the First Sentence. Of course, the First Sentence does not have an explicit textual locus for this determination. Perhaps this would be a reason to have a more constrained definition of 'like products' in connection with the First Sentence.[70]

2.4 *An Interpretative argument for interpreting 'like' and 'DCOS' utilizing modern economic tools, and for interpreting 'like' narrowly to include only products that raise the same regulatory concerns*

The *Border Tax Adjustment* factors are precedent, not treaty language. And of course, precedent is not formally binding in WTO law. As the Appellate Body points out, the *Border Tax Adjustment* factors are tools available to tribunals 'for organizing and assessing evidence relating to the competitive relationship between and among the products'.[71] Below, we propose tools commonly regarded as superior in the economics profession. Of course, the interpretive task of a WTO Panel or the Appellate Body is not to determine what the economics profession believes, but if the member states of the WTO utilize a concept, such as competition, it appears that tribunals should use the best tools available to determine competition.

Under Article 3.2 of the WTO Dispute Settlement Understanding, Panels and the Appellate Body are to utilize the customary rules of interpretation of public international law. In *Japan–Alcoholic Beverages*, the Appellate Body confirmed that Articles 31 and 32 of the Vienna Convention on the Law of Treaties are included in these customary rules of interpretation. Article 31 requires that 'A treaty shall be interpreted in good faith in accordance with the ordinary meaning to

70 See *Japan–Alcoholic Beverages*, at 19–20 (definition of 'like products' for purposes of Article III:2 (first sentence) should be construed narrowly); Aim and Effects, supra note 19.

71 Appellate Body Report, *Philippines–Spirits*, para. 131.

be given to the terms of the treaty in their context and in the light of its object and purpose.' Just as the Appellate Body found in *US–Shrimp* that the definition of 'natural resources' in Article XX(g) of GATT is not 'static' in its content or reference but is rather 'by definition, evolutionary', we might also argue that our understanding of like products and DCOS products may evolve as more reliable and plausible tools are developed by economics. Of course, it is necessary to remain faithful to the overall purpose of the clause interpreted. However, if, as the Appellate Body has consistently asserted, the meaning of these clauses is found in a search for a competitive relationship, it is worth recognizing that our understanding of competitive relationships has grown more reliable and plausible. Why should WTO law not take advantage of this evolution in understanding?

As expressed above, a test for discrimination that only refers to a competition-based product comparison, and a treatment comparison that is inhospitable to nonprotectionist regulatory reasons for differential treatment, would invalidate appropriate and efficient regulation. There appears to be room in SATAP under the Second Sentence, and in 'less favourable treatment' under Article III:4, to include the question of nonprotectionist regulatory rationales for differential treatment. Already in *Japan–Alcoholic Beverages,* the Appellate Body expressed its concern that the First Sentence might excessively invalidate appropriate national measures:

> Because the second sentence of Article III:2 provides for a separate and distinctive consideration of the protective aspect of a measure in examining its application to a broader category of products that are not 'like products' as contemplated by the first sentence, we agree with the panel that the first sentence of Article III:2 must be construed narrowly so as not to condemn measures that its strict terms are not means to condemn.[72]

This concern might lead to an understanding of 'like' for purposes of First Sentence cases as requiring imported and domestic products to be so similar as not to raise different degrees of challenge to nonprotectionist regulatory goals.

This concern arises despite the continued availability of exceptions under Article XX. First, under Article XX the burden of proof is broadly on the respondent, and, second, not all regulatory purposes are included in the list of regulatory purposes in Article XX. Therefore, Article III must avoid invalidating good-faith regulatory distinctions.

3. Economic analysis

The objective of this section is two-fold. First, we will discuss the factors that may be relevant to an empirical assessment of the effect of discriminatory treatment. Second, we will briefly review from an economic standpoint how the Panel and Appellate Body have dealt with the evidence that relates to those factors.

72 *Japan–Alcoholic Beverages*, at 21.

3.1 Assessing discriminatory treatment

In this section, we assume that Article III is concerned with the effect that different taxes on domestic and imported products may have. As discussed above, the Appellate Body has denied that Article III is concerned with effects, emphasizing instead the protection of competitive opportunities. However, we find it hard to give meaning to the protection of competitive opportunities in the absence of the effect that differential taxation may have either under current and/or future demand conditions. Even if the concept of competitive opportunities is understood in terms of an option for foreign producers to sell in the domestic market that is denied by the differential tax, such an option will only be valuable if indeed the differential tax is expected to have an effect on their sales.

As discussed in Neven (2001),[73] the effect of different taxes on different products is formally identical to the effect of a relative increase in the marginal cost of some product. That is, a higher tax on one product can be seen as an increase in the marginal cost of that product. As a result of an increase in the marginal cost of one product (say the imported product), its price but also the prices of the other products (whose marginal cost are kept constant, say the domestic products) will increase.

As one would expect, the extent to which the increase in marginal cost will be passed through to consumers in the prices of both products will be affected by the degree of substitutability between the two products. Other things being equal, the greater the substitutability between the foreign and domestic products, the larger will be the pass-through on both products.[74] With strong substitution, margins will be slim and firms will not be in a position to absorb an increase in cost by a reduction in margins. That is also to say that if foreign and domestic products are close substitutes, the protection granted to domestic firms increases (as measured by the increase in price that they can sustain). One can also easily check[75] that the sales of the foreign firm (as measured by quantities) will fall, so that, in this particular sense, demand is shifted away from foreign firms. The degree of substitution can in turn be captured for instance by the cross-price derivative of demand (more on this later).

However, the degree of product differentiation (as a synonym for the degree of substitution) is not the only factor that will determine the extent to which domestic firms will be protected and demand will be foreclosed from foreign firms. As shown

73 Damien Neven (2001), 'How Should 'Protection' be Evaluated in Article III GATT Disputes?', 17 *European Journal of Political Economy*, 421.

74 The framework used in Neven (2001) assumes symmetric product differentiation among domestic firms and foreign firms. In that framework, a foreign firm is identified by its greater level of cost. A richer model would allow for a different level of product differentiation among domestic firms and between domestic and foreign firms. The effect of domestic competition on the level of protection would also obtain in that framework.

75 Ibid.

in Neven (2001), the degree of rivalry in the domestic markets (as measured for instance by the number of firms) also matters. The less intense competition is in the domestic market (the lower the number of domestic competitors), the greater will be the pass-through to domestic and foreign prices. The pass-through (and hence the protection) will be greatest with a domestic monopoly and least when the domestic market is competitive (assuming that the degree of differentiation between domestic products is less than the differentiation between domestic and foreign products). This arises because a domestic monopolist will take advantage of a price increase by its foreign competitors and will find it attractive to increase its own price. By contrast, in a competitive setting, firms will resist such price increases, which increases would benefit their domestic competitors.

Hence, if the characterization of products as being 'like' or 'directly competitive or substitutable' is meant to refer only to the degree of substitutability between domestic and foreign products, it cannot be used as a sufficient proxy to determine whether differential taxation is likely to have adverse effects on imported products. Domestic products that are very 'like' imported products, but are sold in a competitive market, will enjoy a lower level of protection than less 'like' products sold by a domestic monopoly.

Thus, the effect of discriminatory treatment is a function of three factors: (i) the relative likeness or substitutability of the products, (ii) the relative competitiveness of the product market, and (iii) the magnitude of the tax differential.

3.2 *Likeness or substitutability: market definition*

This naturally raises the question of how to practically assess the effect of discriminatory treatment. Article III's reference to 'like' and 'directly competitive or substitutable products' emphasizes the degree of substitutability or differentiation as a relevant factor. This factor raises a tempting parallel with market definition in antitrust or competition law and indeed the Appellate Body occasionally refers to the 'relevant market'.

At the outset, it is worth spelling out the objective of market definition in antitrust. The formal definition of a relevant market for antitrust purposes (see e.g. the EU notice on market definition[76] or the US horizontal merger guidelines[77]) is that of the narrowest set of products (including the products of the firm under investigation) in which a hypothetical monopolist could profitably increase price by x% (in which x is often specified to be 5% or 10%). This is known as the SSNIP test (small but significant nontransitory increase in price). Even if, in practice,

76 Commission notice on the definition of relevant market for the purposes of Community competition law [Official Journal C 372 of 9.12.1997].

77 US Department of Justice and the Federal Trade Commission, Horizontal Merger Guidelines, 19 August 2010, available at http://www.justice.gov/atr/public/guidelines/hmg-2010.html (last visited July 26, 2012).

the delineation of a relevant market only rarely proceeds by directly estimating the profitability of a price increase over an alternative set of products, the SSNIP test is the organizing principle of market definition.

According to this principle, a relevant market is thus a set of products over which a firm with 100% market share (a hypothetical monopolist) could exercise market power (increase price) to a specified extent. Delineating a relevant market in this way thus acts as a way of calibrating market shares. Indeed, if a market share of 100% would imply a certain exercise of market power, market shares below that level can be interpreted relative to this benchmark. For instance, one could make the inference with some confidence that a market share of, say 50%, in this relevant market will still confer an appreciable degree of market power to the firms concerned (given the presumption, supported by various models of competition and empirical evidence, that there is a positive link between market share and market power).

Of course, market share is only meant to be a first indicator of the market power that a firm may be able to exercise. Other factors are taken into account in order to interpret this market share, including the significance of capacity constraints, the extent to which the products controlled by the firm may be particularly close substitutes for one another, the existence of buyer market power, and the prospects for entry.

To recap, (i) the objective of market definition in an antitrust case is to evaluate the market power that a firm may be able to exercise either in its current form or in a particular counterfactual (for instance a merger), (ii) market definition in antitrust also includes an explicit tolerance level (typically, as mentioned above price rise of some 5% to 10%) for the effect (market power) that it is meant to help evaluate, and (iii) market definition and the calculation of market shares only provide a first proxy for market power. Other factors are taken into account in order to interpret market power.

First, from this perspective, it is striking that the tools of market definition in antitrust cannot be directly transplanted for use in evaluation of the effect of discrimination in the context of Article III. With respect to the latter, the objective is not to assess market power but to assess the extent to which a set of products will benefit from the unfavourable treatment imposed on others (or alternatively, the extent to which a set of products will be harmed by this unfavourable treatment). It is only at a superficial level that the exercises are similar (arising from the observation that in both instances, the degree of substitution between products will matter).[78]

78 Note, however, that there is a direct parallel between the objective pursued under Article III and the objective of assessing the 'distortions of competition' induced by state aids under Article 107 of the Treaty of Rome (which instructs the Commission to identify to what extent competitors of the recipients of state support may be affected).

Second, it is nonetheless instructive to observe that market definition in antitrust includes an explicit tolerance level with respect to market power. Such discipline is probably desirable as a matter of methodology. In the context of the assessment of discriminatory policies, this suggests that any methodology should formulate a benchmark in terms of the extent of discrimination and its effects. A natural candidate in this respect would be the difference in the (excise) tax between domestic and foreign products and the pass-through rate. In the same way that an increase in price (exercise of market power) of $x\%$ is considered to be a concern in antitrust, an increase in price for the domestic product of $x\%$ resulting from a differential tax of $y\%$ (of the initial price) and a pass-through rate of z (with $x = y \times z$) could be considered a source of concern. This approach would thus allow for an explicit comparison of different measures involving different degrees of discrimination. For instance, a discriminatory tax of 2% with a pass-through rate of one-half could be compared with a discriminatory tax of 3% that has a pass-through rate of one-third (as both would yield a price increase of 1%).

Third, in the same way that market power is an increasing function of market share, the pass-through rate is an increasing function of concentration. This suggests that market structure could initially be taken as given in evaluating the scope of products over which a certain pass-through rate would arise. Concretely, assume that a price increase of $x\%$ (say 5%) is considered to be tolerable and that the discriminatory tax is equal to $y\%$ (say 10%) of the price, so that the tolerable pass-through is equal to $z = x/y$ (one half in our illustration). One could then ask what is the scope of products for which the pass-through rate is equal to z (one half), assuming that the domestic market is a monopoly. Indeed, it may be easier to identify the pass-through rate, and hence the scope of the product that would benefit from a price increase of 5%, when it is assumed that all domestic products are sold by a single firm. When this market is found, the extent to which competition in the domestic market would bring down the pass-through rate (and hence the effect of the discriminatory treatment) could then be assessed.

Note, however, that the definition of a relevant market in the counterfactual of a monopolist is possibly more compelling for antitrust purposes; the extent to which a monopolist would find it profitable to increase price (or alternatively would implement a profit-maximizing price of a certain percentage), is solely determined by the optimization of that firm and the demand conditions (the degree of substitution between the product sold by the hypothetical monopolist and the degree of substitution with alternative products). This makes the exercise particularly straightforward (at least at the level of principles). By contrast, the extent to which a hypothetical monopolist controlling domestic products would benefit from the increase in the marginal cost of foreign products involves the evaluation of an equilibrium response (it involves interactions between the foreign firms and the hypothetical monopolist). Hence, the exercise remains intricate and is possibly only marginally easier than a direct approach, in which the degree for pass-through is estimated for the observed competitive conditions.

3.3 *The assessment of evidence by the Panel and Appellate Body*

In this section, we discuss how the Panel and Appellate Body have assessed the evidence on whether domestic and foreign spirits could be considered to be 'like' and 'directly competitive or substitutable'. We pay particular attention to the way in which the Panel and Appellate Body have dealt with quantitative evidence.

Before we discuss this evidence, a couple of remarks may be in order. First, it may be worth noticing that the finding of the Panel and Appellate Body that domestic and foreign spirits are like products is puzzling from the perspective of the extent of tax discrimination. Indeed, taxes on domestic products (14.68 pesos per proof litre) appear to be an order of magnitude (from 10 to 40 times) lower than taxes on imported spirits (from 159 to 635 pesos per proof litre). Such differences in taxes are likely to be reflected in substantial differences in consumer prices (with the prices of foreign spirits as a multiple of domestic items). In principle, such significant price differences are hard to square with the idea that like products are (according to the Appellate Body's own language) 'close to perfectly substitutable'. Indeed, if they were, all consumers would have shifted to the domestic items and imported products would have no sales.

As discussed above, the Appellate Body is concerned about the opposite inference; the Appellate Body argues that products do not appear to be substitutes for one another precisely because of the magnitude of the difference in tax, so that with lower taxes, they would be expected to compete more closely with one another. The intuition behind the Appellate Body's reasoning is clear, namely that if taxes on foreign products were lower, the market shares of the foreign products would be larger. However, the intuition is not robust. As mentioned above, the closer the substitution between the domestic and foreign products, the larger is the pass-through so that with a strong substitution and a large pass-through of taxes which are 10–40 times larger than those imposed on domestic products, the sales of foreign products should essentially have vanished.

The fact that sales of foreign products have not vanished in the face of such strong discrimination is more consistent with the view that the demand for foreign products is not strongly affected by the price of the domestic items (that the products are not close substitutes for one another). Hence, it appears that the reasoning of the Appellate Body is at best incomplete. In particular, the observation that sales have not vanished is difficult to reconcile with the idea that foreign and domestic products are close to perfectly substitutable. If they were, a price difference of a few percentage points would have brought the demand for foreign products to zero.

Our second preliminary remark concerns the evidence that can be used to assess the degree of substitution between products. As mentioned above, the cross-price elasticity of demand between products is the relevant concept to assess substitution (see also Horn and Mavroidis, 2004). In practice, cross-price elasticities may be difficult to estimate econometrically. Demand estimations have only recently become widespread in antitrust investigation and only for those products for which scanner or consumer-panel date are available. Besides the availability of data, these estimations face significant problems (for instance of endogeneity). However, there are numerous alternative pieces of evidence that may be telling and are often used in antitrust investigations. These include the use of natural experiment (like the introduction of new products, out-of-stock periods for particular products, or large discounts) as well as the analysis of price series (co-integration and correlation for instance). Marketing studies and consumer panels, as well as internal strategic documents, often also prove insightful.

The Panel discusses a couple of economic studies that have been submitted by the parties as part of its introductory remarks.[79] These studies (one by Euromonitor International and another by a couple of academics, Abrenica and Ducanes, from the University of the Philippines) are described as attempting to assess the degree of substitution between domestic and foreign products. In the introductory section, the Panel only provides a short description of the studies and quotes some of its conclusions. In particular, the Panel reports that according to the Euromonitor study, with an import price decrease of 25% and domestic increase of 50%, consumers would be '4.9% more willing to purchase imports and 4.0% less likely to purchase domestics'. The Abrenica and Ducanes study is reported as indicating that distilled spirits have low own- and cross-price elasticity and that local and imported brands are nonsubstitutable. The only conclusion drawn from the studies by the Panel (in the introductory section) is that 'despite their shortcomings, both studies suggest that, within the Philippines' market, a simultaneous increase in the price of domestic spirits and decrease in the price of imported spirits, such as that which would result from an equalization in the respective level of the excise tax, could result in the substitution of the consumption of imported spirits in lieu of domestic spirits'.[80]

All this says is the demand for domestic and foreign spirits is not 'pathological' or in other words that it respects the regularity properties expected of any demand system, namely that demand will increase with the price of substitutes and decrease in own price. Surely, the Panel did not need the studies in order to reach that conclusion. One would have expected the Panel to draw some conclusion from the studies, not about the direction of the effects (the observation that the products are not complement), but about their magnitude of the effects (the extent to which the products are substitute).

The studies are further discussed by the Panel in its assessment of whether the products are 'like' and 'DCOS'. In the relevant sections, the Panel provides some information about the methodology of the studies. It appears that the Euromonitor study is based on an (online) survey and that the Abrenica and Ducanes study is

79 See Panel Report, *Philippines–Spirits*, section on factual aspects, paras. 2.31 to 2.45.
80 Ibid., para. 2.45.

based on a conjoint analysis.[81] The Panel also reveals that the studies have been criticized by the opposite parties but does not discuss the merit of these criticisms at any length.[82] The Panel notes that neither of the studies is based on historical data on price and quantities (which it would regard as more reliable). The Panel then observes that the Euromonitor study is 'not an attempt to estimate and provide figures for the cross-price elasticity for imported . . . and domestic . . . distilled spirits', and accordingly seems to attach little weight to the study. It is hard to tell whether the judgment of the Panel is appropriate without being told more about the methodology of the study.

With respect to the Abrenica and Ducanes study, the Panel observes that it estimates cross-price elasticities to be in the range of −0.01 to 0.07. It is not clear whether this is a confidence interval or the result of different estimations (in which case, the first one would be puzzling). The Panel notes that these cross-price elasticities are regarded by the authors as low but does not offer its own view on the matter. In a footnote, the Panel seems to endorse some criticism put forward by the EU regarding this study (in particular regarding possible biases in the choices that respondents were confronted with and the econometric method used to infer the cross-price elasticities).[83] But the footnote does not appear well placed, at the end of a sentence that discusses the price counterfactuals used for some of the conclusions.

Indeed, the Panel seems to be very concerned with the fact that neither of the two studies isolates the effect of a single price change (but rather compares scenarios in which both domestic and foreign prices change). This point is well taken since an increase in consumption for one product which follows a decrease in own price and an increase in the price of substitutes is consistent with the independent demand for the products. It is still a bit puzzling as presumably the conjoint analysis and regressions performed by Abrenica and Ducanes should in principle allow for the evaluation of the effects of single price changes. It should be merely a matter of interpretation of the coefficients.

Hence, the Panel does not provide a detailed discussion of the methodologies used by the studies and the weight that it attaches to their findings. What is even more surprising is then the Panel's conclusion[84] that both 'studies support the proposition that there is a significant degree of competitiveness or substitutability in the Philippines's market between the distilled spirits at issue in the present dispute'. Importantly, the Panel's statement is no longer (as in the introductory section) about the fact that the products cannot be said not to be substitutes but explicitly about the 'significance' of that substitution. How the Panel can, in particular,

81 Ibid., para. 7.55.
82 Ibid., paras. 7.53 and 7.110.
83 Ibid., note 507.
84 Ibid., para. 7.113.

construe the Abrenica and Ducanes study as supporting the finding that there is a significant degree of substitution between domestic and foreign products, despite their own explicit conclusion to the contrary (whose validity is not explicitly denied by the Panel), is really unclear.

Overall, the level of transparency on the analysis performed by the Panel with respect to the economic studies is thus rather poor. This does not allow for proper accountability of the Panel.

3.3.1 Likeness

With respect to likeness, the Appellate Body seems to emphasize at various places that the core concept that would determine its assessment is the 'competitive relationship' between domestic and foreign products. For instance, in discussing the relevance of physical characteristics, the Appellate Body indicates that the Panel examines various criteria 'in order to make a determination about the nature and extent of a competitive relationship between and among the products'. The Appellate Body further notes that 'products that have very similar characteristics may not be like within the meaning of Art III:2 if their competitiveness or substitutability is low, while products that present certain physical differences may still be considered to be like if such physical differences have a limited impact on the competitive relationship between and among the products'.[85]

In discussing the relevance of the raw material used to make the products, the Appellate Body notes that if differences in raw materials 'leave fundamentally unchanged the competitive relationship among the final products, the existence of these differences would not necessarily negate a finding of "likeness" under Art III:2'.[86] Further, in discussing the criteria used by Panels to establish 'likeness' under Art III:2, first sentence, the Appellate Body stresses that these criteria are not exhaustive and are the 'tools available to panels for organizing and assessing the evidence relating to the competitive relationship between and among the products'.[87]

It is not entirely clear, however, what is meant by the 'competitive relationship', which is sometimes distinguished from 'substitutability'. In the context of the framework discussed above, one possible interpretation is that a competitive relationship is simply meant to refer to demand substitution and hence the extent to which different products are close substitutes. According to this first interpretation, a competitive relationship would thus be determined only by the characteristics of consumer demand. Another interpretation is that a competitive relationship refers not only to consumer demand but also to competitive dynamics (and the fact that competitive relationship is sometimes distinguished from substitutability would

85 Appellate Body Report, *Philippines–Spirits*, para. 120.
86 Ibid., para. 125.
87 Ibid., para. 131.

support that interpretation). According to this latter interpretation, 'competitive relationship' would be determined by price responses so that products would be in a competitive relationship when a change in the price of one product prompts a strong response from the supplier of the other products. In terms of the framework discussed above, the competitive relationship would be a function of demand primitives but also of the conditions of competition. We would, of course, naturally favour such an interpretation, given that the protection granted by discriminatory treatment (or the foreclosure of foreign products) is affected by both factors.

Some additional findings by the Appellate Body may be worth discussing. First, the Appellate Body observes that consumer perceptions may be relevant for other dimensions than physical characteristics. The Appellate Body considered that 'while consumer perception of products is highly relevant to the overall determination of likeness under Art III:2, . . . this element may reach beyond the products' properties, nature, and qualities, which concern the objective physical characteristics of the products'.[88] Indeed, consumer preferences and their ultimate choices will be affected by other dimensions beyond the products' physical characteristics, such as its brand image. However, one would expect that brand image is precisely one of the main dimensions by which domestic and foreign spirits differ, which might indeed support the view that domestic and foreign spirits are not 'like'.

The Panel also discusses the argument that 'because of the difference in purchasing power of its population, the Philippine domestic market is segmented into two groups'.[89] According to this argument, the poorer segment of the population would be unable to purchase the imported items. The Panel, however, insists that the argument would rest on evidence that there are two separate population groups with distinct consumption patterns. The Panel questions the plausibility of this, observing that 'the population in the Philippines does not appear to be divided into two separate groups, but is rather distributed along a continuum of income brackets'. This analysis is a bit puzzling.

First, it is clear that disposable income (the budget constraint faced by consumers) is a determinant of consumer choices; consumers with a tight budget constraint can be expected to be both more sensitive to the price of domestic items and less sensitive to the price of imported products (a decrease in the price of foreign products might not induce buyers to switch as they still prefer to buy the domestic item in light of their budget constraint).

Second, the pricing strategy of a domestic firm facing a distribution of income among potential buyers (and hence different own- and cross-price elasticities) depends very much on whether the domestic firm is able to engage in price discrimination. To illustrate, a domestic firm may find it profitable to charge low

88 Ibid., para. 132.
89 Panel Report, *Philippines–Spirits*, para. 7.59.

prices for more price-elastic buyers (the less affluent) and high prices to others, for whom the imported items would be a realistic alternative. In such circumstances, the existence of a segment in which the foreign spirits are a realistic alternative and in which higher prices can be charged might be seen as evidence that, at least for some buyers, domestic firms benefit from the discriminatory taxes (more on this below).[90] Third, in the absence of price discrimination, the domestic firm will have to charge a single price, which will be determined by the aggregate elasticity that it faces. The elasticity will, in turn, be determined by the distribution of consumers. If the majority of consumers are highly elastic, the aggregate elasticity will tend to reflect this, and the optimal price will tend to be low.

Hence, it would appear (i) that if price discrimination is feasible, the existence of different segments might indeed allow the domestic firms to benefit from the discriminatory tax and (ii) that the existence of just two identifiable customer groups is unimportant. What matters is whether price discrimination is feasible, and it may take place across more than two groups. If price discrimination is not feasible, the identification of different customer groups only matters insofar as they will determine the aggregate elasticity.

The Appellate Body's discussion of distribution channels should also be seen in this light. The Appellate Body supports the Panel in attaching little weight to the observation that distribution channels may be different for domestic and imported products and in particular that, unlike imported items, domestic products are also distributed off premises. This difference in distribution channels may be consistent with the view that price discrimination across channels is feasible and that there is a segment of buyers (those consuming spirits at home) for whom foreign spirits are not close substitutes for domestic products.

3.3.2 *Directly competitive or substitutable products*

The question of whether a possible segmentation of the domestic market for spirits may be relevant is further examined by the Appellate Body in its discussion of whether the products are DCOS. The Appellate Body acknowledges that large differences in price between domestic and foreign spirits could demonstrate that they belong to different segments. However, the Appellate Body, in support of the Panel, attaches weight to the finding that there is an overlap in the prices of imported and domestic distilled spirits. The Appellate Body also supported the Panel's finding that evidence of substitution in one segment supports the conclusion that imported and domestic spirits are capable of being substituted in the Philippines.

90 It is unclear from this perspective why the Philippines argued that there are different consumer groups. Its argument may have been that discrimination is not feasible and the weight of elastic consumers is such that the aggregate own-price elasticity of demand for domestic items is high and that the aggregate elasticity of demand for domestic items with respect to the price of foreign items is low.

Evidence of overlapping prices between domestic and foreign products should be interpreted carefully. Even if the Appellate Body is not explicit about its analysis, it may suggest that there is a chain of substitution between different products so that some unbranded, low-quality domestic products are substitutes for higher-quality domestic products, which in turn are substitutes for low-quality imported products, themselves substitutes for higher-quality, branded imported items. The conclusion that products belong to the same relevant market because they are linked by a chain of substitution is a common fallacy in antitrust. Similarly, in the current framework, the existence of a chain of substitution may appear to be consistent with limited competitive interactions between the bulk of domestic and foreign products.

Regarding the segmentation, it is not clear why the 'capability' of being substituted is relevant in the absence of evidence that demand will indeed change over time in such a way that capability to substitute will turn into actual substitution. More generally, one can question the finding of the Appellate Body that the Panel did not have to focus on the most representative segment. This seems to suggest that in the presence of clear segmentation such that different prices apply in the different segments and such that for the largest segment of consumers there is no substitution between the domestic and foreign products, the Appellate Body would still be satisfied with evidence that there is a narrower segment in which domestic and foreign products are substitutes. This would seem questionable at least from the perspective of the assessment of the overall effects on domestic producers (since only a fraction of their sales would then be affected by the discriminatory taxes).

The Appellate Body explicitly considers the significance of the price counterfactual with which it is faced. It observes that taxes on foreign products are 10 to 40 times higher than those applied to domestic products and that actual competition with such differential taxes is probative of 'potential' competition, presumably if differences in taxes were lower. The term 'potential' competition may be a bit misleading here, in particular if reference is made to the antitrust practice, in which potential competition normally refers to entry. What the Appellate Body seems to have in mind here is rather the degree of 'competition' or substitution that would be observed in a different price counterfactual. However, as discussed above, the logic of the Appellate Body is not compelling; it seems to say that because products compete even under such high price differences, they will inevitably compete in a counterfactual in which prices are closer. As mentioned above, what is puzzling is rather that foreign products have any sales at all with such high price differences, if they are indeed such close substitutes to domestic products.

4. Conclusion

WTO jurisprudence relating to like products and DCOS products has tended to focus on a set of criteria derived from the *Border Tax Adjustments* case. These factors – physical characteristics, consumer preferences, end-uses, and tariff classification – are somewhat determinable through ordinary, as opposed to empirical economic, factual determination, although the tendency has been to use cross-price elasticity of demand as at least one way of suggesting consumer preferences. However, the Appellate Body has clearly and consistently stated that these factors are to be used to determine a single underlying question: whether products are in close enough competition to be 'like' or DCOS. Given that there is a more methodologically sophisticated, and more precise and plausible, way to determine the scope of competition, it is difficult to continue to justify using the less sophisticated and precise *Border Tax Adjustment* approach. Implicit in a more precise approach would be the establishment of benchmark degrees of competitiveness for determining like products and DCOS products, respectively.

We have suggested that any methodology for assessing discriminatory taxes should formulate a benchmark in terms of the extent of discrimination and its effects. A natural candidate in this respect would be the tax differential between domestic and foreign products and the pass-through rate. In the same way that market power is an increasing function of market share, the pass-through rate is an increasing function of concentration. This suggests that market structure could be taken as given in evaluating the scope of products over which a certain pass-through rate would arise. When this market is found, the extent to which competition in the domestic market would bring down the pass-through rate (and hence the effect of the discriminatory treatment) could be assessed.

However, a move toward a more sophisticated and precise approach to determining competition would definitively exclude from the determination of like products and DCOS products the question of the regulatory justification for differential treatment. It is entirely possible that products would be in very close competition, but would result in substantial consumption externalities, or even production externalities, that would make it perfectly rational, and desirable, to impose regulatory distinctions.

Therefore, either a new approach to interpretation, or a treaty amendment, would be appropriate to ensure that national measures that are justified in this way are not found to violate Article III of GATT. An interpretative approach would seem readily available that would include in the determination of 'so as to afford protection' in connection with the Second Sentence and 'less favourable treatment' in connection with Article III:4 the consideration of the nonprotectionist regulatory justification of the national measure. Indeed, in *US–Clove Cigarettes*, the Appellate Body, has interpreted 'less favourable treatment' within the context of Article 2.1 of the Agreement on Technical Barriers to Trade, to include an assessment of nonprotectionist regulatory justification.[91]

91 Appellate Body Report, *United States – Measures Affecting the Production and Sale of Clove Cigarettes*, WT/DS406/AB/R, adopted 24 April 2012, para. 182.

However, there is no readily available textual 'hook' on which to hang this consideration in connection with First Sentence cases, and so it may be best to interpret 'like products' very narrowly in connection with First Sentence cases, focusing not just on competition but on the degree to which nonprotectionist regulatory rationales are implicated.

The TBT Panels: *US–Cloves, US–Tuna, US–COOL*

ROBERT HOWSE
New York University School of Law
PHILIP I. LEVY
University of Virginia Darden School of Business

Abstract: In a series of controversial 2011 decisions, WTO DSM Panels sought to reconcile legitimate regulatory interests of the state with various obligations to treat imported products in an even-handed and not unnecessarily trade-restrictive manner. Among the key points of contention were which obligation pertained in each case – national treatment, limits on technical regulations, or rules governing standards. In each case, the Panel imposed significant restrictions on national regulatory practices, and in each case the Panel reasoning was challenged by the Appellate Body. This paper addresses some of the key legal and economic issues raised in the original Panel decisions, leaving the late-breaking Appellate Body decisions for future analysis. Given the unsettled nature of the terrain, the economic analysis focuses primarily on the question of national treatment, while the legal analysis deals with other interesting points that emerge from these rulings, such as the appropriate level of deference to international standards and the legitimacy of labeling requirements.

1. Overview

The three cases we consider together bring to mind the classic Japanese film by Kurosawa, *Rashomon*. In that film, the same past event is recounted in very different ways by different observers. Applying that cinematic device to the three WTO cases at hand, one could tell a generic version of their tale in two ways:

1. A heroic, publically interested domestic government, eager to protect the public, notes that an imported product has noticeably different health and environmental effects than its domestic counterpart. This government, mindful of its neoclassical economic obligation to internalize externalities wherever they are found, crafts

regulations to protect the public from the potential dangers of these imported products. The government is no less concerned about the health and environmental impact of the domestic products; they will be covered by the regulations as well. The impact on imported and domestically produced products may differ, but that is an inescapable effect of the differences in the products.

Or:

2. A conniving and corrupt group of public officials sets out to protect a favored domestic industry from international competition. For whatever reason, foolish predecessors have blocked this country's ability to impose outright protection. But there is still hope. So long as these officials can find plausible differences between the domestic and imported products, they can write regulations that block the imported products, using those differences as justification. Of course, they cannot do this for just any differences (shape, color, etc.). The officials will have to find something legitimate, like some difference in health effects or environmental impact. But this is a problem that creative minds can solve. Whatever the rationale, the goal of promoting domestically produced products over imported ones will be achieved.

In the *US–Tuna II (Mexico)* case,[1] the United States argued that Mexican tuna-fishing methods posed a greater threat to dolphins than those used by US fleets. It adopted labeling regulations that would let consumers choose between tuna that met 'dolphin-safe' standards and tuna that did not. Mexico claimed its fishing methods posed no greater risk and that this labeling approach would either saddle it with unacceptable costs or would effectively exclude it from the market.

In the *Country of Origin Labeling* case (*US–COOL*),[2] the United States imposed regulatory requirements that would let US consumers know from whence their meat came. While various scares about cattle diseases might lead one to think that this was a human health and safety measure, the United States actually argued that it was not, that the intent was just to 'provide consumer information about origin'.[3] Canada and Mexico claimed that this measure was really an attempt at protectionism, one that would make imported livestock more difficult and costly to work with, thereby reducing the demand for their products.

In the *US–Cloves* case,[4] the United States prohibited flavored cigarettes, with exceptions made for tobacco and menthol flavors. The measure was part of the

1 Panel Report, *United States – Measures Concerning the Importation, Marketing and Sale of Tuna and Tuna Products*, WT/DS381/R, adopted 13 June 2012, as modified by Appellate Body Report WT/DS381/AB/R (*US – Tuna II (Mexico)*).

2 Panel Report, *United States – Certain Country of Origin Labelling (COOL) Requirements*, WT/DS384/R / WT/DS386/R, adopted 23 July 2012, as modified by Appellate Body Report WT/DS384/AB/R / WT/DS386/AB/R (*US – COOL*).

3 *US – COOL*, WTDS386R-01, p. 144.

4 Panel Report, *United States – Measures Affecting the Production and Sale of Clove Cigarettes*, WT/DS406/R, adopted 24 April 2012, as modified by Appellate Body Report WT/DS406/AB/R (*US – Cloves*).

Family Smoking Prevention and Tobacco Control Act[5] and was meant to address health concerns about smoking. The US Food and Drug Administration argued that flavored cigarettes had special appeal to young people and made it easier to start smoking, by masking the tobacco flavor. The measure was thus directed at cutting into the more than 400,000 US smoking deaths each year. Indonesia, the primary source for clove cigarettes sold in the United States, argued that this ban unfairly discriminated against its exports, particularly since menthol cigarettes made in the United States were excluded from the ban.

A standard, reductionist economic approach to these questions might argue that any time a similar imported product is afforded worse treatment than its domestic equivalent, there is protectionism at play. That, in fact, is the basis for the 'national-treatment' provision in the General Agreement on Trade and Tariffs (GATT) Article III:4, which reads:

> The products of the territory of any contracting party imported into the territory of any other contracting party shall be accorded treatment no less favourable than that accorded to like products of national origin in respect of all laws, regulations and requirements affecting their internal sale, offering for sale, purchase, transportation, distribution or use.

Yet this begs many questions. What does it mean for products to be similar? Does this mean that treatment must be exactly the same? What if the same treatment (e.g. a labeling requirement) proves significantly more costly for imported products than for domestically produced products? In judging either product similarity or treatment, do we care more about descriptions of the products or measures, or do we care about observed economic effects, such as substitutability in consumption or the effects on price or trade flows? And what of other parts of the GATT that allow for exceptions, particularly in the case of certain noble motives, such as protecting the health of humans, animals, and plants (the subject of GATT Article XX)? Does the given rationale for imposing the restrictions matter? And how do we decide whether the rationale that was offered was the true motivation for the measure, or just a convenient pre-certified excuse that masks protectionist intent?

The challenge for lawyers is at least as difficult. Even if one were to sort out these questions of principle, there are questions of where, exactly, in the texts of agreements or in the case law, these principles are to be found. The governance of regulation is significantly more complicated than the governance of measures such as tariffs and quotas, for the reasons given above. There are sections of text describing national-treatment obligations, sections governing technical barriers to trade, sections covering sanitary and phytosanitary regulation, and sections providing exceptions to the other sections. Lawyers, when arguing these cases

5 Pub. L. 111-31, 2009.

before Panels, tend to include any and all arguments and provisions that might work in their favor. This leads to sprawling, inclusive cases.

It also leads to confusion. The central issues raised in *US–Cloves, US–Tuna II*, and *US–COOL* are not new. They have been taken up over the years in cases such as *Japan–Alcoholic Beverages I*[6] and *II*[7] (1987, 1996), *US–Shrimp*[8] (1998), *Korea–Alcoholic Beverages* (1999),[9] and *EC–Asbestos*[10] (2001). Yet, despite this ample case history, crucial points remained unresolved. The uncertainty was sufficiently great that in each of the three cases handed down in the last year, the Appellate Body promptly overturned at least some of the key legal findings by the Panels.

From the standpoint of those who follow these questions closely, one of the headlines to emerge from this year's decisions is a new emerging standard for how to approach national-treatment cases, one that parallels well-established analytical approaches elsewhere and emphasizes the competitive relationship between products in determining whether they have been afforded 'less favorable treatment'. The Panel rulings also provided substantial new insight into restrictions on Technical Barriers to Trade (TBT). In each of these cases, the complainant succeeded in its claim of a TBT violation, and in each case the Panel considered a number of operative provisions of TBT, including Article 2.1 (National Treatment and Most Favoured Nation (MFN) Treatment), Article 2.2 (the requirement that technical regulations be no more trade-restrictive than necessary to achieve a legitimate objective); and Article 2.4 (the obligation to use international standards as a basis for technical regulations where they exist and where they are relevant and appropriate).

From those who carry placards and denounce the reign of faceless bureaucrats in Geneva, some of the headlines will be quite different. They will be that, once again, the WTO has impinged on the right of national governments to promote health, protect the environment, and inform consumers.

In this report, we will first attempt to extract the significant findings in each of the three cases. Whereas the economic analysis will delve more into the central question of national treatment, the legal analysis will largely focus elsewhere. This is because the three Appellate Body rulings to date have significantly rewritten the legal interpretation offered by the Panels. Thus, the legal aspects of national treatment will be an important topic for next year. This year's economic analysis can play into next year's more comprehensive analysis. For this year, we will also delve into other interesting legal and economic points that emerge from these rulings, such as the

6 BISD, 34th Supp. 83 (1988).

7 *Japan – Taxes on Alcoholic Beverages*, WT/DS 8/WT/DS 10/WT/DS 11.

8 *United States – Import Prohibition of Certain Shrimp and Shrimp Products*, WT/DS 58.

9 *Korea – Taxes on Alcoholic Beverages*, WT/DS 75/WT/DS 84.

10 *European Communities – Measures Affecting Asbestos and Asbestos-Containing Products*, WT/DS 135.

appropriate level of deference to international standards and the legitimacy of labeling requirements.

The next section discusses the key issues in the three cases. Section 3 presents some of the economic questions at issue, while Section 4 focuses on the prominent legal aspects of the rulings. Section 5 concludes.

2. The key issues in the cases

US–Cloves

The context of the *US–Cloves* case is the long-standing and intensifying efforts of the United States to address the immense public-health consequences of tobacco use and addiction through a variety of regulatory approaches. Based on evidence that cigarettes with added flavors have a particular capacity to attract young people to smoking, the United States moved towards the banning of such cigarettes, in particular in the dispute at hand, clove cigarettes, which are almost overwhelmingly foreign-produced; Indonesia, the complainant in this case, having the bulk of the US market share. However, the US measure exempted menthol cigarettes, which are used by a hugely greater number of smokers than cloves. The Panel found that the US measure violated the national-treatment provision of TBT (Article 2.1). It applied a two-step approach, first of all examining whether Indonesian clove cigarettes and US menthol cigarettes were 'like products' and then, having found that they were, it considered whether there was less favorable treatment of cloves than menthol. To determine whether the products were 'like', the Panel used an approach (disapproved before and after this ruling by the Appellate Body) that considers likeness from the perspective of the defending Member's regulatory objectives. Here the objective was taken as preventing young people from getting addicted to cigarettes through their attraction to flavored cigarettes; since both cloves and menthol were flavored, they were like products from this perspective. With respect to less favorable treatment, the Panel found that since the vast bulk of clove cigarettes were imported and menthol cigarettes domestically produced, there was less favorable treatment of the group of imported products in relation to the group of domestic products. In coming to this conclusion, the Panel ignored arguments by the United States that there were significant differences in the regulatory challenges posed, respectively, by bans on clove and menthol cigarettes. Since the latter were already smoked by millions of people, the health issues of dealing with their dependency on a product no longer permitted (and the related issues of a possible black market) made banning menthol a vastly different undertaking than in the case of a specialty product like cloves.

At the same time, the Panel found the US measure justified under Article 2.2 of the TBT. While Indonesia had proposed a variety of other forms of tobacco regulation that it claimed were less restrictive than an outright ban on clove cigarettes, the Panel held that each of these alternatives was merely asserted by

Indonesia as hypothetically open to the United States, but without proof that it was reasonably available and would, in fact, achieve, to the same extent as a ban, the level of protection against the public-health effects of smoking.

The Appellate Body, while considerably modifying the Panel's legal interpretations with respect to TBT 2.1, including the use of regulatory objectives to determine whether products are 'like', upheld the finding of a national-treatment violation. The Appellate Body essentially based its ruling here on the Panel's finding of fact that the United States had not adequately shown that the difference in magnitude and kind of the regulatory challenge, posed by banning menthol cigarettes, justified the decision to ban cloves not menthol as legitimate and nondiscriminatory and therefore as consistent with treatment 'no less favorable'.

US–Tuna II

In *US–Tuna*, Mexico challenged a US measure that monitored and enforced a private voluntary label on tuna, the 'dolphin-safe' label. While Mexico made some polemical claims that the US measure was 'coercive' and was not in the spirit of international cooperation with respect to dolphin conservation under the Agreement on the International Dolphin Conservation Program (AIDCP), a regional intergovernmental regime for dolphin protection, its more precise legal claims focused on two aspects of the US measure. First of all, as interpreted by the US Courts, the US legal framework required the prohibition of the use of the label on tuna marketed in the United States in any instance where the tuna was caught by a method involving encircling or setting upon dolphins. This method is attractive to tuna fishers in the Eastern Tropical Pacific (ETP), where Mexican boats fish for tuna, because in that region dolphins are known to swim with tuna. Mexico argued that by not allowing tuna fished in this way to be certified as dolphin-safe, even if no actual dolphin was killed despite the encircling or setting upon of dolphins, the United States violated Article 2.1 of TBT; since this was a method typically used by Mexican fishers, not allowing it to qualify for 'dolphin-safe' labeling *de facto* limited the competitive opportunities for Mexican tuna in the United States.

Secondly, Mexico claimed that, while the United States had a strict monitoring and enforcement scheme for tuna originating in the ETP, with respect to tuna fished *outside* the ETP the United States allowed the label 'dolphin safe' to be used based upon the self-declaration of the captain of the fishing vessel that no dolphins had been set upon and no dolphins killed. Mexico did produce some credible evidence that there was genuine harm to dolphins from tuna-fishing outside the ETP, thus putting into question the justification for treating tuna from the two geographic regions so different. Since the United States made a distinction based upon geographical origin of the tuna, requiring much stricter regulatory enforcement within the ETP, the area where Mexican tuna was sourced, Mexico argued that there was a national-treatment violation. The Panel tended to conflate these rather different claims into a single claim of *de facto* discrimination with respect to the requirement of not setting on dolphins. While finding that Mexican 'tuna' and US 'tuna' were like products, the Panel rejected the conflated claim, based on the observation that at the time the measure was introduced both US and Mexican fishing boats were using the method of setting upon dolphins, and thus the initial competitive effect on US and Mexican tuna of the banning of this method was the same. The choice of US fishers to avoid the method in order to be able to have their tuna certified as dolphin-safe and the Mexican fishers not to do so was a business decision, and did not reflect any lack of even-handedness in the requirement itself.

A threshold issue in the *Tuna* case was whether the US measure fell within the definition of a 'technical regulation' given that it was not a mandatory labeling scheme; there was no requirement that tuna be labeled for dolphin safety (or unsafety). The measure merely ensured that when the claim 'dolphin-safe' was made, certain criteria were followed that provided an adequate assurance that dolphins were not being killed or hurt. Even though, to use the precise definitional terms of 'technical regulation' in TBT, the US measure did not make the characteristic in question – 'dolphin safety' – mandatory for the product, which was defined as 'tuna' to be marketed in the United States, the Panel found that the measure was a technical regulation because it had *some* mandatory features. This is a very controversial finding, which has now been upheld by the Appellate Body, and we will make some criticisms of it in our analysis below.

Mexico also argued that there was a violation of TBT 2.2 because the US objective of informing consumers and protecting dolphins could be achieved if the United States were to permit both the label that it was now, in effect, imposing as the sole label and the alternative AIDCP dolphin-safe label, the latter allowing tuna to be caught in setting upon dolphins. According to Mexico, consumers could make an informed choice and if they wanted to ensure that tuna was not caught through setting upon dolphins, they could always choose the label certifying to that effect. The Panel held that, while having both labels freely available could create consumer confusion, it would be a less trade-restrictive alternative, provided that this confusion was avoided through a requirement that the label on each can of tuna be accompanied by explanatory language that indicated the precise claims behind the particular label at issue. It is surprising that the Panel would find a violation of 2.2 based on the failure to adopt this information-intensive least-restrictive alternative of explanatory tuna labels, since it was never proposed by Mexico, and never discussed in the pleadings or the hearings.

Finally, Mexico claimed that the United States was in violation of TBT 2.4 because it did not use the AIDCP alternative labeling scheme as a basis for its regulation. Mexico argued that the AIDCP was an international standard within the meaning of TBT 2.4. The Panel held that the AIDCP was an international standardization body, even though it is a regional organization to which only a small subset of WTO adhere, because at a particular point in time in the history of this organization there was a possibility for interested states outside the region to join it as parties to the treaty (this window had long passed). However, the Panel ultimately determined that there was no violation based on the finding that the standard was inappropriate and ineffective to achieve the US objective, since that objective concerned avoiding harms to dolphins explicitly connected to the technique of setting upon them, such as stress and trauma.

The Appellate Body reversed the Panel's finding of a violation of TBT 2.2 and significantly altered its analysis of 2.1 and 2.4, but ultimately found a violation of 2.1; given the rather sharp discrepancy of treatment in the US scheme between tuna fished in the ETP (the operating zone of Mexican tuna fishers) and outside the ETP, the AB held that there was a lack of evenhandedness, constituting a violation of 2.1 based upon the methodology it had set out in *Cloves*.

US–COOL

The *US–COOL* case concerned a mandatory labeling scheme for the country of origin of a number of food products; the dispute however centered on the mandatory labeling of meat. The complainants, Mexico and Canada, claimed that the labeling scheme violated Article 2.2 of the TBT Agreement, in that the challenged measure in fact did not serve to fulfill the objective in question. In the *COOL* case, the United States required that the country of origin of the meat in question be disclosed through the employment of a series of labels applicable to different situations. A US-origin label was to be used to designate 'beef [or] . . . pork . . . derived from an animal that was . . . exclusively born, raised and slaughtered in the United States' (Label A). A 'Multiple Countries of Origin' label was to apply where there is more than one country of origin in that, at different stages, the animal was in different countries – for example, born in Canada and raised in the United States or born and raised in Canada and slaughtered in the United States (Label B). A third label applied where the animal was in the United States only at the stage of slaughter (Label C). A final label addressed the situation where an animal was in a particular foreign country at all stages ('Foreign Origin-D'). Additionally, in the case of ground meat and chicken products, the label must list all countries of origin or all 'reasonably possible' countries of origin. Canada and Mexico argued that this multi-label approach did not fulfill the US objective of providing as clear and accurate information as possible to consumers with respect to the origin of their meat, since the B and C labels and the ground-meat labeling were ambiguous and confusing in indicating to consumers that the meat could come from one or more of a number of countries. Canada and Mexico maintained that to be in fulfillment of the US legitimate objective, i.e. to be 'clear and accurate', labeling would have to indicate not merely the possible range of countries where the animal might have been at some stage, but in respect of each individual package of meat, which country it actually was in at each of the stages and for how long.

The Panel in *COOL* agreed with the complainants that the measure did not serve the US objective of providing consumers with clear and accurate information concerning the national origin of the products at issue, and on this ground it found a violation of 2.2. (As will be discussed more thoroughly below, the legal interpretation underlying this finding is highly questionable.) Under Article XX (*Brazil–Tyres*[11]), a measure must be in relation to an objective covered by the treaty provision, must make a material contribution to that objective, and must be least-trade-restrictive in the sense that there is no reasonably available alternative measure that achieves the level of protection sought by the regulating measure, i.e. reduces the risk to the level deemed acceptable for that society by the authorities of the regulating measure. There is no requirement that the measure achieve the objective sought to the *greatest extent possible*. Yet the *COOL* Panel read this into 2.2 of the TBT Agreement. Indeed, a requirement that a Member's measure achieve a legitimate objective to the greatest extent possible would be inconsistent with the right under TBT of a Member to choose its level of protection, which the Appellate Body has recently in its Report in *US–Cloves* (subsequent to the *COOL* Panel decision) affirmed as fundamental to the object and purpose of the TBT Agreement. A Member could choose a high level of protection, but limitations in resources and other legitimate public-policy objectives might not allow it to fully achieve that level of protection. This is one reason why a Member's level of protection cannot be *simply* inferred from the measures it adopts. The fundamental obligation of least-trade-restrictiveness does not require that a measure achieve a Member's level of protection; it only requires that there be no alternative reasonably available alternative measure that makes an equal (or greater) contribution to the achievement of that level of protection. This criticism of the Panel will be pursued in some detail below. The Panel also made questionable factual assumptions or interpretations about the nature of the labeling scheme and how it would affect consumers' choices.

In reasoning that is extremely difficult to understand, the Panel also found a violation of TBT 2.1, National Treatment. Its reasoning seemed to center on the scenario that a meat producer that wanted to be able to sell some of its meat under the US origin label would, if it also wanted to produce meat products from imported livestock, be faced with regulatory costs in segregating the imported livestock from the domestic livestock in any stage of production taking place in the United States. Otherwise it would compromise its ability to label the meat from the US livestock as of US origin. As a consequence of this additional regulatory cost, the Panel reasoned, imported livestock would be less attractive at the margin than US livestock, thus leading to less favorable treatment of the imported livestock. Here the Panel appears not to have, as it would be expected to, compared the *group* of like imported with the *group* of like domestic products. Thus, some meat producers who found it highly profitable to process foreign-origin meat using US livestock as well, might not do so because of the regulatory costs of segregation involved in using US livestock in addition to foreign livestock. In each instance, it would be market considerations that would determine whether, at the margin,

11 *Brazil – Measures Affecting Imports of Retreaded Tyres*, WT/DS 332.

a particular producer might be inclined to avoid using US or avoid using imported livestock, due to the additional regulatory costs of using both imported and domestic as inputs.

Finally, the Panel dismissed a claim of violation of Article 2.4, largely on burden-of-proof grounds.

The Appellate Body reversed the Panel's finding of a violation of 2.2 of TBT but found a violation of 2.1. Using the methodology it developed in *Cloves*, the AB found a lack of evenhandness in that, where dealing with imported meat, processors would have to fulfill more complex or costly traceability requirements, holding information about each stage of production. This was not justified as a legitimate regulatory distinction because much of the information in question was not strictly speaking needed in order to verify the bona fides of what was being stated on the actual consumer label.

3. Economic questions

At the heart of each of these cases were questions about what makes products similar and, once similarity of products is established, how much flexibility regulators have in dealing with the products.

In the *US–Tuna II* case, there was relatively little question that tuna caught by US fishing fleets and tuna caught by Mexican fleets were directed at the same consumers and were competitive. The differences lay not in the tuna itself, but in the way the tuna was caught. In *US–Cloves*, there was a more serious question of whether products were similar. Clove cigarettes were not only produced in a different place, they had different ingredients and – arguably – a somewhat different target market than menthol cigarettes. In the *US–COOL* case, the United States was not claiming that Canadian or Mexican livestock were different or inferior, only that it was legitimate to require producers to inform consumers about the origin of their beef.

To establish an economic framework that encompasses these questions, it may be useful to start with an abstract ideal and then see how deviations from that ideal affect the analysis.

The ideal of like products and no less favorable treatment

Imagine there are two products that are identical in every respect except the country of origin. This is, in fact, the norm in standard theoretical approaches to trade with homogeneous products; wine is wine, cloth is cloth, and we quickly proceed to compare autarky prices. It has always been an abstraction, however. To really make these products identical, they must have matching dimensions, materials, functionality, methods of production, and even spillovers from those methods of production.

In the case of truly similar products, there would not be economic justification for any different treatment of an imported product once it had crossed the border. There is, of course, a large literature that talks about why a country might want to treat imported goods differently from domestically produced goods (terms-of-trade possibilities, infant-industry arguments, etc.), but efficiency arguments alone would dictate that such distinctions be made at customs posts, which are substantially fewer in number than retail outlets. The issues raised in national-treatment questions – the differential imposition of regulatory or tax requirements on goods once they have entered a country – presume that the countries have, for whatever reason, eschewed the use of tariffs to block the import of foreign tuna, cigarettes, or beef. So there is a baseline economic presumption that identical products should receive identical regulatory and tax treatment.

The reasons for the eschewal of border instruments can matter, however. If, for example, a country has no domestic production in an industry x in year t, it may agree to bind its tariffs at zero. In year $t+10$, a domestic industry may have developed. If, for political-economy or national-welfare reasons, the country's government now wishes to protect industry x, it has at least three prominent options. First, it could just live with its past commitments and rue the shortsightedness of its predecessor. Second, it could try to renegotiate the bound tariff – a potentially problematic process that will bring about lost market access in other sectors. Or, third, it could engage in constrained optimization and adopt a second-best domestic measure that replicated the protectionist effect of the tariff. If it can successfully implement the third strategy, rather than the second, it has effectively denied trading partners the rights for which they bargained when the original tariff binding was set. Blocking such a maneuver is the central rationale for the GATT's national-treatment clause.

Problems in theory

What, then, if we begin to relax the assumption that the products are identical and allow them to differ in certain dimensions. At another extreme, the situation is also easy: if the foreign product is toxic whereas the home product is not, or if the foreign product serves an entirely different function, there is no argument that it should be regulated or taxed in the same way as the domestic product.

The difficult choices lie between these two extremes. If products are truly identical, even a protectionist government will be unable to find grounds on which to discriminate against the foreign goods. If products are significantly different, then there is no objection to different policy treatments. In the space in between, there will be the possibility for distinctions between the similar products, whether for good or ill. What if foreign sugared soda comes in half-liter bottles, but domestic sugared soda comes in only smaller cans?[12] One can imagine a panoply of differences, from product dimensions, to packaging, to manufacturing method, to health effects.

12 The mayor of New York, Michael Bloomberg, recently proposed banning oversized sugared drinks in New York City on health grounds.

At the extreme of protecting human, animal, or plant health, such distinctions are presumed to be legitimate and given excepted status under GATT Article XX. Yet even in this protected realm, it is not clear how different products have to be to permit differential treatment. Suppose a domestic type of cigarette had a 10% chance of causing lung cancer while an imported cigarette had an 11% chance of causing the same cancer. Let us stipulate that this difference is statistically significant. Should a domestic government be permitted to ban the imported cigarette on the basis of its elevated health risk, while permitting the sale of the domestic type? It is actually difficult to argue against such a distinction on strictly economic grounds. We might reject such a policy if we could argue that it was inefficient under any plausible set of societal preferences. But economics has relatively little to offer in terms of positive descriptions of societal preferences.[13] Even under strong assumptions, such as individuals with identical and well-behaved preferences, the approach to something like cigarette smoking involves a tradeoff between negative health impacts and personal freedom. There is no obvious cutoff point at which the health risks become too great. So why could that cutoff point not be a 10.5% chance of lung cancer, leaving domestic cigarettes on one side of the divide and foreign cigarettes on the other?[14]

The objection is more likely to be a practical one. While 10.5%, in the previous example, *could* be the cutoff point, it would seem to be a remarkable coincidence. There would be a strong suspicion, instead, that the small difference in health risks was being used as an excuse for excluding the foreign product and that health concerns were not the true motivation. Further, even if health risks *were* the true motivation and 10.5% were the true cutoff point, the damage done by requiring identical treatment of the domestic and foreign cigarettes would likely be minor. Such a requirement would leave the government with the option of banning both types of cigarettes or allowing both. In either case, the distance between the optimal and the restricted policies would be small.

In their treatise on national treatment, Grossman *et al.* (2012) discuss the different types of errors that could occur when passing judgment on the legitimacy of such a choice:

> One possible mistake is to permit measures that should be declared illegal. The cost of such mistakes are borne by the affected trading partner, and will at least partly take the form of reduced profits of exporters, and consequent losses of

13 The strong statements that are sometimes made about societal preferences generally stem from assumptions, not observations. The strength of the assumptions necessary to make bold statements about welfare gains is one indication of the difficulty posed by more general cases.

14 This example picks a number that neatly divides domestic and foreign producers, and thus invites suspicion. There have been GATT cases along these lines, such as *Canada–Beer*, Panel Report, *Canada – Import, Distribution and Sale of Certain Alcoholic Drinks by Provincial Marketing Agencies*, BISD 39S (1992). The situation would get more complicated if we vary the hypothetical such that some domestic cigarettes have risks over 10.5% and some foreign cigarettes come in below.

> income for other interests associated with the exporting firms. The other type of mistake is to outlaw measures that should be allowed. (p. 38)

They assert that this latter type of error could be very costly, given the importance of regulations in protecting human health or the environment. This last proposition seems problematic. Suppose we have two determinants of public well-being, x and y, and an objective function that gives us a level of well-being for any value of the variable, $W(x,y)$. We can say that variable x is 'important' for well-being if W changes rapidly for a given change in x and that variable y is 'unimportant' because W changes relatively slowly for the same change.[15] If we now consider the possibility of policy errors and consider errors of the same magnitude in x and y, then it would be the case that errors in the important x variable would be more worrying. But there is no particular reason why the threshold one would apply to differences in x and y would be the same. Returning to the carcinogenic cigarettes example above, one might provide greater deference to regulatory distinctions in health exactly because it is more important. This is just to argue that, *contra* Grossman *et al.*, there should *not* be a *general* presumption that outlawing measures that should be allowed would be the more costly mistake, even if such a presumption might be justified in particular contexts where the mistake of outlawing would result in much more grave consequences (such as loss of human life) than the reverse mistake of permitting.

The balance of risks between mistakenly permitting and erroneously banning might be clearer in an example fully lodged in the health sector. Suppose domestic regulation bars the import of a promising experimental drug for HIV/AIDS, on the grounds that the drug has not yet been subject to the stricter domestic clinical-trial regimen. Lives are certainly at stake, but they are at stake in both directions. It is possible that importing the drug would save lives through treatment. It is also possible that there are lethal side effects to the drug that would have been uncovered in more rigorous testing. Thus, the high stakes that are at play with measures concerning human health are not dispositive in either direction.

In the three cases considered in this paper, Panels decided to block the regulatory measures at issue. One of the interesting economic questions to pose for these cases is how costly the decisions might be if, in fact, they were in error.

Policy challenge #1: how to decide if products are sufficiently similar to merit national-treatment protection

It is worth spending a moment on the economic challenges before the Panels in these cases. A first challenge is to determine whether products are 'like'. In fact, depending on the section of the trade agreement under discussion, the legal

15 As this is simply meant to provide a heuristic explanation, we will not worry about what metric one would apply to compare the magnitude of policy changes.

language might instead bring in products that are 'directly competitive or substitutable'. This is the difficult task of attempting to draw a bright line between identical products and those that are obviously distinct.

There are a number of obvious, descriptive measures one might use, as mentioned above, including size, functionality, health impact, and so forth. The question, though, as raised in the cigarette example above, is which of these differences is significant? The problem is that there is no generic answer to this question. The measurement difference between a half-inch wrench and 5/8-inch wrench may seem trivially small, but one may do the job and another may not. For a wrench, that measurement difference can be important; for a hemline, it may not be.

This dependence on the question being asked emerged as a key point in the Appellate Body review of the *US–Cloves* decision. There a crucial question was whether clove and menthol cigarettes were 'like' products. The Panel agreed with the complainant, Indonesia, that they were, in that they could both be smoked. The Appellate Ruling reversed:

> we disagree with the Panel that the end-use of cigarettes is simply 'to be smoked' and agree with the United States that there are more specific end-uses of cigarettes such as 'satisfying an addiction to nicotine' and 'creating a pleasurable experience associated with the taste of the cigarette and the aroma of the smoke'. We consider, however, that, based on the Panel's findings referred to above, it can be concluded that both clove and menthol cigarettes share the end-uses of 'satisfying an addiction to nicotine' and 'creating a pleasurable experience associated with the taste of the cigarette and the aroma of the smoke'. Accordingly, we consider that the more specific products' end-uses put forward by the United States also support the Panel's overall finding that clove and menthol cigarettes are like products.[16]

From an economic standpoint, this seems unsatisfying in its arbitrariness. It is certainly true that the more specific the criteria, the less probable a finding of 'likeness'. Had the Appellate Body progressed on from the 'pleasurable experience of cigarette taste' to the 'pleasurable experience of clove taste' it would have found that menthol cigarettes were different.

The possibility of looking at 'directly competitive or substitutable' in lieu of likeness seems to offer the possibility of bringing objective economic analysis to bear. The *Cloves* Panel and Appellate Body struggled with how one differentiated clove cigarettes from menthol cigarettes and both of them from cigars. One could certainly conduct econometric studies of the elasticity of substitution between products (how likely consumers are to switch in response to relative price changes). One would expect to find that the substitutability between cigars and cigarettes is lower than the substitutability between clove and menthol cigarettes, which would

16 *US – Cloves*, para. 132, p. 51.

in turn be lower than the substitutability between different brands of menthol cigarettes. The apparent precision of point estimates derived from a regression may be reassuring, but an econometric approach would still leave two problems. First, consumer-preference estimates are not always precise. These characterizations are not universal constants, waiting to be discovered (like, for example, the speed of light). They emerge from particular samples in a data set and are based on particular modeling of preferences. Even then, they emerge with error bands.

Of course, there is little we can know with precision and the perfect ought not be the enemy of the good. But this brings up the second problem: even if we assume away any error in estimation, or variability in preferences, there is no obvious economic threshold to establish to determine that products are directly competitive. One may well find that consumers are very willing to switch between different brands of gasoline, but very unwilling to switch between Coke and Pepsi.[17] That could hardly be taken to mean that Coke and Pepsi are not competitive products.

Finally, even if we could determine substitutability with precision and were able to normalize for different products, there would still be the question of what the threshold of significance might be. Ultimately, this would depend on the question one was asking. The upshot is that the fruitless grasping around by Panels and Appellate Bodies is entirely understandable.

Policy challenge #2: Similar treatment, different impact

If products are dissimilar, there is a presumption they can be treated differently through regulation. If products are similar, there is a presumption that they will be treated in like fashion. In the parlance, imported products are expected to receive treatment 'no less favorable' than similar domestic products. Here, though, an additional problem can arise.

To the extent that there are differences between similar products, those differences can mean that similar treatment will have a differential impact. This was a prominent part of the *US–Tuna II* case, though not one on which the complainant ultimately prevailed. The United States argued that it had established a set of requirements for a 'dolphin-safe' label that applied equally. Per the Panel, 'Mexico and the United States agree that the US measures are, on their face, origin neutral'.[18] After citing an earlier Appellate Body decision (*Korea–Beef*) that found

17 This, of course, is a major purpose of advertising: to convince consumers that these two types of soda are not at all the same thing. If advertising is successful, consumers are less willing to switch away from a product when the price goes up. The very malleability of this preference, though, indicates that it cannot fit the role of 'immutable constant'.

18 *US–Tuna II (Mexico)*, para. 4.251, p. 55.

that in some cases like products could receive disparate treatment, the *Tuna* Panel pulled out the double-negative:

> However, the Appellate Body did not state that a measure that does NOT treat domestic and imported like products differently is, for that reason, consistent with the national treatment obligation. That is precisely the effect of the supposedly 'origin neutral' measures at issue in this dispute.[19]

As summarized by the Panel, Mexico alleged *de facto* discrimination in the following way:

> US measures do not, on their face, discriminate on the basis of the foreign country that is the source of particular tuna and tuna products; rather, they discriminate on the basis of where the tuna is harvested and the fishing method. But this has the effect of favouring tuna and tuna products from some countries over others because different countries harvest tuna in different ocean fisheries using different fishing methods.[20]

Although the Panel found that the US labeling approach might have a detrimental impact, this did not constitute 'less favorable treatment'.

> We acknowledge, in this respect, that different products of various origins may be affected differently by a measure that lays down certain product characteristics with which compliance is mandatory. However ... what matters for the purposes of determining whether there is a violation of Article 2.1 is not only the existence of some adverse impact on some imported products, but whether the group of imported products is placed at a disadvantage, in this respect, *compared to* the groups of like domestic and imported products originating in any other country.[21]

Narrow versus expansive interpretations

While these sprawling cases encompass an array of technical issues, there are some themes that have emerged from the literature and that are relevant in the three cases at hand. Grossman *et al.* (2012) note the occasional lack of coherence in the case law, and put forward two potential approaches to interpreting national treatment. The version that may be more concerned with the potential for unduly burdening imported goods, they label 'Interpretation XX' (after Article XX, containing the list of general exceptions to member obligations). This is a more expansive interpretation of the WTO Members' obligation to address the concerns of trading partners (p. 105).

The alternative interpretation they label 'Interpretation III (after Article III, containing the national-treatment clause). This is a narrower interpretation of

19 Ibid., para. 4.252, p. 55.
20 Ibid., para. 7.260, p. 177.
21 Ibid., para. 7.375, p. 205.

Members' obligations. They provide a contrast in keeping with the fishery theme of this section:

> Interpretation XX sees Art. III GATT as a net with fine meshes, and uses Art. XX GATT to evaluate what in the catch should be thrown back to sea. Interpretation III instead lets Art. III GATT take a more select catch, but one that for the most part is meant to be kept. (p. 105)

Thus, faced with the potential for the two types of error described above, Grossman *et al.* opt to tilt away from erroneously dismissing regulation, while the three cases seem to tilt in the opposite direction (away from erroneously permitting protectionism). This is consistent with Grossman *et al.*'s assessment that the penalties for underregulation are likely to exceed the penalties for overregulation, as contested above and as explored below.

First, however, the methodology in the quoted paragraph raises an additional factor to be put in the balance. The narrower interpretation they propose (Interpretation III) uses international efficiency criteria, such as whether the party imposing the regulation could – in theory – compensate the exporting party and still come out ahead (p. 114). A rule of this sort would be very difficult to implement, as it would require careful balancing of welfare changes in both countries. Would one look, for example, at proportionate change in welfare? Or would one conclude that large countries would normally win against small countries, since the same *per capita* gains would sum to a bigger number than matching *per capita* losses.

Such an approach would seem to increase both the complexity of litigation over these points and uncertainty over the outcome. To the extent that this prolongs the process, it offers a particular advantage to those who would use the regulatory process for protectionist ends. Depending on the discount rates of participants, a US administration, for example, might feel confident that it could apply regulatory barriers to afford protection to a favored industry and that, by the time a Panel and an Appellate Body had sorted through all the complications, it would have won its industry several years of commercial advantage.

There would seem to be an asymmetry to this sort of cost. If a relatively simple rule that favors the rights of imported goods is adopted, it would certainly be subject to error, but it is harder to see how it would be subject to abuse.[22]

22 Robert Howse dissents from the policy conclusion that follows from this economic analysis for reasons that relate to considerations of legitimacy both of the WTO system as a whole and the dispute-settlement organs in particular, and the appropriate relationship between WTO competences and domestic institutions, including the legislative branch. For these considerations, he prefers Interpretation III. Nevertheless, the economic analysis above illuminates the difficulty of applying Interpretation III, and in particular how the manner in which the adjudicator appreciates and weighs complex facts may well be decisive to the outcome. This is illustrated by the three cases under discussion.

An economic review of the decisions

In this section, we review the three cases through a particular lens. Following the earlier hypothetical discussion of the balance of costs and benefits surrounding potential judicial error, we take the opportunity to use these cases as data – how costly might it be if the decisions were wrong?

Clove cigarettes

In quick response to the Clove Cigarettes Appellate Body decision, the advocacy group Public Citizen issued a press release condemning the finding:

> The World Trade Organization's (WTO) final ruling today against U.S. efforts to reduce teen smoking shows that our current trade regime is simply incompatible with basic public health regulation ... Countries should not be weakening their public health laws to comply with the anti-health, anti-environmental WTO rules.[23]

Here the depiction of the cost, if one assumes the ruling to be erroneous in its outcome, is the health cost associated with additional smoking. Yet in a national-treatment case, there is another obvious remedy: impose a burden just as onerous on the domestically produced good. The United States could choose to ban menthol cigarettes along with clove cigarettes. It is not hard to see where the political opposition to such a move might come from, but this is just a demonstration of why protectionist motives have a built-in advantage: domestic industry has representation in legislatures while imported products do not. This being said, the political economy in this particular case is exemplified not simply by a powerful domestic industry versus a foreign industry that is not represented domestically but by a small foreign niche industry (cloves) versus a large industry dominated by a relatively small number of multinational firms (menthol).

It does raise the question, however, of whether one should take political constraints as given when assessing the impact of the WTO decision. Is it legitimate to argue that a broader ban on cigarettes is not politically feasible, so the only practical choice is between limiting smoking imperfectly through blocking imports and not limiting it at all? Taking into account these political realities is not necessarily protectionism in the narrow sense that it is motivated by the goal of switching market share from foreign to domestic producers. But it is not even-handed in the sense that it reflects an imposition of a disproportionate burden on foreign economic interests for the achievement of albeit legitimate regulatory goals. The idea of national treatment as treatment no less favorable, in our view, extends beyond a discipline on protectionism in the narrow sense to this somewhat broader

23 Public Citizen, 'Public Citizen Condemns WTO Attack on U.S. Efforts to Reduce Teen Smoking', 4 April 2012, www.citizen.org/documents/release-on-wto-cigarette-ruling-4-4-12.pdf (accessed 6 March 2013).

notion of even-handedness. Even the original conception of the GATT was one not just of eliminating inefficient protection of domestic producers but ensuring that states do not externalize the costs of managing their own social and economic challenges on outsiders.[24] This is evident for example in the treatment of restrictions on *exports*, which are prohibited regardless of whether they have a protectionist effect (such as reducing the price of raw materials to domestic industries in competition with foreign industries). They are banned subject to exceptions such as Article XX(g), conservation of exhaustible natural resources, which notably requires even-handedness, i.e. that such restrictions be imposed in conjunction with restrictions on domestic production and consumption.

Tuna/Dolphin

Environmental groups were no more enthused about the decision in *US–Tuna II*. It was naturally interpreted as disregarding the welfare of dolphins. Yet one of the key points of contention in the case was whether Mexican methods were, in fact, more hazardous for dolphins than those advocated by the United States. Mexico had already subscribed to an international standard for dolphin protection. The problem was that the international standard differed from the US-backed standard.

The marginal environmental cost of the decision, were it considered erroneous, would be the incremental harm to dolphins imposed by following one standard versus the other. While that could, in principle, be large, it seems in this case that it is an instance of the theoretical argument provided above, in which the issue is very important, but the policy change is relatively small (the standard of dolphin protection) and the corresponding change in welfare would be relatively minor. Nevertheless, citizens/consumers may care considerably not only about overall rates of dolphin mortality but also the trauma and other harmful effects that result from the particular technique of setting on dolphins. There is nothing illegitimate in taking account of such preferences, if they exist. Here the Panel was dismissive but without Mexico having produced evidence that most consumers care only about dolphin mortality and not the specific harms to dolphins produced by setting upon them.

Country of origin labeling

As noted above, the *US–COOL* case is distinguished from its contemporaries in that it hinges not on the degree of similarity between the products in question (foreign versus domestic beef), but rather on the alleged differential impact of the labeling requirement on the complainants.[25] Given this alleged differential impact, there was substantial discussion in the Panel Report about the legitimacy of US

24 See Howse (2002).

25 All parties to the case agreed that there were compliance costs to the labeling requirements, though there was disagreement over the magnitude. Panel Report, *US–COOL*, p. 126.

motives. Mexico and Canada both claimed that the United States's true motive in adopting the *COOL* requirement was protectionist.[26] The United States argued that its objective was to provide consumers with information so they could make informed choices. Mexico and Canada then asserted that, even if this were the true objective, it was not legitimate.[27]

It was interesting how tentative this last assertion was. Neither Canada nor Mexico made a blanket claim about the legitimacy of consumer-information requirements. It could be legitimate in certain circumstances, they argued. Mexico even provided some examples: 'for health or safety purposes or for making choices according to cultural or religious beliefs or dietary choices'.[28]

Ultimately, the Panel found that the goal of providing consumer information was legitimate and that country of origin was one type of information that could legitimately be required,[29] but that the *COOL* measure was illegitimate in practice because it failed to convey meaningful origin information.[30]

There are a number of interesting economic points about the arguments and findings. The reasoning of the Panel does not seem to grapple with the relative costs and benefits of allowing such regulation. As will be discussed below in the legal analysis, the Panel disregards entirely the issue of why and to what extent the information could be valuable to consumers. Instead, it merely notes that 'consumers may indeed have preferences for products produced by or originating in particular countries for a variety of reasons'.[31] It also notes that 'a considerable proportion of WTO Members' have origin information requirements.[32] To crudely paraphrase: it's plausible and everybody does it, so it's probably okay.

Yet, from an economic standpoint, this misses some important points. First, just because consumers might be curious does not mean that sating that curiosity is worth the cost. Suppose that consumers were curious about the genealogy of every worker involved in the production of a product; could this too be required? It is hard to see how it would affect consumer choices and it would be very costly to provide, but that is qualitatively similar to the facts of the *COOL* case.

It could be argued that information is at the core of consumer choice. That is true. But it is not obvious where the information has to come from. Where buyers do not trust the voluntary self-disclosure of sellers (the lemons problem) in some circumstances they may be able to rely on nongovernmental third parties (if we wish to purchase products that are kosher or a car that handles well in turns, we can get the necessary information from private sources – kosher-certification bodies

26 *US–COOL*, para. 7.580, p. 144.
27 Ibid., para. 7.623, 7.624, p. 153.
28 Ibid., para. 7.624, p. 153.
29 Ibid., para. 7.641, p. 159.
30 Ibid., para. 7.719, p. 176.
31 Ibid., para. 7.648, p. 161.
32 Ibid., para. 7.650, p. 161.

and auto-review magazines). Of course, due to collective-action problems, and also due to third parties having interests of their own that may not be entirely aligned with those of consumers (agency costs), nongovernmental third parties may not supply the optimal quantity and quality of information. Here one need only think of the controversy surrounding the role of bond-rating agencies in the recent economic and financial crisis. But this does not still tell us about the optimal role for government with respect to consumer information: the government may (as in the case of *Tuna*) monitor and enforce the claims associated with a voluntary industry-based disclosure scheme, or, in the case of *COOL*, mandate the disclosure of certain information in a particular format. We would not necessarily argue that a government should be precluded from requiring provision of information; just because a measure fails a cost–benefit test does not render it illegitimate. However, it is notable that the Panels never really engage in any analysis of the role of government in consumer information relative to other actors.

If one is to assess the potential costs of judicial error as discussed above, the cost of the provision and the availability of alternative sources of information both come into play. If the potential change in welfare from making a choice informed (as opposed to uninformed) by country-of-origin information is small, or if alternative sources of information exist, then the potential loss from erroneously disallowing the reporting requirement will be small. On the other hand, the more onerous the reporting requirement, the greater the cost to erroneously allowing a protectionist regulation to stand. In this case, the Panel may have reached the right result for the wrong reasons.

4. Legal questions

The TBT Agreement concerns, in large part, internal policies and regulations of WTO Members. Disciplining internal regulations in a multilateral system to which states with many different political and social systems adhere is a complex and sensitive matter. While usually advancing legitimate, nonprotectionist governmental objectives, such policies may be more trade-restrictive than necessary to achieve those objectives; and there are cases where they are intentionally designed to advantage domestic interests. In legislating and regulating, governments, particularly in pluralist liberal democracies, attempt to balance the interests of diverse constituencies. Regulations serve diverse objectives and reflect compromises between different groups. In such circumstances, it is not simple to draw a line between internal policies that are legitimate exercises of domestic regulatory autonomy (even if they have some trade-restrictive effects) and those that can be considered a form of protectionism or 'cheating' on the WTO bargain, in that they undermine the market access reasonably expected from commitments on liberalization of border measures in the multilateral trading system.

During the earlier era of the multilateral trading system, based on the General Agreement on Trade and Tariffs (GATT) 1947, the concern with domestic regulation was largely focused on problems of discrimination: against imports in favor of domestic products (national treatment), and between imports from different member states (most-favored nation). The multilateral trading system was viewed as, mostly, a framework for negotiated bindings on the reduction or elimination of discriminatory border measures restricting trade, such as tariffs or quotas. In order to sustain such a bargain, it was necessary to ensure that member states did not 'cheat' on, or circumvent, these commitments through reintroducing measures amounting to import-discrimination in their domestic policies. The official theology of the trading system sanctioned complete regulatory autonomy and wide regulatory diversity: as long as they did not discriminate, member states were free to adopt whatever approach to domestic regulation they saw as appropriate. This outlook was well-suited to an international regime such as the GATT, which lacked the institutions, expertise, or explicit mandate to engage in 'positive integration' through regulatory rapprochement or harmonization.[33]

It is notable, however, that not even the nondiscrimination norm is an absolute constraint on regulatory autonomy in the GATT regime. In practice, it is largely impossible to determine, in a given case, which regulatory distinctions amount to impermissible 'discrimination', and which do not, without reference to *some* benchmarks or standards for, crudely speaking, 'legitimate' regulation. Consider debates about the meaning of 'like' products in the national-treatment obligation, such as whether social, environmental, ethical, and health considerations may be taken into account in determining whether products are 'like' for purposes of domestic regulatory treatment. Moreover, policies that violate national treatment or MFN might be justified, under certain conditions, where necessary or rationally related to particular policy objectives such as public morals, health, or the conservation of exhaustible natural resources. Judging the necessity or rationality of a particular regulatory device necessarily entails reviewing and appraising a set of domestic regulatory choices informed by diverse concerns (culture, social and community structures, administrability, the constitutional system, etc.).

In part due to recognition of this difficulty, as well as the related instability of the nondiscrimination norm as a means of disciplining domestic policy, two of the specialized agreements that emerged out of the Uruguay Round[34] gave a significant role to international standards as a means of managing the interface between domestic regulation and trade liberalization in the case of trade in goods. These were the Agreement on Technical Barriers to Trade (TBT) and the Agreement on Sanitary and Phytosanitary Measures (SPS). The international standards were imported in various ways from non-WTO standardization regimes, such as

33 For an economic perspective on the nondiscrimination norm as a basis for addressing regulatory trade 'barriers', see Horn (2006).

34 The Uruguay Round negotiations ran from 1986 to 1994, culminating in the Marrakech Declaration and Final Act of 15 April 1995, announcing the creation of the WTO.

the International Standards Organization (ISO) or the Codex Alimentarius, as normative benchmarks for judging the acceptability of WTO Members' domestic regulations from the viewpoint of trade liberalization.

The Agreement on Technical Barriers to Trade (TBT) covers technical regulations, standards, and conformity assessment with both technical regulations and standards (the definitions of each of these terms was an issue in the *Tuna* case, and we will address that below). TBT imposes obligations additional to those in the GATT. It is possible that the obligations of the TBT could apply simultaneously to those of GATT, provided the measure in question falls under the definitions in both agreements. The TBT Agreement's provisions are aimed at government regulations, and they also include a Code of Conduct for nongovernmental standardizing bodies.

Article 2.1 includes a National Treatment and MFN obligation stated in rather different language than Articles III:4 and I of the GATT respectively:

> Members shall ensure that in respect of technical regulations, products imported from the territory of any Member shall be accorded treatment no less favourable than that accorded to like products of national origin and to like products originating in any other country.

Unlike the GATT, there is no equivalent to Article XX, which would allow measures to be justified even if they provisionally violated III:4 or I where necessary to achieve certain legitimate objectives. This is an important structural difference. The provision of TBT that is akin to GATT Article XX in its language is Article 2.2, but this Article, far from functioning as an exception to Article 2.1, imposes an *additional* obligation of least-trade-restrictiveness.

Article 2.2 reads:

> Members shall ensure that technical regulations are not prepared, adopted or applied with a view to or with the effect of creating unnecessary obstacles to international trade. For this purpose, technical regulations shall not be more trade-restrictive than necessary to fulfil a legitimate objective, taking account of the risks non-fulfilment would create. Such legitimate objectives are, inter alia: national security requirements; the prevention of deceptive practices; protection of human health or safety, animal or plant life or health, or the environment. In assessing such risks, relevant elements of consideration are, *inter alia*: available scientific and technical information, related processing technology or intended end-uses of products.

The various qualifications on the substantive criterion of necessity – for example ('taking account of the risks nonfulfilment would create') least trade-restrictive – distinguish the TBT Agreement from Article XX of the GATT, which provides a means of justifying measures that have already been found to violate some provision of the GATT. Since it is not a matter of 'saving' measures that have already been impugned, the burden of proof is logically on the complainant to show that a less-restrictive alternative does exist, which would fulfill the defending Member's legitimate objective.

Under 2.2, the obligation to ensure the least-trade-restrictiveness of regulations is relative to the kinds of risks that would arise in the absence of the regulations. Deliberation about the choice of regulatory instrument can be a costly and time-consuming process. How far a Member should be expected to go in exhausting all the regulatory alternatives to find the least-trade-restrictive alternative is logically related to the kind of risk it is dealing with. Where what is at stake is a well-established risk to human life itself, a Member may be expected to act rapidly, rely on the scientific acquis to a large extent, and tend towards the more obviously effective and enforceable kinds of regulatory tools, as opposed to the more sophisticated and speculative ones.

It is important to note that Article 2.2 explicitly lists among the relevant elements of consideration in assessing risk 'available scientific and technical information'. This suggests that a WTO Member is not required to adopt or even explore a less-restrictive alternative that has not been shown as effective in achieving its legitimate objective on the basis of existing scientific and other relevant information.

Because 2.1 and 2.2 are autonomous but cumulative obligations, it follows that:

1. Even if a measure is consistent with 2.2 and the least-trade-restrictive to achieve a Member's legitimate objective, it may still be a violation of 2.1 national treatment or MFN treatment.
2. Conversely, in principle, a measure that is nondiscriminatory and indeed not in violation of any other norm of TBT may be scrutinized for whether it is least-trade-restrictive under 2.2.

These differences between GATT and TBT mean that, unless interpreted with great caution and sensitivity, TBT could be considerably more intrusive on domestic regulatory choices than the GATT. TBT raises the possibility that nondiscriminatory measures may be impugned. Also, the structure of TBT, as noted, makes national treatment and least-trade-restrictiveness separate obligations (rather than least-trade-restrictiveness being a defense or exception to other obligations like national treatment as in GATT). This leads to the possibility that even if it has not been shown to be unnecessarily trade-restrictive under 2.2 (and thus quite likely justifiable under the GATT Article XX exception), a measure may still end up in violation of TBT. This outcome seems at odds with the tolerance of regulatory diversity (and indeed the Panel in *Tuna/Dolphin* and the Appellate Body in *Cloves* ended up ruling the US measures impermissible even though they found, in effect, that these measures had not, under 2.2, been shown to be more trade-restrictive than necessary to achieve a Member's legitimate objective).

One of the key disciplines of the TBT Agreement is the obligation for WTO members to use relevant 'international standards' as a 'basis' for their technical regulations, unless the international standards are ineffective or inappropriate (Article 2.4). Yet international standards themselves are mostly of a voluntary nature and do not result, in most cases, in binding treaty commitments; quite a few of these standards are the creation of nongovernmental bodies, or private/public partnerships where industry is the driving force. By virtue of Article 2.4 of the TBT Agreement, a very broad range of normative material, including privately generated norms in some cases, is converted or transformed into an international legal obligation.

In *dicta* in the *EC–Sardines*[35] ruling, the Appellate Body has suggested that a 'very strong and substantial' relationship may be required between domestic regulations and international standards to satisfy the obligation under TBT 2.4 to use international standards as a 'basis'; the Appellate Body has clearly implied that international standards have considerable, automatic legal force in the WTO. The TBT Agreement nowhere defines international standards, nor does the Agreement attempt to list the international regimes that qualify to promulgate international standards within the meaning of TBT 2.4. (The Appellate Body ruling in *Tuna/Dolphin* does now state some judicially invented criteria to determine which international regimes qualify under TBT 2.4).

US–Cloves

National Treatment – objective assessment

Due to the Appellate Body ruling, we will not discuss in depth the findings of the Panel with respect to national treatment. Yet we do think it is relevant to note, at least as a legal issue, the manner in which the Panel dealt with some of the facts. Article 11 of the DSU places Panels under a legal duty to make an objective assessment of the matter. They cannot ignore facts properly pleaded by the parties nor give contradictory or incoherent reasons for their findings.

The United States had presented evidence that, at the margin, clove cigarettes posed additional health risks. Here is the Panel's response:

> Nonetheless, the evidence filed by the United States suggesting that the presence of eugenol and coumarin in clove cigarettes makes them more harmful to health does not lead us to a different conclusion in terms of toxicity. Regardless of whether eugenol and coumarin might allegedly cause further health problems, the principal reason why cigarettes create health risks is the inhalation of combusted substances, which may cause different types of cancer, different types of cardiovascular disease and various respiratory diseases and harms, among others.[36]

This statement is totally illogical. It makes no sense at all in terms of the analysis of health risks. Basically, the Panel is saying that, since all cigarettes are dangerous, a WTO Member – even if it has compelling evidence that, at the margin, one kind poses some special health risks that others do not pose – cannot distinguish in regulation between the two. The irrationality or incoherence in stating that

35 Appellate Body Report, *European Communities – Trade Description of Sardines*, WT/DS231/AB/R, adopted 23 October 2002, DSR 2002:VIII, 3359.

36 *US – Cloves*, para. 7.184.

evidence of additional health risks does not affect toxicity suggests that the Panel could, in this particular instance, have been found in violation of Article 11 of the DSU; the Panel was at least under a duty to assess the significance of this additional toxicity in terms of the risks that the United States was concerned with in its regulation, rather than simply dismissing it as irrelevant. But the United States did not plead this specifically before the Appellate Body.

A related concern in the manner in which the Panel dealt with the facts is a lack of clarity concerning the burden of proof with respect to whether banning menthol would entail regulatory challenges of an entirely different order or scale than banning cloves. The Panel held, as noted, that the United States had not provided convincing evidence that banning a product to which millions of people were addicted would pose a very different and much more daunting regulatory challenge than banning cloves. The Panel seems to have assumed that once Indonesia demonstrated a differential impact on imported cigarettes relative to the group of domestic 'like' products, the burden of proof would shift to the United States to explain the distinction that resulted in the differential treatment in a nonprotectionist way. The Appellate Body in *Cloves* seems to have made a similar assumption. In any case, the United States might well have assumed that it would be a matter of common sense that if one immediately cuts off legal access to a product to which a large population is addicted, that a number of significant regulatory challenges would ensue.

Consider the following reasoning of the Appellate Body, albeit interpreting a different legal provision in the SPS treaty (the complainants pointed out that though the EU banned hormone-fed beef it did not ban products where the same or higher levels of hormones occurred naturally, such as broccoli):

> 221. We do not share the Panel's conclusions that the above differences in levels of protection in respect of added hormones in treated meat and in respect of naturally-occurring hormones in food, are merely arbitrary and unjustifiable. To the contrary, we consider there is a fundamental distinction between added hormones (natural or synthetic) and naturally-occurring hormones in meat and other foods. In respect of the latter, the European Communities simply takes no regulatory action; to require it to prohibit totally the production and consumption of such foods or to limit the residues of naturally-occurring hormones in food, entails such a comprehensive and massive governmental intervention in nature and in the ordinary lives of people as to reduce the comparison itself to an absurdity. (emphasis added)[37]

Instead of clarifying what kind of proof would be required beyond commonsense intuition of the difference between banning cloves and banning menthol, the *Cloves* Panel invented its own theory as to why the difference did not matter: menthol

37 Appellate Body Report, *EC Measures Concerning Meat and Meat Products (Hormones)*, WT/DS26/AB/R, WT/DS48/AB/R, adopted 13 February 1998, DSR 1998:I, 135.

smokers could simply switch to regular (unflavored) cigarettes, thus avoiding either the need for public-health measures to treat their dependency or to address the possibility of a black market in menthol. There was no evidence in the record, however, to suggest that this would be the actual behavioral result of banning menthol.

TBT 2.2

Reinforcing the approach to least-trade-restrictiveness taken by the Appellate Body in cases such as *EC–Asbestos* and *Brazil–Tyres* with respect to Article XX of the GATT, the *Clove* Panel emphasized that an alternative measure less restrictive of trade must be one capable of being implemented at reasonable cost in the real world: it is not enough for the complainant to assert the existence of a hypothetical or theoretical less trade-restrictive alternative in order to establish a violation of TBT 2.2. If this is the case for Article XX, it must be *a fortiori* true of TBT 2.2, because, not being in the nature of an exception, the initial burden of proof with respect to all the elements is on the complaining party. Thus, the Panel held: 'The problem is that the mere listing of two dozen alternative measures without more does not show that such measures would make an equivalent contribution to the achievement of the objective at the level of protection sought by the United States. We further note that Indonesia does not specify whether it is any one of these measures, or some combination of these measures, or all of these measures, that would be the alternative measure(s).'[38] Here the Panel's findings seem correct. Indonesia's pleadings were not precise or detailed enough to allow for an evaluation of whether any particular alternative measure (or some combination of them) could function in the real world at reasonable cost to achieve the level of protection sought by the United States.

Tuna

The definition of a technical regulation

In *EC–Asbestos* and *EC–Sardines*, the Appellate Body, interpreting the text of the TBT Agreement, set out and applied a three-part test for the determination of whether a measure is a 'technical regulation'.[39] The first step involves ascertaining an 'identifiable product' to which the measure applies. The second step is to determine that the measure is a document that lays down product characteristics. The third step is to determine whether the measure is 'mandatory'.

38 *US – Cloves*, para. 7.423.

39 Appellate Body Report, *European Communities – Measures Affecting Asbestos and Asbestos-Containing Products*, WT/DS135/AB/R, adopted 5 April 2001, DSR 2001:VII, 3243, para. 67; Appellate Body Report, *European Communities – Trade Description of Sardines*, WT/DS231/AB/R, adopted 23 October 2002, DSR 2002:VIII, 3359, paras. 175–176.

Applying the first prong of this test, the Panel majority in *US–Tuna* found that there was an 'identifiable product' to which the measure applied, and that this 'identifiable product' was '*tuna*' or '*tuna product*'.[40] While the reasoning of the Panel to support its finding that 'tuna' or 'tuna product' is the relevant 'identifiable product' is sparse, it appears that this finding was consistent with the positions of both parties to this dispute.[41] In its application of the second and third steps, however, the majority erred.

In the case of the second step, the Panel wrongly characterized the measure as a document laying down a product characteristic.[42] The measure complained of by Mexico in its Request for a Panel, and as clarified in its various written submissions and oral statements before the Panel, was in the first instance the ruling of a US federal court concerning the assessment by US officials of conformity with the standards set out in the Dolphin Protection Consumer Information Act, and, second, with the various steps that the US government took to bring itself into compliance with that ruling.[43] At various points in the proceedings, Mexico underlined that it had no dispute with the standards in question themselves, provided that conformity with those standards was assessed in a manner that was, effectively, rendered illegal by the *Earth Island* court ruling.[44]

The *Earth Island* ruling is, plainly, not a document setting down product characteristics. Rather, the ruling concerns the acceptable parameters of executive discretion in the interpretation of a US statute that requires that US authorities assess and assure the conformity of market actors with a voluntary standardization scheme, *where those market actors have freely decided to participate in that scheme*. The *Earth Island* court did not explore necessary characteristics of tuna products entitled to the dolphin-safe label, but instead focused on the continued refusal of the Executive Branch to follow the instructions of both the legislature and

40 Panel Report, *United States – Measures Concerning the Importation, Marketing and Sale of Tuna and Tuna Products*, WT/DS381/R, adopted 13 June 2012, as modified by Appellate Body Report WT/DS381/AB/R, para. 7.62.

41 See First Written Submission of the Mexican States, para. 196 (noting that tuna products 'is the identifiable group of products to which the document applies'); Answers of the United States of America to the Second Set of Questions from the Panel to the Parties to Panel Question 121 at para. 44 ('The panel should look at the market of tuna products in general.')

42 Panel Report, *US–Tuna II (Mexico)*, para. 7.76.

43 Request for Establishment of a Panel by Mexico, *United States – Measures Concerning the Importation, Marketing and Sale of Tuna and Tuna Products*, WT/DS381/4 (10 March 2009) (identifying the Ninth Circuit decision in *Earth Island Inst.* v. *Hogarth* and the regulations enacted to implement it, as the measures in question); First Written Submission of the Mexican States, para. 121 (same).

44 See First Written Submission of the Mexican States, para. 128 (noting that, prior to the court decision, the US statute would have allowed tuna caught in sets where dolphins were killed or injured, but 'such possibility was rendered inapplicable by the 2007 Court decision in *Hogarth*'); Mexico's Response to First Set of Panel Questions, Question 53, para. 157 ('The statute and regulations originally provided a certain degree of discretion to the US Executive Branch to modify the dolphin-safe labeling standard, but the court ruling in *Earth Island* v. *Hogarth* removed that discretion.')

the judiciary in carrying out specific studies.[45] The court restricted the Executive Branch's discretion to change the rule, not because it sought to define what constituted a 'dolphin-safe' tuna product, but because 'the government's intransigence in following Congress's mandate renders this case one of the rare circumstances where generic remand is not appropriate'.[46] The subsequent administrative action complained of by Mexico is merely the consequence of the operation of the rule of law within the US constitutional and administrative system, whereby the judiciary controls the acceptable limits of discretion of the executive in the interpretation and application of federal statutes. Of course, this does not mean that the United States is not responsible for court decisions of this kind under its WTO obligations; however, here the role of the courts is such that the proper characterization of the judicial action under 2.2 is as going to 'conformity assessment' (what is required to conform to a certain nongovernmental standard such that one can nonfraudulently or nonmisleadingly identify one's product with that standard) and not to 'technical regulation'.

The mischaracterization of the *Earth Island* court ruling and its subsequent implementation (as required by US law) as 'a document laying down product characteristics' flows in part from a legal error identified by the minority panelist. The Panel failed to read Article 2 of the TBT Agreement in light of its context, within the meaning of Article 31 of the Vienna Convention on the Law of Treaties, as interpreted by the Appellate Body of the WTO.[47] *Thus, the Panel failed to consider as 'context' the TBT Agreement as a whole.* The Panel made the fatal error of not considering the relationship of Article 2 of the TBT Agreement to Article 5, which concerns 'Conformity with Technical Regulations and *Standards*'.[48] Article 5.1 explicitly governs the obligations of central-government bodies where 'positive assurance of conformity with technical regulations *or standards* is required'.[49] *Thus, contrary to what the Panel majority seems to have assumed, the involvement of central government administration in assurance of conformity with a standard – i.e. with a* ***voluntary*** *norm as defined in the TBT Agreement – does* ***not*** *convert that norm into a technical regulation.* There are important differences between state responsibility with respect to conformity assessment under 5.1 on the one hand and 'technical regulations' under 2.2 on the other. For example, and most apposite to the facts of this dispute, TBT 5.1 defines the concept of unnecessary obstacle to

45 *Earth Island Inst.* v. *Hogarth*, 494 F.3d 757, 762 (9th Cir. 2007) (noting that the Executive Branch had already been instructed in a previous case to carry out statutorily-specified studies regarding the impact on dolphin populations of purse-seine fishing and had still failed to do so).

46 Ibid., at 770.

47 Vienna Convention on the Law of Treaties, Article 31(1), 23 May 1969, 1155 U.N.T.S. 331.

48 Agreement on Technical Barriers to Trade, Art. 5, GATT Doc. MTN/FA II-AIA-6 (15 December 1993) [hereinafter TBT Agreement] *in* Final Act Embodying the Results of the Uruguay Round of Multilateral Trade Negotiations, GATT Doc. MTN/FA (15 December 1993), 33 I.L.M. 9 (1994) (emphasis added).

49 Ibid., at Art. 5.1 (emphasis added).

trade differently than it is defined in TBT 2.2. Thus, according to TBT 5.1.2: 'conformity assessment procedures shall not be more strict or be applied more strictly than is necessary to give the importing Member adequate confidence that products conform with the applicable technical regulations or standards, taking account of the risks non-conformity would create'.[50]

The language of both the *Earth Island* ruling and the subsequent regulations signals that the central concern of the government was the assessment of conformity with the label requirements. The court stressed that to change the label, the Executive Branch was required to provide 'affirmative scientific evidence that the purse-seine fishery was not significantly impacting the dolphin population'[51] and that 'Congress's clear intent was to have the findings based on science alone'.[52] In finding the data insufficient and contrary to what Congress requested, the court noted that the Executive's evidence identified a number of possible ways that the purse-seine fishery could possibly adversely impact dolphin populations to find that 'the data does not furnish a rationale for, or evidence to support, the Secretary's finding'.[53] The court thus assessed the Executive Branch's evidence to determine whether purse-seine fishing in the ETP did not cause harm to dolphin populations, and thus conformed to the requirements of the voluntary 'dolphin-safe' labeling standard as defined by Congress. The implementing regulations 'govern[] the requirements' for the 'dolphin-safe label' and apply to tuna products that 'claim[] or suggest[] that tuna contained in the products were harvested using a method of fishing that is not harmful to dolphins'.[54] The regulations then set out in remarkable specificity, by method and location, what tuna-harvesting methods qualify for the label and allow for new scientific findings to further inform those requirements.[55] Both the court decision and the regulations show a preoccupation with scientific evidence demonstrating that particular harvesting methods do not adversely impact dolphin populations before they can be allowed to use the dolphin-safe label. This suggests that the mandatory requirements set out in both the ruling and the regulations are simply those that 'give the importing Member adequate confidence that products conform with the applicable technical ... standards'.[56] This does not mean, however, that the Member has implemented a technical regulation.

With respect to the third step in determining whether a measure is a technical regulation under TBT, the Panel also erred. As the Appellate Body made clear in *EC–Sardines*, in order to be characterized as 'mandatory' under the third step,

50 Ibid., at Art. 5.1.2.
51 *Earth Island Inst.*, 494 F.3d at 765.
52 Ibid., at 768.
53 Ibid., at 766–767.
54 50 C.F.R. §§ 216.90–216.91.
55 Ibid.
56 TBT Agreement, art. 5.1.2.

compliance with the characteristic laid down in the document must be mandatory *with respect to the 'identifiable product'*.[57] This follows logically from the pivotal role of the concept of 'identifiable product' in the determination of whether a measure is a 'technical regulation', as articulated by the Appellate Body in *EC–Asbestos* and *EC–Sardines*. This concept delineates the relevant product class that is subject to enforcement or compliance action by the authorities of the Member taking the measure. In *EC–Sardines*, the identifiable product was held to be 'preserved sardines';[58] in order for 'preserved sardines' to be sold in the EC, they had to conform to the product characteristic in question.[59] In the instant dispute, the identified product is tuna – and yet tuna does not have to conform to the product characteristic at issue in order to be sold in the United States, as the minority panelist points out.[60]

Unfortunately, deviating from the thrust of its previous jurisprudence, the Appellate Body has now upheld the Panel's finding that the US measure in *Tuna* is a 'technical regulation', based on the notion that any mandatory element makes a measure a technical regulation. But can it possibly make sense to impose the same strict disciplines where the government is merely facilitating the implementation of a scheme where the norms in question originate from private actors as are appropriate where the decision to create the norm emanates from governmental rather than private actors, and government has shaped the norm at every stage? This is not in the least to say that where government plays a verification role with respect to voluntary schemes it should escape WTO disciplines altogether. But the approach of the Panel would convert virtually every kind of labeling or certification scheme into a technical regulation, thus making the separate disciplines that apply to standards and conformity assessment largely irrelevant or at least making their role in contrast to those concerned with technical regulations rather obscure or uncertain.

National Treatment

While, as noted, we do not intend to consider in detail the legal interpretations of the Panels concerning TBT 2.1, given the Appellate Body rulings in *Cloves, Tuna/Dolphin*, and *COOL*, one aspect of the Panel's findings on national treatment that was not directly addressed by the Appellate Body and raises important doctrinal considerations is the finding that there was no treatment less favorable of Mexican duty by virtue of the requirement of not setting upon dolphins since at the time the measure was enacted this practice was engaged in by US fishers as well as Mexican ones. Thus, if they wanted to use the label, fishers from both countries would be

57 Appellate Body Report, *EC–Sardines*, para. 185.
58 Ibid., para. 182.
59 Ibid., para. 190.
60 Panel Report, *US–Tuna II (Mexico)*, para. 7.161.

faced with adaptation costs. This consideration of the state of affairs at the time of the enactment of the measure might well be probative concerning protectionist intent at that time (of course, there could still be protectionism, if the regulator knew or supposed that for some reason the adaptation costs would be manageable by domestic fisheries but unsustainable by the Mexican fishery). But if we put the issue of protectionist intent aside, is it appropriate to determine state responsibility for treatment no less favorable based solely upon conditions existing at the time of enactment? There is a troubling implication for state responsibility that flows from the availability under WTO law (as it is generally interpreted) of only prospective relief. We can grasp this implication by considering, on the hypothetical, that foreign manufacturers respond by adapting their behavior and (at some real cost) meeting the energy efficiency standard that the domestic industry was already performing to. Assuming the imposition on foreign producers of a standard that domestic ones were already producing to was characterized as a violation of TBT 2.1, once the foreign industry has adapted and is producing to the required standard there is a strong argument that there is no continuing breach of 2.1. Unless one constructs a continuing-breach theory that the foreign manufacturers remain less competitive in the sense that they have to recoup the costs of adapting to the energy-efficiency standard through on-going higher prices, there is no effective state responsibility for the costs having been imposed in the first place.

TBT 2.2

Legitimate objective

The Panel accepted the United States dual objective of protecting dolphins and informing consumers as legitimate under TBT 2.2. It rejected Mexico's suggestion that an objective that involves placing pressure on producers elsewhere in the world to change their environmental practices (or governments to change their policies) is not 'legitimate' under TBT. This renders the approach to TBT consistent with the approach to Article XX of the GATT articulated in paragraph 121 of the *Shrimp/Turtle* Appellate Body ruling, where the Panel rejected the product/process distinction as a basis for limiting the general exceptions available to WTO Members under Article XX. One might argue that, in *Tuna*, the Panel went even further towards consigning the product/process distinction to irrelevance in that it found that process-based measures did not violate an operational norm as opposed to simply saying their justification as an exception might be entertained.

This relates to a very cogent point that has been made by Joost Pauwelyn.[61] The definition of a technical regulation under TBT includes 'product-related' PPMs (Process and Production Methods). Some commentators had suggested that 'product-related' meant that the processes would affect the physical characteristics

61 International Economic Law and Policy blog, at www.worldtradelaw.net (last visited 7 November 2012).

of the product. This interpretation assumes what one might call the PPM mythology that somehow the essence of a product is defined by its physical identity (as to how it has affected all manner of interests through its lifestyle). In *Tuna*, no one questioned that the labeling measure was 'product-related'. This is the correct interpretation of 'product-related'. As one of us (Howse) has argued previously, the qualification 'product-related' merely indicates that the TBT Agreement does not discipline PPMs *unrelated to traded goods*. For example, a PPM that addressed methods of production that is only traded as a service (such as the advice of a multinational consulting engineering firm as to how to safely operate a mine that provides raw materials to domestic industries) would not be covered by TBT, since TBT is a *lex specialis* to trade in goods. Similarly, PPMs that are traded only as intellectual property (such as process patents) would be governed by TRIPS but not TBT.

Finally, the Panel made it clear that protection of the life and health of animals is a legitimate objective under TBT 2.2 even where the goal is not the conservation of an endangered species (or instrumental to human economic interests or human health interests). This is an important recognition of animal welfare as a legitimate objective under TBT, and will have implications for the *Seal Products* dispute between Canada and Norway and the EU. Thus, the *Tuna* Panel held:

> [T]he protection of dolphins may be understood as intended to protect animal life or health or the environment. In this respect, a measure that aims at the protection of animal life or health need not, in our view, be directed exclusively to endangered or depleted species or populations, to be legitimate. Article 2.2 refers to 'animal life or health' in general terms, and does not require that such protection be tied to a broader conservation objective. We therefore read these terms as allowing Members to pursue policies that aim at also protecting individual animals or species whose sustainability as a group is not threatened.[62]

By the appellate stage, Mexico appeared to have basically conceded that protecting dolphins on this basis was a legitimate objective under TBT.

Least restrictive alternative/objective assessment

Article 11 of the DSU requires a Panel to make an 'objective assessment of the matter'.[63] A Panel may not make a finding on a matter that is not before it. To do so is a serious violation of due process, as the parties have not had an opportunity to

62 *US – Tuna II (Mexico)*, para. 7.437.

63 DSU, Art. 11, Dispute Settlement Rules: Understanding on Rules and Procedures Governing the Settlement of Disputes, Marrakesh Agreement Establishing the World Trade Organization, Annex 2, The Legal Texts: The Results of the Uruguay Round of Multilateral Trade Negotiations 354 (1999), 1869 U.N. T.S. 401, 33 I.L.M. 1226 (1994).

address the matter in the Panel proceedings.[64] An objective assessment also requires that a Panel's findings have a basis in the evidence on the record.[65] The finding in paragraph 7.575 is inconsistent with the requirements in Article 11 of the DSU in both these respects. First of all, *it is a finding on a matter that the Panel did not have before it*. Secondly, there is a *complete lack of evidence on the record* to support the finding.

In paragraph 7.575 of its Report, the Panel describes and finds to be less restrictive of trade and capable of fulfilling the US legitimate objectives, an alternative regulatory scheme with the following features: the United States would continue to ensure compliance with the 'dolphin-safe' designation but instead would permit two separate labeling and certification schemes, each of which defined 'dolphin-safe' in a somewhat different manner.[66] The labels in each case would be required to disclose to consumers the relevant meaning of 'dolphin-safe' that corresponded to the particular tuna in question.[67] In a note to paragraph 7.575, the Panel acknowledges that allowing the US and AIDCP labels to operate in tandem without more information, Mexico's proposed alternative, would be confusing.[68]

The less trade-restrictive alternative put forward by Mexico in its first and second submissions is significantly different from the complex scheme described by the Panel in paragraph 7.575. In paragraph 224 of its first submission, far from putting forth an alternative regulatory scheme for the United States that would be less trade-restrictive, Mexico claims that the US measures are in their entirety more trade-restrictive than necessary because '*in the absence of the US measures*, the preservation of dolphin stocks in the ETP fishery will continue to be accomplished by the requirements and procedures of AIDCP'.[69] In Mexico's second submission to the Panel, Mexico reiterates its claim that a technical regulation is entirely unnecessary to fulfill the US objectives: 'A less trade restrictive way of fulfilling the objectives would be to create dolphin safe standards *rather than* a technical regulation.'[70] In other words, the US objectives can be fulfilled by the operation of voluntary standards by the various labeling and certification schemes, with no requirement of government action through technical regulations. There is certainly

64 Appellate Body Report, *Chile – Price Band System and Safeguard Measures Relating to Certain Agricultural Products*, WT/DS207/AB/R, adopted 23 October 2002, DSR 2002:VIII, 3045 (Corr.1, DSR 2006:XII, 5473), para. 174.

65 Ibid., para. 172; Appellate Body Report, *United States – Countervailing Duties on Certain Corrosion-Resistant Carbon Steel Flat Products from Germany*, WT/DS213/AB/R and Corr.1, adopted 19 December 2002, DSR 2002:IX, 3779, para. 142.

66 *US–Tuna II (Mexico)*, para. 7.575.

67 Ibid.

68 Ibid., para. 7.575 n. 815 ('The Panel recognizes that without additional information in the labels, the US and AIDCP dolphin-safe logos may be confused with one another.')

69 First Written Submission of the Mexican States, para. 244 (emphasis added).

70 Second Written Submission of the Mexican States, para. 210 (emphasis added).

no suggestion that Mexico's alternative would entail the new regulatory step of requiring that dolphin-safe designation be accompanied by an explanation on the label of the meaning of that designation. Mexico's claim is different: namely, that through the operation of the voluntary schemes in question, combined with market incentives, consumers will be at least as well informed as under the current measure, while trade will be less restricted. However, as noted above, the Panel expressly rejected Mexico's proposed alternative as confusing.[71]

An examination of the first and second set of questions to the Panel reveals that the Panel never asked the parties to comment on whether the kind of scheme concocted by the Panel in paragraph 7.575 was reasonably available, whether it would fulfill the US objectives to the same extent, and whether it would be less restrictive of trade. Instead, in its first set of questions to the parties, the Panel asked the United States about the adequacy of the AIDCP to achieve its objectives.[72] These questions are consistent with asking the United States to comment on Mexico's actual claim concerning the unnecessary trade-restrictiveness of the US measures, namely that as long as the AIDCP existed and functioned properly, the US measure was entirely unnecessary. An examination of Mexico's responses to the Panel's questions at the first and second Panel hearings reveals that neither the questions nor Mexico's responses disclose any consideration of the kind of alternative regulatory scheme concerning which the Panel made a finding in paragraph 7.575. In response to a question regarding whether Mexico thought the retailers would accept tuna products carrying the AIDCP label, Mexico communicated its intention that the two labels operate side by side without further explanation: 'It would be enough to simply clearly designate the labels "AIDCP Dolphin-safe" and "US Dolphin-safe" and let the retailers and final consumers make a buying decision based on that information.'[73] This statement is accompanied by a pictorial example of the AIDCP label, which conveys none of the information contemplated by the Panel in paragraph 7.575.[74]

A careful comparison of the finding in 7.575 of the Panel Report with Mexico's own submissions concerning alternative measures less restrictive of trade shows clearly that the alternative measure on which the Panel ruled was one that was never pleaded or considered in the Panel proceedings, and was one on which neither the United States nor Mexico had an opportunity to comment on or adduce evidence.

71 Panel Report, *US–Tuna II (Mexico)*, para. 7.575 n.813.

72 First Set of Questions from the Panel to the Parties, Questions 26 and 27. Question 26 inquired into the capability of the AIDCP label to meet its objective of progressively reducing dolphin mortality in the agreement area, and Question 27 asked the United States to compare the objectives of the AIDCP with those of its own statute governing use of the dolphin-safe label. Ibid.

73 Answers of the Mexican States to the Second Set of Questions from the Panel to the Parties to Panel Question 109, para. 62.

74 Ibid.; see also Exhibit MEX-121.

Thus, not surprisingly, the Panel's finding in 7.575 has *no basis in evidence on the record.* The Panel presumed, without any evidentiary foundation, that consumers would be at least as well informed or better informed than under the scheme challenged by Mexico, if they were presented with two different labels designating tuna as dolphin-safe, with dolphin-safe meaning different things in each case. The Panel *assumed* that if tuna were required to carry on its label an explanation of what the dolphin-safe designation meant in each case, consumer confusion would be avoided.[75] The Panel refers to 'information asymmetries' between producers and consumers and adopts – again without any argumentation or evidence by the parties on this matter – the view that such asymmetries are reduced and consumers protected in their bargains through the disclosure of more information.[76] Without any evidence on the record to support this finding, the Panel concluded that, as a result of this additional information, '[w]ell-informed consumers would be in a better position to use their purchasing power to influence the way tuna fisheries and canners operate'.[77]

As Hadfield *et al.* summarized in a 1998 article in the *Journal of Consumer Policy*,

> information and information asymmetries has been a staple of consumer protection analysis for well over thirty years. There is, however, a crucial distinction between earlier thinking about the role of information asymmetries and modern information theory. Early analysis saw in information asymmetries a brute inequality between buyers and sellers; resolution of this inequality, through the provision of information to buyers, it was thought would restore the balance and eliminate the bargaining disadvantage. Modern information theory, however, recognizes the subtle and complex ways in which information affects the dynamics of markets and bargaining settings and also recognizes the cost of being informed as an irreducible component of market transactions. (footnote omitted) These modern insights illuminate the paradox of attempting to use costly information procedures ... to solve the problems created by the cost of becoming informed.[78]

Thus, depending on the manner in which consumers process additional information, and the way it is presented, they can end up making more- rather than less-distorted consumption decisions. If the information cost of understanding the meaning of 'dolphin-safe' becomes too high for example, consumers might end up switching from tuna to substitute products. In a rigorous study of 'dolphin-safe'

75 Panel Report, *US–Tuna II (Mexico)*, para. 7.575 ('[The additional information] would contribute to informing consumers about the precise dolphin-safe characteristics.')

76 Ibid. ('In our view, [the additional information] would enhance the ability of dolphin-safe labels to remedy market failures arising from asymmetries of information between tuna producers, retailers, and final consumers in the US market.')

77 Ibid.

78 Hadfield *et al.* (1998: 139).

labeling, based on the principles of modern information economics, Teisl *et al.* (2002: 350–352) describe how, in response to concerns about dolphins, US consumers were switching from tuna to substitute products until, eventually, the 'tuna-safe' labeling scheme won their confidence and resulted in increased market share for canned tuna in the United States.

How would US consumers respond to the coexistence of multiple labeling schemes with manifestly different meanings to the 'dolphin-safe' designation, as proposed by the Panel? How would they process the information the Panel suggests would have to be contained on each tuna label? In order to make a finding concerning the effect of the alternative measure on the fulfillment of the US legitimate objectives as well as its effect on trade, there would need to be *some* evidence on the record that is probative as to these questions of consumer behavior.

In the absence of any evidence on the record, the Panel substituted its own dogmatic (and outdated) view of information economics. This is a manifest and egregious departure from the Panel's duty under Article 11 of the DSU to make an objective assessment of the matter. If anything, the evidence from the relevant economic literature suggests that any uncertainty or variance with respect to the meaning of the standards associated with a given label could create very significant consumer confusion.[79] This need not mean that under Article 11 the Panel had a duty to consider any particular economic study or type of evidence; at the same time, the finding of the Panel depended upon controversial and questionable assumptions and dogmas, which were never explored in the proceedings and which the parties had no opportunity to question or contest.

The alternative measure invented by the Panel in paragraph 7.575 would entail the creation of a new label for all tuna that bears the 'dolphin-free' designation, which would be redesigned to contain additional information concerning the meaning of 'dolphin-free' in the case of that particular label. In effect, all tuna on the US market carrying the 'dolphin-free' designation would have to be relabeled. Whether or not the alternative measure invented by the Panel was reasonably available, whether it would fulfill to the same extent the legitimate objectives of the United States, *and* its relative trade-restrictiveness would require *some* consideration of the costs on sellers of tuna imposed by the Panel's new labeling requirement, as well as the regulatory costs to the United States of assuring that all tuna sold as 'dolphin-safe' did indeed bear a label setting out the correct information. That there is no evidence on the record concerning such costs further aggravates the Panel's dereliction of its duty under Article 11 of the DSU.

Article 13 of the DSU provides Panels with ample powers to seek information. The Panel posed extensive sets of questions to both parties after both the first and second hearings. The lack of any reference to evidence in the record to support the Panel's finding in paragraph 7.575 is conspicuous. But, as suggested, it is not

79 Harbaugh *et al.* (2011).

surprising – since this finding was concerning a matter that was never put before the Panel by the parties.

TBT 2.4

International standardization body

In its consideration of Mexico's claims under TBT 2.4, the Panel found, based in part on the determination that the AIDCP was 'open' to all WTO Members (a finding now reversed by the Appellate Body), that the AIDCP was an international standardization body.[80] The Panel made the legal interpretation that openness to all WTO Members includes a situation where the existing members of a body may, at their discretion, decide to accept a WTO Member as a new member of that body.[81] This understanding of openness is empty and trivial. *Any* standardization body could, in theory, decide at its whim, on the basis of consensus, to increase its membership. Thus, if the criterion that a body be 'open' to all WTO Members could be satisfied by the possibility that a body could invite at its discretion any WTO Member that so desires to join, it would be largely lacking in legal meaning. It would afford no legal security whatever to WTO Members that they are able to participate, if they so choose, in the formulation of standards that, under TBT 2.4, they are legally required to use as a basis for their technical regulations.

The Panel also suggested that the criterion of 'openness could be fulfilled if, during a certain temporal window, all WTO Members had an opportunity to choose to join the body.[82] The United States has ably, in its Appellant Submission, explained why, in fact, it is incorrect that, even during the temporal window referred to by the Panel, the AIDCP was open to all WTO Members.[83] Be that as it may, the legal interpretation of the Panel that 'open' to all WTO Members could include a situation where that body was open at a particular historical point in time to all Members is fundamentally defective – and not only for the rather simple reason that it is inconsistent with the use of the present tense 'is' in the TBT provision being interpreted.

80 Panel Report, *US–Tuna II (Mexico)*, para. 7.693.

81 Ibid., para. 7.691 ('[T]he AIDCP remains open to accession to any State ... that is invited to accede to the Agreement on the basis of the parties' decision. To this day, the AIDCP membership is therefore open on a non-discriminatory basis to the relevant bodies of at least all WTO Members in accordance with the principle of openness.')

82 Ibid. (concluding that because the AIDCP membership was open from May 1998 until May 1999 to states whose vessels fished in the Agreement Area without restrictions on who could fish in the area, the AIDCP was open to all WTO Members).

83 Appellant Submission of the United States, *United States – Measures Concerning the Importation, Marketing and Sale of Tuna and Tuna Products*, WT/DS381 (20 January 2012), para. 142 (noting that even had the period for signature of the AIDCP been the same as when the resolution was developed, other WTO Members who might have had an interest other than fishing (such as consumer or conservation interests) were ineligible to become parties).

First of all, a state may well not have been a WTO Member while this temporal window was open (a significant number of states have acceded to the WTO relatively recently); a state might only seek compelling reasons to seek membership in the standardization body in question once it joined the WTO, and assumed the obligation in 2.4 to use international standards. The Panel's interpretation would allow such a body to deny membership on the basis that it was not sought and/or achieved during the historical window in question.

Second, a state might not have existed during a particular historical window; in such a case, it would have had no effective opportunity whatever to join the standardization body in question, even though now, having achieved statehood and acceded to the WTO, it is bound to use as a basis the standards promulgated by that body.

Third, paragraph 4 of Annex I refers to openness to 'the relevant bodies of all WTO Members'. Relevant bodies include, evidently in this context, domestic standardization bodies. Not all WTO Members have domestic standardization bodies; some developing-country Members have instituted such bodies only recently, and others do not yet have them. If the requirement of openness were satisfied by having maintained such openness during a particular historical window, then WTO Members who did not have 'relevant bodies' before that window closed would be prevented from participating in the creation of standards that they would be required by TBT 2.4 to use as a basis for their technical regulations.

This last consideration reminds us that the Panel never, in fact, properly turned its mind to the precise wording of paragraph 4, Annex I of the TBT Agreement. In particular, the Panel never considered the significance of the language 'relevant bodies' in the provision in question. The use of the expression 'relevant bodies of WTO Members' in paragraph 4, Annex I, reflects the fact that, in many WTO Members, standardization bodies are not state organs; indeed, this recognition is explicit in Articles 3 and 8, inter alia, which address the standardization and conformity assessment activities of nongovernmental bodies. *Membership* in the AIDCP is limited to states and regional economic organizations; no other reading of Article XXVI of the AIDCP is possible. A standardization body that does not have the international legal personality of a state or regional organization is per se prevented from Membership in the AIDCP (and always was).[84] Such a nongovernmental standardization body would be relegated to the status of an Observer, with very limited participatory rights, and no decisionmaking rights, as determined by Annex X of the AIDCP. We note, finally, that the Appellate Body reversed the Panel's findings under Article 2.4.

84 Indeed, even if for purposes of attribution under ILC Articles a standardization body's conduct could be attributable to a state, for example where it is exercising elements of governmental authority or acting under the direction of the state, this would still not provide the requisite international legal personality required for membership in AIDCP, which clearly limits membership to states and regional economic organizations.

Use of non-WTO law by the Panel

The Panel's finding in paragraph 7.575 also hinged on certain conclusions about the meaning, effect, and compliance with the AIDCP. These determinations are to be found, inter alia, in paragraphs 7.598, 7.608–7.612, and 7.615. The Panel's observations in these paragraphs represent explicit or implicit determinations regarding the meaning of the law of the AIDCP, the nature of the United States's obligations under the AIDCP, Mexico's compliance with the AIDCP, and the actual effect of the law of the AIDCP.

In light of its detailed examination of the requirements of the AIDCP and the obligations of parties to the treaty, the Panel concluded that 'allowing compliance with the AIDCP requirements to be advertised in addition to the current US label' would not result in a lower level of protection than the US label alone.[85] The Panel employed the AIDCP as an indispensable legal benchmark in determining that the US measure was more trade-restrictive than necessary and thus that the United States was in violation of TBT 2.2.

Article 11 of the DSU requires that the Panel 'make an assessment of the conformity with the relevant covered agreements'. Article 3.2 of the DSU explains what a Panel is required to do in order to make such an assessment, which includes interpreting the covered agreements in accordance with the customary rules of interpretation of public international law. Accordingly, the Panel's assessment of conformity under Article 11 must be governed by use of the sources of international law as determined by Article 38 of the Statute of the International Court of Justice and the Vienna Convention on the Law of Treaties.[86]

In making determinations or assumptions concerning the meaning and effect of the AIDCP and concerning compliance of states parties, the Panel failed completely to articulate the basis on which, under customary international law that relates to the interpretation of treaties, it was entitled to consider the AIDCP in coming to the conclusion that the United States had breached a provision of a WTO-covered agreement. In the *Mexico–Taxes on Soft Drinks* case, the Appellate Body indicated that the WTO dispute-settlement organs have a very limited or circumscribed jurisdiction to make determinations concerning whether states parties are in conformity with non-WTO legal rules.[87] In the ruling, the Appellate Body noted that it saw 'no basis in the DSU for panels and the Appellate Body to adjudicate non-WTO disputes'.[88]

One way in which a Panel may consider non-WTO law is as 'other relevant rules of international law applicable between the parties', as set out in Article 31(3)(c) of

85 Panel Report, *US–Tuna II (Mexico)*, para. 7.615.

86 Palmeter and Mavroidis (1998).

87 Appellate Body Report, *Mexico – Tax Measures on Soft Drinks and Other Beverages*, WT/DS308/AB/R, adopted 24 March 2006, DSR 2006:I, 3 [*hereinafter Mexico–Taxes on Soft Drinks*], para. 56.

88 Ibid.

the *Vienna Convention on the Law of Treaties*.[89] As the Appellate Body has held in *EC–Aircraft*, the expression 'parties' in 31(3)(c) should not be read so as to *exclude* the consideration of international legal rules that are not binding on all Members of the WTO (this effectively overrules the approach on this issue of the earlier, widely criticized *EC–Biotech* Panel[90]). However, the Appellate Body also found that the WTO dispute-settlement organs should exercise caution when they consider non-WTO international legal rules that are binding only on a subset of WTO Members. Before making its determinations concerning the AIDCP, the Panel utterly failed to balance the important systemic considerations that the Appellate Body set out in *EC–Aircraft*[91] as at play in any decision to take into account non-WTO legal rules that are not applicable between all Members of the WTO. Indeed, as noted, it did not even set out the legal basis in the *Vienna Convention on the Law of Treaties* for its reliance on non-WTO law. This utter failure represents a violation of the duty of the Panel under Article 11 of the DSU.

The Panel did not appreciate that in judging the United States's compliance with the provisions of a WTO-covered agreement in relation to the legal rights and obligations, and the effects, of a different treaty regime, it was engaged in a delicate exercise of constructing a relationship between two separate international legal regimes, with important implications for what the International Law Commission has called 'fragmentation'. It completely ignored the United States's submissions that the AIDCP was a separate and distinct international legal regime that could not be simplistically employed to judge the conformity of the United States with the TBT Agreement. The AIDCP contains certain provisions for settlement of disputes and interpretation of the treaty. At times, in its submissions, Mexico presented the dispute before the Panel as a dispute concerning the United States's compliance with its obligations under the AIDCP. The Panel never turned its mind to whether the WTO rather than the AIDCP was the appropriate forum for this dispute, given Mexico's reliance on the AIDCP as well as its assertions about the consistency of the conduct of the United States with its undertakings in that non-WTO treaty regime.

Finally, in the *US–Shrimp* case, the Appellate Body considered the terms of a regional agreement that the United States had entered into with certain WTO Members as evidence that WTO Members nonparties of the agreement had been treated worse, and thus subject to discrimination within the meaning of the

89 Vienna Convention on the Law of Treaties, art. 31(3)(c), May 23, 1969, 1155 U.N.T.S. 331.

90 Panel Report, *European Communities – Measures Affecting the Approval and Marketing of Biotech Products*, WT/DS291/R, WT/DS292/R, WT/DS293/R, Add.1 to Add.9, and Corr.1, adopted 21 November 2006, DSR 2006:III–VIII, 847.

91 Appellate Body Report, *European Communities and Certain Member States – Measures Affecting Trade in Large Civil Aircraft*, WT/DS316/AB/R, adopted 1 June 2011, para. 845 ('[O]ne must exercise caution in drawing from an international agreement to which not all WTO Members are party.')

chapeau of Article XX of the GATT.[92] Although the ruling described the obligations of the Inter-American Convention in some detail, the Appellate Body concluded this examination demonstrated that 'consensual and multilateral procedures are available and feasible for the establishment of programs for the conservation of sea turtles'.[93] It used the Convention solely as a 'convincing demonstration' that the United States had negotiated seriously with some parties and had not done so with others.[94]

Especially in its 21.5 Report, the Appellate Body made it very clear that the terms of the regional agreement merely constituted some evidence of the kind of treatment that the United States might have offered, on a nondiscriminatory basis, to the claimants. In rejecting Malaysia's claim that the Panel below established a new legal standard, the Appellate Body explicitly reaffirmed that the Convention was only to be used as 'a basis for comparison' in terms of negotiating efforts and in no way 'transform[ed] the Inter-American Convention into a "legal standard"'.[95] The Appellate Body was therefore exceedingly careful to indicate that it was *not* imposing the other agreement as a juridical norm that was indispensable or decisive in assessing whether the United States was in compliance with the provisions of the covered agreements at issue in the dispute.

Cloves

TBT 2.2 Objective assessment

As noted above, the Panel in *COOL* found that the United States was in violation of TBT 2.2 because its measure did not achieve the US stated objective of clear and accurate information concerning the national origin of the products at issue. We would observe at the outset that, to the extent that Article 2.2 of TBT is considered to require the same kind of inquiry as Article XX of the GATT, the legal interpretation underlying this finding is highly questionable. Under Article XX (*Brazil–Tyres*), a measure must be in relation to an objective covered by the treaty provision, must make a material contribution to that objective, and must be least-trade-restrictive in the sense that there is no reasonably available alternative measure that achieves the level of protection sought by the regulating measure. There is no requirement that that measure achieve the objective sought to the *greatest extent possible*. Yet the *COOL* Panel read this into 2.2 of the TBT Agreement. Indeed, a requirement that a Member's measure achieve a legitimate objective to the greatest extent possible would be inconsistent with the right under

92 Appellate Body Report, *United States – Import Prohibition of Certain Shrimp and Shrimp Products*, WT/DS58/AB/R, adopted 6 November 1998, DSR 1998:VII, 2755, paras. 169–171.

93 Ibid., para. 170.

94 Ibid., paras. 171–172.

95 Appellate Body Report, *United States – Import Prohibition of Certain Shrimp and Shrimp Products – Recourse to Article 21.5 of the DSU by Malaysia*, WT/DS58/AB/RW, adopted 21 November 2001, DSR 2001:XIII, 6481, para. 130.

TBT of a Member to choose its level of protection, which the Appellate Body has recently in its Report in *US–Cloves* (subsequent to the *COOL* Panel decision) affirmed as fundamental to the object and purpose of the TBT Agreement. A Member could choose a high level of protection, but limitations in resources and other legitimate public-policy objectives might not allow it to fully achieve that level of protection. This is one reason why a Member's level of protection cannot be *simply* inferred from the measures it adopts. The fundamental obligation of least-trade-restrictiveness does not require that a measure achieve a Member's level of protection; it only requires that there be no alternative reasonably available alternative measure that makes an equal (or greater) contribution to the achievement of that level of protection.

But this brings us to the way in which the Panel in *COOL* interpreted the US objective of 'clear and accurate information'. The Panel viewed this language as if it were stating a level of protection rather than an objective. Thus, it understood the United States to mean by the objective of clear and accurate information, that the United States was seeking the provision of the most detailed, or perhaps the greatest amount of information possible to consumers about the national origin of the products in question. The Panel identified the supply of the most, or the most detailed, information possible with a level of protection suggesting that consumers should be as perfectly informed as possible in their consumption decisions.

The Panel never contemplated that, due to the way that consumers process information, and the costs involved in doing so, consumers might end up being less perfectly informed if more information is supplied, due to the information-overload problem. A more simplified presentation of information might well be easier for consumers to process correctly, and thus might result in their consumption decisions more perfectly reflecting their preferences.[96] As Mulholland and Sylvan suggest: 'Market research ... in products as diverse as jams and retirement savings, suggests that past a point, when provided with more choice and information, we either walk away from markets, choosing not to choose or we choose randomly.'[97]

This relates to a more general consideration to which the Panel appeared completely oblivious, as noted above in the economic analysis: what counts as 'clear and accurate information' or the most 'clear and accurate' information is relative to the purpose for which the information is used and its *value* for that purpose. What counts as 'clear and accurate information' about the working of a computer will be different depending on whether the addressee is a hardware engineer, a software designer, a computer-science student, or a consumer. There are many empirical studies that suggest that governments often mandate disclosure of information that in fact has little value to consumers in their consumption

96 See, e.g., Wansink *et al.* (2004); Héroux *et al.* (1988).

97 'Section I: Setting the Context', OECD Roundtable on Economics for Consumer Policy, Summary Report, 26 July 2007, p. 11.

decisions. Is mandating the supply of largely worthless information to consumers a legitimate objective under TBT?

The legitimate regulatory objective here was consumer protection. This, rather obviously, means that the information is intended to facilitate consumers aligning their purchase decisions with their preferences to the greatest extent possible. What kind of labeling scheme achieves this objective depends on the nature of those preferences. It might be the case that some consumers are simply curious about the national origin of the products they buy: they get utility from the satisfaction of that curiosity (and I admit that in most democracies there would probably not be strong support for imposing significant regulatory costs on producer interests to satisfy an exogenous preference for knowledge about the national origin of products. It is more plausible to assume that the national origin of the products is related in some way to the utility of consumption of the product). What *kind of information* will allow consumers to best align their consumption decisions with their preferences will depend crucially on how their preferences related to the national origin of products. *But this is a question the Panel never addressed.*

Some consumers may be nationalistic or xenophobic. They may inherently gain more utility when they purchase goods produced in their own country simply out of nationalistic sentiment. Or they may be prejudiced against the majority ethnic or religious group of some particular country and so have a disutility from purchasing their products. We have serious doubts that facilitating such decisions based on nationalistic considerations is a 'legitimate objective' compatible with the objective and purpose of the WTO and, in particular, the disciplines on trade in goods that are inherently anti-protectionist in normative orientation. While the complainants in *COOL* did in fact argue that there was a protectionist motivation behind the country-of-origin labeling scheme, and the Panel dismissed the evidence that they provided in this regard (connected to legislative history), the Panel did not consider explicitly whether the preferences of consumers for products of a particular national origin might be protectionist and therefore whether facilitating consumption decisions that reflect such preferences might not be a 'legitimate' objective under TBT 2.2.

In fact, however, as some of the evidence presented by the United States suggested, in the case of meat products, consumers are concerned with the national origin of the products because they regard national origin as a proxy for safety and other aspects of quality. Indeed, the available evidence suggests that US consumers *will* only pay a premium for country-of-origin labeled beef to the extent that they believe beef from certain countries to be safer and of higher quality than other countries.[98] Moreover, consumer surveys suggest that a very high percentage of US consumers believe that US meat is fresher and safer than meat from other sources. According to Loureiro and Umberger (2007), 'U.S. meat is perceived to be the safest

98 Umberger (2004).

relative to meat from Argentina, Australia, Canada, Denmark, Mexico, and New Zealand. Nonetheless, meat from Canada, Australia, and New Zealand still received an average rating as "safe", but meat produced in Mexico and Argentina was not rated as safe'. On the other hand, there is a group of consumers who prefer grass-fed beef, which is more likely to be from Canada or Argentina as opposed to the United States.

If the value of information about national origin of meat to US consumers is entirely that of enabling them to use national origin as a proxy for safety and other quality attributes, it would make no sense to interpret the US goal of providing as much clear and accurate information as possible as requiring the provision of disclosure to extend to information that is irrelevant to consumers because it does not assist them in using national-origin information in this way. In effect, the United States would be imposing costs on producers to provide information that is worthless to consumers. This would not be consistent with the overall objective of consumer protection. The manner in which the Panel seemed to abstract from essential questions about the value of the information to consumers may be attributable in part to the US curious insistence that consumer health and safety were not among its regulatory objectives in the case of the *COOL* requirements.

Let us take the consumer concern with safety first of all. It is reasonable to assume that all stages in the production of meat can affect safety. A risk-averse consumer would thus get the most clear and accurate information from a country-of-origin label that specifies the country of origin as American where all the stages of production have occurred in the United States. Certainly such a consumer would be seriously misled by a 'made in America' label where *only* the slaughter of the animal occurred in the United States, since the great bulk of the practices and regulations affecting the ultimate safety of the meat – the consumer's central concern – would be in another, or other, jurisdictions.

What about the B and C labels, which the Panel characterized as not providing valuable information or creating ambiguity or confusion? Label B tells the consumer that the meat in question may have originated in a limited subset of countries. As far as the truly risk-averse consumer is concerned, label B serves the useful purpose of warning them that, although the meat in question may partly be from the country they identify as safest, there is a possibility that this is not the case. The risk-averse consumer will therefore know to choose A or D (to the extent that the D label refers to a country of origin other than the United States that the consumer associates with the highest degree of food safety).

However, there may be a somewhat less risk-averse consumer who does not always require meat from the country of origin that she identifies as having the highest safety standard. She may be willing to trade off some additional risk for a lower price or other attributes. At the same time, this consumer may still be concerned enough about safety that she may want to avoid meat that has been produced in whole or in part in countries she identifies with a serious lack of safety. From the perspective of this consumer, the information in label B is 'clear and accurate'. She will be able to know whether there is a possibility of the meat originating in whole or in part from a country that she identifies with safety concerns that would dissuade her from consuming the meat. For example, if this consumer finds Canada and the United States acceptable for safety but not Mexico, then a label that says that the product may be meat of either the United States or Canada will communicate information that is clear, accurate, and of value to the consumer, just as will a label that the meat may be any of US, Canadian, or Mexican origin. In other words, the consumer will always have clear and accurate information concerning whether the meat comes from a country that is *un*acceptable to her with regard to safety.

Now let us take label C. This label indicates that all stages of production other than slaughter have occurred outside of the United States. There is nothing inherently lacking in accuracy or clarity about this information. It would be of value to a consumer who is willing to be satisfied that application at the border of US sanitary and phytosanitary standards to the live animal is sufficient to deal with safety concerns about other countries that arise at the prior stages of production, but who values the information that the slaughter of the animal has occurred in the United States as an indication of greater safety at that stage. Risks that some consumers consider as of paramount importance, such as E. coli contamination, may be identified closely with slaughterhouse practices. This kind of contamination often garners a great deal of public and media attention.[99]

In sum, once we consider the use by consumers of national-origin information as a proxy for safety, the Panel is wrong (paragraph 7.707) to suggest that labels that indicate the possible, as opposed to actual, origin of meat (label B in this case) do not communicate clear or accurate information to consumers or that such labels contribute to confusion or uncertainty. Similarly, the Panel is wrong to suggest that there is any lack of clarity as to the information being communicated by labels B and C. Both labels, it is true, list more than one country of origin. Label B does so in such a way to communicate to the consumers all of the countries whose conditions, practices, and regulations *may* have influenced the safety of the meat in question, whereas label C assures the consumer that, whatever other country the live animal may originate from, the safety of the slaughter stage is determined by US conditions, practices, and regulations. Of course, consumer heuristics are complex, and it might turn out that the presentation of the information in question on B and C could be such as to create confusion or ambiguity as to which information is being communicated by which label. But the Panel admitted that the complainants had not presented any actual empirical evidence of consumer confusion.

Let us now consider quality attributes other than safety. These attributes may be affected by various stages in the production process, breeding stock, corn-fed vs. grass-fed, etc. The requirements for Labels A and D, which apply to claims that

99 Roberts *et al.* (1999).

meat originates from a single country, prevent consumers from being misled that the stage(s) in production that are relevant to the quality attributes they are concerned with occurred in the country they identify with those attributes, by specifying that all stages of production must have occurred in that country. Labels B and C admittedly are less useful to consumers who are concerned with some nonsafety quality attribute they are seeking and that they identify with a particular country.

It is true that such consumers would gain further information from a label that specifies the country where each stage of production occurred for the actual meat in the package. However, the complexity of such a label, if we follow the general lessons of behavioral law and economics in this area, might be such as to deter the consumer from effectively using the information; at the same time, the regulatory costs entailed in this degree of traceability could be considerable. In sum, the Panel was wrong to think (as it seemed implicitly to do) that a reasonable regulator pursuing the goal of information being as clear and accurate as possible would require that each stage of production be specifically traceable to the country at which that stage took place. There is empirical evidence that consumers place considerably less value on very specific traceability than on more general assurances concerning the characteristics of products.[100]

Finally, the Panel cited as a further example of confusion or ambiguity the fact that in the case of commingling (the slaughter together of animals of both domestic and foreign origin) labels B and C were permitted to be used interchangeably. Yet why should this be confusing? From the point of view of the consumer who wants to know all the countries whose conditions, practices, and regulations may have affected the safety of the meat, B and C are equally informative. It is just that label C provides an additional piece of information, namely that the slaughter stage took place in the United States. As indicated above, this information will be useful to one particular group of consumers, those who are particularly concerned with safety at the slaughter stage. But this additional piece of information does not in any way obscure or make harder to process the basic information concerning the possible countries that may have affected the safety of the meat at some other stage of its production. Whether a producer chooses, in the case of commingled meat, to use label C would presumably depend on whether he or she believes that the information would lead some relevant group of consumers to prefer meat that they know has been slaughtered in the United States.

To conclude the discussion of the *COOL* case, the Panel's conclusion that the US measure did not correspond to the US goal of as clear and accurate information as possible concerning national origin was based on several errors of understanding and analysis – first of all, ignoring that the meaning of clear and accurate information where the goal is consumer protection depends on the way in which

100 See Hobbs (2003).

consumers use information; second, assuming that more information necessarily enhances accuracy and clarity from the relevant consumer point of view; and, third, not appreciating that the design of a labeling scheme may target different groups of consumers with overlapping, but not identical, interests in the kind of information without being ambiguous or confusing.

5. Conclusions

We began this paper with the observation that these are cases where it is far from obvious, from either the design of the measure or the broad policy, whether the measures are legitimate idealistic government regulation in the public interest or insidious if somewhat hidden protectionism. Depending on one's particular bias or perspective, one could look at the measures and the surrounding facts in very different ways. However the legal tests are refined by the Appellate Body, much will depend on the characterization of the measures and the facts related to them by the Panels. As we have shown, gauging the various effects of these kinds of measures on different market actors – consumers, foreign producers, domestic producers, and downstream processors – is a delicate and complex exercise.

While, as noted, Panels are bound in their fact-finding by the duty to make an objective assessment of the matter, and are also bound by the Appellate Body jurisprudence on the burden of proof, etc., the panelists do not normally (indeed very rarely) have a background as triers of fact or trial advocates. Even less are they likely to have the expertise to evaluate complex economic impacts. It is difficult to come to any conclusion but that the panelists in this case approached the measures and the surrounding facts with a *presumption* of protectionism. In the United States, against which the Panels decided in all three cases, judicial review of regulation would normally be done by experienced judges, assisted by law clerks who are the leading graduates of the best law schools. While US administrative law is complicated, and neither of us is a specialist in that field, some degree of deference to agency expertise and to the democratic process is evident in the approach to complex regulatory choices. US agencies are generally required to take into account, and treat fairly, affected economic interests, whether domestic or foreign. *More* intrusive review by an international body, which is *further* removed from the democratic will and legitimate political institutions than the domestic courts, may still be useful for protecting some politically *under*-represented foreign economic interests; but it is also likely to raise among other constituencies justified legitimacy concerns that cannot easily be solved within the confines of the existing WTO treaties and dispute-settlement practices. Some Appellate Body decisions have, as a matter of legal doctrine, directed Panels towards a greater sensitivity toward, if not actual deference to, the reasoned regulatory choices of domestic regulators and agencies (*EC–Hormones; Brazil–Tyres*). But the value of these decisions is limited in cases where the devil is in the details, the facts are not obvious in pointing to protectionism, and where the system persists in naming panelists who are not professional adjudicators and who tend to have a deregulatory bias, easily presuming protectionism in the presence of complexity and ambiguity.

References

Grossman, G. M., H. Horn, and P. C. Mavroidis (2012), 'Legal and Economic Principles of World Trade Law: National Treatment', in ALI, *Legal and Economic Principles of World Trade Law: The Genesis of the GATT, the Economics of Trade Agreements, Border Instruments, and National Treatment, Report to ALI.*

Hadfield, G. K., R. Howse, and M. J. Trebilcock (1998), 'Information-Based Principles for Rethinking Consumer Protection Policy', *Journal of Consumer Policy*, **21**(2): 131–169.

Harbaugh, R., J. W. Maxwell, and B. Roussillon (2011), 'Label Confusion: The Groucho Effect of Uncertain Standards', *Management Science*, **57**(9): 1512–1527.

Héroux, L., M. Laroche, and K. L. McGown (1988), 'Consumer Product Label Information Processing: An Experiment Involving Time Pressure and Distraction', *Journal of Economic Psychology*, **9**(2): 195–214.

Hobbs, J. E. (2003), 'Traceability and Country of Origin Labelling', Policy Dispute Information Consortium 9th Agricultural and Food Policy Information Workshop, Montreal, 25 April.

Horn, H. (2006), 'National Treatment in the GATT', *American Economic Review*, **96**(1): 394–404.

Howse, R. (2002), 'From Politics to Technocracy and Back Again: The Fate of the Multilateral Trading Regime', *American Journal of International Law*, **96**(1): 94–117.

Loureiro, M. L. and W. J. Umberger (2007), 'A Choice Experiment Model for Beef: What US Consumer Responses Tell Us about Relative Preferences for Food Safety, Country-of-Origin Labeling and Traceability', *Food Policy*, **32**(4): 496–514.

Palmeter, D. and P. C. Mavroidis (1998), 'The WTO Legal System: Sources of Law', *American Journal of International Law*, **92**(3): 398–413.

Roberts, T., S. A. Malcolm, and C. A. Narrod (1999), 'Probabilistic Risk Assessment and Slaughterhouse Practices: Modelling Contamination Process Control in Beef Destined for Hamburger', *Probabilistic Safety Assessment PSA '99: Risk-Informed Performance-Based Regulation in the New Millennium*, Mohammad Modarres (ed.), 809–815.

Teisl, M. F., B. Roe, and R. L. Hicks (2002), 'Can Eco-Labels Tune a Market? Evidence from Dolphin-Safe Labeling', *Journal of Environmental Economics and Management*, **43**(3): 339–359.

Umberger, W. J. (2004), 'Will Consumers Pay a Premium for Country-of-Origin Labeled Meat?', *Choices*, 4th quarter.

Wansink, B., S. T. Sonka, and C. M. Hasler (2004), 'Front-Label Health Claims: When Less is More', *Food Policy*, **29**(6): 659–667.

Yet Another Nail in the Coffin of Zeroing: *United States – Anti-Dumping Administrative Reviews and Other Measures Related to Imports of Certain Orange Juice from Brazil*

KAMAL SAGGI
Vanderbilt University
MARK WU
Harvard Law School

Abstract: This paper analyzes Brazil's WTO challenge to the methods undertaken by the United States in calculating anti-dumping duties in administrative reviews and other investigations of Brazilian orange juice. The dispute resulted in a Panel ruling that conforms with earlier Appellate Body decisions outlawing the use of 'weighted average to transaction' zeroing in such reviews. However, we note that the Panel's stance was driven largely from a desire to preserve 'stability and predictability' within the system, suggesting a practical recognition of the shadow of past Appellate Body decisions on the same legal question. In addition, we argue that to understand fully the effects of zeroing, it is important to account for the underlying reasons behind observed price changes in the market. We show that zeroing is more likely to convert a negative dumping determination into a positive one when price changes are driven by variations in demand relative to when they are driven by variations in the cost of exporting. In the present case, Brazilian exporters of orange juice experienced an increase in (residual) demand for their product since, by reducing the local supply of round oranges, adverse weather conditions in the United States made it difficult for US orange-juice producers to meet local demand.

1. Introduction

Over the past decade, the United States has played a game of 'cat and mouse' when it comes to the use of 'zeroing' in anti-dumping proceedings. As will be described below in greater detail, zeroing is a methodology employed by governments in

The authors are grateful for comments received from Mark Sanctuary, our discussant, Tom Prusa, and other participants at the 2012 American Law Institute conference on WTO Case Law.

anti-dumping investigations in which transactions with negative dumping margins are not allowed to offset those with positive margins. As a result, when aggregating transactions, the use of zeroing causes the weighted average dumping margin to be higher than it would be without zeroing. This leads to higher anti-dumping margins, much to the chagrin of US trading partners.

Beginning with the *US–Softwood Lumber V*[1] complaint brought forth by Canada in 2002, numerous WTO Appellate Body (AB) decisions have found the US practice of zeroing to be impermissible under WTO rules. The US has consistently interpreted each ruling against it narrowly, eliminating the practice of zeroing in the specific factual context under the legal complaint, but keeping the practice alive in other situations where the context differed ever so slightly. This narrow compliance behavior, in turn, has sparked additional cases, resulting in additional rulings against the use of zeroing. This incrementalist approach toward outlawing zeroing by the AB has resulted in large resource costs, for the litigants as well as the WTO as an institution (Bown and Sykes, 2008). Because of the importance of the US as an export market and the prevalence of zeroing in US anti-dumping investigations, many trading partners have willingly expended litigation resources in an attempt to stop this US practice.

US–Orange Juice (Brazil)[2] is yet another one in this extensive line of cases. At the time the Panel issued its report, 20 zeroing disputes had already come before WTO Panels.[3] All but two of these disputes have involved the US as the defendant (with the EU being the defendant in the remaining two cases). While the EU discontinued the practice of zeroing after losing its cases, the US boldly marched on with its strategy of narrow compliance, changing its use of zeroing in anti-dumping proceedings only to the extent necessary to bring its measure into compliance with the WTO ruling.

However, there is hope that *US–Orange Juice (Brazil)* may indeed be among the last of this long line of WTO litigation involving the US as a defendant on zeroing. On 6 February 2012, US Trade Representative Ron Kirk announced that the US had reached agreements with the EU and Japan to end longstanding WTO disputes

1 *United States – Final Dumping Determination on Softwood Lumber from Canada*, DS264 [*US–Softwood Lumber V*].

2 *United States – Anti-Dumping Administrative Reviews and Other Measures Related to Imports of Certain Orange Juice from Brazil*, DS382 [*US–Orange Juice (Brazil)*]

3 For a review of the WTO cases on zeroing and its impact, see Bown and Prusa (2011). Note that besides the 18 cases listed in Table 14 of Bown and Prusa (2011), two other cases had also come before a WTO panel before the issuance of the panel report: *US – Corrosion-Resistant Carbon Steel Flat Products (Korea)*, DS420 [*US–Carbon Steel Flat Products (Korea)*] and *US – Shrimp and Diamond Sawblades From China*, DS422 [*US–Shrimp and Diamond Sawblades (China)*]. A 21st zeroing dispute was filed after this panel report was issued, *United States – Anti-Dumping Measures on Certain Frozen Warmwater Shrimp from Vietnam*, DS429 [*US – Frozen Warmwater Shrimp (Vietnam)*].

(*US–Zeroing (EC)*,[4] *US–Zeroing (Japan)*,[5] and *US–Continued Zeroing*[6]) over zeroing.[7] Under these recently concluded agreements with the EU and Japan, the US Department of Commerce (DOC) finally completed the process – which began in December 2010 – of ending the use of zeroing in most anti-dumping proceedings.[8] Since the AB has repeatedly found the use of zeroing by the US to be inconsistent with WTO rules, had the US not agreed to end the practice of zeroing, it would have been hit with retaliatory trade measures by the EU and Japan that would have potentially resulted in hundreds of millions of dollars of lost exports. The threat of retaliatory sanctions appears to have put the contentious issue of zeroing mostly to bed, at least for now.[9]

With the EU having already discontinued the practice of zeroing and the US now having committed to do so in most contexts, it is to be hoped that this controversial practice has been consigned to the realm of history. It is hard to imagine other nations, particularly smaller ones, choosing to adopt zeroing, given that two giants of the trading system (the US and EU) have failed to defend its use at the WTO. In our view, the US decision to abandon zeroing in almost all of its anti-dumping proceedings is welcome news. Ridding the WTO system of zeroing removes an onerous burden from the shoulders of the dispute-settlement system. The litigation resource cost of zeroing has been tremendous on an already taxed dispute-settlement system; zeroing has accounted for almost 20% of AB reports (Bown and Prusa, 2011).

Given the stream of commentary about past zeroing cases, both in past studies in this series and elsewhere, what insights then are there to add from the *US–Orange Juice* decision, potentially one of zeroing's last gasps? We offer three points: First, while the Panel in *US–Orange Juice* certainly recognized that zeroing is prohibited in several forms of anti-dumping reviews, it cast doubt as to whether the AB may have overreached in its earlier *US–Zeroing (Japan)* decision when finding zeroing to be a violation of the 'fair comparison' requirement of Article 2.4 of the WTO Anti-Dumping Agreement (ADA). Rather than challenging the AB directly,

4 *United States – Laws, Regulations and Methodology for Calculating Dumping Margins (Zeroing)*, DS294 [*US–Zeroing (EC)*].

5 *United States – Measures Relating to Zeroing and Sunset Reviews*, DS322 [*US–Zeroing (Japan)*].

6 *United States – Continued Existence and Application of Zeroing Methodology*, DS350 [*US–Continued Zeroing*].

7 Press Release, Office of the US Trade Representative, 'United States Trade Representative Ron Kirk Announces Solutions to Years-Old Zeroing Disputes, Demonstrating Commitment to Export Growth and Job Creation' (6 February 2012).

8 Note that in Section 6, we discuss the possibility that the DOC may still have left itself the leeway to use this practice in one particular form of anti-dumping case, that in which there is 'targeted' dumping by a producer in a given region or over a particular time period.

9 As Prusa and Rubini's chapter (forthcoming) discusses, a number of zeroing disputes against the United States remain because the US DOC's new rules on margin calculations applied only prospectively. Thus, several countries have brought disputes concerning zeroed margins in pre-existing cases in order to obtain an adverse finding to force the US DOC to calculate non-zeroed margins for the products.

however, this decision highlights how Panels, at least on longstanding issues such as zeroing where the AB has made its views clear, feel increasingly constrained by the shadow of past AB rulings. Even if Panels are not formally bound by AB rulings, a *de facto* form of vertical *stare decisis* has taken hold in certain areas where panelists are concerned about the systemic costs to the WTO dispute-settlement regime of repeatedly challenging the AB's prior rulings, only then to be overturned.

Second, while the economics of zeroing are transparent and largely well understood, we note that the costs of zeroing differ depending on the context in which the practice is applied. When zeroing eliminates high price observations with larger export volumes, the damage that results is greater than in the case where zeroing eliminates high price observations with lower export volume. In other words, zeroing poses a greater potential problem in situations where the price increase of the exporter's good (which necessitates the importer's use of zeroing) is driven by changes in consumer demand rather than changes in the cost of exporting.

Finally, while we express cautious optimism that the WTO dispute-settlement regime may be seeing its last set of its zeroing challenges,[10] we note that the door remains open for a potential re-emergence of zeroing in a limited context.[11] Nevertheless, despite this opening, it appears that momentous litigation battles over zeroing are winding down, with future battles to be fought in negotiating rooms rather than courtrooms.

2. Background summary of the dispute

2.1 Past WTO challenges on zeroing

To understand the impact of zeroing, one needs to first understand what occurs during the investigation of an anti-dumping case. After a complaint has been filed alleging dumping by a foreign producer, the investigating authority compares the prices of export transactions with the 'normal' value of the product. If the former is lower than the latter, then the foreign producer is found to have 'dumped' its product. The ADA allows 'normal' value to be determined in various ways, depending upon the circumstances. These include reference to home-country prices, third-country prices, and/or a constructed price approach.

Prices will fluctuate with time based on a number of factors, including, but not limited to, input price fluctuations, foreign exchange fluctuations, changes in

10 Given the US strategy of only calculating non-zeroed margins in a pre-existing case following an adverse WTO finding for that particular case, there may still be several zeroing challenges ahead. Nevertheless, these disputes will be fairly easy to resolve, as evidenced by the quick Panel decisions rendered in *United States – Anti-Dumping Measures on Polyethylene Retail Carrier Bags from Thailand*, DS383 [*US–PET Bags (Thailand)*] and *United States – Use of Zeroing in Anti-Dumping Measures Involving Products from Korea*, DS402 [*US–Zeroing (Korea)*].

11 See *supra* note 8 and *infra* Section 6.

market demand conditions, etc. In comparing the price of export transactions with the normal value over a period of time, the investigating authority will encounter fluctuations in the export price over the investigation period. Disputes over zeroing arise from what happens in those instances when the investigating authority finds that the export price is actually higher than the normal value. It can treat such instances as 'negative dumping', meaning that it can use these instances to offset other instances of 'positive' finding (i.e., when the export price is lower than the 'normal value'). Or it can simply set the value to zero for that instance. This latter practice is what is known as 'zeroing'. Its significance is that its use can dramatically alter the results of an anti-dumping investigation and the calculation of anti-dumping margins to be levied.

Why is this? When investigating an allegation of dumping, investigating authorities must consider a series of export price observations over a period of time. The WTO Committee on Anti-Dumping Practices has adopted a recommendation that 'the period of data collection for dumping investigations normally shall be 12 months, and, in any case, no less than six months, ending as close to the date of initiation as is practicable'.[12] Investigating authorities are free to deviate from this investigation, but it is clear that they must consider more than a single observation. Because their dumping determination is based on a series of observations in which prices fluctuate, how these particular observations are treated matters when determining the average of these interactions.

Consider, then, an example series where some observations are ones where the export price is higher than the normal value, but most are instances where they are lower.[13] The former is what is to be expected, whereas the latter constitutes 'dumping' under WTO law. Normally, in determining the average of these observations, the instances of 'negative dumping' would be used to offset those instances of positive dumping. However, where zeroing is deployed, that is not the case. With zeroing, provided there are instances of positive dumping in the series, the investigation will inevitably result in a positive finding of dumping. Moreover, zeroing leads to a higher anti-dumping margin. This is again due to the fact that incidences of 'negative dumping' are set back to zero, so as to minimize their ability to serve as an offset to incidences of positive dumping. As a result, the practice of zeroing has been highly controversial and has been attacked in several prior cases.

To complicate the picture further, investigating authorities have taken different approaches when comparing the price of export transactions with normal value to determine the dumping margin and to calculate anti-dumping duties. Article 2.4.2 of the ADA recognizes three possibilities. The first is to compare 'the weighted

12 Committee on Anti-Dumping Practices, *Recommendation Concerning the Periods of Data Collection for Anti-Dumping Investigations*, adopted 5 May 2000, G/ADP/6, at para. 1(a).

13 Those who prefer to see an example with numbers may wish to skip ahead and read Example 1 in *infra* Section 4.

average normal value with a weighted average of all comparable export transactions'. The second is to compare 'normal value and export prices on a transaction-to-transaction basis'. The former is known as the 'weighted average to weighted average' (W–W) approach, whereas the latter is known as the 'transaction to transaction' (T–T) approach. Either of the two approaches is fine under the ADA. A third approach, however, may be used only in the limited circumstance where 'authorities find a pattern of export prices which differ significantly among different purchasers, regions or time periods, and if an explanation is provided as to why such differences cannot be taken into account by the use of a weighted average-to-weighted average or transaction-to-transaction approach'. Under this condition, investigating authorities are allowed to compare a 'normal value established on a weighted average basis' to 'prices of individual export transactions'. This third possibility, available only under limited circumstances, is known as a 'weighted average to transaction' (W–T) approach.

Prior to the entry into force of the ADA on 1 January 1995, the United States and other major users of anti-dumping generally calculated anti-dumping margins using the W–T approach.[14] However, as noted, the ADA constrained WTO members from using the W–T approach except under exceptional circumstances. In response, the US DOC adopted a new approach, known as 'model' zeroing. Under model zeroing, the product alleged to have been dumped is subdivided into a series of models. For example, a product may be subdivided into models on the basis of differences in physical characteristics, consumer preferences, and/or end use. A 'weighted average-to-weighted average' comparison is then conducted for each model rather than for the product as a whole. This model-specific W–W approach has come to be known as 'model' zeroing. In contrast, where the analysis is not performed on a model-to-model basis, the approach has been described as 'simple' zeroing. By nature, the T–T approach falls under the 'simple' zeroing category. So too does the W–T approach, even where the weighted-average normal value used is one for a model of the product; this is because the export price to which it is being compared is not model-specific.

Thus, the method of comparison which results in the use of zeroing may differ. A complaint brought before the WTO may be attacking one or more of these three different comparison approaches used in determining the dumping margin.

Another area of potential difference in the fact pattern of a WTO zeroing case is the type of investigation in which zeroing is used. So far, we have spoken of an anti-dumping investigation in general terms. However, anti-dumping investigations occur under various different contexts. Specifically, zeroing has been used in five different types of anti-dumping investigations. (1) The first type is the original investigation, i.e. the investigation conducted after the initial petition for anti-dumping remedies is filed. (2) A second type is an interim review or changed-

14 See Prusa and Vermulst (2009) at 222.

circumstance review. Article 11.2 of the ADA stipulates that this must occur 'upon request by any interested party which submits positive information substantiating the need for a review' so long as 'a reasonable period of time has elapsed since the imposition of the definitive anti-dumping duty.' (3) A third type is an administrative review. Under Article 9.3 of the ADA, an investigating authority is permitted, but not required, to determine the amount of the anti-dumping duty assessed on a foreign producer on a retrospective basis. In other words, the duty determined at the end of the original investigation is considered to be only an estimate, but the actual duty levied is determined at a later date retroactively. The administrative review is the process through which the actual duty, calculated retroactively, is determined. Because the US uses this approach, several of the WTO zeroing cases against the US, including this one, have targeted the practice of zeroing in administrative reviews. (4) A fourth type is a sunset review. Article 11.3 of the ADA stipulates that anti-dumping duties be terminated after five years, unless a sunset review initiated before then finds 'that the expiry of the duty would be likely to lead to continuation or recurrence of dumping and injury'. (5) A final type is a new-shipper review. These are reviews, as authorized by Article 9.5 of the ADA, for the purposes of determining individual dumping margins for new exporters that did not export during the period of investigation but are from a country against which anti-dumping duties have been applied.

This complicated web of possibilities has meant that the fact patterns of past WTO zeroing cases will often vary, with the type of comparison methodology and the type of investigation serving as key areas of difference. Unlike the European Union, which eliminated the use of zeroing altogether after losing the *EC–Bed Linens*[15] case, the US has chosen to comply with WTO rulings narrowly, by eliminating the use of zeroing for the particular factual circumstance in which it was challenged and lost. If a trading partner then sought to eliminate the US practice of zeroing in a different fact context, it was forced to bring another case. This has resulted in a series of prior AB rulings on US zeroing practices, which form the backdrop for this dispute. What follows below is a quick review of these cases, with particular attention given specifically to the type of zeroing methodology and the type of investigation at issue in each of the cases in which the AB has ruled against the US.

First, in *US–Softwood Lumber V*, the AB invalidated the use of model zeroing under the W–W methodology in original investigations by the US DOC.[16] The US then deployed simple zeroing under the T–T methodology instead, arguing that it was complying with the ruling by eliminating the offending W–W model zeroing measure. This argument was then challenged in compliance proceedings under

15 *European Communities – Anti-Dumping Duties on Imports of Cotton-Type Bed Linen from India*, DS141 [*EC–Bed Linens*].

16 Appellate Body Report, *US–Softwood Lumber V*, WT/DS264/AB/R, 11 August 2004.

Article 21.5 of the DSU.[17] Again, the US lost. Eventually, this led the US to eliminate the use of zeroing in original investigations.

However, recall that original investigations are but one of the five different types of anti-dumping investigations in which zeroing may be used. The US continued to retain the practice of zeroing in these other contexts, including administrative reviews under Article 9.3 of the ADA as well as new-shipper reviews under Article 9.5 of the ADA. The former is especially important because the US, as noted above, assesses anti-dumping duties retrospectively, as allowed under Article 9.3.1. The original investigation establishes only a deposit rate that the importer must pay, but the actual duty is determined in these subsequent administrative reviews. Thus, what truly matters for most foreign producers is whether the US employs zeroing in the administrative reviews.

US practices in Article 9.3.1 administrative reviews have been challenged in two separate cases, *US–Zeroing (EC)* and *US–Zeroing (Japan)*. In *US–Zeroing (EC)*, the AB addressed the use of W–T simple zeroing in administrative reviews, both as applied and as such. It found that the use of the W–T zeroing as applied by the US in 16 administrative reviews was inconsistent with Article 9.3 of the ADA and GATT Article VI:2.[18] The AB also declared moot the Panel's earlier ruling that the W–T simple-zeroing methodology as such in administrative reviews did not violate provisions of the GATT and the ADA.[19] In *US–Zeroing (Japan)*, the AB again affirmed that W–T simple zeroing is not allowed in administrative reviews. It held that the use of W–T simple zeroing as applied in 11 administrative reviews was inconsistent with several provisions of the ADA (Articles 2.1, 2.4, 9.1, and 9.3) as well as GATT Articles VI:1 and VI:2.[20]

Despite the two AB rulings against it, the US continued to engage in zeroing in administrative reviews. While proceedings challenging US noncompliance progressed, the Europeans filed a follow-up case, *US–Continued Zeroing (EC)*. Again, the Europeans challenged the US practice of using W–T simple zeroing in administrative reviews, along with several other issues. The AB's ruling was circulated in February 2009, after Brazil had already filed its complaint in this case. Just as before, the AB ruled against the US. In 34 of the 37 administrative reviews challenged by the EC, the AB found the use of W–T simple-zeroing methodology violated Article 9.3 of the ADA and GATT Article VI:2.[21] In two instances, the

17 Appellate Body Report, *US–Softwood Lumber V*, Article 21.5, WT/DS264/AB/RW, 15 August 2006.

18 Appellate Body Report, *US–Zeroing (EC)*, WT/DS294/AB/R, 18 April 2006 at para. 135.

19 Ibid., para. 227 (declaring moot the Panel's finding regarding Articles 1, 2.4, 2.4.2, 9.3, 11.1, 11.2, and 18.4 of the ADA and GATT Articles VI:1 and VI:2).

20 Appellate Body Report, *US–Zeroing (Japan)*, WT/DS322/AB/R, 9 January 2007 at para. 176.

21 Appellate Body Report, *US–Continued Zeroing*, WT/DS350/AB/R, 4 February 2009 at paras. 316 and 353.

AB chose not to complete the analysis, and, in the other instance, the AB held that the challenge of a preliminary measure was premature.[22]

In addition to opining on the use of W–T simple zeroing in Article 9.3.1 administrative reviews, the AB used these cases to rule on zeroing in a number of other factual contexts. In *US–Zeroing (Japan)*, Japan also challenged the US DOC's use of W–T simple zeroing in new-shipper reviews; the AB held this practice to be illegal.[23] Japan also challenged US practices in two sunset reviews in which the US relied upon administrative reviews that had used the W–T simple-zeroing methodology. The AB found that such practice violated Article 11.3 of the ADA.[24] In *US–Continued Zeroing (EC)*, the EU also had challenged the US DOC's use of W–W model zeroing in sunset reviews. The AB found the US at fault in eight of 11 sunset reviews in which the US had employed the W–W model-zeroing methodology.[25] In the remaining three instances, the AB again found the challenge of a preliminary measure to be premature.[26]

With the AB consistently ruling against the US on zeroing, why is the beast not yet dead? How is it that we get to yet another zeroing dispute? The main reason is US delay in complying with the AB's rulings. At the time of Brazil's complaint, the US had not yet signaled its intention to comply with the WTO rulings against its zeroing practices. This intransigence led the EU and Japan to press ahead with compliance proceedings under Article 21.5 of the DSU for *US–Zeroing (EC)* and *US–Zeroing (Japan)*; each proceeding was then subsequently appealed to the AB.[27] After winning the compliance proceedings, the EU and Japan sought DSU authorization for retaliation.[28] It was not until February 2012, when the European and Japanese retaliation threats became real, that the US finally backed down. By then, Brazil had already pressed ahead with its own case.

A second reason is the US practice of reading the AB's holding to apply narrowly to only the particular anti-dumping measures being challenged in the case. This meant that even were the US to eliminate the use of W–T simple zeroing with respect to the particular anti-dumping measures challenged by the EU and Japan, its other trading partners lacked confidence that the US would do so in administrative reviews concerning their products. To be certain that the US DOC would stop using W–T simple zeroing in administrative reviews for a particular

22 Ibid., paras. 207–12 and 354–7.

23 Appellate Body Report, *US–Zeroing (Japan)* at paras. 166 and 169 (finding violations of Arts. 2.4, 9.3, and 9.5 of the ADA and Art. VI:2 of the GATT).

24 Ibid., para. 186.

25 Appellate Body Report, *US–Continued Zeroing* at paras. 382–3.

26 Ibid., paras. 207–12.

27 Appellate Body Report, *US–Zeroing (EC)*, Article 21.5, WT/DS294/AB/RW, 14 May 2009; Appellate Body Report, *US–Zeroing (Japan)*, Article 21.5, WT/DS322/AB/RW, 18 August 2009.

28 Request for Recourse to Article 22.2 of the DSU by the European Union, *US–Zeroing (EC)*, Article 22.6, WT/DS294/35, 2 February 2010; Communication from Japan, *US–Zeroing (Japan)*, Article 22.6, WT/DS322/37, 5 May 2010.

Brazilian product, Brazil needed to file its own case. In a way, the US, through its strategy of narrowly interpreting AB rulings on zeroing, was testing its trading partners to see if the cost of zeroing was large enough that it would be willing to burn through costly litigation resources. The Brazilian government, having already tasted the political and economic gains of earlier WTO victories against the US, decided that it was worth forging ahead. Under this context, yet another zeroing dispute arose.

2.2 *The global orange-juice industry*

This particular zeroing case concerns orange juice. The orange-juice market is dominated by producers from two countries – Brazil and the United States. Together, they account for the lion's share of global production. The trade orientation of the industries in the two countries is very different. Domestic demand for pre-squeezed orange juice is small in Brazil.[29] As a result, most of the orange juice produced in Brazil is for export. Brazil supplies over 80% of the global orange-juice exports (USDA, 2007), and Brazilian firms have invested substantial sums in building a fleet of tankers used solely to transport frozen orange juice (Sterns and Spreen, 2010, 170). In contrast, the US is the world's largest consumer of orange juice. Most of the orange juice produced by US firms is for the domestic market, where its major competitors are the Brazilian producers.

The orange-juice industry in Brazil is highly concentrated. In crop year 2004–05, four firms (Coinbra, Cutrale, Citrosuco, and Montecitrus) accounted for approximately 85% of the total production of Brazilian orange juice (USITC, 2006, VII-6). As part of the anti-dumping investigation challenged in this dispute, the US DOC investigated the export practices of three of these firms – Cutrale, Fischer (which owns Citrusco), and Montecitrus – and applied zeroing when calculating the firm's dumping margins. Ironically, while high concentration levels typically raise concerns about monopoly pricing – which tends to be high – the position of the US DOC and the US International Trade Commission (ITC) was that the prices charged by Brazilian firms were *so low* that they caused material injury to the domestic orange-juice industry.[30]

Because the US is the world's largest consumer of orange juice, it is an important export market for Brazilian orange juice. The vast bulk of shipments by Brazilian producers to the US are of frozen orange juice, rather than non-frozen orange juice. Several of the major Brazilian producers have wholly owned or related processing

29 Brazilians prefer to drink orange juice that is freshly squeezed rather than pre-squeezed. They will squeeze oranges themselves at home or purchase from retailers juice that is freshly squeezed before them (USITC, 2006, VII-4 n. 12). Thus, there is little demand for pre-squeezed or frozen orange juice in Brazil.

30 Note that in 2011, long after the ITC determination was made and following the WTO case's conclusion, the Brazilian orange-juice industry further consolidated; a merger between Citrusco and Citrovita has resulted in the creation of the world's largest orange-juice producer. See White and Kassai (2011) and *Hispanically Speaking News* (2011).

affiliates in the US. However, the importance of the US market should not be overstated. In 2003, the year prior to the filing of the anti-dumping petition by the US citrus producers and processors, exports to the US represented only 20% of total Brazilian exports of frozen orange juice.[31] By contrast, exports to the largest and most important export market, the EU, represented over 52% of total Brazilian exports of frozen orange juice.[32]

In the non-frozen orange-juice segment (which represented 18% of total Brazilian orange-juice exports in 2003), the US market was even less important. In 2003, exports of non-frozen orange juice to the US represented a mere 1% of total Brazilian exports.[33] In contrast, 99% of non-frozen exports were destined for the EU.[34] The Brazilian share of the domestic US market in the not-from-concentrate orange-juice market was tiny – rising from a mere 1% in crop year 2001–02 to 3.3% in 2004–05.[35] Even when added with the frozen orange-juice segment, the Brazilian share of the US market was barely over 15% in 2004–05.[36]

Thus, while low-tariff access to the US market affected the business interests of Brazilian orange-juice producers, the zeroing case did not represent a 'make-or-break case' for the Brazilian orange-juice industry. Instead, Brazil's motivation to bring forward this challenge was likely driven by the desire to strike another blow against the US for zeroing, and, in doing so, reap the domestic political gain of another WTO victory against the US. In addition, large US beverage manufacturers (e.g., Coca-Cola and PepsiCo) are important buyers of Brazilian orange juice worldwide and presumably would want the benefit of lower duties for its US imports.[37] One can further speculate whether Brazil may have also been motivated to bring the case in order to cultivate favor with American multinational corporations that operate downstream on the supply chain.

2.3 *Factual aspects of the case*

The specific zeroing practices challenged in this dispute arose out of a 2004 petition filed by a collection of US citrus producers and processors. That petition alleged that Brazilian producers of certain orange juice were dumping their product in the US and materially injuring domestic producers. Upon receiving this petition, the US DOC began an investigation in February 2005, resulting in case number A-351-840.

31 Calculations by authors based on information provided in the UN Comtrade database for HS-200911.

32 Ibid.

33 Calculations by authors based on information provided in the UN Comtrade database for HS-200919.

34 Ibid.

35 See Table IV-5 in USITC (2006).

36 Ibid.

37 For example, Tropicana (owned by PepsiCo) and Minute Maid and Simply Orange (owned by Coca-Cola Co.) are sold not only in the US but also throughout Europe and Asia. See Kiernan and McKay (2012).

On 24 August 2005, the DOC issued a preliminary determination of dumping, which levied anti-dumping duties between 24.62 and 60.29% on Brazilian producers.[38] This was followed by a final determination on 13 January 2006 that revised the final anti-dumping duties downward to between 9.73% and 60.29%.[39]

Because the US employs a retrospective approach to assessing anti-dumping duties, the US collects only a 'security' in the form of a cash deposit at the time of entry. This cash deposit rate (CDR) represents an estimate of the importer's final anti-dumping duty payment.[40] Once a year, interested parties are allowed to request an administrative review to determine the final payment due for the relevant period of review. This payment is known as the importer-specific assessment rate (ISAR). The administrative review is also conducted by the US DOC, pursuant to Article 9.3.1 of the ADA. If no such review is requested, then the final anti-dumping duty assessed is the estimated rate, and the cash deposit collected as security are used to pay the duty owed.[41]

Brazilian orange-juice producers requested such an administrative review. The First Administrative Review was completed on 11 August 2008.[42] During this review, the US DOC employed W–T simple zeroing in calculating the dumping margins, CDRs, and ISARs. On 27 November 2008, Brazil requested consultations with the US at the WTO.[43] Brazil specifically challenged the DOC's use of W–T simple zeroing in calculations for two of the major Brazilian exporters, Cutrale and Fischer.

While the WTO consultations proceeded, Brazilian orange-juice producers requested a second administrative review the following year. On 22 May 2009, before the Second Administrative Review was completed, Brazil requested further consultations with the United States with regard to the use of zeroing in the original anti-dumping duty investigation as well as in the Second Administrative Review.[44] Brazil also requested consultations regarding the continued use of the United States zeroing procedures in successive anti-dumping proceedings pertaining to the imports of certain orange juice from Brazil. The Second Administrative Review was completed on 11 August 2009.[45]

38 'Notice of Preliminary Determination of Sales at Less Than Fair Value, Postponement of Final Determination, and Affirmative Preliminary Critical Circumstances Determination: Certain Orange Juice from Brazil', 70 Fed. Reg. 49557 (24 August 2005).

39 'Notice of Final Determination of Sales at Less Than Fair Value and Affirmative Final Determination of Critical Circumstances: Certain Orange Juice from Brazil', 71 Fed. Reg. 2183 (13 January 2006).

40 Panel Report, *US–Orange Juice (Brazil)*, WT/DS382/1, para. 7.83.

41 Ibid.

42 'Certain Orange Juice from Brazil: Final Results and Partial Rescission of Anti-Dumping Duty Administrative Review', 73 Fed. Reg. 46584 (11 August 2008).

43 Request for Consultations by Brazil, *US–Orange Juice (Brazil)*, WT/DS382/1, 1 December 2008.

44 Request for Consultations by Brazil, *US–Orange Juice (Brazil)*, WT/DS382/1/Add.1, 27 May 2009.

45 'Certain Orange Juice from Brazil: Final Results of Anti-Dumping Duty Administrative Review', 74 Fed. Reg. 40167 (11 August 2009).

The W–T simple-zeroing methodology deployed by the DOC and challenged by Brazil operated as follows.[46] Recall that, in determining whether dumping is occurring and calculating the dumping margin for a given exporter, the investigating authority needs to compare the export price with normal value. The DOC used a computer program to sort through the data necessary to make this comparison. This program computed a weighted-average normal value (WANV) each month for each exporter. The program then performed a series of W–T comparisons for each exporter. In other words, it compared the export price of a specific transaction for a given exporter to the WANV corresponding to that exporter for the month in which the transaction occurred. For every instance in which the normal value was higher than the export price, the computer program was instructed to set the result of this comparison to zero. The results were then aggregated and then divided by the total number of export transactions to figure out the weighted-average dumping margin. Because of the zeroing, the dumping margin was higher than it would have been otherwise.

Brazil's complaint charged that the US DOC's use of W–T simple zeroing in the two administrative reviews violated several WTO treaty provisions, namely Articles 2.4 and 9.3 of the ADA and Article VI:2 of the GATT 1994. Furthermore, Brazil alleged that the US DOC's continued use of W–T simple zeroing in successive anti-dumping proceedings, including the original investigation and subsequent administrative reviews, violated the same WTO provisions as well as Article 2.4.2 of the ADA.

As expected, the ensuing consultations failed to resolve the dispute. The US, as previously mentioned, gave no indication in 2009 of any intention to abandon its practice of zeroing in administrative reviews, despite the AB's rulings against it in *US–Zeroing (EC)* and *US–Zeroing (Japan)*. Therefore, on 20 August 2009, Brazil formally requested that the Dispute Settlement Body (DSB) establish a Panel with regard to the original investigation of the aforementioned dumping case, its two administrative reviews, as well as the continued use of zeroing by the US in anti-dumping proceedings. The Panel was established on 25 September 2009. After conducting its hearings, the Panel issued its report on 25 March 2011.

The Panel, not surprisingly, ruled in favor of Brazil. It held that with respect to the two administrative reviews at issue, the use of W–T simple zeroing by the US violated Article 2.4 of the ADA because it did not allow for a 'fair comparison' between export price and normal value.[47] The Panel further held that the continued use of zeroing under the Orange Juice Order also violated Article 2.4 of the ADA.[48] With respect to Brazil's other claims concerning Articles 2.4.2 and 9.3 of the ADA

46 Panel Report, *US–Orange Juice (Brazil)*, para. 7.85.
47 Ibid., paras. 7.155–7.161.
48 Ibid., para. 7.193.

and GATT Article VI:2, the Panel exercised judicial economy and chose not to examine the claims.[49]

3. The shadow of past Appellate Body rulings

Was the Panel's ruling that the US practice of zeroing violated Article 2.4 of the ADA correct? The provision states:

> A fair comparison shall be made between the export price and normal value. This comparison shall be made at the same level of trade, normally at the ex-factory level, and in respect of sales made at as nearly as possible the same time. Due allowance shall be made in each case, on its merits, for differences which affect price comparability, including differences in conditions and terms of sale, taxation, levels of trade, quantities, physical characteristics, and any other differences which are also demonstrated to affect price comparability.

The key question, as far as Article 2.4 of the ADA is concerned, is whether the practice of W–T simple zeroing allows for a fair comparison to be made.

As the Panel noted, this was the fifth case in which the question of the US DOC's use of W–T simple zeroing in administrative reviews has arisen.[50] Questions over the legality of W–T simple zeroing in periodic administrative reviews have also surfaced in *US–Zeroing (EC), US–Zeroing (Japan), US–Stainless Steel (Mexico)*,[51] and *US–Continued Zeroing*. In all four of these cases, the complainant had alleged that W–T simple zeroing violated Article 2.4 of the ADA. The central legal question, therefore, was anything but novel.

In several of these earlier decisions, the Panel and the Appellate Body (AB) have disagreed in their views on the consistency of W–T simple zeroing with respect to several provisions of the ADA and GATT. We summarize the results of these disagreements in Table 1.

Brazil, like past complainants of the US practice of zeroing in administrative reviews, raised claims that the US practice violated Articles 2.4 and 9.3 of the ADA as well as Article VI:2 of the GATT 1994. A review of the past rulings shows that in each of the four prior decisions, the AB has confirmed that W–T simple zeroing in administrative reviews is inconsistent with Articles 9.3 of the ADA and Article VI:2 of the GATT 1994. On the other hand, in three of the past four cases, the AB has declined to comment fully on the consistency of simple zeroing in periodic administrative reviews with Article 2.4 of the ADA. The AB has refused to endorse the view of several Panels that W–T simple zeroing is not inconsistent with

49 Ibid., para. 7.194.

50 Ibid., para. 7.130.

51 *US – Final Anti-Dumping Measures on Stainless Steel from Mexico*, DS344 [*US–Stainless Steel (Mexico)*].

Table 1. Past rulings on the consistency of simple zeroing in US administrative reviews (i.e., Article 9.3.1 reviews)

	Panel ruling	Appellate Body ruling
US–Zeroing (EC) [DS294] (as applied in 16 reviews)	Found that simple zeroing in administrative reviews is not inconsistent with Articles VI:2 of the GATT 1994 and Articles 2.4, 9.3, 11.1 and 11.2 of the ADA.	Reversed the Panel's finding with respect to Articles VI:2 of the GATT 1994 and Article 9.3 of the ADA, finding instead a violation. Upheld the Panel's finding concerning Articles 11.1 and 11.2 of the ADA, as well as the third to fifth sentences of Article 2.4 of the ADA. Declined to rule on the consistency of simple zeroing with the first sentence of Article 2.4 of the ADA.
US–Zeroing (Japan) [DS322] (as such and as applied in 11 reviews)	Found that simple zeroing in administrative reviews is not inconsistent with Articles VI:1 and VI:2 of the GATT 1994 and Articles 2.1, 2.4, and 9.1–9.3 of the ADA both as such and as applied in 11 periodic reviews.	Reversed the Panel's findings on both the as-such and as-applied claims. Found instead that simple zeroing is inconsistent with Article VI:2 of the GATT 1994 and Articles 2.4 and 9.3 of the ADA for both the as-such and as-applied claims. Declined to complete the analysis on claims regarding Article VI:1 of the GATT 1994 and Articles 2.1, 9.1, and 9.2 of the ADA.
US–Stainless Steel (Mexico) [DS344] (as-such claim and as-applied in five reviews)	Found that simple zeroing in administrative reviews is not inconsistent with Articles VI:1 and VI:2 of the GATT 1994 and Articles 2.1, 2.4, and 9.3 of the ADA both as-such and as-applied in five periodic reviews.	Reversed the Panel's finding on both the as-such and as-applied claims. Found instead that simple zeroing is inconsistent with Article VI:2 of the GATT 1994 and Article 9.3 of the ADA for both the as-such and as-applied claims. Found it unnecessary to rule on the claim concerning Article 2.4 of the ADA.
US–Continued Zeroing [DS350] (as applied in 29 reviews)	Ruled that simple zeroing in administrative reviews violated Article VI:2 of the GATT 1994 and Article 9.3 of the ADA. Applied judicial economy with respect to other claims, including Article 2.4 of the ADA.	Upheld Panel ruling on Article VI:2 of the GATT 1994 and Article 9.3 of the ADA. Declined to make additional findings on Article 2.4 of the ADA.

Article 2.4 of the ADA, overturning such a Panel ruling on three occasions. But more frequently than not, the AB has declined to complete the analysis so as to be able to explain why zeroing in administrative reviews is inconsistent with Article 2.4.

Only in *US–Zeroing (Japan)* did the AB address this issue, albeit briefly. The AB stated, 'If anti-dumping duties are assessed on the basis of a methodology involving comparisons between the export price and the normal value in a manner which results in anti-dumping duties being collected from importers in excess of the amount of the margin of dumping of the exporter or foreign producer, then this methodology cannot be viewed as involving a "fair comparison" within the meaning of the first sentence of Article 2.4.'[52] The AB then implied that the use of W–T simple-zeroing methodology would result in a duty being charged that was higher than the amount of the margin of dumping, because simple zeroing did not allow sales where the export price was higher than normal value to be properly taken into account.[53] Thus, it was 'unfair' and in violation of Article 2.4 of the ADA.

If there is one area where *US–Orange Juice (Brazil)* advances the discussion of the zeroing jurisprudence further, it is with respect to the issue of why exactly W–T simple zeroing is inconsistent with Article 2.4's requirement that a 'fair comparison' be undertaken. Recognizing that past cases had already discussed Article 9.3 of the ADA and Article VI:2 of the GATT 1994 extensively, the Panel chose to pass on those claims, on the ground of judicial economy. Instead, it focused its energy on discussing whether W–T simple zeroing was consistent with Article 2.4 of the ADA.

Yet, even on this question, the Panel did not consider itself entirely free to make up its own mind. Despite the limited discussion in the AB opinion in *US–Zeroing (Japan)*, the AB had clearly answered the question. Use of W–T simple zeroing in administrative reviews for the sake of retrospective duty assessment under Article 9.3.1 of the ADA was not permissible. This was true for both as-such and as-applied claims. The Panel therefore recognized,

> Although adopted panel and Appellate Body reports do not bind WTO Members beyond parties to a particular dispute, the Appellate Body has expressed the view that ensuring 'security and predictability' in the dispute settlement system, as contemplated in Article 3.2 of the DSU, implies that, absent cogent reasons, an adjudicatory body will resolve the same legal question in the same way in a subsequent case. Indeed, the Appellate Body has held that 'following the Appellate Body's conclusions in earlier disputes is not only appropriate, but is what would be expected from panels, especially where the issues are the same' … Institutionally, the fact that all Appellate Body reports overturning panel findings on the question of 'zeroing' have been adopted by the DSB implies acceptance by all WTO Members of their contents, and bestows upon them systemic legitimacy.[54]

52 Appellate Body Report, *US–Zeroing (Japan)*, para. 168.

53 Ibid., paras. 154–55 (cited in para. 168 as a cross-reference explanation for the AB's rationale for its ruling on the claim concerning Article 2.4 of the ADA).

54 Panel Report, *US–Orange Juice (Brazil)*, para. 7.132 (citations omitted).

The Panel, rightly in our opinion, recognized that although it was not bound by *US–Zeroing (Japan)*, the AB's prior proclamation on the very question did serve as a source of legitimate consideration (and constraint) on its deliberations. The excerpt above quoted by the Panel notes the AB's expectation, as stated in *US–Oil Country Tubular Goods Sunset Reviews* and repeated in subsequent cases, that where the legal issues is identical, Panels are expected to follow the AB's prior conclusions.[55] Thus, while the Panel could choose to deviate from the AB's past ruling that W–T simple zeroing in administrative reviews contravened Article 2.4 of the ADA, doing so would largely be a reflection of the Panel's obstinacy. Unless its ruling was crafted in such a way as to convince the AB that its past decision was wrong, it would simply be overruled.

Indeed, in *US–Stainless Steel (Mexico)*, the AB, when discussing a Panel's deviation from an established AB ruling on similar facts, noted, 'Ensuring "security and predictability" in the dispute settlement system, as contemplated in Article 3.2 of the DSU, implies that, absent cogent reasons, an adjudicatory body will resolve the same legal question in the same way in a subsequent case.'[56] In a subsequent zeroing case, *US–Continued Zeroing*, the Panel, while affirming that it was not bound to follow vertical *stare decisis*, nevertheless recognized that neither 'should a panel make a finding different from that in an adopted earlier Panel or Appellate Body report on similar facts and arguments without careful consideration and examination of why a different result is warranted, and assuring itself that its finding does not undermine the goals of the system'.[57]

This Panel appears to have taken these directives seriously. It recognized that it was not bound to follow the past precedent as laid forth by the AB in *US–Zeroing (Japan)*. But if it was to deviate from that ruling, it also recognized that it would need to elaborate on a set of cogent reasons for why such a deviation was necessary, given the costs triggered in terms of undermining 'security and predictability' of the dispute-settlement system. The Panel, therefore, stopped short of deviating and tempting the AB to overrule it. Instead, it simply offered a much more elaborate discussion of the arguments on both sides of the question of whether W–T simple zeroing in administrative reviews under Article 9.3.1 of the ADA was inconsistent with the 'fair comparison' obligation of Article 2.4 of the ADA.

Such a move falls squarely within the range of the Panel's discretion. Article 11 of the DSU directs that a Panel 'should make an objective assessment of the matter before it, including an objective assessment of the facts of the case and the applicability of and the conformity with the relevant covered agreements, and

55 Appellate Body Report, *United States – Sunset Reviews of Anti-Dumping Measures on Oil Country Tubular Goods from Argentina*, WT/DS/268/AB/R, 29 November 2004, para. 188.

56 Appellate Body Report, *US–Stainless Steel (Mexico)*, WT/DS344/AB/R, 30 April 2008, para. 160.

57 Panel Report, *US–Continued Zeroing*, para. 7.180.

make such other findings as will assist the DSB in making the recommendations or in giving the rulings provided for in the covered agreements'. Given the arguments raised by both the US and Brazil on this question, to analyze the various points raised is exactly what is to be expected of a Panel that takes its charge to perform an 'objective assessment' seriously.

The Panel identifies two questions raised by Brazil's challenge: (1) '[W]hether the obligation in the first ... sentence of Article 2.4 to ensure a "fair comparison" between export price and normal value applies outside of the context of what is described in the remainder of the provision, namely beyond the selection of transactions and use of adjustments to account for differences between export price and normal value which affect their comparability'; and (2) If yes, then 'whether the use of "simple zeroing" to calculate a margin of dumping is unfair'.[58]

The first question is whether the 'fair comparison' obligation is a narrow or broad requirement. A narrow reading of the obligation would mean that it is specific to the contexts mentioned in Article 2.4, namely: (a) the selection of transactions to be used for comparing export price to normal value and (b) the use of adjustments when making such a comparison. A broad reading would encompass other contexts beyond Article 2.4, including retrospective duty-assessment proceedings under Article 9.3.1.

On this question, we see the shadow of past AB rulings. In *US–Zeroing (Japan)*, when examining the same question, the Panel declared that 'the requirement of a fair comparison set out in the first sentence of Article 2.4 is an independent legal obligation that is not defined exhaustively by the specific requirements set out in the remainder of Article 2.4 and is not limited in scope to the issue of adjustments to ensure price comparability', noting that a previous Panel in *US–Zeroing (EC)* had reached a similar conclusion.[59] This position was then endorsed implicitly by the AB, as reflected by the fact that the AB then proceeded to assess the compatibility of zeroing in retrospective duty assessment (which is not discussed in the remainder of Article 2.4) with the 'fair comparison' obligation of Article 2.4.[60] Moreover, in *US–Zeroing (EC)*, the AB had explicitly stated that 'the legal rule set out in the first sentence of Article 2.4 is expressed in terms of a general and abstract standard. One implication of this is that this requirement is also applicable to proceedings governed by Article 9.3'.[61] The answer to the first question therefore had been clearly answered by the AB in the past. The obligation applied broadly.

The Panel, in deciding this question, referenced the rationale given in past WTO rulings. It discussed a point noted in the *US–Zeroing (EC)* rulings that the

58 *US–Orange Juice (Brazil)*, para. 7.140.
59 Panel Report, *US–Zeroing (Japan)*, para. 7.157.
60 Appellate Body Report, *US–Zeroing (Japan)*, para. 168.
61 Appellate Body Report, *US–Zeroing (EC)*, para. 146 (citation omitted).

'fair comparison' reference in the first sentence of Article 2.4, which serves as a chapeau to the rest of the provision, must be doing some work beyond addressing the price comparisons expressed in the remainder of the provision.[62] To interpret the provision as not having any independent meaning beyond the scope of price comparison adjustments discussed in Article 2.4 would render the sentence inutile. Hence, the Panel declared that 'fair comparison' obligation 'must apply to discipline the "comparison" between export price and normal value *whenever* undertaken during an anti-dumping proceeding, including during duty assessment'.[63] The obligation therefore extends to the comparisons made in Article 9.3.1 retrospective duty assessment determinations of the sort at issue in this case.

However, while the Panel referenced these past AB rulings, it is not altogether clear that the Panel necessarily agreed fully with the AB's past interpretation. One of its Panel members went so far as to emphasize his view that 'the correct interpretation of the "fair comparison" requirement set out in the first sentence of Article 2.4 is not as clear as previous Panels and the Appellate Body appear to have suggested'.[64] He noted that the first sentence of the chapeau must be interpreted in light of the context of the rest of the chapeau, including the last sentence which also makes reference to a 'fair comparison'. In his opinion, an examination of the fuller context suggests that the scope of Article 2.4 is limited to that of price comparability and adjustments and not that of an enlarged scope encompassing Article 9.3 administrative reviews. As a result, the panelist declared that he 'finds there to be strong grounds to doubt the broad interpretation of the scope of the "fair comparison" requirement made by previous Panels and the Appellate Body'.[65]

Yet, despite apparently holding the view that past Panels and the AB got it wrong on the first question, this panelist did not go so far as to declare his disagreement vehemently. Instead of trying to convince his fellow panelists to join him in challenging the correctness of the past rulings, or expressing a dissent (had he failed in this endeavor), the panelist resigned himself to accepting the subordinate role of the Panel in the WTO dispute-settlement hierarchy. He noted, despite his intellectual objections, 'that, on balance, and in light of the systemic considerations [concerning security and predictability in WTO dispute settlement proceedings], the view of the Appellate Body should be followed on this issue'.[66] This reflects the

62 Panel Report, *US–Orange Juice (Brazil)*, para. 7.142.

63 Ibid (emphasis added). Note that the Panel further added in footnote 240 the clarification that this does not mean 'that a "comparison" between export price and normal value is *required* in *all* anti-dumping proceedings'.

64 Ibid., para. 7.143.

65 Ibid.

66 Ibid.

extent to which the norm of a *de facto* vertical *stare decisis* has taken hold in the mind of panelists, at least with respect to an issue such as zeroing where the AB has made its position adamantly clear.

Is this behavior to be welcomed? On the one hand, where countless litigation resources have been expended on this single topic of zeroing and where the AB has clearly indicated its willingness to overturn Panel rulings that are inconsistent with its prior rulings, perhaps it is the right call. Doing so avoids the cost of yet another appeal on a topic already adjudicated in an earlier case. Yet, on the other hand, in establishing the AB, countries explicitly rejected modeling the WTO dispute-settlement regime along the lines of a common-law regime where the rulings of an appellate court carry the weight of *stare decisis*. Among the advantages of the WTO model is that it gives future Panels the power to reexamine previously decided questions and to highlight ways in which past Panels and the AB may have erred. But this advantage holds only if panelists actually exert this power. Where they find themselves unwilling to do so out of fear that they will be overturned by the AB, then it is the regime itself that suffers.

On balance, we find that on this particular question, the panelist's behavior is, from a pragmatic perspective, the right course of action. By highlighting his intellectual disagreement, he is drawing attention to arguments that the past AB ruling on this question may be wrong. In that sense, he is not abdicating his responsibility to raise questions about the correctness of past rulings. Yet, on this particular question, he recognizes that, even were his view to prevail, this would be immaterial to the outcome of this dispute. Even if the US's actions on simple zeroing were found not to violate Article 2.4 of the ADA because the scope of the provision's 'fair comparison' requirement does not encompass the proceedings at hand, the US zeroing practices are still likely to be inconsistent with other WTO obligations, namely Article 9.3 of the ADA and Article VI:2 of the GATT 1994. Thus, the outcome of this dispute does not turn on this question per se. To flag the issues for the AB to reconsider at a later date, if necessary, seems to be the right call, at least when compared to the alternative of forcing all sides to march yet again down the road of expending resources for an appeal where the overall outcome will not change, even if this question is decided differently. We would disagree, were it the case that we would expect many more future challenges on this same legal question. In that situation, the importance of getting the law right would outweigh any questions of resources. But in this particular instance, the odds of such future challenges appear to be minimal, given the recent changes announced in US zeroing practices.

On the second question of whether the use of W–T simple-zeroing methodology in assessing the anti-dumping duty in Article 9.3.1 administrative reviews actually violated Article 2.4, again, the Panel recognized the shadow of the AB's past ruling in *US–Zeroing (Japan)*. It highlighted the fact that the AB had previously found that the use of W–T simple-zeroing methodology was not fair because it 'would result in duty collection from importers in excess of the margin of dumping established in accordance with Article 2'.[67] This Panel, as a result, decided the question the same way, noting that its decision was based in part on its 'taking into account important systemic concerns'.[68] This, of course, is shorthand for stating that it again did not wish to disturb the 'security and predictability' of WTO jurisprudence on this question, given that the AB had already ruled on it and would likely overrule any disagreement with its ruling.

Yet, again, the Panel expressed some reservation with the correctness of the AB's prior ruling. It signaled its agreement with the US argument that the concept of 'fairness' is highly malleable and context-dependent.[69] The Panel highlighted language from the *US–Softwood Lumber V* Panel suggesting that were the W–T simple zeroing as well as the W–W model-zeroing methodologies both acceptable, then even if the W–T approach resulted in a higher margin than the W–W approach, it could not be deemed inherently unfair.[70] In contrast, were the former prohibited but the latter accepted, then it would be unfair. Thus, according to the Panel, the second question turns on the question whether the W–T simple-zeroing methodology is an acceptable mode of comparison under the ADA.[71]

The Panel then pointed out that the AB, upon examining this question in past disputes, had answered this question in the negative. Yet, the Panel's decision reads more like a resignation of the fact that the Panel is constrained by the AB's prior answer than an enthusiastic affirmation of the AB's interpretation. Relying on the interpretation norms of the Vienna Convention on the Law of Treaties, the Panel first highlighted the fact that there is textual ambiguity. The Panel declared, 'In our view, the language of Article 2.1 of the AD Agreement and Article VI:1 of the GATT 1994 is drafted in such general terms that render both provisions potentially capable of either of the two conceptions of "dumping" advanced by the parties' – with one being that comparisons must be made for a product on the whole (i.e., W–W model zeroing) and the other that they can also be transaction-specific (i.e., W–T simple zeroing).[72]

Given this textual ambiguity, the Panel then turned to the object and purpose of the agreement. The Panel elaborated on several reasons why it thought the drafters of the provision may have viewed a transaction-specific approach as acceptable. First, the Panel noted that GATT negotiators and ADA negotiators may have

67 Ibid, para. 7.146 (citing Appellate Body Report, *US–Zeroing (Japan)*, para. 168).
68 Ibid, para. 7.153.
69 Ibid., para. 7.152.
70 Ibid., para. 7.151 (citing Panel Report, *US–Softwood Lumber V*, para. 5.74).
71 Ibid., para. 7.153.
72 Ibid., para. 7.91.

viewed the term 'product' as having a transaction-specific meaning, since they clearly had expressed such a view when using the term in other treaty provisions outside of the anti-dumping context.[73] Second, the Panel also noted that an approach which required only a product-on-the-whole approach (i.e., W–W model zeroing) for Article 9.3.1 retrospective reviews of anti-dumping duties 'seems to be incongruent and not in keeping with how prospective normal value systems have traditionally operated'.[74] Third, on the historical background to this issue, the Panel expressed 'sympathy for the view that a transaction-specific notion of "dumping" was recognized by the Contracting Parties to the GATT 1947' which subsequently signed the Tokyo Round Anti-Dumping Code.[75] The Panel then concluded that its analysis strongly suggests that the 'Members held, if not accepted, differing views about what "dumping" meant at the time of the closure of the Uruguay Round'.[76]

In short, the Panel was not convinced that W–T simple zeroing was necessarily forbidden and that the only acceptable methodology is the W–W model-zeroing approach. But having seen other Panels challenge the AB's interpretation only to be overturned, the Panel did not dare to pick yet another fight with the AB. It went about as far as it could go in terms of expressing its doubts about the wisdom of the AB's prior judgment, only to then concede that it would follow the AB's prior ruling, since the AB has made its views clear. In short, the Panel acquiesced to the AB's decision on the legal question because doing so would best guarantee the 'security and predictability' of the WTO dispute-settlement system.[77]

Again, while not bound by vertical *stare decisis*, the Panel report in *US–Orange Juice (Brazil)* indicates the influential power that past AB rulings have on future Panel decisions. Even where the Panel may disagree with the AB's past jurisprudence, it may decide that the costs of raising a challenge are too great and damaging to the system for it to bother. This is especially true in an issue such as zeroing, where the questions have been litigated repeatedly and the AB has stuck to its position firmly despite Panel challenges. Instead, as this Panel has done, the panelists may simply articulate their doubts, but, at the end of the day, follow the AB's approach because of the need for 'security and predictability' in dispute settlement.

73 Ibid., para. 7.108 (noting how 'the drafters of the GATT understood the meaning of the word 'product' could have a transaction-specific meaning in the particular context of customs valuation, which in turn also suggests that it cannot be categorically excluded that negotiators may have held the same view about the meaning of 'product' when it appears' in the ADA and GATT Article VI).

74 Ibid., para. 7.112.

75 Ibid., para. 7.124.

76 Ibid., para. 7.126.

77 Ibid., para. 7.133.

4. The economics of zeroing: anything left to say?

The textbook illustration of dumping in international trade usually compares a firm's pricing behavior across two national markets or the price in the export market with the fair value of the product (often measured by its cost of production with a reasonable allowance for profit). As is well known, if a firm is confronted with different demand conditions in two countries (usually captured by differences in the elasticity of demand), then it is optimal for it to engage in international price discrimination. When such discrimination manifests itself as a lower price in the foreign market, the firm is said to be 'dumping'.

The international-price-discrimination-based textbook illustration of dumping is special in many regards. Perhaps its most important limitation is that it presents a *snapshot* comparison of two distinct prices at a point in time. Given only two prices, determining dumping becomes a trivial task: is the price abroad lower than that in the firm's domestic market or not? Of course, in the real world, firms export and sell domestically over multiple time periods, and changes in underlying market conditions often necessitate price adjustments on their part.

In a world of multiple price observations, the most obvious way to define dumping over any particular time period requires a method for aggregating all of the price observations within that time period. At its core, WTO disputes over zeroing – of which there have been many – reflect a disagreement with respect to the method used for *aggregating the information* contained in a particular set of price observations.

An example helps.

Example 1: Suppose a Brazilian firm exports to the US market for four time periods (for instance, months) and alters its price once every period. Furthermore, let the firm's price in Brazil (when converted to dollars) or the fair normal value of its product be constant over this time period at $65 per unit.

Suppose further for simplicity that the firm exports 50 units of output in each time period. The value of total exports over all four periods is easily calculated to be $13,000.

Table 2 shows how the firm's price in the US changes over the relevant time horizon.

Table 2. Effects of zeroing

Time period	US price	Units of US Sales	Dumping margin	Dumping margin with zeroing
1	$50	50	$15	$15
2	$80	50	$–15	$0
3	$80	50	$–15	$0
4	$50	50	$15	$15

According to Table 2, the firm is dumping in the US in periods 1 and 4 but not in periods 2 and 3. The weighted average dumping margin (WADM) can be easily calculated by weighing the DM in each period by the associated export sales and dividing by the value of total export sales. Given the information in Table 2, the WADM equals zero, since the positive dumping margins (DMs) in periods 1 and 4 exactly offset the negative ones in periods 2 and 3 and sales are equal across all periods. Since the WADM is zero (rather than positive), a dumping investigation based on it would find that no dumping has occurred.

How does zeroing fit into the process? The practice of zeroing essentially assigns zeros to all negative dumping margins when calculating the WADM, which in turn has repercussions for both the determination of dumping as well as the level of anti-dumping duty that is eventually imposed. In this example, if the dumping margin in periods 2 and 3 is set to zero, the WADM ends up being 11.54%, which would indicate that the firm is indeed dumping in the US market. Thus, if the dumping investigation incorporates zeroing, then it finds dumping even though the WADM in the absence of zeroing actually equals zero.

For economists, who are generally quite opposed to anti-dumping (and for good reason), the practice of zeroing seems to make a bad policy even worse. As such, it is difficult to conceive of *any* circumstances under which zeroing can help reduce the harm caused by anti-dumping. As Example 1 indicates, it is conceptually clear that zeroing can lead an importing nation to find in favor of dumping even when there is no dumping on average. Furthermore, by inflating the dumping margin, zeroing can also lead to higher anti-dumping duties.

In addition to these well-understood points, Bown and Prusa (2011) make two additional observations about the consequences of zeroing. First, zeroing tends to treat the price in the firm's domestic market (or the fair market value) different from what it actually is. This is because whenever the firm's foreign price is above that in its domestic market, a zeroing policy enacted by the foreign country treats the firm's price there as being the same as its price in its domestic market since, by definition, zeroing sets the dumping margin to zero for such pairs of price observations. Such manipulation of market data is problematic for obvious reasons. Second, they correctly note that 'zeroing is driven by price variations' and that if 'the foreign firm charged exactly the same price for all transactions, then zeroing would not matter'. Thus, to understand the consequences of zeroing, one needs to take a closer look at the causes and consequences of price variations (which we do below).

What arguments do supporters of zeroing make in its defense? Perhaps the most common argument is based on an analogy between zeroing and speeding. Briefly speaking, according to this rationale, it is appropriate to disregard periods of negative dumping margins, since these do no harm to domestic industry, just as driving below the speed limit does not generate undue risks for others (assuming that the speeding limit is optimally chosen by society with that goal in mind to begin with). When a driver speeds by a traffic police car, all previous driving instances where the driver *did not* break the speed limit do not affect the police officer's decision to determine whether or not a traffic violation has occurred at that particular instant. Such a course of conduct on the part of the police officer is reasonable because *each and every speeding incident* has the potential to cause serious harm to others. But is dumping like speeding? In other words, by charging a low price for a day (or even a month), can a foreign firm cause material damage to the local industry? In our view, in their analysis of *Softwood V zeroing* case between Canada and the US, Bown and Sykes (2008) correctly note that 'individual transactions at "dumped" prices are generally of no concern whatsoever. They are simply not analogous to dangerous behaviors such as speeding that are properly subjection to sanction.'

Indeed, for the speeding analogy to be a suitable defense of zeroing, a single instance of dumping ought to be sufficient to do significant damage to domestic. It is difficult to conceive of any real market in which this would be true. Even the typical monopolization concern with respect to dumping (often expressed in the somewhat sensationalistic phrase 'predatory dumping') is not credible in the context of an isolated instance of dumping. As Bown and Sykes (2008) note, 'anti-dumping duties are routinely used in industries where monopolization concerns are fanciful'. Indeed, if a foreign firm were to charge a very low price for a short time with the intention of driving out a domestic competitor, it is unlikely to make much headway, since the domestic competitor will not shut down even when it is suffering losses in the short run, since it would want to avoid having to incur entry/start-up costs in the future. And if the low price charged by the foreign firm were to be permanent, there is again no reason to impose an anti-dumping duty, since a country imports precisely those goods that other countries can produce more cheaply than it can. The possibility of harm exists only in a limited set of circumstances where the foreign firm is able to sustain a low price for a considerable period so as to chase the domestic competitors out of the market and then erect high barriers to entry, so as to preserve a monopoly on the market. In practice, this is difficult to execute, especially with the penalties under competition laws serving a deterrent against any such action.

Despite the fact that most economic commentators tend to agree that anti-dumping is simply another form of protectionism that should be generally avoided and that, if used, dumping ought to be defined on the basis of all price observations that span the relevant time period, the WTO's dispute-settlement process has struggled to come to terms with the appropriate definition of dumping. Indeed, even informed parties have disagreed over this issue: as we noted earlier, the decisions of previous WTO Panels that have decided zeroing disputes have often been over-turned by the Appellate Body (AB), which has repeatedly ruled that the notion of dumping applies to the 'product as a whole' and ought to be based on the *entire set of price observations* over the relevant time period. Thus, the AB has ruled that a country cannot pick and choose price observations in a manner that is unambiguously biased in favor of finding dumping. As should be clear from the discussion above, we are in agreement with this position of the AB, at least generally in contexts where transaction-specific considerations are not mentioned in the ADA, even though several WTO Panels have struggled with the issue and expressed skepticism over the AB's approach.

As we noted above, many analysts have noted that zeroing inflates dumping margins and thereby leads to more affirmative findings of dumping and the eventual application of higher anti-dumping duties. What we want to argue next is that the issue is not just that of ignoring instances where prices are high on average; it may also be important to account for *why* prices fluctuate in the first place. In particular, the consequences of zeroing when price fluctuations are driven by changes in market demand conditions, are likely to be somewhat different than when they are driven by changes in costs of accessing foreign markets (for instance, due to changes in factor markets, technology, transportation costs/trade barriers, or the exchange rate).

As we will demonstrate below, this distinction matters. If high prices in export markets are caused by increases in demand, then they are correlated with high export sales; whereas when they are caused by an increase in costs of exporting, they are correlated with low export sales. We show below that the nature of this correlation between prices and export sales affects the WADM in a way that makes zeroing a relatively more insidious policy than when price fluctuations are driven by changes in market demand as opposed to costs. Thus, the relative harm done by zeroing would be greater in the former scenario.

Consider first the case where prices changes are driven by variations in market demand over time.

Example 2 (when demand changes drive prices): Let the demand curve in the US during periods of low demand (periods 1 and 4) be given by $p=100-q$ while that in periods of high demand (periods 2 and 3) by $p=160-q$. For simplicity, normalize the marginal cost (MC) of exporting to zero and consider the price decisions of a Brazilian firm.

The profit-maximizing Brazilian firm sets marginal revenue equal to marginal cost, which means that in periods of high demand it solves $MR=160-2q=MC=0$. This implies that the firm's exports to the US in periods 2 and 3 equal 80 units each. Similarly, in periods 1 and 4 it solves $100-2q=0$, which gives its exports as $q=50$. As can be observed from Table 3 below, price in the US market equals \$50 in periods 1 and 4 and \$80 in periods 2 and 3 (found by solving the relevant demand curves for p, given the firm's sales). The total value of exports over all four periods equals \$17,800.

As in Example 1, let the firm's price in its home market (i.e., Brazil) be constant at \$65, because demand is assumed to not fluctuate there over time. Given this, the firm's dumping margin (DM) in the US is positive in periods 1 and 4 (it equals \$15), whereas it is negative in periods 2 and 3 and (it equals \$–15). Thus, the firm dumps in periods 1 and 4 but not in periods 2 and 3.

Table 3. Effects of zeroing when demand changes drive price changes

Time period	US price	Units of US sales	Dumping margin	Dumping margin with zeroing
1	$50	50	$15	$15
2	$80	80	$–15	$0
3	$80	80	$–15	$0
4	$50	50	$15	$15

Using the information in Table 3, the WADM is calculated to be –5.1%. Thus, a dumping determination based on either the WADM would find in favor of the firm (i.e., that no dumping occurred in the US).

With zeroing, however, the negative DMs are excluded from the calculation and the ADM as well as the WADM under zeroing end up being 8.4%, which would then indicate that dumping did occur.

A comparison of Examples 1 and 2 yields two insights. First, the WADM is lower in Example 2 even though prices are the same in both cases. This is intuitive: high price observations are accompanied by higher sales levels in Example 2 and therefore carry a greater weight when calculating the WADM. Second, zeroing tends to inflate the WADM to a greater degree in Example 2 (from –5.1% to 8.4%) precisely because it drops observations that carry more weight in the absence of zeroing.

Now consider the case where the changes in export prices are induced by fluctuations in the cost of exporting.

> *Example 3 (when cost changes drive prices):* Suppose US market demand in all periods is given by $p = 100–q$. Further suppose that the *MC* of exporting fluctuates over time. In periods 1 and 4, *MC* equals zero (as in example 1) while in periods 2 and 3 it equals $60.
>
> From Example 1, we know that the firm's sales in periods 1 and 4 equal 50 units each with the associated price of $50. In periods 2 and 3, the firm's exports are found by solving $MR = 100–2q = 60$ which gives $q = 20$ and $p = 100–20 =$ $80.
>
> Observe that, by design, the price levels over the four periods are the same across all three examples: in periods 1 and 4 the price equals $50, whereas in periods 2 and 3 it equals $80. However, in the current example, the high prices in periods 2 and 3 are associated with *lower* sales levels of 20 each, whereas in Example 2 they are associated with *higher* sales levels of 80 each.

Table 4 presents the relevant calculations for this example.

Using the information contained in Tables 3 and 4, it is easy to show that even though the price observations are the same in both cases, the WADM is not. When demand variations drive price changes (i.e., in Table 3), the WADM is actually –5.1% (without zeroing), whereas it is 11.0% when price variations are induced by cost changes (i.e., in Table 4). In other words, a dumping investigation based on

Table 4. Effects of zeroing when cost changes drive price changes

Time period	US price	Units of US sales	Dumping margin	Dumping margin with zeroing
1	$50	50	$15	$15
2	$80	20	$–15	$0
3	$80	20	$–15	$0
4	$50	50	$15	$15

the WADM in Example 2 would *not* find dumping, whereas it would find dumping in the current example even though the observed prices are the same in both cases!

Intuitively, when demand increases drive price changes, the high price observations (i.e., those for which the DM is negative) end up receiving a greater weight in the calculation of the WADM relative to the case where cost changes are the driving factor.

An important observation can be made from Tables 3 and 4: while zeroing leads to a reversal in the sign of the WADM under the demand case (from –5.1% to 8.4%), it does not do so under the cost case (where the WADM goes from 11% to 18.3%). *Thus, zeroing is more likely to convert a negative finding regarding dumping into a positive one when price changes result from demand changes as opposed to cost changes.*

While the two examples are rather specific, the insight that they are based on is fairly general: when zeroing eliminates high price observations with larger export volumes, it will tend to do more damage relative to the case where it eliminates high price observations with smaller export volumes.

Which of these two scenarios is more applicable in a particular case would depend upon the context. In the present case, weather shocks in the US reduced the output of local OJ producers, thereby leaving larger residual demand for Brazilian exporters. Thus, it was a negative supply shock to the domestic OJ industry in the US that translated into a larger residual demand curve facing Brazilian exporters, which in turn led to an increase in their exports. Furthermore, it is well known that the material-injury test applied during dumping investigations is often based on rising import volumes doing serious harm to domestic industry (as opposed to falling import volumes). This suggests that the demand scenario described in Example 2 might be more relevant for a typical anti-dumping case relative to the cost scenario described in Example 3.[78] Of course, zeroing tends to have the strongest effect on the outcome of the dumping investigation precisely when it

78 Of course, reductions in the cost of exporting can also lead foreign exporters to increase their sales volumes but such increases in sales would be accompanied by price decreases as opposed to price increases. As a result, such observations would *not* be dropped under a zeroing policy.

eliminates high price observations associated with large export sales by foreign sellers.

5. Resolving the orange-juice dispute

The US chose not to appeal the Panel's rulings. On 28 December 2010, a few months before the Panel decision was rendered, the US DOC had already issued a notice, pursuant to Section 123(g) of the Uruguay Round Agreement Act, seeking comments on a proposal to modify its methodology for calculating anti-dumping margins and duty assessments involving the elimination of zeroing.[79] With this policy shift already underway, the US did not find it necessary to appeal the Panel's decision, especially given that the AB had already made its position on the legal issues clear in prior rulings.

On 17 June 2011, the Dispute Settlement Body adopted the Panel's recommendations and rulings. The US was given until 17 March 2012, to implement the recommendations and rulings. A month prior to this deadline, the US DOC issued its policy change that discontinued the use of zeroing in administrative reviews, new shipper reviews, expedited anti-dumping reviews, and sunset reviews.[80] As noted earlier, the US did so in order to avoid retaliation from the EU and Japan stemming from the earlier WTO zeroing cases. The US then informed the WTO that the policy modification also addressed the outstanding issues in this dispute.

At the same time, the US ITC was engaged in a sunset review of the anti-dumping order against certain Brazilian orange juice. This review resulted in an ITC decision in March 2012 to terminate the anti-dumping duties on Brazilian orange juice altogether; the termination was to be effective as of 9 March 2011.[81] Based on the US DOC policy change on zeroing and the ITC's decision to terminate anti-dumping duties on Brazilian orange juice altogether, the two countries entered into an agreement on 3 April 2012, stating that they had resolved their dispute.[82]

From an economics standpoint, there was little justification for the anti-dumping duties against Brazilian orange juice or the use of zeroing in determining and calculating those duties. At no point did Brazilian orange-juice producers pose an anti-competitive threat. As noted earlier, at the start of the imposition of anti-dumping duties, the Brazilian share of the US domestic orange-juice market

79 'Anti-Dumping Proceedings: Calculation of the Weighted Average Dumping Margin and Assessment Rate in Certain Anti-Dumping Duty Proceedings', 75 Fed. Reg. 81533 (28 December 2010).

80 'Anti-Dumping Proceedings: Calculation of the Weighted-Average Dumping Margin and Assessment Rate in Certain Anti-Dumping Duty Proceedings', Final Modification, 77 Fed. Reg. 8101 (14 February 2012).

81 US International Trade Commission, 'USITC Makes Determination in Five-Year (Sunset) Review Concerning Certain Orange Juice from Brazil, Press Release, 14 March 2012); 'Revocation of Anti-dumping Duty Order: Certain Orange Juice from Brazil', 77 Fed. Reg. 23659 (20 April 2012).

82 'Understanding Between Brazil and the United States Regarding Procedures Under Articles 21 and 22 of the DSU, WT/DS382/11' (10 April 2012).

hovered around 15%. Moreover, the share was not steadily increasing. Instead, it had fluctuated – increasing to 15.9% in crop year 2002–03, before falling to 10.7% in 2003–04, before rising back up again the following year.[83] Nor were the anti-dumping duties particularly effective in stemming the flow of Brazilian orange juice into the American market. Even after the preliminary anti-dumping duties were imposed in 2005, Brazilian orange-juice imports continued to rise. In 2007, the US imported a record $270 million in frozen Brazilian orange juice. This represented more than a doubling from the $129 million imported in 2002, and a more than three-fold increase over the recent low of $85 million in 2004.[84]

Such fluctuations are not surprising given that round oranges, the variety most commonly used for producing orange juice, are a highly perishable commodity. Supply conditions in orange-juice production are intimately linked to variations in the crop volume of round oranges. This link is so strong that growers of round oranges were found by the ITC to be part of the domestic industry when making its injury determination. As the dissenting commissioners in the ITC's injury investigation noted 'the impact of weather and other factors on the US crop resulted in significant volatility in US round orange production during the period examined'.[85] It was this underlying volatility, rather than any anti-competitive behavior, that indirectly led to changes in imports of orange juice from Brazil via its effect on domestic production of orange juice in the US.[86] When crop volumes of domestic round oranges fall, Brazilian orange-juice imports increase, even if anti-dumping duties raise costs. The main effect of the anti-dumping duties in this instance was not protection for American orange-juice producers, but rather higher prices for downstream American consumers.

Therefore, it is clear that the anti-dumping duties against certain Brazilian orange juice were not economically necessary nor were they welfare-enhancing. Moreover, since zeroing in administrative reviews, at least in the early years, was practiced in the face of increasing export volumes due largely to demand changes resulting from exogenous shocks (in the supply of round oranges), we suggest that the damage from zeroing was greater in this context than it would be in others. The termination of anti-dumping duties for certain Brazilian orange juice is therefore welcome news. It has, along with other market forces, brought orange-juice futures down 40% in 2012, which should be welcome news for consumers.[87]

83 See Table IV-5 in USITC (2006).

84 See UN Comtrade database for HS-200911.

85 USITC (2006) at 39.

86 Ibid. This view finds support in the empirical analysis of Carter and Mohapatra (2006) who find that FCOJ imports from Brazil were larger when domestic supplies in the US were relatively low. Similarly, they also find a strong negative correlation between domestic FCOJ inventories in the US and imports from Brazil. Finally, they show that imports of FCOJ from Brazil did not have a significant impact on the price of orange juice in the US over the relevant time period, a finding that is consistent with the position of dissenting USITC commissioners.

87 Wexler (2012).

6. Concluding thoughts: so is this the end of the WTO zeroing disputes?

Does *US–Orange Juice (Brazil)*, along with *US–Shrimp (Vietnam)*,[88] represent the end of the zeroing disputes at the WTO? Technically, the answer remains no. Four cases remain pending before the WTO concerning US zeroing practices: *US–Zeroing (Korea), US–Carbon Steel Flat Products (Korea), US–Shrimp and Diamond Sawblades (China)*, and *US–Frozen Warmwater Shrimp (Vietnam)*.

Yet, the DOC's announcement on 14 February 2012, that it would discontinue the practice of zeroing in administrative reviews (under Article 9.3.1 of the ADA) as well as new shipper reviews, expedited anti-dumping reviews, and sunset reviews will certainly lessen the probability of further conflicts. The era of major substantive battles over US zeroing practices may be drawing to a close.

Two points are worth noting. In order to enjoy the benefits of the DOC's policy eliminating zeroing in administrative reviews, foreign producers subject to anti-dumping duties must request a review during the window of the product's annual review. By placing the impetus on producers rather than making this review automatic, larger foreign producers with the financial means to request and participate in the annual retrospective reviews are placed at an advantage. The smaller producers that fail to expend resources to call for an administrative review in which zeroing is not done will still find themselves subject to CDRs calculated on the basis of zeroing. Countries should therefore seek to ensure that all their exporters subject to anti-dumping duties will seek an administrative review and assist smaller exporters, who may be resource constrained, with such reviews. Otherwise, the effects of zeroing may continue to linger on.

Second, even if the zeroing disputes disappear altogether, the issue is not altogether dead. The US continues to seek, albeit with little or no support, a clarification that zeroing is allowed through Doha Round negotiations. To the extent that the ghost of zeroing continues to hover, it will be increasingly in the rooms of the Rules Negotiation.

Still, in light of the fact that a US negotiating proposal on zeroing is unlikely to succeed, when the history of zeroing is written years from now, what may be most significant about *US–Orange Juice (Brazil)* may not be the decision itself, but the way in which the Panel flagged concerns about past AB decisions without openly disagreeing. On a longstanding issue, the Panel, though not bound by the AB, recognized and accepted its subordinate role. In doing so, it helped deliver yet another nail in the coffin of the WTO's longest-running dispute-settlement drama.

88 *United States – Anti-Dumping Measures on Certain Shrimp from Vietnam*, DS404.

References

Bown, C. P. and A. O. Sykes (2008), 'The Zeroing Issue: A Critical Analysis of Softwood V', *World Trade Review*, 7(1): 121–42.

Bown, C. P. and T. J. Prusa (2011), 'US Anti-dumping: Much Ado About Zeroing', in W. J. Martin and A. Mattoo (eds.), *Unfinished Business? The WTO's Doha Agenda*, London: CEPR and World Bank, pp. 355–92.

Carter, C. and S. Mohapatra (2006), 'The Sunshine State versus Brazil: Economics of Orange Juice Trade', Department of Agricultural and Resource Economics, University of California.

Crowley, M. and R. Howse (2010), 'US–Stainless Steel (Mexico)', *World Trade Review*, 9(1): 117–50.

Hispanically Speaking News (2011), 'Brazil Will Allow Merger of Orange Juice Companies', 15 December 2011, available at http://www.hispanicallyspeakingnews.com/notitas-de-noticias/details/brazil-will-allow-merger-of-orange-juice-companies/12583/.

Kiernan, P. and B. McKay (2012), 'Coke, Pepsi Attempt to Ease O.J. Fears', *Wall Street Journal*, 13 January: B1.

Prusa, T. J. and L. Ribini (forthcoming), 'United States – Use of Zeroing in Anti-Dumping Measures Involving Products From Korea: It's Déjà Vu All Over Again', *World Trade Review*.

Prusa, T. J. and E. Vermulst (2009), 'A One-Two Punch on Zeroing: *US–Zeroing (EC)* and *US–Zeroing (Japan)*', *World Trade Review*, 8(1): 187–241.

Prusa, T. J. and E. Vermulst (2011), 'United States – Continued Existence and Application of Zeroing Methodology: The End of Zeroing?', *World Trade Review*, 10(1): 45–61.

Sterns, J. A. and T. H. Spreen (2010), 'Evaluating Sustainable Competitive Advantages in Brazilian and US Processed Citrus Supply Chains: An Application of Porter's Diamond Framework', *International Journal on Food System Dynamics*, 2: 167–75.

United States Department of Agriculture (USDA) (2007), 'Orange Juice: Foreign Agricultural Service, World Markets and Trade Report.'

US International Trade Commission (USITC) (2006), '*Certain Orange Juice From Brazil*', Publication 3838, Washington, DC.

Wexler, A. (2012), 'Orange Juice Feels Supply–Demand Squeeze', *Wall Street Journal*, 18 May: B4.

White, A. and L. Kassai (2011), 'Citrovita, Citrosuco Win EU Approval For Orange-Juice Deal', May 4, available at http://www.bloomberg.com/news/2011-05-04/citrovita-citrosuco-win-eu-approval-for-orange-juice-deal.html.

United States – Use of Zeroing in Anti-Dumping Measures Involving Products from Korea: It's déjà vu all over again

THOMAS J. PRUSA

Rutgers University and NBER

LUCA RUBINI

University of Birmingham

Abstract: This paper analyzes the dispute between Korea and the United States regarding the method of calculating anti-dumping duties. The case mirrors other recent WTO disputes involving zeroing. Even though it ceased zeroing in original investigations in December 2006, the United States implemented the policy change only prospectively. As a result, the margins applied to the products in this dispute remained unchanged because they had been calculated prior to the policy change. The United States did not contest Korea's claims. The Panel confirmed that zeroing was used and, following the long line of Panel and Appellate Body rulings, found the practice inconsistent with the Anti-Dumping Agreement. After the Panel Report was adopted, the United States recalculated the margins without zeroing. It, however, refused to refund unliquidated cash deposits that were based on zeroing, highlighting the United States's continued lukewarm compliance with WTO rulings on zeroing. This dispute offers an opportunity to ponder on weaknesses of the WTO Dispute Settlement and the ability of one Member to take advantage of it. Since the facts and their legal assessment were undisputed, why was litigation necessary? Can compliance with WTO law be improved with broader findings and more incisive remedies?

[I]nternational legal arrangements have relatively more in common with the law of primitive societies studied by anthropologists, in which litigation is still emerging as a rather tenuous alternative to dispute resolution by force. International litigation is an institution of indeterminate character. It is not an inevitable response to legal disputes, nor does it supply a conclusive outcome.[1]

The views expressed in this paper are those of the authors and all omissions and errors are also of the authors. We would like to thank Dukgeun Ahn, Sungioon Cho, Jim Durling, Gary Horlick, Rob Howse and Seong-Joong Kim for helpful discussions.

1 Robert E. Hudec (1987), '"Transcending the Ostensible": Some Reflections on the Nature of Litigation Between Governments', 72 *Minnesota Law Review*, 211, 212–213.

1. Introduction

United States – Use of Zeroing in Anti-Dumping Measures Involving Products from Korea[2] is another WTO dispute involving the United States's practice of zeroing negative dumping margins in calculating overall weighted-average margins of dumping.[3] In this dispute, the measures at issue are the final determinations, amended final determinations, anti-dumping duty orders, and amended anti-dumping duty orders imposed by the United States in relation to imports of the three products: stainless-steel plate in coils (SSPC), stainless-steel sheet and strip in coils (SSSSC), and diamond sawblades (DS).[4]

At first blush, the dispute is seemingly superfluous because the United States [US] ceased zeroing in original investigations [OI] almost three years before Korea requested consultations.[5] Why would Korea complain about zeroing when the US had already stopped zeroing? The conflict hinges on the particular way the US changed its domestic law to eliminate zeroing. Although the US stopped zeroing in OI in December 2006, it did so only prospectively; that is, the US's new rules only apply to margin calculations performed after the implementation date.[6] According to the US, all anti-dumping [AD] margins computed prior to the date of its policy change, including the margins in this dispute, were unaffected by the WTO's prior determinations.

US–Zeroing (Korea) has many parallels with *US–PET Bags (Thailand)*.[7] While the current dispute is somewhat more complicated than *US – PET Bags (Thailand)*,

2 *United States – Use of Zeroing in Anti-Dumping Measures Involving Products from Korea*, WT/DS402/R, adopted 24 February 2011 (hereafter, *US–Zeroing (Korea)*).

3 Over the past decade, the WTO Appellate Body has heard at least 20 disputes involving various types of zeroing and each time has found that the practice violates the WTO Anti-Dumping Agreement. All but two of the cases have involved the United States as respondent. For a review of WTO cases involving zeroing, see Chad P. Bown and Thomas J. Prusa (2011), 'US Anti-Dumping: Much Ado about Zeroing', in William J. Martin and Aaditya Mattoo (eds.), *Unfinished Business? The WTO's Doha Agenda*, London: CEPR and the World Bank, pp. 355–392.

4 *US–Zeroing (Korea)*, para. 2.1.

5 'Anti-Dumping Proceedings: Calculation of the Weighted-Average Dumping Margin During an Anti-Dumping Investigation, Final Modification', Federal Register, 71: 248 (27 December 2006), pp. 77722–77725 (hereafter, '2006 Modification'). The effective date of this final modification was 16 January 2007.

6 To be more precise, the 2006 Modification reads: 'The Department will apply this final modification in all current and future antidumping investigations as of the effective date.' All three cases in this dispute had their OI margins calculated prior to this date and hence were not subject to the new rules.

7 Panel Report, *United States – Anti-Dumping Measures on Polyethylene Retail Carrier Bags from Thailand*, WT/DS383/R, adopted 18 February 2010, DSR 2010:IV, 1841 (hereafter, *US–PET Bags (Thailand)*). For an analysis of that dispute, see Thomas J. Prusa and Edwin Vermulst (2012), 'United States – Anti-Dumping Measures on Polyethylene Retail Carrier Bags from Thailand: A Cat in the Bag', **11:2** *World Trade Review*, 257–271.

Table 1. Key dates in US proceedings

	Product		
	SSPC	SSSSC	DS
Petition Initiated	27 April 1998	13 July 1998	21 June 2005
Final OI AD Duty (W-W method)	31 March 1999 (amended 28 August 2001)	8 June 1999 (amended 28 August 2001)	22 May 2006 (amended 24 March 2010)
Final Injury	12 May 1999	28 July 1999	11 July 2006 (remanded 13 January 2009)
AD Order	21 May 1999 (amended 11 March 2003, 2 April 2003, and 24 April 2003)	27 July 1999	4 November 2009

the raison d'être for both disputes is identical[8] – the US Department of Commerce [USDOC] will calculate non-zeroed margins for preexisting cases only after an adverse finding for each particular case. In both *US–Zeroing (Korea)* and *US–PET Bags (Thailand)*, all evidence indicates that the US perceived it had no chance to prevail at the WTO Dispute Settlement Body [DSB]. In its prior decisions, the WTO Appellate Body [AB] unfailingly had found zeroing to be inconsistent with the WTO Anti-Dumping Agreement [ADA].[9] The US did not contest the claims in either *US–Zeroing (Korea)* or *US–PET Bags (Thailand)*. In fact, the US acknowledged it had used zeroing when calculating dumping margins in both disputes. Yet, in both disputes the US refused to recalculate the margins upon receipt of the consultation request. As best we can tell, *US–Zeroing (Korea)* and *US–PET Bags (Thailand)* were both *legal formalities* required by USDOC's narrow implementation of WTO rules.

The timing of events highlights the basis for the dispute. As seen in Table 1, the USDOC made final AD margin calculations for all three cases prior to the policy change. In SSPC and SSSSC, the order was in effect long before the USDOC policy change; however, due to legal challenges involving the injury determination, the DS AD order went into effect after the policy change (but, as noted, the USDOC had calculated the OI AD margin before the December 2006 policy change).

In this dispute, Korea challenged the US's continued use of zeroing. On 24 November 2009, Korea requested consultations with the US (Table 2). Consultations were held in December 2009 and February 2010, but failed to resolve the dispute. Korea requested the establishment of a Panel in April 2010.

8 Two issues make this dispute somewhat more complicated. First, unlike *US–PET Bags (Thailand)* there was not a pre-dispute agreement as to how the Panel's decision would be implemented. Second, this dispute involves three cases rather than just a single claim.

9 Bown and Prusa, 'US Anti-Dumping', Table 14.2, supra at note 3.

Table 2. Key dates in WTO dispute

Event	Date
Korea requests consultations	24 November 2009
US and Korea fail to resolve dispute in consultations	December 2009 to February 2010
Korea requests WTO Panel	08 April 2010
Final Panel Report circulated	18 January 2011
Final Panel Report adopted	24 February 2011
'Reasonable period of time' for implementation established	17 June 2011
New AD duties implemented	October 2011 and November 2011
US refuses to recalculate margins for unliquidated cash deposits	February 2012

The final Panel Report was circulated in January 2011 and adopted by the DSB in February 2011. In March 2011, the US announced it intended to implement the DSB's recommendations. Korea and the US were able to agree on the 'reasonable period of time' for implementation by July 2011. The US recalculated the margins on DS in October 2011 and on SSPC and SSSSC in November 2011. On 8 December 2011, the US reported to the DSB that it had 'fully implemented' the DSB's recommendations and rulings. While not within the scope of the investigation, Korea requested that the US refund unliquidated cash deposits based on the zeroed margins. To date, the US has refused to do so.

Given that (i) the dispute covers extremely well-trodden ground,[10] (ii) neither party challenged the Panel to push the envelope on zeroing, and (iii) the Panel's reasoning simply restated previous AB and Panel opinions, we find ourselves with little to say about zeroing beyond what has been previously stated. Instead,

10 Legal and economic summaries of previous zeroing disputes include Merit E. Janow and Robert W. Staiger (2003), 'European Communities – Anti-Dumping Duties on Imports of Cotton-Type Bed Linen from India', in Henrik Horn and Petros C. Mavroidis (eds.), *The WTO Case Law of 2001*, Cambridge: Cambridge University Press; Gene M. Grossman and Alan O. Sykes (2006), 'European Communities – Anti-Dumping Duties on Imports of Cotton-Type Bed Linen from India: Recourse to Article 21.5 of the DSU by India', in Henrik Horn and Petros C. Mavroidis (eds.), *The WTO Case Law of 2003*, Cambridge: Cambridge University Press; Chad P. Bown and Alan O. Sykes (2008), 'The Zeroing Issue: A Critical Analysis of *Softwood V*', **7:1** *World Trade Review*, 121–142; Thomas J. Prusa and Edwin Vermulst (2009), 'A One-Two Punch on Zeroing: *US–Zeroing (EC)* and *US – Zeroing (Japan)*', **8:1** *World Trade Review*, 187–241; Meredith Crowley and Robert Howse (2010), '*US–Stainless Steel (Mexico)*', **9:1** *World Trade Review*, 117–150; Bernard Hoekman and Jasper Wauters (2011), 'US Compliance with WTO Rulings on Zeroing in Anti-Dumping', **10:1** *World Trade Review*, 5–43; Thomas J. Prusa and Edwin Vermulst (2011), 'United States – Continued Existence and Application of Zeroing Methodology: The End of Zeroing?', **10:1** *World Trade Review*, 45–61; Prusa and Vermulst, 'United States – Anti-Dumping Measures on Polyethylene Retail Carrier Bags from Thailand', supra at note 7.

our commentary will focus on three subordinate issues. First, how should the Panels handle undisputed claims? What is the real issue with such claims? Second, what does the US's insistence on adverse finding before it will recalculate margins imply for the WTO DSU, its remedies, and other member countries? Third, is it reasonable to expect the US to refund unliquidated cash deposits that were based on OI margins calculated with zeroing?

In the next section, we review the claims and summarize the Panel's findings. Next, we discuss how the US implemented the Panel's recommendations. We then offer commentary on the ancillary issues associated with this dispute.

2. Claims and Panel findings

Zeroing refers to the practice of replacing the actual amounts of dumping that yield negative dumping margins with a value of zero prior to the final calculation of a weighted-average margin of dumping for the product under investigation with respect to the exporters under investigation. Zeroing drops transactions that have negative margins from the numerator and hence increases overall dumping margins and the resulting size of the applied anti-dumping duty.[11] While there are several forms of zeroing,[12] the present case concerned the relatively simple form of model zeroing under the weighted-average-to-weighted-average comparison method in original investigations.

Korea claimed that the USDOC had used the model-zeroing methodology to determine the final dumping margins for individually investigated Korean exporters whose margins of dumping were not based on total facts available, in violation of Article 2.4.2 of the ADA.[13] In particular, Korea claimed that the USDOC (i) identified different 'models', i.e., types, of products based on the most relevant product characteristics; (ii) calculated weighted-average prices in the US and weighted-average normal values in the comparison market on a model-specific basis for the entire period of investigation; (iii) compared the weighted-average normal value of each model to the weighted-average US price for that same model; (iv) calculated the dumping margin for an exporter by summing up the amount of dumping for each model and then dividing it by the aggregated US price for all models; and (v) set to zero all negative margins on individual models before summing the total amount of dumping for all models.[14]

The US *did not contest* Korea's claims. It acknowledged the accuracy of Korea's description of the USDOC's use of zeroing and recognized that in *US–Softwood*

11 Prusa and Vermulst, 'A One-Two Punch on Zeroing', supra at note 10, provide an extended discussion of how zeroing affects the calculated margin.

12 See, e.g., ibid.; Edwin Vermulst and Daniel Ikenson (2007), 'Zeroing under the WTO Anti-Dumping Agreement: Where Do We Stand?', 2:6 *Global Trade and Customs Journal*, 231–242.

13 *US–Zeroing (Korea)*, paras. 2.2–2.7.

14 Ibid., para. 7.3.

Lumber V[15] the AB found that the use of zeroing with respect to the average-to-average comparison methodology in investigations was inconsistent with Article 2.4.2 by interpreting the terms 'margins of dumping' and 'all comparable export transactions' in an integrated manner. The US also acknowledged that reasoning was equally applicable in the present case.[16]

The Panel considered that the issues raised in the present case were very similar to those addressed by the Panels in *US–Shrimp (Ecuador)*,[17] *US–Shrimp (Thailand)*,[18] and *US–PET Bags (Thailand)* and agreed with the approach adopted by those Panels.[19]

The Panel then first considered its role under Article 11 of the DSU, in light of the fact that the US did not contest Korea's claim. Article 11 of the DSU describes the role of Panels in DSB proceedings requiring that the 'Panel should make an objective assessment of the matter before it, including an objective assessment of the facts of the case and the applicability of and conformity with the relevant covered agreements and make such other findings as will assist the DSB in making the recommendations or in giving the rulings provided for in the covered agreements'. Notwithstanding the US's decision not to contest Korea's claim, the Panel explained that it was bound by Article 11 of the DSU to make 'its own objective assessment of the matter before it, including an objective assessment of the facts and the applicability of and conformity with the covered agreements as required by Article 11 of the DSU'.[20]

The Panel consequently adopted the approach followed by the Panel in *US–Shrimp (Ecuador)*.[21] The Panel thus reasoned that, in the absence of effective refutation by the defending party, it is still required for the complaining party to present a *prima facie* case. The Panel could thus only rule in favor of Korea if it was satisfied that Korea had made a *prima facie* case regarding its zeroing claim.[22]

In order to establish that the USDOC zeroed in the present case, Korea referred to a computer program used by the USDOC to calculate dumping margins. The Panel found, in that respect, that the computer program indeed indicated the use of zeroing by the USDOC. The Panel furthermore repeated that the US had

15 Appellate Body Report, *United States – Final Dumping Determination on Softwood Lumber from Canada*, WT/DS264/AB/R, adopted 31 August 2004, DSR 2004:V, 1875 (hereafter, *US–Softwood Lumber V)*.

16 *US–Zeroing (Korea)*, para. 3.2.

17 Panel Report, *United States – Anti-Dumping Measure on Shrimp from Ecuador*, WT/DS335/R, adopted on 20 February 2007, DSR 2007:II, 425 (hereafter, *US–Shrimp (Ecuador)*).

18 Panel Report, *United States – Measures Relating to Shrimp from Thailand*, WT/DS343/R, adopted 1 August 2008, as modified by Appellate Body Report WT/DS343/AB/R, WT/DS345/AB/R, DSR 2008: VII, 2539 (hereafter, *US–Shrimp (Thailand)*).

19 *US–Zeroing (Korea)*, para. 7.17.

20 Ibid., para. 7.8.

21 *US–Shrimp (Ecuador)*, paras. 7.7–7.11.

22 *US–Zeroing (Korea)*, para. 7.19.

acknowledged the accuracy of Korea's description of the USDOC's use of zeroing. The Panel therefore concluded that it was satisfied that Korea had demonstrated that the USDOC zeroed in the measure at issue.[23]

The Panel then verified whether Korea had established that the methodology used by the USDOC was indeed the same in all legally relevant aspects as the methodology reviewed by the Appellate Body in *US–Softwood Lumber V*. Korea relied on the description of the methodology used in the USDOC's notice of preliminary determination of sales at less than fair value, as well as the computer program used to determine the dumping margins. According to the Panel, this was sufficient evidence to establish that the USDOC performed the actions as claimed by Korea in points (i) to (v) above.[24]

The Panel considered that the absence of any denial by the US and the above-mentioned evidence established that Korea had demonstrated that the methodology applied by the USDOC in calculating the margins of dumping that were not based on total facts available was the same as the methodology that the Appellate Body in *US–Softwood Lumber V* had found to be inconsistent with Article 2.4.2 of the ADA.[25]

Finally, the Panel verified whether Korea had established that the methodology applied by the USDOC was inconsistent with Article 2.4.2 of the ADA. The Panel considered, in that respect, that while it was not strictly speaking bound by the reasoning in prior Panel or AB Reports,[26] adopted Reports do create 'legitimate expectations' among WTO members and found that following the AB conclusions in earlier Reports would not only be appropriate but would also be what would be expected, especially where the issues are the same.[27]

The Panel referred to the Panel Report in *US–Shrimp (Ecuador)* with regard to the AB's reasoning in *US–Softwood Lumber V* concerning the compatibility of zeroing with Article 2.4.2 of the ADA.[28] The AB in *US–Softwood Lumber V* had found that it was clear from the texts of Article VI:1 of the GATT 1994 and Article 2.1 of the ADA that dumping is assessed in relation to the product as a whole as defined by an investigating authority and cannot be found to exist only for a type, model, or category of that product. The AB in *US–Softwood Lumber V* on that basis concluded that the treatment of comparisons for which the weighted-average normal value is less than the weighted-average export price as 'non-dumped' comparisons was not in accordance with the requirements of Article 2.4.2 of the ADA.

23 Ibid., para. 7.22.

24 Ibid., paras. 7.23–7.26.

25 Ibid., para. 7.27.

26 Since 'there is not a system of precedent within the WTO dispute settlement system', *US–Zeroing (Korea)*, para. 7.31.

27 Ibid., para. 7.30.

28 *US–Shrimp (Ecuador)*, paras. 7.38–7.39.

The Panel also noted that the Panel in *US–Shrimp (Ecuador)* found that there was a consistent line of AB Reports that holds that zeroing in the context of the weighted-average-to-average methodology in original investigations was inconsistent with Article 2.4.2 of the Anti-Dumping Agreement.[29]

The Panel therefore concluded that given that the issues raised in the present case were identical in all material respects to those addressed by the AB in *US–Softwood Lumber V*, Korea had established a *prima facie* case that the use of zeroing by the USDOC was inconsistent with Article 2.4.2 of the ADA, because the USDOC did not calculate those dumping margins on the basis of the product as a whole, taking into account all comparable export transactions.[30]

3. US implementation

With the adverse WTO Panel ruling, the USDOC proceeded to recalculate the AD margins. On 17 June 2011, Korea and the US informed the WTO that they had mutually agreed that the US would comply with the Panel's recommendations and rulings no later than 1 December 2011.[31] On 19 December 2011, the US reported that it had fully implemented the Panel's recommendations and rulings within the reasonable period of time agreed by the parties.[32]

The table below (Table 3) summarizes the dumping margins with and without zeroing. The order on diamond sawblades and stainless-steel plate in coils was revoked; both participating firms in stainless-steel sheet and strip in coils had their AD order revoked; however, because one Korean firm (Taihan) did not participate, margins for that firm were based on facts available and a duty remains in place.

While the US implemented the AB ruling, the fact that the US requested six months to recalculate the margins reflects its continued foot dragging with respect to zeroing decisions. We imagine that only a few minutes were needed for the USDOC to re-run its AD margins computer program with the zeroing code commented out. Yet, the US took months to implement.[33]

Moreover, the US already knew (at least) in November 2009 (when the consultations with Korea started) it would have to recalculate the margins. Yet, it refused to do so until months after the Panel made its perfunctory decision. This allowed it to levy zeroing-distorted margins for another 24 months after the consultations request.

29 *US–Zeroing (Korea)*, para. 7.34.

30 Ibid., paras. 8.1–8.2.

31 *US–Zeroing (Korea)*, WT/DS402/6, 22 June 2011.

32 *US–Zeroing (Korea)*, WT/DS402/7, 9 December 2011.

33 The fact that Korea accepted and agreed to this time frame as 'reasonable' suggests that it could not do anything to force the US to implement more promptly. Nor, arguably, could the WTO DSU. Although obviously from a legal standpoint nothing prevents immediate implementation, the 'reasonable period of time' to implement DSU obligations is the recognition of the political and practical adjustment required by compliance.

Table 3. OI weighted-average anti-dumping duty margins, with and without zeroing

Exporter/manufacturer	OI W. Avg. margin (with zeroing)[1] %	OI W. Avg. margin (without zeroing)[2] %
Diamond sawblades		
Ehwa	8.80	0
Shinhan	16.88	0
Hyosung	6.43	0
All others	11.10	0
Stainless-steel plate in coils		
Pohang Iron and Steel	6.08	0.55 (*de minimis*)
All others	6.08	0.55 (*de minimis*)
Stainless-steel sheet and strip in coils		
Pohang Iron and Steel	2.49	0
Inchon Iron and Steel	0	0
Taihan Electric Wire	58.79 (facts available)	58.79 (facts available)
All others	2.49	19.60

Notes: [1] Diamond Sawblades, from 71 Fed. Reg. 29310 (22 May 2006) and as amended 75 Fed. Reg. 14126 (24 March 2010); Stainless Steel Plate in Coils and Stainless Steel Sheet and Strip in Coils from 66 Fed. Reg. 45279 (28 August 2001).
[2] Diamond Sawblades, from 76 Fed. Reg. 66892 (28 October 2011); Stainless Steel Plate in Coils and Stainless Steel Sheet and Strip in Coils from 76 Fed. Reg. 74771 (1 December 2011).

4. Analysis of Panel's decision

Bown and Prusa document that between the first zeroing dispute of 1998 and early 2010 nearly 20 WTO disputes have involved zeroing.[34] Consequently, there are numerous WTO AB rulings on the issue and also a considerable body of legal and economic analyses of zeroing.[35]

The key phrase is contained in Article 2.4.2 of the ADA:

> the existence of margins of dumping during the investigation phase shall normally be established on the basis of a comparison of a weighted average normal value

34 Bown and Prusa, 'US Anti-Dumping', supra at note 3.

35 Including Janow and Staiger, 'European Communities – Anti-Dumping Duties on Imports of Cotton-Type Bed Linen from India'; Grossman and Sykes, 'European Communities – Anti-Dumping Duties on Imports of Cotton-Type Bed Linen from India'; Bown and Sykes, 'The Zeroing Issue'; Prusa and Vermulst, 'A One-Two Punch on Zeroing'; Prusa and Vermulst, 'United States – Continued Existence and Application of Zeroing Methodology'; Crowley and Howse, '*US–Stainless Steel (Mexico)*'; and Hoekman and Wauters, 'US Compliance with WTO Rulings on Zeroing in Anti-Dumping' – see supra at note 10; Prusa and Vermulst, 'United States – Anti-Dumping Measures on Polyethylene Retail Carrier Bags from Thailand' – see supra at note 7.

> with a weighted average of prices of all comparable export transactions or by a comparison of normal value and export prices on a transaction-to-transaction basis.[36]

The case does not add much to the existing WTO rulings on zeroing. We agree with Prusa and Vermulst who stated:

> the Appellate Body was arguably correct in prohibiting the use of zeroing under the main methods of Article 2.4.2 of the ADA[37]

and with Prusa and Vermulst who wrote:

> We agree with the legal justification logic behind the AB's decisions – given that this case largely follows the script developed in prior cases, this should not be surprising. Further, as we have argued in the past, we also believe that standard economic statistical inference methods demand that all transactions be included in a 'fair' comparison.[38]

With nothing new to add to the existing commentary on zeroing, we instead discuss several related issues in this case that raise broader questions with respect to the WTO DSU system and build on Prusa and Vermulst who commented on the very similar *US–PET Bags (Thailand)* decision.

4.1 *The real issue of undisputed claims*

Even though the US had not contested Korea's claim, the Panel nevertheless considered it necessary, in accordance with the approach of previous Panels,[39] to satisfy itself – albeit in a summary fashion – that Korea had discharged its burden of proof, establishing a *prima facie* case. All this under Article 11 DSU, which requires the Panel to make 'an objective assessment of the matter before it, including an objective assessment of the facts of the case and the applicability of and conformity with the relevant covered agreements and make such other findings as will assist the DSB in making the recommendations or in giving the rulings provided for in the covered agreements'.[40] It therefore followed the analysis we have outlined in Section 2 above.

The analysis covers some nine of the 17 pages of the Report, and most of it is taken up by quotations from previous AB and Panel Reports.

36 Article 2.4.2, *Agreement on the Implementation of Article VI of the General Agreement on Tariffs and Trade 1994*.

37 Prusa and Vermulst, 'A One-Two Punch on Zeroing', p. 188, supra at note 10.

38 Prusa and Vermulst, 'United States – Continued Existence and Application of Zeroing Methodology', pp. 46–47, supra at note 10.

39 *US–Shrimp (Ecuador); US–Shrimp (Thailand)*. Compare David Palmeter and Petros C. Mavroidis (2004), *Dispute Settlement in the World Trade Organization* (second edn), Cambridge, UK: Cambridge University Press, p. 145.

40 *US–Zeroing (Korea)*, para. 7.15.

The Panel did ensure that a violation had occurred. This was made easy by the uncontested nature of the facts and the clear and undisputed illegality of the practice of zeroing. Indeed, the US's recognition of the breach already significantly contributed to making the establishment of Korea's *prima facie* case easier. In other words, the threshold is *naturally* lower for complainants faced with undisputed claims.

Thus, even though one could argue the necessity of analyzing an undisputed claim, what can in fact be challenged is the depth of the assessment of the breach. One could certainly envisage a more straightforward procedure, particularly in a paradigmatically simple dispute such as this one. Arguably, as the EU suggested, one step further could have been taken without any major breach of the rules of evidence. In consideration of the undisputed description of facts and of their legal assessment, the Panel might well have found that there was no dispute in the first place and move to its rulings and recommendations without much further ado.[41]

Whatever it may be, no serious analysis was required and indeed no significant clarification of the law made by the Panel. From an economic viewpoint, no significant amount of resources were used (or wasted) because of the Panel's analysis – but for time. And, in a context where compliance is taken to be only prospective (and normally commences only after the expiration of a 'reasonable period'), time does matter.[42]

In other words, the fact that the claim was both factually and legally undisputed raises other questions, going beyond the necessity for Panels to perform their (in such circumstances) pretty straightforward review. Why, despite the parties were in agreement with respect of the breach, was litigation necessary in the first place? Is it a desirable use of the WTO Dispute Settlement System? If not, what could be done to improve the situation?

4.2 Implications of USDOC's insistence on adverse finding before recalculating margins, retrospective remedies, and continuing breach

The USDOC announced it would cease zeroing in original investigations on 27 December 2006; the effective date of this final modification was 16 January 2007. Since that time, in each of the WTO disputes involving zeroing in OI (all commenced before the change in policy), the US has not contested the claims. Nevertheless, the US has insisted that the WTO DSB make a ruling in each case

41 *US–Zeroing (Korea)*, para. 7.10.

42 Although the simplicity of the case certainly meant that the time requested for the proceedings was shorter than would otherwise have been. For example, after consulting the parties, the Panel decided not to hold a second substantive meeting with the parties. See para. 1.6 of the Panel Report. The Panel stage thus lasted eight months rather than the usual average of 14.7 months. See Henrik Horn, Louise Johannesson, and Petros C. Mavroidis (2011), 'The WTO Dispute Settlement System (1995–2010): Some Descriptive Statistics', 45:6 *Journal of World Trade*, 1107–1138.

before it recalculates margins that were originally computed before the policy change.

From a political viewpoint, the continuous involvement of the US in zeroing cases can be explained in the following way. Domestic action, which is rational (assuming the compliance with international obligations contributes to the broad domestic-welfare outcome expected from them) but unpopular (because it decreases the welfare of well-defined and organized stakeholders), becomes possible if governments present it as an inescapable international commitment. As Mavroidis notes:

> one cannot exclude the cases where recourse to dispute settlement is done on commitment grounds; the defendant prefers to lose and comply using the WTO as an excuse for behavior that it would not have otherwise adopted for domestic political economy reasons.[43]

With another language, to some extent the continuing litigation on zeroing – nearly 20 WTO Disputes, the sheer majority of which has the US as defendant – could be explained as an instrument for 'temporizing', as Hudec called it:

> Thus, any device which helps to smooth the process by which the losers learn to accept their losses actually makes a valuable contribution to the cohesion, and thus the well-being, of the entire collective entity. It also keeps politicians in office, of course.[44]

For all practical purposes, however, the WTO Dispute Settlement Body is paying the price for the US's overly narrow implementation of the zeroing decisions. By way of comparison, in the aftermath of the *EC–Bed Linen* zeroing dispute, which also involved model zeroing, the EU offered interested parties affected by zeroing in other EU cases the opportunity to request a review. It also refrained from applying model zeroing after the adoption of the AB Report.

The US's approach has important economic consequences. The US implementation means that zeroing-inflated anti-dumping duties will continue to be assessed on many existing cases. According to Prusa and Vermulst, there are as many as 200 cases with zero-inflated anti-dumping duties that have not yet been recalculated. Of this set, perhaps 20 have sufficiently low margins to warrant bringing a WTO dispute.[45] In effect, the US implementation shifts the cost of compliance on to its trading partners (via the costs required to pursue the dispute) and to the WTO DSB.

From a legal viewpoint, there are two orders of considerations: the first on remedies, the second on breach.

43 Petros C. Mavroidis (2012), 'A Little Bit Less Conversation and a Little More Action (Property and Liability Rules in the DSU Review of the WTO)', draft on file with the author.

44 Hudec, 'Transcending the Ostensible', p. 218, supra at note 1.

45 Prusa and Vermulst, 'United States – Anti-Dumping Measures on Polyethylene Retail Carrier Bags from Thailand', supra at note 7; and Bown and Prusa, 'US Anti-Dumping', supra at note 3, argue that only cases where removing zeroing will result in *de minimis* margins are suitable WTO disputes.

First, as we have noted above, time plays in favor of the defendant in the WTO DSU. The US narrow approach to implementation to the repeated (eventually accepted) condemnation of zeroing methodology by the WTO DS underlies this case and mirrors the entrenched and (among Members) virtually universal view that WTO DS's rulings are for the future only and that remedies do not have any retrospective or retroactive effect.[46]

Although the suggestion that remedies could have some retrospective effect is highly controversial in the WTO,[47] in no less than five cases GATT Panel Reports in the field of anti-dumping and countervailing duties retroactive remedies were imposed.[48] We agree with Mavroidis's assessment of the perverse disincentive a weak remedy has for illegally imposed anti-dumping duties:

> what is the incentive for a WTO Member to respect the anti-dumping disciplines if it knows that, at worst, it risks seeing itself obliged to stop some four years down the road imposing duties that were illegally rendered in the first place?[49]

As noted by Prusa and Vermulst:

> the prospective nature of WTO remedies limits their effectiveness, as the US zeroing saga abundantly shows.[50]

One certainly can question whether each and every case concerning anti-dumping duties based on zeroing methodology involves the issue of retrospectiveness. It may be argued that for certain administrative investigations that are not concluded – for example, when the duty or liability has only been provisionally

46 For an extensive discussion, see Petros C. Mavroidis (2000), 'Remedies in the WTO Legal System: Between a Rock and a Hard Place', **11:4** *European Journal of International Law*, 763–813; Piet Eeckhout (2009), 'Remedies and Compliance', in Daniel Bethlehem, Donald McRae, Rodney Neufeld, and Isabelle Van Damme (eds.), *The Oxford Handbook of International Trade Law*, Oxford, UK: Oxford University Press, pp. 437–459.

47 A good example is the reaction to the Panel Report in *Australia – Subsidies Provided to Producers and Exporters of Automotive Leather – Recourse to Article 21.5 of the DSU by the United States*, WT/DS126/RW and Corr.1, adopted 11 February 2000, DSR 2000:III, 1189. See the DSB's discussion on the adoption of the Panel Report, WT/DSB/M/75.

48 The first case was *New Zealand* v. *Finland* (the *Transformers* case). On these GATT cases see Ernst-Ulrich Petersmann (1993), 'International Competition Rules for the GATT/WTO World Trade and Legal System', **27:6** *Journal of World Trade*, 35–86; Norio Komuro and Edwin Vermulst (1997), 'Anti-Dumping Disputes in the GATT/WTO: Navigating Dire Straits', **31:1** *Journal of World Trade*, 5–43. The political difficulties ensuing a finding that a retroactive repayment of illegally imposed duties can impose clearly come out from the Panel Report, *Guatemala – Definitive Anti-Dumping Measures on Grey Portland Cement from Mexico*, WT/DS156/R, adopted 17 November 2000, DSR 2000:XI, 5295, paras. 9.6–9.7. See Petros C. Mavroidis, Patrick A. Messerlin, and Jasper M. Wauters (2008), *The Law and Economics of Contingent Protection in the WTO*, Cheltenham, UK and Northampton, MA: Edward Elgar Publishing, pp. 258–260.

49 Mavroidis, 'A Little Bit Less Conversation and a Little More Action', supra at note 43.

50 Prusa and Vermulst, 'United States – Anti-Dumping Measures on Polyethylene Retail Carrier Bags from Thailand', supra at note 7.

determined – there is no need to talk of the retrospective effect, since the effect of the declaration of illegality would affect a pending situation.

Whatever it may be, it is reasonable to assume that, if WTO remedies have had some retrospective effects, the US would have more quickly changed its domestic laws so as to end this long zeroing litigation.[51] Further, it looks intuitive that, if this remedial possibility would have been available and the US had not changed its policy, we would have had even more zeroing complaints against the US.

Secondly, it may be asked whether the narrow approach to implementation to WTO rulings finding the zeroing methodology illegal may constitute a case of breach 'having a continuing character'.

In public international law, this breach 'extends over the entire period during which the act continues and remains not in conformity with the international obligation'.[52] As noted over and over above, the fact that US laws, by providing zeroing as the methodology to calculate dumping, were illegal under WTO has been repeatedly found by Panels and the Appellate Body. This was not contested but acknowledged by the US itself. It could therefore be argued that the breach of the relevant WTO laws has continued over time (by applying the same policy to the same and different investigations) and, for what matters to Korea, was still lasting in the anti-dumping investigations at issue in DS 402.

Bown and Sykes underlined the implications of the initial piecemeal approach of the WTO rulings on zeroing, comparing it with a more expansive approach that might have clarified the full scope of permissibility and impermissibility of zeroing across all of the procedures of the anti-dumping process in which it might be used.[53] The deference of this approach can be understood. One of its negative implications, however, has been to blur the continuity of lack of compliance of US laws with WTO law. In more recent cases (*US–Continued Zeroing (EC)*,[54] *US–Zeroing (Japan)*,[55] and *US–Zeroing (EC)*),[56] the complainants made very expansive claims against the practice. The WTO AB's decisions now imply that the practice of zeroing is inconsistent except under exceptional circumstances.[57]

51 See the negotiating proposal of Canada, TN/RL/GEN/37, which *inter alia* suggests that, in case of an anti-dumping or countervailing-duty measure found WTO law-inconsistent, the relevant Member 'should be obliged to apply the compliant measure to all past entries and, where application of the compliant measure yields lower duty liability, to refund all excess anti-dumping and/or countervailing duties collected pursuant to the original (WTO-inconsistent) measure'.

52 Article 14 of the International Law Commission's Articles on State Responsibility. See James Crawford (2002), *The International Law Commission's Articles on State Responsibility Introduction, Text and Commentaries*, Cambridge, UK: Cambridge University Press, pp. 135–140.

53 Bown and Sykes, 'The Zeroing Issue', supra at note 10.

54 *United States – Continued Existence and Application of Zeroing Methodology*, WT/DS350.

55 *United States – Measures Relating to Zeroing and Sunset Reviews*, WT/DS322.

56 *United States – Laws, Regulations and Methodology for Calculating Dumping Margins ('Zeroing')*, WT/DS 294.

57 This discussion is based on Bown and Prusa, 'US Anti-Dumping', supra at note 3.

Although the practical implications of a ruling of continuing breach are not substantial, its clear and symbolic value and signal cannot be underestimated.

4.3 *The policy change of February 2012: all is well that ends well?*

Zeroing has also been an issue for duty calculations in periodic 'administrative reviews'. Under US AD law, the USDOC will, upon request, periodically conduct 'administrative reviews' of an AD order for purposes of (i) calculating the exact dumping margin for each exporter on entries covered by that review, and (ii) recalculating the duty deposit rate for future entries. Reviews are carried out indefinitely until the AD order is either completely or partially revoked. Typically, either domestic firms or foreign exporters will request a review within the first few years after the order was imposed.

The December 2006 policy change only affected zeroing in OI. The US only agreed to stop zeroing on administrative reviews in February 2012.[58] The relevant timetable reads:

> The Final Rule and Final Modification for Reviews will be effective and applicable to all reviews pending before the Department for which the preliminary results are issued after April 16, 2012. The Department will further apply the *Final Rule and Final Modification of Reviews* to all sunset reviews pending before the Department for which either the preliminary results or expedited final results of sunset review are issued after April 16, 2012. This methodology will be used in implementing the findings of the WTO panels in *US-Zeroing (EC)*, *US-Zeroing (Japan)*, *US-Stainless Steel (Mexico)*, and *US-Continued Zeroing (EC)*, with respect to any antidumping duty proceedings conducted pursuant to section 129 of the URAA. This methodology will also be applicable to any reviews currently discontinued by the Department if such reviews are continued after April 16, 2012 by reason of a final and conclusive judgment of a US Court.

This policy change should result in most countries simply requesting an administrative review rather than pursuing WTO litigation since a successful WTO ruling essentially just forces the US to perform a non-zeroing calculation.[59]

Since, however, as the zeroing saga shows, compliance with WTO rulings is often erratic, one cannot exclude the fact that Member governments will continue WTO litigation under Article 21.5 of the DSU claiming lack of full compliance as to refund of duties after the 'Reasonable Period' ended.

58 'Antidumping Proceedings: Calculation of the Weighted-Average Dumping Margin and Assessment Rate in Certain Antidumping Duty Proceedings; Final Modification', Federal Register, 77:30 (14 February 2012), pp. 8101–8114.

59 The only difference is that the margins are calculated for different periods of time. A recalculated OI margin would be based on a different (earlier) set of transactions than an administrative-review margin calculation. This timing difference is unlikely to generate a WTO dispute.

4.4 Unliquidated cash deposits: taking WTO DSU recommendations seriously

The US is unique in that it uses a retrospective system to compute duties while most other WTO members use a prospective system. Bown and Prusa argue that the differences in the duty-assessment systems in the EC and US partly explain why they responded differently to the WTO rulings.[60] In the prospective system, the dumping margin is established on the basis of the original investigation. In the retrospective system used by the United States, the dumping margin calculated in the initial investigation only establishes the deposit rate. The actual dumping margin is established during an administrative review.

An issue that emerged in the implementation phase was the appropriate way to handle cash deposits that had been collected (based on zeroing methodology) but had not yet been liquidated. The US will not implement with regard to what it considers a previous violation. The US believes it is sufficient to abandon zeroing on a forward-looking basis and that this implementation is enough to comply. The US's position is particularly problematic in this case.

For SSPC and SSSSC, there had been no shipments for many years and thus there were no deposits that could potentially be refunded. However, for diamond sawblades there were unliquidated cash deposits and these deposits could be potentially refunded. Recall that the US changed its policy regarding zeroing in OI in December 2006. Due to legal appeals, the cash-deposit order on sawblades began in January 2009, only after the US Court of International Trade remanded the USITC's negative injury determination. In other words, the US began to collect AD deposits over two years after it ceased zeroing in original investigations.

While unliquidated deposits were not in the scope of the dispute, Korea requested that the US refund the unliquidated deposits but the US refused. The instance of refusal to refund the unliquidated cash deposits is another clear example of the US's narrow approach to implementation of WTO zeroing decisions.

Certainly, a not-too-narrow reading of the standard recommendation to bring the measures (i.e., final determinations, amended final determinations, anti-dumping duty orders, and amended anti-dumping duty orders) in conformity with its obligations under the Anti-Dumping Agreement does involve the repayment of sums collected on the basis of those orders and of a calculation that has been found illegal. In other words, there are no reasons to disturb the principle of *no ultra petita*. The refund of sums collected on the basis of a methodology that has been expressly found to be illegal is a *reasonable and direct consequence* of the ruling of illegality.

60 Bown and Prusa, 'US Anti-Dumping', pp. 373–374, supra at note 3. This would depend on the fact that the retrospective system may amplify the effect of zeroing on dumping margins thus possibly explaining the US's resistance to implement WTO rulings.

The US refusal to refund the unliquidated cash deposits may also represent a good example of the weakness of the WTO DSU at the remedy level, which has been noted above. If WTO remedies were retroactive, it can reasonably be argued that the US would not be able to refuse repayment. But, even without invoking the far-reaching and emotion-stirring notion of retroactivity, it could be argued that since, in the US retrospective system to compute duties, cash deposits are collected only on the basis of the provisional determination of the initial investigation and do not reflect the actual dumping margin (which is established only during an administrative review), the procedure would still be current and subject to review.

5. Concluding comments: how strong is the law coming out from the WTO DSU?

The Panel's decision in *US–Zeroing (Korea)* does not have significant legal or economic interest with respect to the issue of zeroing. In its decision, the Panel simply restated long-standing (and numerous) Appellate Body views on the inconsistency of zeroing with Article 2.4.2 of the ADA.

After at least 20 disputes and more than 13 years of WTO litigation which repeatedly confirmed the illegality of zeroing, it comes as welcome news that the US finally decided to also stop zeroing in administrative reviews. Hopefully, for the health of the WTO DSU, this long-simmering irritant has come to an end.

What starkly emerges from this zeroing-litigation saga is a more general consideration of the weakness in the WTO DSU system and of the ability of one country to take advantage of it. Important questions can be made. Why do countries litigate although the law is clear and the facts undisputed? How much stronger is domestic politics than international legal obligations? To what extent does the current WTO DSU system reflect or favor this state of affairs? And, more importantly, what could be done to prevent, in the future, long-lasting foot-dragging like that witnessed with the US and zeroing? Would broader findings that any continuity of the illegality be established make any difference? Would complainants ask for this, and would Panels and the Appellate Body promptly respond to the call? Further, would a change of view on the lack of retrospective effects of remedies in the WTO help? In public international law, we do have retrospective remedies since the *Chorzow Factories* decision of the International Court of Justice in 1929. Why is this so difficult in the WTO? Is it because the WTO DSU is *lex specialis* to the general rules of State responsibility? Or is there any other reason that makes countries reluctant to be subject to more robust remedies in the WTO? Although certainly politically sensitive, would a statement that duties calculated on the basis of zeroing should be recalculated and any sum levied repaid be so revolutionary? In a word – how binding and strong is the law coming out from a WTO dispute? And – crucially – how binding and strong do its Members want it to be?

How Easy Is an Easy Case for a Complainant? Comment on *US–Zeroing (Korea)* DS402

JORGE A. HUERTA-GOLDMAN

Carouge, Switzerland

Abstract: This article is about how easy a WTO case is when the defendant concedes the claims, the description of the facts, and the evidence presented by the complainant. In *US–Zeroing (Korea)*, the United States did just that. We explore whether Korea obtained any additional benefit by having an easy case. We identified some small benefits at the preparation stage of the case arising from the favourable precedents and shorter time frames only at the Panel stage. There were, however, some additional costs for the complainant stemming from the Panel's reasoning when it addressed case law. In our opinion, benefits were few. Korea was obliged in any case to engage in two years of multilateral procedures before three old measures, which were not defended by the defendant, were revoked.

At the 2012 American Law Institute conference on WTO law in Florence, I discussed the case *US–Zeroing (Korea)*[1] presented by Prusa and Rubini. I developed two issues. First, how easy is a dispute where the defendant has conceded the challenge by the complainant? Second, to what extent can WTO legal remedies be applied retrospectively? The two questions are closely related. The first issue explores whether Korea obtained any additional benefit by having an easy case where the defendant conceded the complaint – i.e., *US–Zeroing (Korea)*. As the benefit is small, the second issue takes on greater relevance: whether WTO legal remedies may be applied retrospectively so as to cover part of the consequences of the illegal measure, especially in cases where even the defendant conceded the complaint. This article is about the first element. The second is addressed in a forthcoming separate article.

In *US–Zeroing (Korea)*, the United States (US) knew before the judgment that the measure was WTO illegal. This is confirmed by the fact that it conceded the

The author is a law practitioner and researcher on trade and investment (www.tilpa.ch). The opinions expressed in this work are entirely those of the author, and he alone is responsible for the accuracy of the information. We would like to thank participants at the ALI Conference on WTO Law 2012, EUI, Florence, Italy, for their comments and guidance in writing this article. Also, we would like to thank Peter Bennett.

1 *United States – Use of Zeroing in Anti-Dumping Measures Involving Products from Korea*, WT/DS402/R, adopted 24 February 2011 (hereafter, *US–Zeroing (Korea)*).

issues of law and the issues of fact presented by Korea in that dispute. Despite that, the US maintained the anti-dumping (AD) duties and let Korea undertake the WTO Dispute Settlement (DS) process before revoking the AD orders.

Korea claimed that the US applied zeroing in the three original investigations of products coming from Korea. It alleged violation of Article 2.4.2 of the ADA through the use of zeroing in the original investigations when determining the dumping margin through the methodology of weighted average to weighted average.[2] The US did not contest Korea's description of the zeroing methodology, the evidence, or the legal claim.[3] Also, strong and clear precedents supported Korea's case of violation.[4]

1. Upstream

Korea had to prepare evidence, study the measures, develop the claims, and assess the case law before initiating the dispute. At the time of preparation of the case, Korea did not know whether the US would concede its complaint. Had Korea not presented the case properly, most probably the US would not have conceded the complaint. This suggests that the case was not easier for Korea at the preparatory stage.

But, Korea had the guidance from strong precedents that have ruled on identical measures and claims.[5] Certainly, this was an advantage when determining sufficiency of evidence, and clarity of claims. But it was the precedents that gave advantage and not the *US–Zeroing (Korea)* dispute itself.

2. Time table

First, the Panel eliminated the second substantive meeting with the parties after consulting with them. This made the case shorter for Korea. We consider this to be a benefit.[6]

2 The products concerned were stainless-steel plate in coils ('SSPC'), stainless-steel sheet and strip in coils ('SSSS'), and diamond sawblades. See *US–Zeroing (Korea)*, paras. 1.1, 2.1, and 7.26.

3 A similar situation with respect to uncontested claims occurred in Panel Report, *United States – Antidumping Measures on Certain Shrimp and Diamond Sawblades from China*, WT/DS422/R and Add.1, adopted 23 July 2012. The Panel noted, at para. 7.5, that: 'the panels in *US – Shrimp (Ecuador)* and, subsequently, *US – Shrimp (Thailand), US – Anti-Dumping Measures on PET Bags*, and *US – Zeroing (Korea)* were presented with a similar situation. Indeed each of these panels examined claims, unopposed by the United States, that were virtually identical.'

4 See Panel Report in *US–Zeroing (Korea)*, paras. 1.1, 3.2, and 7.27 and US communication dated 9 December 2011 (WT/DS402/7). Korea's request for consultations was presented on 24 November 2009. Its request for a Panel is from 8 April 2010. Finally, the US revoked the AD order on Steel Plate and Steel Sheet in November 2011, and on Sawblades in December 2011.

5 See Panel Report in *US – Zeroing (Korea)*, paras. 3.2 and 7.27.

6 See ibid., para. 1.6.

Figure 1. Overall time frames

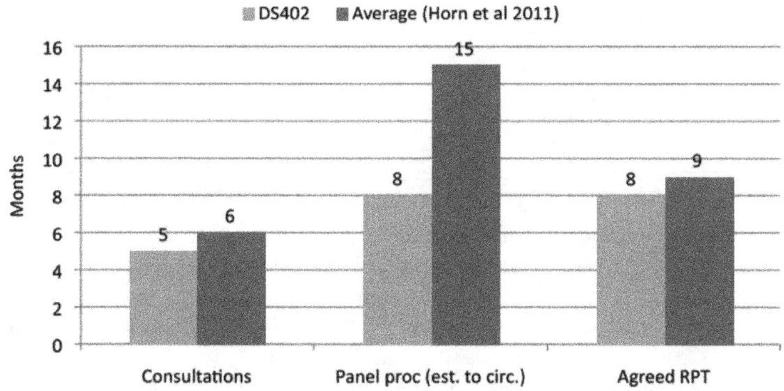

Note: 'Panel proc (est. to circ.)' means Panel proceeding (establishment to circulation).

Second, Figure 1 shows the overall time frames of the case at issue and the average of WTO DS cases (based on information from Horn *et al.*, 2011).[7] The only period that is significantly shorter is the Panel stage. Seven months less is a benefit for Korea. But, no significant benefit is shown at the consultations stage, or after a reasonable period of time (RPT).

3. Adjudication

There are some additional costs for Korea in the adjudicative Panel process. First, the AB has indicated that adjudicators may use uncontested facts to draw a ruling on the matter.[8] But, the Panel decided not to follow such practice in order to comply with the need for an objective assessment of the matter under Article 11 of the DSU. If the AB uses undisputed facts to complete the legal analysis, this may suggest that the AB does not consider that a violation of Article 11 of the DSU occurs when a Panel draws on undisputed facts.

Second, the Panel decided not to categorize this undisputed matter as a mutually agreed solution (MAS), as it was concerned to meet the obligation to make an objective assessment under Article 11 of the DSU. This interpretation by the Panel may wrongly suggest that if the parties agree that there is a violation and the Panel reflects this in the Report, there is a risk of violation of Article 11 of the DSU. Further research is needed on the scope of MAS and Panels' treatment of

7 The averages are based on: Henrik Horn, Louise Johannesson, and Petros C.Mavroidis (2011), 'The WTO Dispute Settlement System 1995–2010: Some Descriptive Statistics', 45:6 *Journal of World Trade*, 1107–1138.

8 See the Appellate Body Report in *European Communities – Export Subsidies on Sugar*, WT/DS265/AB/R, WT/DS266/AB/R, WT/DS283/AB/R, adopted 19 May 2005, DSR 2005:XIII, 6365, at para. 337. It 'has declined to complete the legal analysis where "the factual findings of the panel and the *undisputed facts* in the panel record" did not provide a sufficient basis for the legal analysis by the Appellate Body' (emphasis added).

Table 1. Time frames on implementation

Order	Initiation to revocation of AD	Req. Consul.[1] to revocation of AD
Steel Plate[2]	13 years 7 months	2 years
Steel Sheet[3]	13 years 4 months	2 years
Sawblades[4]	6 years 7 months	2 years 1 month

Notes:
1 Korea's request for consultation is from November 2009.
2 For Steel Plate, the AD order was initiated in April 1998, and the revocation took place in November 2011.
3 For Steel Sheet, the AD order was initiated in July 1998, and the revocation took place in November 2011.
4 For Sawblades, the AD order was initiated in June 2005, and the revocation took place in December 2011.
Source: Based on Thomas S. Prusa and Luca Rubini (2013), *United States – Use of Zeroing in Anti-Dumping Measures Involving Products from Korea*: It's déjà vu all over again, *World Trade Review*, this issue.

undisputed facts – already accepted by the AB – and undisputed claims, such as the case at issue.

Finally, the Panel added a new step in determining a WTO violation. The Panel's test is whether the measure violates WTO law (see for instance Articles 7 and 19 of the DSU). The Panel covered that in two sections of its Report: whether the US zeroed (para. 7.21 et seq.) and whether the zeroing methodology used is inconsistent with Article 2.4.2 of the Antidumping Agreement (para. 7.28 et seq.). But, it included an additional section on whether the methodology used by the US in this case was the same as the one used in *US–Softwood Lumber V*, which represented the strong precedent (para. 7.23 et seq.). It seems that the Panel inserted an additional step for cases with strong precedents: the need to prove that the two measures are the same. If this practice is adopted in future cases, there will be a two-step process for cases without strong precedents and a three-step process for cases with strong precedent.

4. Implementation

Table 1 shows the time frames on implementation. Two years from the request for consultations to the revocation of the order seems a short period. As noted in Table 1 above, the Panel procedure was faster than the average, which was a benefit for Korea. But, this is still far from perfect as revocation took two years of multilateral procedures despite the fact that there was no disagreement by the parties that the measure was WTO-illegal.

Finally, for two products, 13 years elapsed between the time of initiation of the AD investigation and the revocation of the AD order; and, for the other product, it was six years. The date of initiation of the AD order is relevant in light of

Article 5.8 of the Anti-Dumping Agreement (ADA) that: '[a]n application ... **shall be rejected** and an investigation **shall be terminated** promptly as soon as the authorities concerned are satisfied that there is not sufficient evidence of ... dumping'. The investigations were not recent.

5. Conclusion

Korea was guided by a strong precedent in its favour – very useful as complainant – and obtained a shorter Panel process. At the adjudicative stage, it had some extra costs. The costs do not appear to be significant in an easy case, but in complex cases they could be onerous for a complainant. Finally, two years of multilateral proceedings to revoke three old measures, where the defendant conceded the complaint, calls for an assessment of WTO legal remedies. I agree with Prusa and Rubini that there is a need for more studies on whether the WTO legal remedies may be applied retrospectively.

US – Anti-Dumping Measures on Certain Shrimp from Viet Nam: A Stir-Fry of Seafood, Statistics, and *Lacunae*

TOMER BROUDE
Hebrew University of Jerusalem
MICHAEL MOORE
George Washington University

Abstract: This unappealed Panel Report deals with now standard controversies involving US zeroing practices, but also involves a number of novel problems in administrative reviews of US anti-dumping orders that transcend zeroing issues. Most importantly, this dispute highlights the economic, legal, and statistical importance of sample-selection bias when calculating 'all others' rates for exporters that were not queried during dumping investigations. Sampling is particularly problematic in this dispute since US investigators found only zero and *de minimis* margins in the administrative reviews, a situation in which the relevant provision of the Anti-Dumping Agreement appears to provide no guidance (an apparent '*lacuna*'). The Panel did not directly deal with the key sample-selection issues in the case, and so we provide an alternative legal and statistical analysis. These issues are likely to become more important as the practice of zeroing is phased out in the United States. Indeed, sampling may well be the new zeroing.

1. Introduction: much more than zero(ing)

At first glance *United States – Anti-Dumping Measures on Certain Shrimp from Viet Nam* (*US–AD Shrimp*)[1] could easily be mistaken for simply yet another in the long series of 'zeroing' disputes adjudicated by the WTO dispute-settlement system. Ever since India filed a case in *EC–Bed Linen* (2001),[2] at least 16 distinct

We would like to thank participants Chad Bown, Niall Meagher, Tom Prusa, and Edwin Vermulst for helpful discussion about an earlier draft. All errors are of course our own.

1 Panel Report, *United States – Anti-Dumping Measures on Certain Shrimp from Viet Nam*, WT/DS404/R, adopted 2 September 2011.

2 Appellate Body Report, *European Communities – Anti-Dumping Duties on Imports of Cotton-Type Bed Linen from India*, WT/DS141/AB/R, adopted 12 March 2001, DSR 2001:V, 2049.

complaints have been filed at the WTO relating to variants of the zeroing methodology used in dumping calculations.[3] In such investigations, authorities ascribe a 'zero' margin to any transaction where the export price exceeds the 'normal' price (i.e., in which the dumping margin is negative), thereby inflating the resulting calculated dumping margin (Voon, 2011). The vast majority of these complaints have been brought against the US, which has proven reluctant to amend its methodologies and only recently announced significant changes in policy and legislation (Cho, 2012).

US–AD Shrimp can indeed be read as a late chapter in the zeroing saga. Viet Nam complained against the use of zeroing in the calculation of dumping margins, both 'as applied' and 'as such', referring both to the implications of zeroing used during the original investigation, and to the WTO consistency of zeroing employed in subsequent periodic administrative reviews. On these issues, the Panel, whose Report was not appealed by either the US or Viet Nam, generally followed the lines of analysis set out by the Appellate Body in prior jurisprudence, finding US zeroing practice to be WTO-inconsistent.[4] Besides one or two relatively minor points, the Panel in *US–AD Shrimp* was not asked to rule on any particularly novel issues relating to zeroing in dumping calculations.[5]

However, *US–AD Shrimp* has several dimensions of interest that transcend the question of zeroing. In particular, as we shall set out in more detail below, the dispute provides us with an opportunity to analyze the statistical, economic, and legal implications of sample-selection practices employed by investigating authorities in anti-dumping proceedings.

Under the terms of the second sentence of Article 6.10 of the Anti-Dumping Agreement (ADA),[6] Members may limit their investigation to a sample of relevant firms when faced with a large number of enterprises involved in the product market under investigation (sometimes known as 'limited examination'). In structural-legal terms, this possibility is an exception to the general rule whereby the investigating authorities should determine 'an individual margin of dumping for each known exporter or producer concerned of the product under investigation',[7] but sampling

3 For legal and economic analyses of zeroing in anti-dumping cases, see Bown and Sykes (2008), Prusa and Vermulst (2009), Prusa and Vermulst (2011), and Bown and Prusa (2011).

4 See *US–AD Shrimp*, paras. 8.1(b) and (c).

5 As the Panel noted understatedly, *US–AD Shrimp* was 'not the first time US practices in relation to zeroing have come before a WTO panel'. However, the facts of the case were 'unusual' in that all of the individually calculated dumping margins in the relevant administrative reviews were either zero or de minimis, thus raising the question of whether zeroing is WTO-inconsistent even when it does not lead to the imposition of duties on firms with an individually calculated dumping margin (see *US–AD Shrimp*, para. 7.82). We address this issue in Section 2.2.2.

6 Agreement on Implementation of Article VI of the General Agreement on Tariffs and Trade 1994, Annex 1 A, Marrakech Agreement establishing the World Trade Organization, 15 April 1994, Final Act Embodying the Results of the Uruguay Round of Multilateral Trade Negotiations, Legal Instruments: Results of the Uruguay Round, 6, 6–18; 33 I.L.M. 1140, 1144–1153 (1994).

7 Article 6.10 ADA, first sentence.

is hardly an uncommon practice among investigating authorities. Indeed, it is so common that Viet Nam argued against US Department of Commerce's repeated use of limited examinations in anti-dumping investigations as having 'effectively turned the general rule in the first sentence of Article 6.10 ADA (i.e., that an individual margin should be determined for each exporter/producer) into an exception, and the exception under the same provision into a general rule'.[8]

The way domestic administrators select the sample of individually assessed firms may have crucial repercussions on firms left outside of the sample because, in accordance with Article 9.4 ADA, the anti-dumping duty rate imposed upon the imports of the latter (the 'all others' rate) is linked to the dumping margins calculated with respect to the former. Moreover, exporters may still face the 'all others' rate even if they are willing to offer their own data for use by domestic authorities to calculate firm-specific rates, if investigators find that to conduct such an individual calculation would be 'impracticable', as determined by the investigators themselves. The practical consequences of this selection process could be dramatic: in the second and third administrative reviews of *US–AD Shrimp*, only two and three Vietnamese firms, respectively, were investigated in detail. The weighted average of this exceedingly small sample was then applied to dozens of other Vietnamese firms that were not queried about their particular economic conditions. Sample selection therefore raises interrelated questions involving both statistical analysis, on the one hand, and fairness and due process, on the other.

Surprisingly, the Article 6.10 ADA parameters for sample selection and limited examination have not merited significant interpretation in either WTO jurisprudence or academic analysis,[9] and have only received peripheral attention from WTO Members concerned with reforming the ADA.[10] Furthermore, the terms established by Article 9.4 ADA for the calculation of the 'all others' rate are, in certain circumstances, very vague, to the point that the Appellate Body has identified a '*lacuna*' in the clause.[11]

These special circumstances – *viz*, when all the dumping margins calculated for the selected firms are either zero or *de minimis* – are strongly linked to the question

8 See *US–AD Shrimp* at para. 7.154. We address this issue in some more detail in Section 2.2.3 On rule-exception normative relationships in WTO law generally, see Broude (2007).

9 But see Panel Report, *Argentina – Definitive Anti-Dumping Measures on Imports of Ceramic Floor Tiles from Italy*, WT/DS189/R, adopted 5 November 2001, DSR 2001:XII, 6241, paras. 6.86–6.105, discussing the duty established by Article 6.10 ADA to establish an individual dumping margin for firms included in the sample.

10 See in particular WTO, Negotiating Group on Rules, TN/RL/GEN/46, *Issues Related to Article 6.10, Including 'Limited Examination', and Article 9.4 'All Other's Rate'*, Paper from Brazil; Chile; Hong Kong, China; Israel; Japan; Republic of Korea; Norway; Switzerland; Separate Customs Territory of Taiwan, Penghu, Kinmen, and Matsu; and Thailand, 10 June 2005.

11 See Appellate Body Report, *United States – Anti-Dumping Measures on Certain Hot-Rolled Steel Products from Japan*, WT/DS184/AB/R, adopted 23 August 2001, DSR 2001:X, 4697 (hereafter *US–Hot-Rolled Steel*), paras. 125–126. We address this issue in additional detail in Section 4 below.

of sample selection. It is on the statistical and interpretative issues associated with Articles 6.10 and 9.4 ADA, and the relationship between them, that most of our analysis in this article will focus.

Before turning to a more detailed examination of *US–AD Shrimp*, we wish to briefly dwell on two aspects of the dispute's economic and political context.

First of all, the dispute was the first complaint filed by Viet Nam at the WTO dispute-settlement system, soon after its accession to the WTO on 11 January 2007.[12] Indeed, the dispute relates to an original anti-dumping investigation that the US conducted *prior* to Viet Nam's accession. The 'Socialist Republic of Viet Nam' is a socialist/communist state lacking a tradition of participation in the international legal system but with an economic system that is undergoing a complex transition to liberalization and exposure to market forces while retaining a centralized political structure (the so-called 'socialist-oriented market economy', building on the *Doi Moi* economic reforms of the late 1980s and 1990s (Gantz, 2007). While monitoring the economic benefits of WTO accession (Vo Tri Thanh and Nguyen Anh Duong, 2009), Viet Nam's filing of the complaint in *US–AD Shrimp* represents a strong signal that it regards dispute settlement in the WTO as a legitimate and worthwhile means for enforcing its rights and promoting its interests in international trade, perhaps in emulation of the strategy of 'aggressive legalism' that has been attributed to Japan and Korea as well as post-WTO accession China (Pekkanen, 2001; Gao, 2005). Viet Nam's demeanor in *US–AD Shrimp* suggests that it should be regarded as a sophisticated player in the WTO, and as has been pointed out by some commentators, the case has implications for the way trade partners will treat Viet Nam as a 'non-market economy' (NME) in the WTO,[13] in all sectors of importance to Viet Nam's economic development (Do Thanh Cong, 2010).

Second, again as a matter of political and economic context, the dispute discussed in this paper related to the international market for shrimp products, and as such is interconnected with a number of other WTO disputes. Since the late 1990s, demand for shrimp products has increased significantly, eagerly satisfied by exporters in various Asian countries, ultimately resulting in lower prices (Do Thanh Cong, 2010). Import controls imposed by Europe in the early 2000s, based on health concerns relating to the antibiotic treatment of farmed shrimp in countries of origin, diverted significant Asian output to North America (Debaere, 2010), with significant harm to the US shrimp industry, which led to successful petitions for

12 Consultations in the dispute were requested by Viet Nam on 1 February 2010; see *US – Anti-Dumping Measures on Certain Shrimp from Viet Nam – Request for Consultations*, WT/DS404/1, 4 February 2010.

13 A WTO Member's characterization as an NME will affect the way other Members conduct anti-dumping investigations with respect to imports from the NME Member. This issue was specifically addressed in Viet Nam's accession documents; see *Accession of Viet Nam – Report of the Working Party on the Accession of Viet Nam*, WT/ACC/VNM/48, 27 October 2006, paras. 254–255.

anti-dumping duties imposed by the US (Keithly and Poudel, 2008). Part of the exporting countries' reaction to these duties is now on the books of WTO jurisprudence. Thus, *US–AD Shrimp* should be read against the backdrop of a total of seven complaints relating to US anti-dumping duties on shrimp products brought separately to the WTO by China, Ecuador, India, Thailand, and Viet Nam (including a recent follow-up complaint to *US–AD Shrimp* brought by Viet Nam),[14] some of which deal with zeroing issues. The shrimp-farming industry is an extremely important export sector for Viet Nam, and the US is a chief export market;[15] Viet Nam's interests in bringing the complaint in this case are clear. However, it is worth bearing in mind that the dispute is part of a larger legal campaign by shrimp-exporting developing and emerging economies against US anti-dumping practices perceived as protectionist in a sector important for their economic development.

The article will proceed as follows. In Section 2, we will set out the relevant legal background of the dispute, including an exposition of the main practices of the US Department of Commerce (the 'USDOC') as the investigating authority; the legal basis of the complaint by Viet Nam; the US response and interventions by third parties where relevant; and the main findings of the Panel in its Report, including a critique of the Panel's hermeneutic approach to the sample-selection issues. In Section 3, we will critically analyze the issue of sample selection in limited examinations under Article 6.10 ADA, with an emphasis on insights from statistical methodologies. In Section 4, we will discuss the so-called '*lacuna*' in Article 9.4 ADA with respect to the 'all others' rate of anti-dumping duties, suggesting a role for statistical analysis in the interpretation of that provision. Section 5 concludes.

2. Legal issues in *US–AD Shrimp*

2.1 Relevant USDOC practices

Understanding the US system of anti-dumping investigations will be critical in analyzing the *US–AD Shrimp* dispute. The USDOC bears the legal responsibility for investigating alleged dumping by exporters from foreign countries.[16] The agency calculates dumping margins in three situations: (1) original investigations, when first determining whether anti-dumping duties should be imposed, and at which rates; (2) periodic administrative reviews, which, subject to certain terms, take place on the anniversary of the original anti-dumping order; and (3) five-year

14 See *United States – Anti-Dumping Measures on Certain Shrimp from Viet Nam – Request for Consultations by Viet Nam*, WT/DS429/1, 27 February 2012.

15 See the *Business Times* (Viet Nam) (2012).

16 See Title VII of the Tariff Act of 1930 (19 U.S.C. 1671 et seq.).

'sunset' reviews, when the termination of the original order is at issue.[17] In each type of investigation, the USDOC in principle compares the export price to the US for each foreign exporter with the 'normal' price of the good, which can be the price in the home market, a third market (if there are insufficient sales for a valid comparison in the home market), or a constructed production-cost calculation (if there are insufficient instances of the other outcomes).[18] These comparisons necessarily require detailed information about foreign firms' pricing and cost data.

The USDOC conducts its investigations according to two categories of exporting states. 'Market economy' cases involve foreign firms operating in economies where prices are deemed under US law to provide accurate signals about the efficient allocation of resources. In contrast, exporters operating in 'non-market economy' (NME) cases are considered to have unreliable pricing and cost information so that USDOC investigators must use third-country surrogates to calculate the dumping margins. Viet Nam is considered an NME by US authorities and hence subject to the latter sets of procedures.[19]

Administrative reviews are the particular focus of *US–AD Shrimp*. The role of administrative reviews is especially important and derives from the 'retrospective' duty-assessment system operated by the US, whereby, upon importation, a cash deposit for anti-dumping duty liability is collected, but actual anti-dumping duties are assessed only at a later date. This assessment takes place in the periodic administrative review, which may be requested by interested parties every year, during the anniversary month of the original anti-dumping order. In an administrative review, the USDOC assesses the importer's liability for anti-dumping duties retrospectively on a transaction-specific basis. If no review is requested, the duty is assessed at the full rate of the cash deposits.[20] We discuss the procedures for NME administrative reviews below in more detail within the specific context of the *US–AD Shrimp* dispute.

Specific outcomes for individual NME exporters subject to anti-dumping orders in administrative reviews depend on several factors.[21] Figure 1 sets out a detailed decision tree tracing them.

17 Details of US standard procedures can be found in the Antidumping Manual (US Import Administration (2009) (the ADM)). For a description and critique of the US anti-dumping regime, see Barfield (2005).

18 See ADM, Chapter 6; and Article 2.2 ADA.

19 Section 771(18) of the Tariff Act of 1930 (*supra* at note 16) defines NME as 'any foreign country that the [USDOC] determines does not operate on market principles of cost or pricing structures, so that sales of merchandise in such country do not reflect the fair value of the merchandise'. The USDOC classifies states as either market economies or NMEs under its own terms (see ADM, Chapter 10). In footnote 27 in the *US–AD Shrimp* Panel Report, the Panel expressed 'no opinion on the WTO-consistency of the USDOC's classification of certain countries, including Viet Nam, in such a category'.

20 See *US–AD Shrimp*, para. 7.12.

21 These procedures are discussed in detail in Department of Commerce (DOC) (2009).

Figure 1. US administrative review process for non-market economies

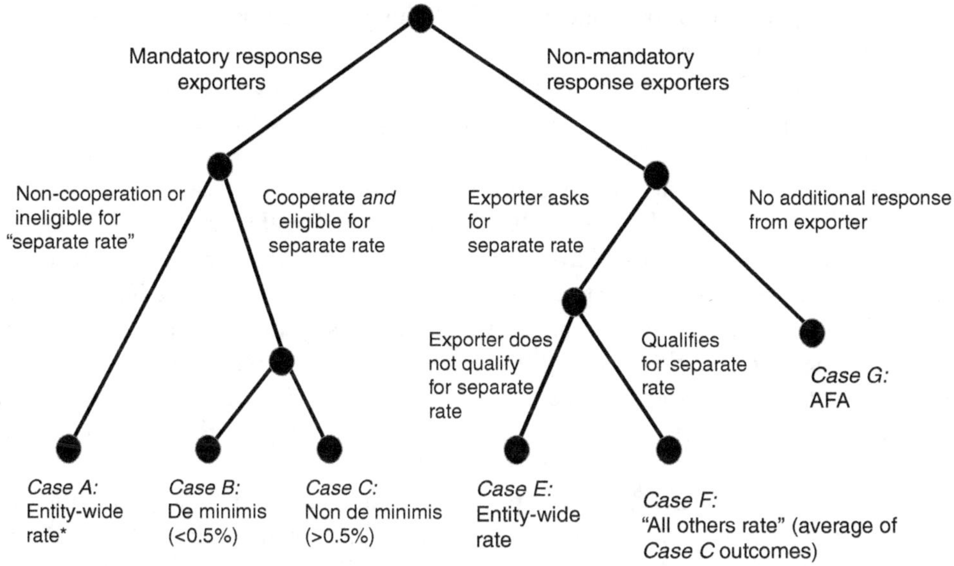

Upon the request of an interested party (in the US, or a foreign exporter) the USDOC will launch an administrative review of the original anti-dumping order. The USDOC begins from the (rebuttable) presumption that all firms in the NME will receive an 'entity-wide rate' (EWR), unless they can show to the USDOC's satisfaction that their exports are sufficiently independent of government control. Firms that meet these independence criteria may be eligible for a 'separate rate' determined independently from the entity-wide rate.

The USDOC initially sends a 'quantity and value' questionnaire to all foreign exporters that have been either: (a) identified by petitioners, or (b) those exporters who themselves have requested a review. The requested information will include the volume and value of exports to the US of the product subject to the existing anti-dumping order.[22]

The USDOC's investigators also determine how many foreign firms they will choose to examine in detail for the formal dumping investigation in the administrative review. In practice, the number of foreign firms investigated is limited by how many resources the USDOC chooses to devote to the case. Typically, investigators will choose a very small number of foreign exporters, who become 'mandatory respondents' for the formal review. As in the original

22 In more recent cases, the USDOC has relied on detailed data gleaned from official customs records, as in the third administrative review in *US–AD Shrimp*. See DOC (2009).

investigations, only the largest exporters of the product in question to the US are considered for this category. Note that an exporter requesting an administrative review is not guaranteed to be one of the firms that the USDOC will select to receive a detailed questionnaire.

These 'mandatory respondent' firms may then choose to cooperate or not in the full-scale dumping investigation by providing detailed data (e.g., about input quantities) to the USDOC.

Mandatory respondents selected in the administrative review that do not cooperate (as determined by the USDOC investigators) will necessarily receive the EWR, which is normally the 'Adverse Facts Available' (AFA) rate determined for similarly noncooperative selected respondents in the initial investigation. The USDOC also considers that mandatory respondents that cooperate but cannot show that they are eligible for a 'separate' rate, are subject to the EWR. Both types of NME exporters are depicted as Case A in Figure 1. The margins assigned to them are deemed 'unrepresentative' and so are not included in the subsequent 'all others' rate.

Mandatory respondents that do respond adequately to the questionnaire and are deemed by the USDOC as eligible for a 'separate rate' will receive a firm-specific margin calculated in the administrative review. As in original investigations, the USDOC chooses a surrogate country it considers to be at a similar level of economic development, whose input prices are then applied to the input quantities reported by the cooperating firms, in order to calculate a dumping margin. If the specific foreign firm's calculated margin is less than a 0.5% *de minimis* rate (rather than the 2% *de minimis* rate applicable in original investigations), then that firm is not subject to an anti-dumping duty at all (Case B in Figure 1). Margins above the *de minimis* rate are also the basis of the anti-dumping duty going forward to at least the next administrative review for these mandatory-response exporters (Case C in Figure 1).

The procedures for mandatory respondents in market-economy investigations parallel the process below with the exception that there is no need to determine whether a particular exporter is eligible for a 'separate rate'. All mandatory respondents either receive an individually calculated rate or, if they do not cooperate, the AFA rate.

Let us turn now in detail to procedures used for the *non*mandatory response firms in NME cases.

All firms not queried during the administrative review and that do not request separate-rate eligibility by default receive the EWR based on AFA (Case G in Figure 1). In conventional market-economy cases, all nonqueried firms normally would receive an 'all others' rate based on a weighted average of nonzero and non-*de minimis* margins.

A nonmandatory respondent may volunteer to provide information to the USDOC that may establish its eligibility to avoid the EWR. If the USDOC rejects this contention, then the firm receives the EWR (Case E in Figure 1). This outcome may also occur if the USDOC determines it is not 'practicable' to analyze more firms in the administrative review.

A nonmandatory response foreign firm that does qualify for a separate rate is designated as Case F in Figure 1. In this instance, the USDOC typically does not conduct a new investigation using that firm's individual data. Instead the USDOC will apply an 'all others' rate based on a weighted average of Case C outcomes, i.e., based on the data of other mandatory-response firms eligible for a separate rate. In a market-economy case, such a firm would receive a margin based on a separate investigation using data provided by the individual exporter. This distinction makes clear that the procedures for determining the 'all others' rate is of particular importance in an NME case such as *US–AD Shrimp*.

2.2 *Certain issues addressed by the US–AD Shrimp Panel*

2.2.1 *Factual background and the measures challenged*

US–AD Shrimp relates mainly to the WTO-consistency of final determinations made by the USDOC in the second and third administrative reviews regarding certain frozen and canned warm-water shrimp from, *inter alia*, Viet Nam, published on 1 February 2005. As already noted, in the original investigation and order, the USDOC treated Viet Nam as an NME. It further determined that it was impracticable to examine all Vietnamese exporters of shrimp, opting instead for a limited examination of four mandatory respondents accounting for the largest volume of exports during the period of investigation. Three of these mandatory respondents cooperated with the USDOC and each received individually calculated dumping margins ranging from 4.30% to 5.24% (i.e., Case C outcomes in Figure 1). These were used to calculate the 'all others' rate of 4.57%, while the rate applied to all firms considered to be a part of the Viet Nam-wide NME was 25.76%, a rate determined on an AFA basis (Case A outcomes).[23]

The second and third administrative reviews were the first such reviews relating to shrimp exports during a period subsequent to Viet Nam's WTO accession on 11 January 2007. The second administrative review, published on 9 September 2008, included individual investigations of only *two* mandatory respondents, both of which revealed zero or negligible dumping margins. The USDOC applied either the same 4.57% 'all others' rate from the original investigation (for Case F outcomes) or the 25.76% Viet Nam-wide rate to firms not eligible for a 'separate rate' (i.e., Cases A, G, and E).

In the third administrative review, issued on 19 September 2009, the USDOC conducted individual investigations for only *three* mandatory respondents, once again finding only *de minimis* dumping margins of between 0.08% and 0.43%. Non-mandatory respondents eligible for a separate rate received the much higher

23 See *US–AD Shrimp*, para. 7.24.

4.57% 'all others' rate from the original investigation. The remaining firms were not considered eligible for a separate rate and therefore received the 25.76% Viet Nam-wide rate from the original investigation.[24]

With respect to these USDOC anti-dumping determinations, Viet Nam made four sets of claims relating to: the use of zeroing methodology, limited examination of selected mandatory respondents, application of the 'all others' rate to nonselected firms, and Viet Nam-wide entity rate. We discuss these claims in this order in the following pages, critiquing some of the hermeneutical choices made by the Panel.

2.2.2 *Zeroing methodologies in administrative reviews – the blurring of the lines between 'as such', 'as applied', and 'continued use' complaints*

Viet Nam attempted a general claim against the 'continued use of challenged practices', inspired by the relative success of a prior WTO case brought by the EU against a series of 18 US anti-dumping determinations involving zeroing.[25] However, the *US–AD Shrimp* Panel rejected this claim as a preliminary matter upon the request of the US, finding that such 'continued', ongoing USDOC conduct had not been sufficiently identified by Viet Nam as a measure at issue in its request for a Panel, so that it lay outside the Panel's Terms of Reference.[26] The Panel then exercised judicial economy with respect to the general question of whether a 'continued use of challenged practices' measure could be subject to challenge in the WTO, though citing the Appellate Body's acceptance of this possibility in the *US–Continued Zeroing* case.[27]

On the merits of Viet Nam's separate 'as applied' challenge to USDOC zeroing practice, the Panel followed prior jurisprudence[28] and sided with Viet Nam and several Third Parties (India, Japan, Korea) in finding that 'simple zeroing' exercised by the USDOC in administrative reviews with respect to individually examined exporters was a violation of the 'fair comparison' requirement of Article 2.4 ADA. Indeed, this was found to be the case even when all individually calculated dumping margins were determined to be either zero or *de minimis*, and no duties were assessed and levied in practice. The US had argued that if dumping margins were

24 See ibid., paras. 7.26–7.27.

25 Appellate Body Report, *United States – Continued Existence and Application of Zeroing Methodology*, WT/DS350/AB/R, adopted 19 February 2009, DSR 2009:III, 1291 (hereafter *US–Continued Zeroing*).

26 *US–AD Shrimp*, para. 7.68.

27 Ibid., para. 7.69.

28 See *US–AD Shrimp*, para. 7.91, referring to Appellate Body Report, *United States – Sunset Review of Anti-Dumping Duties on Corrosion-Resistant Carbon Steel Flat Products from Japan*, WT/DS244/AB/R, adopted 9 January 2004; Appellate Body Report, *United States – Final Dumping Determination on Softwood Lumber from Canada – Recourse to Article 21.5 of the DSU by Canada*, WT/DS264/AB/RW, adopted 1 September 2006; and Appellate Body Report, *United States – Measures Relating to Zeroing and Sunset Reviews*, WT/DS322/AB/R, adopted 23 January 2007.

zero or *de minimis*, one could not say that they had been inflated, but according to the Panel, '[e]ven in cases where no anti-dumping duties are assessed, the application of zeroing distorts the prices of certain export transactions, because export transactions made at prices above normal value are not considered at their real value'.[29] This finding elevates the practice of zeroing, when challenged 'as applied', to one of a *per se* character, in the sense that the WTO-inconsistency of the practice is not dependent on its effects upon anti-dumping duties actually levied.

This *per se* 'as applied' finding can be difficult to logically distinguish from the subsequent finding by the Panel with respect to Viet Nam's claim that the US 'zeroing methodology' in periodic administrative reviews is a rule or norm of general and prospective application that is inconsistent with the ADA 'as such'.[30] Viet Nam submitted this 'as such' claim, facing a higher threshold of proof because the challenged measure (zeroing methodology in periodic reviews) is not clearly expressed in the form of a written document.[31] In order to confirm that USDOC adopts zeroing methodology as *a general and prospective* matter, the Panel relied upon evidence of the application of zeroing *in practice*, stating at one stage that the evidence shows that 'the USDOC will always apply zeroing'[32] and that the 'application of zeroing in administrative reviews extends well beyond the mere repetition of a practice in specific cases and rather substantiates Viet Nam's allegation that the USDOC maintains a deliberate policy to this effect'.[33] This is in line with prior Appellate Body jurisprudence whereby evidence of the existence of a general and prospective rule or norm amenable to challenge 'as such', may include 'proof of [its] systematic application'.[34]

However, taken as a whole, the challenges against zeroing in *US–AD Shrimp* raise questions about the soundness of the analytical distinctions between the three separate claims made by Viet Nam, as assessed by the Panel: (1) the 'continued use of challenged practices' (rejected by the Panel on procedural grounds as lying outside its terms of reference); (2) the claim of 'as applied' inconsistency bearing in effect a *per se* character; and (3) the claim of 'as such' inconsistency, substantiated to large extent on the practice of zeroing 'as applied'. In *US–Continued Zeroing*,[35] the Appellate Body opined that the distinction between 'as such' and 'as applied' is a 'heuristic device' that 'however useful, does not define exhaustively the types of measures that may be subject to challenge in WTO dispute settlement. In order to

29 See *US–AD Shrimp*, para. 7.93.

30 Ibid., para. 7.142.

31 The Appellate Body elaborated upon this higher standard of proof in Appellate Body Report, *United States – Laws, Regulations and Methodology for Calculating Dumping Margins (Zeroing)*, WT/DS294/AB/R, adopted 9 May 2006, and Corr.1, DSR 2006:II, 417 (hereafter *US–Zeroing (EC)*), para. 198.

32 See *US–AD Shrimp*, para. 7.117.

33 Ibid., para. 7.115.

34 See *US–Zeroing (EC)*, para. 198.

35 *US–Continued Zeroing*, para. 179, *supra* at note 25.

be susceptible to challenge, a measure need not fit squarely within one of these two categories, that is, either as a rule or norm of general and prospective application, or as an individual instance of the application of a rule or norm'. Thus, the 'continued use' of zeroing in successive proceedings resulting from 18 anti-dumping orders, was considered to be susceptible to challenge in a Panel procedure without being classified as either 'as such' or 'as applied'. The problem we note in *US–AD Shrimp*, however, is not the recognition of new categories of measures which may be challenged, but rather the interpretation of such categories in ways that blur the distinctions and create significant overlaps between them.

For present purposes, the importance of the Panel's findings of both 'as such' and 'as applied' ADA-inconsistency of USDOC zeroing methods in periodic administrative reviews lies in the role they returned to play in the evaluation of Viet Nam's claims regarding the validity of the 'all others' rate of anti-dumping duties applied to nonindividually assessed firms, as explained in Section 2.2.4.

2.2.3 *Limited examination of mandatory respondents – presumptions of statistical validity instead of substantive scrutiny*

USDOC's practice of limited examination is based on Article 6.10 ADA, which permits investigating authorities to diverge from the general rule of a comprehensive individual dumping-margin determination (established in the first sentence of that provision) '[i]n cases where the number of exporters, producers, importers or types of products involved is so large as to make such a determination impracticable' (as provided in the second sentence). Article 6.10 ADA states that the examination of dumping margins may then be limited:

> either to *a reasonable number of interested parties or products* by using samples which are *statistically valid* on the basis of information available to the authorities at the time of the selection, *or* to the largest percentage of the volume of the exports from the country in question *which can reasonably be investigated.* (Emphases added.)

Article 6.10 ADA therefore attempts to strike a balance between the burden that comprehensive examinations place on investigating authorities' limited resources, on the one hand, and the implications of limited examination for the rights of exporting firms not individually investigated, on the other. It does so by: (a) restricting limited examinations to situations in which a comprehensive examination would be 'impracticable', as a threshold matter; and (b) demanding that limited examination be executed with respect to a sample of firms that conforms to alternative requirements of either statistical representativeness or to maximal coverage in terms of export volume.

In challenging the USDOC's practice of limited examination, one might therefore have expected Viet Nam to directly question the satisfaction by USDOC of either or both of these conditions, i.e., by claiming that a comprehensive examination of individual dumping margins was not impracticable, and/or by claiming that the sample of mandatory-response firms selected by USDOC was neither statistically valid nor of the largest export coverage still enabling reasonable investigation. Importantly, however, as noted by the US[36] and emphasized by the Panel, this was not the case: 'Viet Nam is not challenging the USDOC's determination that it was "impracticable" to examine all known exporters and producers. Nor is Viet Nam challenging the number of exporters or producers which the USDOC included in its limited sample.'[37] Indeed, the Panel expressly noted that it proceeded to evaluate Viet Nam's claims on the presumption that USDOC's limited examinations in the second and third administrative reviews were consistent with the requirements of Article 6.10 ADA, although it did not positively determine this. For the record, the Panel quoted (noncritically) the justification given by USDOC in its decisions to pursue only limited examination, in reference to the 'significant workload' imposed upon it by 'numerous concurrent antidumping proceedings', conducted under conditions of scarce resources.[38] With respect to the sample quality and size employed in the limited examinations, the Panel merely noted, as a matter of fact, that in the second administrative review USDOC had examined two Vietnamese exporters accounting for 34% of total exports of relevant firms; and that in the third administrative review, it had selected three exporters of an unspecified share in total exports.

In short, absent a direct challenge by Viet Nam to the fulfillment by USDOC of the Article 6.10 ADA conditions for recourse to and conduct of limited examination, the Panel acted narrowly within its terms of reference and consequently adopted a fully deferential approach towards the USDOC's decisions in this respect, with no substantive scrutiny of those conditions. In Section 3, we provide an analysis of these questions from a statistical and economic perspective. Moreover, we will here briefly suggest that the Panel could have, and perhaps should have, addressed the substance of Article 6.10 ADA conditions for limited examination within the context of Viet Nam's claims as actually made (i.e., without a direct challenge).

Viet Nam claimed that the way USDOC applies limited examination under Article 6.10 ADA led to violations of the substantive rights of nonselected firms derived from other provisions of the ADA, namely under Article 9.3 (restriction of anti-dumping duties to margins calculated under Article 2 ADA), Article 11.1 (imposition of anti-dumping only when necessary to counteract dumping causing injury), and Article 11.3 ADA (termination of definitive anti-dumping duties after five years subject to 'sunset' review). Viet Nam was in essence arguing that because these provisions implicitly require findings to be made for individual firms (a point that was itself contested by the US), repeated limited examination that necessarily

36 See *US–AD Shrimp*, para. 7.158.
37 Ibid., para. 7.164.
38 Ibid., para. 7.156.

entails exclusion of nonmandatory respondent firms constitutes a denial of their substantive rights.

This claim can technically be reduced to the question of the relationship between the rule of comprehensive individual examination established in the first sentence of Article 6.10 ADA, the exception of limited examination allowed by the second sentence of that provision, and the substantive rights established in other ADA provisions. The Panel followed some of the parties' arguments in this vein and pursued this line of analysis, which leads to a dichotomous logical choice between two interpretative extremes. Either, as Viet Nam argued, the Article 6.10 ADA allowance for limited examination cannot release the investigating authority from its substantive obligations towards nonselected firms under Articles 9 and 11 ADA, because such an interpretation of the exception would render *the rule and those additional provisions* meaningless; or, as argued by the US, the exception trumps those substantive individual-firm rights (to the extent that they exist under Articles 9 and 11 ADA), and any other interpretation would render the Article 6.10 ADA second-sentence *exception* meaningless. Between these two possibilities, the Panel chose to grant effect to the exception, rejecting Viet Nam's claim.[39]

We believe another, more nuanced approach could have been adopted, one that better takes into account the role of Article 6.10 ADA in striking the balance we have alluded to above, between investigative burdens, on the one hand, and individual-firm procedural and substantive rights in anti-dumping investigations. This balance is first and foremost regulated by the conditions of impracticability and statistical validity or reasonable sample size established by the second sentence of Article 6.10 ADA with respect to the exercise of limited examination. Indeed, at one end of the spectrum, if simply none of these conditions were fulfilled, limited examination would certainly be ADA-inconsistent and all individual-firm rights would *ipso facto* remain intact. At the other end of the spectrum, if both conditions were perfectly fulfilled – and in particular the requirements of sample quality and size – it could be said that the exercise of individual-firm rights would be redundant and unduly burdensome.

However, given the relative fluidity of the tests of impracticability and sampling, there may well be intermediate situations in which imperfect sampling, (imperfect, either because it was not entirely justified, or because it was not properly conducted) would cause a disproportionate infringement of at least some excluded firms' rights. For example, if the sample included only large firms, to the exclusion of all small firms – whose capacity to engage in dumping can be very different – and could only be rectified by individual examination.[40] We analyse the issue of

39 Ibid., para. 7.167.

40 To be sure, individual examination in such circumstances could be achieved through voluntary responses by nonselected firms, under the terms of Article 6.10.2 ADA. However, as we have seen in Section 2.1, in a USDOC NME investigation, a voluntary response could at best result in the responding

appropriate sampling in more detail in Section 3, but the point made here is that the question raised by Viet Nam's Article 6.10 ADA claim could not have been fully examined by the Panel in isolation from the evaluation of the degree of conformity of USDOC limited examination with the conditions of the second sentence of Article 6.10 ADA.

Furthermore, although (as already noted) no violation of Article 6.10 ADA was claimed by Viet Nam, the arguments of both parties to the dispute referred to the balancing role of Article 6.10 ADA and the fulfilment of its conditions. Viet Nam argued that 'the USDOC made no effort in the proceedings at issue to balance its right to conduct limited examinations with the interests and rights of Vietnamese respondents to have duties assessed based on individual margins and to obtain a company-specific review in order to demonstrate the absence of dumping'.[41] The US stressed that Article 6.10 ADA permits the investigating authority to limit its examination 'whenever the conditions for doing so are met, i.e., where the number of exporters/producers makes determinations of individual margins for all exporters/producers "impracticable"'.[42] Nevertheless, the Panel limited its finding to stating that 'the use of limited examinations is governed exclusively by the second sentence of Article 6.10', not only refraining from evaluating the fulfilment of those conditions, but also effectively depriving that provision of its broader context within the ADA and ignoring the impact of limited examination upon individual-firm rights.

Viet Nam's second claim on the conduct of limited examination related to USDOC's treatment of nonmandatory response firms who had volunteered information. Article 6.10.2 ADA requires investigating authorities to assess individual dumping margins for such nonmandatory respondents, except 'where the number of exporters or producers is so large that individual examinations would be unduly burdensome to the authorities and prevent the timely completion of the investigation'. The final sentence of Article 6.10.2 ADA further provides that '[v]oluntary responses shall not be discouraged'. The provision should be understood as a partial response to the potential infringement of individual-firm rights as a result of exclusion from limited examination, and as an extension of the balance between investigative burden and exporting firms' rights, as discussed above. Thus, a firm fearing that the dumping margins calculated on the basis of mandatory responses would be higher than its individual dumping margin (which may in fact be *de minimis*, zero, or negative) may voluntarily provide information on its sales, and benefit from individual assessment. Only if the investigating authority is faced with such a large number of responses as to defeat the purpose of

firm receiving the 'all others' rate, rather than the 'entity-wide' rate; and as we shall see below, the *US–AD Shrimp* Panel rejected Viet Nam's claims regarding the application of Article 6.10.2 ADA.

41 See *US–AD Shrimp*, para. 7.147.

42 Ibid., para. 7.158.

limited examination, may requests for individual assessment based on sufficient information be denied.

Viet Nam argued that USDOC treated submissions of voluntary responses in reliance upon its original evaluation of the reasonable scope of the investigation under Article 6.10 ADA, where it should have separately determined the number of additional voluntary responses that its investigative capacities could absorb; USDOC policy in this respect provided no flexibility towards nonmandatory respondents and was therefore tantamount to a discouragement of voluntary submissions.[43] In its defence, the US made the factual argument whereby in practice no full voluntary submissions were received from nonmandatory respondents in either the second or third administrative review. It further denied that any action or indeed inaction on its part had constituted a discouragement of voluntary responses.[44]

The Panel's task with respect to the Article 6.10.2 ADA claims by Viet Nam was on its face relatively simple. Indeed, because no voluntary responses had been submitted, the Panel found that obligations under the first sentence of Article 6.10.2 ADA were not 'triggered'.[45] No persuasive evidence of 'discouragement' of voluntary submissions had been presented by Viet Nam. The Panel therefore rejected Viet Nam's claims. One point in the Panel's reasoning merits further scrutiny, however, because it bears upon the relationship between the mandatory respondent sample selection in limited examination under Article 6.10 ADA, on the one hand, and the scope for additional voluntary responses under Article 6.10.2 ADA, on the other. Viet Nam argued that USDOC's 'explicit statement that it cannot and will not examine more than the identified number of companies will of course dissuade companies from seeking examination on a voluntary respondent basis'.[46] This argument, too, was rejected by the Panel, relying on the legitimacy of the USDOC decision to limit its examination, a decision which in itself could not, in its view, constitute evidence of a discouragement of voluntary responses. Here again we observe that the conformity of USDOC's sample of firms selected for limited examination with the requirements of Article 6.10 ADA was assumed by the Panel rather than determined on its merits. An examination of the quality and size of the sample could have led to the conclusion that it was overly restrictive or unrepresentative. While the most obvious remedy for such a finding would have been an expansion of the group of mandatory respondents, we contend that such an unjustifiably narrow sample could also lead to an indirect 'chilling effect' on firms not included in the original sample. We note again that we will expand on the statistical analysis of limited-examination sampling in Section 3.

43 See ibid., paras. 7.172–7.175.
44 See ibid., paras. 7.176–7.178.
45 See ibid., para. 7.183.
46 See ibid., para. 7.185.

2.2.4 *The application of the 'all others' rate to nonselected firms*

Viet Nam also made claims regarding the 'all others' rate applied by USDOC in the second and third administrative reviews, i.e., the rate applied to non-Mandatory respondents who had requested a separate rate and provided information (Case F in Figure 1). Notably, in the second and third administrative reviews, the individual rates calculated for the mandatory respondents were ultimately all *de minimis* – less than 0.5%. Nevertheless, in these reviews USDOC chose to apply the 4.57% rate derived from the original investigation (applied as well in the first administrative review) to most nonselected Vietnamese firms, considering this approach to be 'a reasonable method which is reflective of the range of commercial behaviour demonstrated by exporters of the subject merchandise during a very recent period'.[47]

Under the terms of Article 9.4 ADA, the 'all others' rate shall not exceed 'the weighted average margin of dumping established with respect to the selected exporters or producer', excluding any zero and *de minimis* margins and margins based on AFA. The question therefore arises, whether the 'all others' rate selected by USDOC was not in excess of the relevant average margin. The determination of this margin is in itself a matter of uncertainty, when all applicable dumping margins are zero or considered *de minimis* and hence excluded from the calculation. It would appear to be unclear how the 'all others' margin can be calculated when all individual margins are excluded, and the Appellate Body has indeed characterized this situation as a '*lacuna*'.[48] We will analyze this issue in more detail in Section 4. However, it is important to note that the question was not directly tackled by the Panel. The main claim addressed by the Panel was that the 'all others' rate was determined on the basis of dumping margins calculated with the use of zeroing. This claim was somewhat complicated by the US assertion that ADA disciplines did not in any event apply to this rate because USDOC had simply continued to apply the 'all others' rate calculated prior to Viet Nam's accession to the WTO. The intertemporal argument was rejected by the Panel, however, because the evidence showed that USDOC had made 'a new and distinct' determination of the 'all others' rate in each administrative review, subsequent to Viet Nam's WTO accession.[49] Because the use of zeroing in the calculation of dumping margins for mandatory respondents had already been factually established, and the Panel considered it to be inconsistent with Article 9.4 ADA to determine the maximum allowable 'all others' rate on the basis of dumping margins calculated with the use of zeroing, Viet Nam's claim regarding the 'all others' rate was accepted by the Panel. Additional claims by Viet Nam were not addressed by the Panel on the basis of 'judicial economy'.[50]

47 See ibid., paras. 7.197–7.198.
48 See *US–Hot-Rolled Steel, supra* at note 11.
49 See *US–AD Shrimp*, paras. 7.221–7.223.
50 See ibid., para. 7.229.

2.2.5 *The application of the 'Viet Nam-Wide Entity' rate*

Finally, Viet Nam made claims regarding the rate of antidumping duties levied upon shrimp exporters considered to be part of the 'Viet Nam-wide' NME entity, assimilated to the very high 'AFA' rate (cases E and G in Figure 1) rather than the 'all others' rate. Here, too, with all individually calculated margins being either zero or *de minimis*, the US argued that Article 9.4 placed no constraints on the nature of a maximum allowable rate, and that it therefore could not be in violation of Article 9.4 ADA.[51] The Panel did not accept this argument, finding instead that nothing in Article 9.4 ADA, *lacuna* notwithstanding, sanctioned a separate rate for nonindividually assessed firms that was not the 'all others' rate, and that USDOC unjustifiably applied a higher AFA rate to numerous Vietnamese firms. US arguments whereby the AFA rate was applied due to lack of cooperation by firms were rejected, *inter alia* due to strong indications that the AFA rate would have been employed by USDOC in any case.[52]

We turn now to a more detailed analysis of the two main issues raised in *US–AD Shrimp*, in our view: the sampling of firms for the purposes of limited examination, and the treatment of the so-called *lacuna* in Article 9.4 ADA.

3. Statistical sampling in anti-dumping investigations and reviews

3.1 *Dumping investigations: divergence from the ideal*

The most interesting issues underlying *US–AD Shrimp* revolve around sample-selection bias in dumping investigations. The procedures laid out above and summarized in Figure 1, and the practices challenged in the dispute as just described, make clear that the USDOC only calculates individual dumping margins on a small subset of foreign exporters. The USDOC uses the results from this small sample of investigated firms to calculate the 'all others' rate for nonsampled firms. The culling process to identify the particular group of enterprises included in the sample as mandatory respondents, to assess whether mandatory respondents have been cooperative 'enough', and to determine which firms are eligible for separate rates in an NME investigation, all raise substantive issues about how representative this sample might be. These procedures are especially important for NME exporters since the best rate that nonsampled firms may receive is the 'all others' rate.

This process can easily lead to sampling bias for at least two reasons. First, the firms that are used to calculate the 'all others' rate are chosen by the USDOC neither randomly nor with statistical representativeness in mind. Second, the information required by the USDOC is costly to collect so that some foreign firms,

51 See ibid., para. 7.242.
52 See ibid., para. 7.274.

particularly small ones, may decide not to cooperate on a simple cost – benefit basis.

One of the basic principles of the ADA is that dumping margins are based on the pricing decisions of individual foreign exporters. As mentioned above, Article 6.10 ADA requires that 'authorities shall, as a rule, determine an individual margin of dumping for each known exporter'. The accurate calculation of such margins necessarily demands important data that can be acquired only from foreign firms themselves.

In an ideal world, the investigating authority would obtain full information at no cost with respect to each foreign firm exporting the product into the domestic market. The authority would institute procedures that were simple and each foreign firm would cooperate fully with the authority in a timely fashion. Such an ideal outcome would result in every exporter being treated on the basis of its individual data.

Commercial and legal realities diverge importantly from this ideal world. First, information frequently is costly to obtain and collect, both for the investigating authority and for responding foreign firms. Second, foreign firms cannot be compelled to respond to inquiries from domestic investigators about activities taking place outside the authorities' jurisdiction. Third, the investigating agency cannot be forced to use information provided by every foreign firm. This combination of costly information and noncompulsion means that there are frequent instances where only a portion of the underlying commercial reality is used when assessing dumping margins and the resulting duties. Finally, in the case of an NME like Viet Nam, the domestic investigating authority must determine whether price information provided by a particular exporter can be used to calculate dumping margins at all, i.e., whether a particular foreign firm is eligible for a 'separate rate'.

Let us turn first to the problems faced by the USDOC when there might be many exporters subject to a dumping investigation, with consequent high information and administrative costs. These issues are relevant for both NME and market-economy cases.

The second sentence of Article 6.10 ADA explicitly allows for investigating authorities to limit their examination in such instances to a 'reasonable number' of exporters that either: (a) represents 'the largest percentage of the exports ... which can reasonably be investigated', or (b) is 'statistically valid.' The results from these investigations can then be used to determine the 'all others' rate applied to nonsampled firms. As a general principle, the US has chosen the former of these two approaches.

The underlying idea behind the second sentence of Article 6.10 ADA is that the data used to calculate the 'all others' rate should be representative. On the one hand, sampling the 'largest percent' of exports is an implicit attempt to obtain information that reflects the broad realities of the market. While the ADA does not specify a particular percentage that would satisfy the criteria, the intention that it be large enough to approximate broader market conditions is clear. The second option of a 'statistically valid' sample makes this even more explicit. And since these are alternatives, one might reasonably expect that they have the same intent – to collect information about some firms that can be applied appropriately to exporters not surveyed by domestic authorities.

The number of firms that can be included under either approach of Article 6.10 ADA depends on the administrative burden on the investigating authority. However, it is important to note that the extent of these burdens is largely determined by the particular procedures adopted by the investigators themselves. The USDOC could streamline the process so that its self-imposed burdens could be lowered and it could investigate many more foreign exporters. For example, the US choice of using a retrospective system (i.e., where the final anti-dumping duties are based on pricing behavior over the previous year) increases the costs for USDOC to calculate dumping margins (and for foreign firms to provide that information) since data must be collected throughout each year.

In any event, the high cost of conducting an investigation has meant in practice that the USDOC only investigates a small number of firms. (For example, recall that only *two* Vietnamese firms were included in the second administrative review.) The USDOC must choose which specific firms to include in its sample. As noted above, standard USDOC practice is first to obtain export quantity and value data from as many exporters as possible. The USDOC then chooses to send detailed questionnaires only to a limited group of the target country's very largest exporters to the US for the actual dumping investigations. These firms are chosen without consultation with exporters.[53] Moreover, as we have emphasized above, the USDOC approach to *only* consider a limited sample of the very largest firms and USDOC's approach to selecting these firms were not in dispute in the case. There is, however, nothing to suggest that considering only the largest firms is an appropriate methodology for the 'all others' rate from a statistical standpoint though it arguably is consistent with the Article 6.10 ADA provision allowing limited examination if it focuses on a 'reasonable' number of firms representing the 'largest' export percentage.

Indeed, there may be something systematically different about the very largest firms that make them quite distinct from other firms in the overall population. Perhaps the larger firms are more likely to price aggressively or smaller firms have higher costs, both of which could alter the dumping margins in a systematic way.[54]

53 Article 6.10.1 ADA notes that '[a]ny selection of exporters, producers, importers or types of products made under this paragraph shall *preferably* be chosen in consultation with and with the consent of the exporters, producers, or importers concerned' (emphasis added). This 'preference' is not reflected in USDOC procedures.

54 Recent international-trade research has focused increasingly on heterogeneity among firms. Two classic studies include Melitz (2003) and Helpman *et al.* (2004).

A second complication of sample selection arises because some foreign firms may refuse to provide information about their pricing and costs. An investigating authority thereby might be stymied while trying to assess a particular dumping margin. In order to encourage cooperation, the ADA included a provision to use other information for assessing the dumping margins of nonresponsive foreign firms, that can even be seen as punitive or coercive in nature – the 'adverse facts available' AFA route.[55] In practice, AFA often has consisted of the pricing allegations lodged by domestic petitioners, who would likely claim that they faced very high dumping margins. Indeed, an exporter might not have an incentive to cooperate and provide actual data if it is chosen for the sample as long as the AFA allegations were lower than its actual dumping margin.[56]

Moreover, the use of AFA includes yet another source of potential sample-selection bias that muddies the waters of assessing 'average' dumping margins for use in the 'all others' rate. First, the foreign firm's choice of whether or not to provide data is not as simple as we have just suggested. Collecting information that satisfies the domestic agency is costly for the exporting firm. In addition, domestic investigators have at least some discretion about how burdensome that process is for firms and thereby potentially could influence which exporters ultimately choose to cooperate. They also have the final say as to whether foreign firms have been cooperative 'enough' to avoid necessarily high AFA margins. The upshot is that those firms who choose to cooperate may not be like other nonsampled firms. On the one hand, they might have higher dumping margins than even the domestic firms allege, making AFA a relatively attractive proposition. On the other hand, they might be discouraged from cooperating by excessively burdensome procedures established by the investigating agency itself.

3.2 *Selecting a more representative sample*

The 'statistically valid' approach contained in the second sentence of Article 6.10 ADA would be more attractive in principle than simply examining a small number of the largest firms. When choosing a sample that is statistically valid, that group should reflect the different types of individual firms in the underlying population. In addition, the choice of investigated firms within representative subgroups should be random. The analyst should also weigh the sampling outcomes by their share in the overall population.[57] For example, if 'large' firms represent half of exports, then no more than half of the weighted-average 'all others' dumping margin should be based on such larger firms.

55 See Article 6.8 and Annex II ADA.

56 For a discussion about foreign firms' decision to cooperate in anti-dumping investigations see Moore (2005) and Moore and Fox (2010).

57 Public-opinion polls routinely take such considerations into account. For example, suppose a country's citizens are 50% female. If a particular random sample were 75% male, then one would want to adjust the weights on the outcomes so that females were not underrepresented in the final results.

Another way to avoid the problems of using unrepresentative data would be to allow nonsampled firms to volunteer information that can be used to calculate a firm-specific rate and contribute to the assessment of the 'all others' rate. This of course increases the administrative burdens on domestic investigators, but it also raises a further complication. In particular, which type of foreign firm would more likely be asked to submit such data? Any firm with dumping margins below the 'all others' rate based upon the dumping margins of the cooperating mandatory respondents would clearly have an incentive to provide such data. Exporters with higher margins would not volunteer information but could potentially benefit from self-reporting low-margin firms if their data were added to the 'all others' calculation.

The ADA embodies many of these considerations in the final text. As noted above, Article 6.10 ADA allows domestic agencies to investigate only some firms, implicitly because of the practical costs of investigating all exporters. The ADA also allows individual nonsampled exporters to offer information voluntarily to provide information but still nods in the direction of domestic-agency investigation costs by allowing it to ignore this information if it is not 'practicable' to conduct the investigation. But while the ADA allows for individually investigated exporters to receive their own firm-specific dumping margins, it does exclude AFA and less than *de minimis* (including zero) margins in the calculation of the 'all others' rate, implicitly because these are, by definition, considered nonrepresentative of the underlying population of exporters. In passing, we would note that the exclusion of AFA-based margins is justified in this respect, because such margins are not based on full data. The exclusion from the 'all others' rate of zero and *de minimis* margins based on individual-firm investigations is less justifiable from a statistical viewpoint, though this is allowed explicitly in Article 9.4 ADA.

A final complication in NME cases is that the USDOC determines which firms are eligible for a 'separate rate' and not subject to the entity-wide rate, which is usually based on AFA. The USDOC determines which of the mandatory respondents are eligible for the separate rate and therefore included in the sample of individually investigated firms. This means that domestic investigators have additional leeway about which particular firms are included in the sample in an NME case.

In addition, nonmandatory respondents in NME cases may ask for a separate rate (and to be eligible for the 'all others' rate) but the USDOC makes the decision whether firms are eligible. These provisions increase the discretion of the USDOC and add another potential layer of sample-selection bias. In addition, these nonmandatory respondents deemed eligible for a separate rate can do no better than receive the (potentially flawed) 'all others' rate; the USDOC normally does not conduct a new investigation for such firms. This raises the stakes in NME cases about the appropriate methodology for sampling when calculating 'all others' rates.

Table 1 (a). Hypothetical original non-market economy investigation

	Sales	Actual dumping margin	Government controlled	Cooperate with USDOC	Margin calculated by USDOC	Final margin	Mandatory response firm
Firm 1	100	15	Yes	NA		10[a]	Yes
Firm 2	100	8	Yes	NA		10[a]	Yes
Firm 3	100	4	No	Yes	4	4	Yes
Firm 4	100	1	No	Yes	0	0	Yes
Firm 5	50	8	No	NA		10[a]	No
Firm 6	50	0	No	NA		10[a]	No

Notes: [a] 'Entity-wide rate' (normally equal to 'adverse facts available' (AFA) rate) equal to 10% by assumption.

Table 1 (b). Hypothetical administrative review non-market economy investigation

	Sales	Actual dumping margin	Government Controlled	Cooperate with USDOC	Margin calculated by USDOC	Final margin	Figure 1 outcome
Firm 1	100	15	Yes	NA		10[a]	Case A
Firm 2	100	8	Yes	NA		10[a]	Case A
Firm 3	100	0	No	Yes	0	0	Case B
Firm 4	100	0	No	Yes	0	0	Case B
Firm 5	50	0	No	NA		10[a]	Case G
Firm 6	50	0	No	NA		?	Case F

Notes: [a] 'Entity-wide rate' (='adverse facts available' (AFA) rate).

3.3 *A hypothetical numerical example*

In Table 1, we also include hypothetical results of an original investigation and administrative review in an NME case such as *US–AD Shrimp*.

We assume that Firms 1 through 4 are 'large' firms that each export 100 units to the US. Firms 5 and 6 are small and export only 50 units. In the ideal situation, Firms 4 and 6 would not face anti-dumping duties in the original investigation because of either zero or *de minimis* margins; all other firms would face anti-dumping duties ranging from 4% to 15%.

In panel (a) of Table 1, we include assumptions about the original investigation, including whether a foreign firm is eligible for a separate rate under provisions of US law, either as a mandatory respondent, or as a firm voluntarily cooperating with the investigation. Consistent with the discussion above, we assume that administrative costs preclude the USDOC from investigating all firms. In addition, we assume that Firms 1 and 2 are government-controlled exporters.

We assume that Firms 1 through 4 were mandatory respondents. Firms 1 and 2 did not cooperate in the original investigation so they receive an entity-wide AFA rate, assumed for concreteness to equal 10%. Firms 3 and 4, having cooperated with the investigation, are eligible for a separate rate, with a *de minimis rate* for Firm 4. Firms 5 and 6 did not ask for a separate rate under NME procedures and so are assessed the entity-wide rate of 10%.

In panel (b) of Table 1, we illustrate one possible outcome in an administrative review in an NME context similar to the issues faced in *US–AD Shrimp*. We have assumed that (government-controlled) Firms 1 and 2 do not change their pricing decisions after the original investigation and so continue to engage in dumping at the original rate. All other firms adjust their pricing decisions so that they are no longer dumping. Suppose that Firms 3 and 4 are those chosen by USDOC for investigation in the administrative review, since they are the two largest exporters qualifying for a separate rate as would be the case under USDOC normal procedures. We assume that Firm 5 has not asked for a separate-rate investigation in the administrative review so that it continues to receive the AFA entity-wide rate.

One of the core issues of *US–AD Shrimp* is illustrated by the situation facing Firm 6. If Firm 6 does not request a separate-rate determination under USDOC NME procedures, then it simply receives the EWR of 10% (based on AFA) and there are no further decisional complications.

However, if Firm 6 *does* ask for a separate rate, and qualifies in the judgment of the USDOC, then the USDOC faces a problem. In this particular example (which mirrors the facts of *US–AD Shrimp*), there are no outcomes that normally would be used by the USDOC to calculate an 'all others' rate, i.e., Firms 3 and 4 have zero dumping margins (Case B outcomes in Figure 1) and Firms 1, 2, and 5 have rates based on AFA (Cases A and G outcomes in Figure 1). There are no Case C outcomes on which to base the 'all others' rate in this NME administrative review using standard USDOC procedures. The question becomes what would be a reasonable and statistically representative approach for the 'all others' rate for Firm 6.

One approach, and which in fact was used in the second and third administrative reviews of *US–AD Shrimp*, would be to look back to the 'all others' rate from the original investigation (4% in Table 1 (a)). This has clear statistical problems. First, the margin is based on a single observation for a larger exporter. Second, the margin is calculated based on the market conditions in an earlier period. One might certainly expect that the behavior of exporters would be influenced by the imposition of anti-dumping duties and overall market conditions such as changing demand and supply conditions, etc.[58]

58 A perverse result of this approach taken by USDOC is that Firm 6 may face *higher* margins if other firms *eliminate* their own dumping. Suppose, instead of eliminating dumping, Firm 3 lowers its actual dumping margin during the administrative-review period to 1%. Firm 6 then would face a 1% margin since there is now an observation that meets the standard NME 'all others' rate procedures in administrative reviews.

Alternatively, this problem could be solved by USDOC requesting that Firm 6 provide input quantity data so the agency could calculate a true separate rate as would be done for a Case C type firm in Figure 1. This would allow the outcomes for Firm 6 to be based on its own contemporaneous economic realities. However, it is important to note a potential downside of this effort to accommodate Firm 6. Suppose that this is a small firm that would find it difficult to collect the requisite information for its own investigation by the USDOC. If these costs are so high that it chooses not to cooperate, it will now face the AFA rates (of 10% in this example) rather than the 'all others' rate of 4% from the original investigation.[59]

If investigators decide not to ask for relevant information from Firm 6, then at least one would hope that they adopt a procedure that would approximate a sample that yielded results plausibly 'representative' of Firm 6 behavior. For example, they could look to recently acquired information from exporters during the period of investigation, which would be relevant information about recent Firm 6 behavior. Indeed, USDOC would have on hand the results of investigations from Firms 3 and 4, which could be used to establish the separate rate for Firm 6, which in this case would be a margin of 0%.

This discussion makes clear that many of the underlying issues in *US–AD Shrimp* transcend the problems of this particular dispute (and importantly, are unrelated to zeroing methodologies). Domestic investigators have the qualified right under the ADA to limit the number of exporters that are queried for firm-specific data used to calculate dumping margins. In US practice, this means that other exporters, even those willing to voluntarily provide information of their own to investigators, will face potentially unrepresentative 'all others' dumping rates. This problem is exacerbated by a US tendency, evident in all stages of the investigations and reviews in the present case, to query only the largest exporting firms, which could have very different economic characteristics than nonsampled firms.

A useful reform would be for the US to simplify the process of calculating dumping margins. This would not only lower the administrative costs that the USDOC would face but would increase the number of foreign firms that could potentially provide information that would result in more accurate dumping margins. An increase in the number of investigated firms would also reduce the chances of the USDOC facing the awkward circumstance that arose during the administrative reviews that triggered the *US–AD Shrimp* dispute, where there were no nonzero, *de minimis*, or AFA margins on which to base the 'all others' rate. In short, the USDOC has at its disposal the means – and methods, should it elect to employ them – to minimize the use of unrepresentative samples that both burden foreign exporters and risk nonconformity with the ADA.

59 Note that the facts of *US–AD Shrimp* are even more extreme. As noted above, the original 'all others' rate was 4.57% compared to 25.76% for the AFA rate.

Furthermore, we believe that it is possible and indeed desirable to incorporate the insights of the above statistical analysis into the legal principles of Article 6.10 ADA. It is therefore to some extent unfortunate that Viet Nam, in this dispute, did not directly challenge USDOC's sampling practices in its investigations and administrative reviews, and that the Panel did not see fit to address the fundamental question of whether USDOC's limited examination satisfied the conditions set out in Article 6.10 ADA, employing, for example, the logic of legal interpretation suggested in Section 2.2.3. It remains to be seen to what extent the issue of sampling will be dealt with in the recently launched follow-up dispute; in the request for consultations, Viet Nam specifically mentioned 'the practice of limiting the number of respondents selected for individual examination to only a small fraction of the total number of companies seeking individual review', as one of the measures it intends to challenge.[60]

4. Dealing with 'Lacuna' in Article 9.4 ADA

We now turn to discuss the supplementary problem of calculating an 'all others' rate under special circumstances such as posed in *US–AD Shrimp*. As already noted, under Article 9.4 ADA, the 'all others' rate shall not exceed 'the weighted average margin of dumping established with respect to the selected exporters or producers', excluding any zero and *de minimis* margins and margins based on AFA. How then can such a ceiling on the 'all others' rate be calculated, when *all* the individually calculated margins are zero, *de minimis*, or AFA? In mathematical terms, this would mean calculating the weighted average of an 'empty set', and the average of an empty set is not well-defined mathematically. Indeed, it can be characterized as an empty set in itself. The ceiling for the 'all others' rate would therefore be a nonexistent figure. It would thus appear that in these circumstances Article 9.4 ADA does not in itself define a ceiling for the 'all others' rate. However, from a mathematical perspective, the absence of a defined ceiling is not the same as an unlimited ceiling of infinity.

In *US–Hot-Rolled Steel*, the AB took note of this problem by stating that Article 9.4 ADA presented a *lacuna*:

> This *lacuna* arises because, while Article 9.4 *prohibits* the use of certain margins in the calculation of the ceiling for the 'all others' rate, it does not expressly address the issue of *how* that ceiling should be calculated in the event that *all* margins are to be *excluded* from the calculation, under the prohibitions. (Original emphases).[61]

60 See *United States – Anti-Dumping Measures on Certain Shrimp from Viet Nam – Request for Consultations by Viet Nam, supra* at note 14.

61 See *US–Hot-Rolled Steel*, at para. 126, *supra* at note 11.

The AB then did not deem it necessary to fill this *lacuna*, in the circumstances that arose in that case.

This celebrated reference to a *lacuna* in Article 9.4 ADA is in some respects unfortunate. Article 9.4 ADA, in our view, does not represent a *lacuna* in any meaningful respect. The fact that Article 9.4 ADA produces an 'empty set' or undefined figure for the establishment of a specific ceiling does not mean that adjudicators are faced with a *lacuna*. A *lacuna* would emerge only if there were *no* legal (WTO) rules that could be applied to the facts at hand. Clearly, this is not the case: the imposition of anti-dumping duties at an 'all others' rate is still subject to the more general rules of the ADA, even in the absence of a calculable ceiling. We agree with previous commentators on *US–Hot-Rolled Steel* (Pauwelyn, 2003; van Damme, 2009) that so long as a measure is subject to some WTO law and within the jurisdiction of the WTO dispute-settlement system, there is no *lacuna*, and no scope for a *non liquet* (a decision not to decide) on such grounds. This determinedly positivistic position conforms with more general understandings of the limited potential for *lacunae* in international law (Lauterpacht, 1958; Stone, 1959; Weil, 1997). It would also appear to be the position adopted by WTO adjudicators in subsequent cases, including *US–AD Shrimp*.

Article 9.4 ADA is a specific provision applying in the exceptional circumstances of limited examination. There is no reason to assume that when Article 9.4 ADA itself proves inoperable, the broader context of the ADA does not have purchase, both as applicable law and as interpretative context. In a subsequent case, *US–Zeroing (EC) (Article 21.5–EC)*,[62] the Appellate Body acknowledged this by stating that:

> [T]he fact that all margins of dumping for the investigated exporters fall within one of the categories that Article 9.4 directs investigating authorities to disregard, for purposes of that paragraph, does not imply that the investigating authorities' discretion to apply duties on non-investigated exporters is unbounded. The lacuna that the Appellate Body recognized to exist in Article 9.4 is one of a specific method. Thus, the absence of guidance in Article 9.4 on what particular methodology to follow does not imply an absence of any obligation with respect to the 'all others' rate applicable to non-investigated exporters where all margins of dumping for the investigated exporters are either zero, *de minimis*, or based on facts available.[63]

In this case as well, the AB exercised a form of judicial economy, relieving it of the need to establish precisely what the methods for and boundaries of calculating the 'all others' rate in these circumstances are. However, it was unequivocal in

62 See Appellate Body Report, *United States – Laws, Regulations and Methodology for Calculating Dumping Margins (Zeroing) – Recourse to Article 21.5 of the DSU by the European Communities*, WT/DS294/AB/RW and Corr.1, adopted 11 June 2009, DSR 2009:VII, 2911.

63 Ibid., para. 453.

establishing that the calculation of the 'all others' rate remained subject to ADA disciplines, the specific '*lacuna*' of Article 9.4 ADA notwithstanding.

In *US–AD Shrimp*, the Panel followed the AB's guidance, interpreting it 'to mean that if an investigating authority limits its investigation and applies an "all others" rate to non-selected exporters, its discretion in doing so is not unlimited'. From this the Panel deducted that 'the margins of dumping which are used to establish the maximum allowable "all others" rate must be ones which, at the time the "all others" rate is applied, conform to the disciplines of the Agreement'.[64] Hence the Panel's conclusion that an 'all others' rate based on margins calculated with the use of zeroing methodology were ADA-inconsistent.

What are the implications of these interpretations of Article 9.4 ADA – overcoming its nature as an erstwhile *lacuna* – for the future application of the provision? What would be the ground rules if the margins had *not* been calculated using zeroing? In other words, if circumstances such as those that arose in *US–AD Shrimp* occur again, what are the bounds of calculation of an 'all others' rate in the face of an 'empty set'? We suggest that this question should best be addressed taking Article 6.10 ADA and the question of statistical validity and representativeness of limited examination as the most relevant context. The two provisions are inextricably tied to each other – it is the practice of limited examination permitted under Article 6.10 ADA that necessitates Article 9.4 ADA, which refers to it explicitly.

If the exporters and/or producers selected (by USDOC, in the present case) are indeed a broad, statistically valid sample, as envisaged by Article 6.10 ADA, the fact that they all had zero or *de minimis* is significant. It would imply that the nonindividually calculated firms might very well have produced a similarly low dumping margin, if they had undergone individual review. Similarly, if all mandatory respondents' dumping margins were calculated on an AFA basis, this would imply that their real dumping margins are at least as high, and the investigative authority could perhaps impose a relatively high 'all others' rate, subject to other ADA rules.

This link between Articles 6.10 and 9.4 ADA gains support from a surprising source: the US claims in *US–AD Shrimp*. The US defended its 'all others' rate by arguing that its selection of the 'all others' rate from the original investigation and first administrative review constituted 'a reasonable method which is *reflective of the range of commercial behaviour demonstrated by exporters* of the subject merchandise during a very recent period'[65] and that 'there is no reason to find that

64 See *US–AD Shrimp*, para. 7.215.

65 Final Determination in the Second Administrative Review, p. 52275, Exhibit Viet Nam-15 to *US–AD Shrimp*; see also Issues and Decision Memo in the Second Administrative Review, p. 19, also Exhibit Viet Nam-15 to *US–AD Shrimp*.

it is not *reasonably reflective of potential dumping margins for the non-selected companies*' (emphases added).[66]

We agree with this contention at a theoretical level: when all individually calculated dumping margins have been excluded by virtue of Article 9.4 ADA, the 'all others' rate should be 'reasonably reflective' of real commercial behaviour. However, we believe the best way to warrant this reflectiveness is by ensuring that the individually calculated dumping margins under Article 6.10 ADA are statistically valid and representative, as explained in depth in Section 3 above.

5. Conclusions

With the apparent demise of USDOC's zeroing methodology, it seems inevitable that the WTO system and its Members will turn their attention to other distortive practices pursued by investigating authorities in anti-dumping proceedings. The dispute in *US–AD Shrimp* demonstrates that the wholesale use of 'limited examination' under Article 6.10 ADA and the application of 'all others' rates to a large number of exporting firms constitutes such a distortive practice, leaving much to the potentially unprincipled discretion of the authority, and leaving many exporting firms with irrelevantly high dumping margins, and no recourse to administrative review in the Member imposing the anti-dumping duties.

In this paper, we have argued for a more rigorous application of the principles of statistical validity and representativeness in limited examination, and also shown how these principles can be the subject of judicial review by the WTO dispute-settlement system. This also applies to the calculation of 'all others' rates, even in specialized circumstances. While the *US–AD Shrimp* dispute itself did not address these issues directly or forcefully enough, in our view, it can be expected that future disputes, in particular Viet Nam's follow-up complaint now being in process at the WTO, will provide better opportunity for their clarification. Sampling may well be the new zeroing.

References

Barfield, C. (2005), 'Anti-dumping Reform: Time to Go Back to Basics', *The World Economy*, 28(5): 719–737.

Bown, C. P. and A. O. Sykes (2008), 'The Zeroing Issue: A Critical Analysis of Softwood V', *World Trade Review*, 7(1): 121–142.

Bown, C. P. and T. J. Prusa (2011), 'US Anti-dumping: Much Ado About Zeroing', in Will Martin and Aaditya Matto (eds.), *Unfinished Business? The WTO's Doha Agenda*, Washington, DC: The World Bank, pp. 355–392.

Broude, T. (2007), 'Genetically Modified Rules: The Awkward Rule–Exception–Right Distinction in *EC–Biotech*', *World Trade Review*, 6(2): 215–231.

66 Issues and Decision Memo in the Second Administrative Review, p. 19, Exhibit Viet Nam-15 to *US–AD Shrimp*.

Business Times (Viet Nam) (2012), 'Vietnam's Shrimp Export Reaches $436Mln In Q1/2012', 17 May 2012, available at http://businesstimes.com.vn/vietnams-shrimp-export-reaches-436mln-in-q12012/ (last visited 28 November 2012).

Cho, S. (2012), 'No More Zeroing?: The United States Changes its Antidumping Policy to Comply with the WTO', *ASIL Insights*, **16**(8): 1–7.

Debaere, P. (2010), 'Small Fish – Big Issues: The Effect of Trade Policy on the Global Shrimp Market', *World Trade Review*, **9**(2): 353–374.

Department of Commerce (2009), 'Certain Frozen Warmwater Shrimp from the Socialist Republic of Vietnam: Issues and Decision Memorandum for the Final Results of the Third Antidumping Administrative Review', Public Document IA/NME/9: IG.

Do Thanh Cong (2010), 'Catfish, Shrimp, and the WTO: Vietnam Loses its Innocence', *Vanderbilt Journal of Transnational Law*, **43**(5): 1235–1264.

Gantz, D. A. (2007), 'Doi Moi, the VBTA & WTO Accession: The Role of Lawyers in Vietnam's No Longer Cautious Embrace of Globalization', *The International Lawyer*, **41**(3): 873–890.

Gao, H. S. (2005), 'Aggressive Legalism: The East Asian Experience and Lessons for China', in Henry Gao and Donald Lewis (eds.), *China's Participation in the WTO*, London: Cameron May, pp. 315–351.

Helpman, E., M. J. Melitz, and S. R. Yeaple (2004), 'Export versus FDI with Heterogeneous Firms', *The American Economic Review*, **94**(1): 300–316.

Keithly, W. R. Jr. and P. Poudel (2008), 'The Southeast USA Shrimp Industry: Issues Related to Trade and Antidumping Duties', *Marine Resource Economics*, **23**(4): 459–483.

Lauterpacht, H. (1958), 'Some Observations on the Prohibition of "*Non Liquet*" and the Completeness of the Law', in F.M. van Asbeck *et al.* (eds.), *Symbolae Verzijl: Présentées au Professeur J.H.W. Verzijl à l'Occasion de son LXX-ième Anniversaire*, The Hague: Martinus Nijhoff, pp. 196–221.

Melitz, M. J. (2003), 'The Impact of Trade on Intra-Industry Reallocations and Aggregate Industry Productivity', *Econometrica*, **71**(6): 1695–1725.

Moore, M. O. (2005), '"Facts Available" Dumping Allegations: When Will Foreign Firms Cooperate in Antidumping Petitions?', *European Journal of Political Economy*, **21**(1): 185–204.

Moore, M. O. and A. K. Fox (2010), 'Why Don't Foreign Firms Cooperate in US Antidumping Investigations?: An Empirical Analysis', *Review of World Economics*, **145**(4): 597–613.

Pauwelyn, J. (2003), *Conflict of Norms in Public International Law: How WTO Law Relates to Other Rules of International Law*, Cambridge: Cambridge University Press.

Pekkanen, S. M. (2001), 'Aggressive Legalism: The Rules of the WTO and Japan's Emerging Trade Strategy', *The World Economy*, **24**(5): 707–737.

Prusa, T. J. and E. Vermulst (2009), 'A One-Two Punch on Zeroing: *US–Zeroing (EC)* and *US–Zeroing (Japan)*', *World Trade Review*, **8**(1): 187–241.

—— (2011), 'United States – Continued Existence and Application of Zeroing Methodology: The End of Zeroing?', *World Trade Review*, **10**(1): 45–61.

Stone, J. (1959), 'Non Liquet and the Function of Law in the International Community', *British Yearbook of International Law*, **35**: 124–161.

US Department of Commerce (2009), *Import Administration Antidumping Manual*, available at http://ia.ita.doc.gov/admanual/index.html (last visited 28 November 2012).

Van Damme, I. (2009), *Treaty Interpretation by the WTO Appellate Body*, Oxford: Oxford University Press.

Vo Tri Thanh and Nguyen Anh Duong (2009), 'Vietnam after Two Years of WTO Accession: What Lessons Can Be Learnt?', *ASEAN Economic Bulletin*, **26**(1): 115–135.

Voon, T. (2011), 'Orange Juice, Shrimp, and the United States Response to Adverse WTO Rulings on Zeroing', *ASIL Insights*, **15**(20): 1–7.

Weil, P. (1997), '"The Court Cannot Conclude Definitively . . .": *Non Liquet* Revisited', *Columbia Journal of Transnational Law*, **36**(1–2): 109–119.

www.ingramcontent.com/pod-product-compliance
Lightning Source LLC
LaVergne TN
LVHW080022210926
848481LV00011B/3090
* 9 7 8 1 1 0 7 6 1 7 2 2 3 *